The State of
Asian Pacific America

The State of Asian Pacific America:

Reframing the Immigration Debate

A Public Policy Report

Bill Ong Hing

Ronald Lee

Editors

LEAP Asian Pacific American Public Policy Institute

and

UCLA Asian American Studies Center

1996

Leadership Education for Asian Pacifics (LEAP), Inc.
327 East Second Street, Suite 226
Los Angeles, CA 90012-4210

UCLA Asian American Studies Center
3230 Campbell Hall, 405 Hilgard Avenue
Los Angeles, CA 90095-1546

ISBN: 0-934052-26-3

Cover design: Fresh Graphics

Table of Contents

Preface

The State of Asian Pacific America: Reframing the Immigration Debate is the third major joint public policy research report produced by our two institutions — Leadership Education for Asian Pacifics (LEAP) and the UCLA Asian American Studies Center. We hope this policy study, like others we have already released and those we will publish in the future, will serve to inform public discussions and shape public policy deliberations about the most important and compelling policy issue-areas facing the nation's rapidly growing and diverse Asian Pacific American population.

This report is being released during a year when heightened governmental and public attention is focused on our nation's immigration policies. The U.S. Senate and House of Representatives are expected to debate and vote on major legislative bills which would lead to sweeping changes in the numbers and characteristics of future immigrants, and immigration could become one of the most contentious and emotion-laden topics of discussion during the 1996 presidential elections. And although there is a sizable body of rigorous and insightful social science research on immigration and the adaptation and contributions of immigrants to American society, the public debate on immigration has often been swayed by speculation, misinformation, and ideological advocacy. This is clearly unfortunate because immigration has played an indispensable role in our nation's past and present greatness and uniqueness, and would likely contribute significantly to the realization of our nation's finest and fullest future potential.

This policy report is intended to respond to the significant public interest in immigration issues by providing the most comprehensive empirical analysis of the contemporary Asian Pacific American immigration experience. By doing so, we are interested in infusing the policy decision-making process with fresh and accurate information as well as rigorous analysis of recent Asian Pacific immigrants and refugees, who have accounted for over a third of all legal immigrants and most refugees who have joined our society since 1970. As Professor Bill Ong Hing, the principal investigator of the study writes, "This project concerns controversy, context, and information. The controversy is over policies related to immigration and immigrants. In addressing the controversy, one goal is to place the debate in proper context; and another is to provide more information that will enable the public and policy makers to make informed judgments."

The report focuses on four highly significant, but largely misunderstood aspects of the contemporary Asian Pacific immigration experience:

the patterns of demographic growth and diversification, the high rates of entrepreneurial activity, the short-term and long-range economic and social benefits from their high educational attainment levels, and the extremely high rates of naturalization and electoral participation which they exhibit in relation to increased acculturation. Through the use of state-of-the-art quantitative and qualitative research methods, these empirical findings challenge an array of harmful and inaccurate myths that have been promulgated in recent years about not only Asian Pacific immigrants and refugees, but also other groups of new Americans. In sharing this information, as well as providing the proper policy and analytical contexts, we hope this report will contribute to reframing our nation's current immigration debate.

To be sure, immigration has had an unprecedented, multifaceted impact on the Asian Pacific American population during the past few decades. From a largely American-born group of 1.5 million in 1970, the Asian Pacific population has been transformed through large-scale immigration to a predominantly foreign-born population of 7.3 million in 1990 (with projections that they will reach 11 million by 2000, and nearly 20 million by 2020). This demographic impact of immigration is visible in many parts of the nation — from Lowell, Massachusetts to the San Gabriel Valley in Southern California, and from Houston, Texas to La Crosse, Wisconsin. At the same time, recent Asian immigrants have gained substantial media notoriety such as during the 1992 Los Angeles civil unrest when thousands of Korean and other Asian businesses were targeted and destroyed, as well as in the horrifying discovery of Thai women garment workers who toiled in slave-like conditions in El Monte, CA. However, the vast majority of recent Asian Pacific immigrants are not in the media spotlight, although their contributions to this society are substantial. Asian Pacific Americans, for example, represent a sizable proportion of the physicians and other health care workers in America's public health system, as well as the engineers and scientists in the nation's advanced technological and scientific sectors.

Recent efforts to drastically change existing immigration policies have generated deep anxiety and concern among a broad cross-section of Asian Pacific American community-based organizations and leaders across the nation. They have joined with other organized groups and leaders to advocate against legislation which would substantially curtail legal immigration, and would virtually eliminate long-standing family reunification provisions. Over a million Asian Pacifics, who have been on waiting lists for upwards of ten years seeking to be reunited with their families would be affected. They also have raised concerns about recent efforts within Congress to deny a number of social service benefits to legal immigrants who have yet to become naturalized. We hope this report provides relevant information and analysis to further illuminate the indispensable benefits which American society has gained from immigration.

Like our other joint policy research activities and publications, this report reflects the special strengths and goals of our two institutions. The UCLA Asian American Studies Center, established in 1969, is one of four ethnic studies centers at UCLA, and one of the nation's oldest programs in Asian American Studies. Through its research, teaching, publishing, library acquisitions, and public educational activities in fields ranging from literature to urban planning, the faculty staff, and students of the Center have sought to advance scholarly and policy understanding of Asian Pacific Americans.

LEAP is a nonprofit organization founded in 1982 to develop, strengthen, and expand the leadership roles played by Asian Pacific Americans within their own communities as well as in mainstream institutions. LEAP's mission to achieve full participation and equality for Asian Pacific Americans through leadership, empowerment and policy is being realized through the innovative Leadership Management Institute (LMI), the Community Development Institute (CDI), and the nationally recognized Asian Pacific American Public Policy Institute (APA•PPI).

We would like to pay special tribute to Professor Bill Ong Hing of Stanford University Law School for serving as the principal investigator of this major policy report, and for coordinating this important research endeavor. We also would like to thank the researchers for this project, as well as the individuals who worked on producing this publication. Finally, we would like to express our gratitude to the Board of Directors of LEAP and the Faculty Advisory Committee of the UCLA Asian American Studies Center for their continued support of our joint policy research endeavors.

Don T. Nakanishi, Ph.D.
Director
UCLA Asian American Studies Center

J.D. Hokoyama
President and Executive Director
Leadership Education for Asian Pacifics

Acknowledgements

We wish to thank the following individuals and institutions who have provided their generous support to the Asian Pacific American Public Policy Institute and have made this study possible:

The Andrew W. Mellon Foundation provided major funding for this study. The Ford Foundation and the Joyce Mertz-Gilmore Foundation also contributed major funds for the project. We also wish to thank the Carnegie Corporation of New York, The Ford Foundation, and The James Irvine Foundation for their continued support of LEAP and the Asian Pacific American Public Policy Institute, and for making this project possible. We wish to acknowledge the support of the following funders: ARCO Foundation, Rockwell International Corporation, Hughes Electronics Corporation, Pacific Bell, Equitable Foundation, William Penn Foundation, GTE Foundation, Kaiser Permanente of Southern California, and the Minneapolis Foundation.

Many people contributed to the successful completion of this project. Besides the various researchers whose articles are presented in this volume, others contributed to the quality of the final product. In addition to our own review, the papers were scrutinized by Michael Fix, Jeffrey Passel, and Wendy Zimmerman of the Urban Institute, Morrison Wong, chair of the Sociology Department at Texas Christian University, and economist Masao Suzuki of Mills College. Paul Ong, who co-authored two pieces in this study, helped with the initial conception of the project. We thank them for their helpful insights and suggestions. The editorial assistance of Diane Yen-Mei Wong was superb. And the technical assistance of Yvonne Yazzie was indispensable. Our thanks to Fresh Graphics for the layout and cover design.

In planning this volume, several meetings were held in New York, Los Angeles, San Francisco, and Washington, D. C., where dozens of community workers, leaders, academics, and residents provided suggestions and guidance. We also had the benefit of discussions with individuals from Houston, Chicago, Phoenix, and Seattle. Their input was invaluable, and our only regret is that we were unable to address all of the relevant issues that were raised in those meetings and discussions. Clearly, more research is in order on behalf of Asian Pacific America. Hopefully, we will be presented with more opportunities in the near future to look at other questions related to immigrants (documented and undocumented), the society, and the economy.

Finally, the individuals at LEAP deserve special recognition for their dedication to the project at every stage. We wish to thank J.D. Hokoyama and John Y. Tateishi, project director, for recognizing the need for this study, taking the initiative to launch the project, and sustaining it over a two year period with constant vision and emotional support. We also wish to thank Gena A. Lew and Linda Akutagawa for their invaluable technical assistance and administrative support throughout the project. And finally, we are indebted to Suzanne J. Hee, project coordinator, for her skillful management in working with the writers and the project team, and for her perseverance in seeing the final product through to its completion.

The Editors

Reframing the Immigration Debate: An Overview

by Bill Ong Hing[*]

This project concerns controversy, context, and information. The controversy is over policies related to immigration and immigrants. In addressing the controversy, one goal is to place the debate in proper context; and another is to provide more information that will enable the public and policymakers to make informed judgments.

Immigration has reached levels not witnessed since the first decade of the century. And since 1965, those reaching the nation's borders have been dominated by Asian Pacific and Latino emigres. From 1971 to 1990, nearly nine million immigrants entered from Asian and Latin American countries, contributing to phenomenal growth in Latino and Asian Pacific American growth in the United States. The Latino population increased by 141 percent over the 20-year period to reach 9 percent of the total U.S. population, while the Asian Pacific American population grew a striking 385 percent to comprise 2.9 percent of the population. By the year 2000, Asian Pacific America is projected to represent 4 percent of the total.[1]

Asians and Pacific Islanders have made up over a third of all legal immigration to the United States since 1970. After 1975, most refugees admitted to the country have been Southeast Asian. This phenomenon has produced several results: (1) a surge in the Asian Pacific American population that is now predominantly foreign born; (2) a change in the demographic character of many parts of the United States; (3) an impact on educational institutions; (4) changes in languages we hear and foods we eat; (5) a transformation in the characteristics and types of businesses; and (6) an influence on many other social, economic, and political institutions. Undoubtedly, in some quarters, the influx of Asian and Pacific immigrants and refugees has contributed to a backlash against immigrants and immigration policies.

---

[*] Bill Hing is an Associate Professor at Stanford Law School and serves as the Executive Director of the Immigrant Legal Resource Center. Many thanks to Irene Chang, Selena Dong, Melanie Erasmus, and Margaret Lin for excellent research assistance.

A certain level of anti-immigrant sentiment has always been a part of the nation's heritage. As economic times get rough and many longtime residents observe social changes that cause discomfort, the level, however, can reach fever pitch. Daily front-page coverage of immigration issues makes it obvious that we are at one of those levels today.

The Project

As one effort to begin addressing the social and economic concerns swirling in the current debate, this volume covers four topics specific to Asian Pacific America: demographics, entrepreneurs, education, and citizenship. The research papers presented certainly do not provide every answer to every question that is important to the debate over immigrant and immigration policy. They certainly, though, provide a good deal of information not previously shared or understood. And by doing so, the papers prompt us to place the controversy in proper perspective.

Part I is a detailed demographic picture of Asian Pacific American communities. Sociologists Lawrence Shinagawa and Robert Jiobu bring us up to date on available data, while offering a variety of perspectives that provide us a new understanding of the various Asian Pacific American communities. They both pay particular attention to the impact that immigration laws and immigrants have on the characteristics of Asian Pacific America.

Shinagawa and Jiobu remind us that today's fastest growing racial community was once the subject of abhorrent exclusion laws that brought growth to a virtual standstill for groups such as Chinese, Koreans, and Asian Indians. After 1965, the population of Asian Pacific America surged but certainly not due to anything foreseen by policymakers of the 1960s. Today Asian Pacific immigrants are about 40 percent of all immigrants; combined with Latinos, the two groups make up well over 80 percent of all immigrants to the United States.

The amount of data provided by Shinagawa and Jiobu is impressive. They include numerous tables and charts that are helpful for understanding the profiles of various Asian Pacific communities. Different groups tend to favor different metropolitan areas of the country, such as Pakistanis in New York and Washington, and Vietnamese in California. Shinagawa's maps reveal the distribution of Asian Pacific Americans across the continent as well as the density in New York and California. While figures for the aggregate Asian Pacific America suggest high levels of educational attainment, a separate study of communities such as Cambodians, Tongans, and Laotians reveals a much different picture. The fact that the median ages for U.S.-born Korean Americans and Cambodian Americans are 9 and 4.7, respectively, reminds us just how new much of Asian Pacific America is. A majority of every group (except the Hmong) rates itself as speaking English well or very well, a point that suggests that acculturation market forces or immigrants' own desires to learn English are quite strong. Labor force participation rates for Asian Pacific America are higher than average, as are household incomes. But per capita income among Asians is lower in areas of high concentration of Asian Pacific Americans. Perhaps the most important contribution of the papers by Shinagawa and Jiobu, however, is their reminder that Asian Pacific America is tremendously diverse.

Shinagawa and Jiobu's accounts make us wonder about the intent behind many of today's restrictionist proposals. Since immigration has fueled the communities' growth since 1965, is the intent to curtail that growth? Certainly many advocates of restrictive immigration policies are motivated by a protectionist sense of economics, but how many other restrictionists are motivated because of growth related specifically to immigration, and how many of those are motivated by the current ethnic composition of immigration?

Part II begins an inquiry into an area that is often neglected in the popular debate over immigrants and immigration policy—the contributions of immigrant entrepreneurs. More often than not, the controversy over the economic impact of immigrants is framed in terms of job competition, wage depression, and public costs. As law and economics specialist Shubha Ghosh points out, highly-publicized studies purporting to report on the economic impact of immigrants do not even attempt to measure benefits that immigrant entrepreneurs may 'pour back into public coffers and employment rolls.

Ghosh's paper provides a theoretical framework for thinking about contributions of immigrant entrepreneurs. Small, immigrant-owned businesses are an important part of the economy; and the number owned by Asian Pacific Americans has surged. Between 1982 and 1987, the number of Asian Pacific American-owned businesses grew by almost 90 percent. By the late 1980s, their total sales and receipts were over $33 billion annually, they had a payroll of $3 billion, and over 350,000 employees. By creating regional markets, immigrant entrepreneurs increase gross national product. Simply put, the likely positive impact that these immigrants have on job creation, tax contributions, property values, and the overall economy is too substantial to ignore.

Ghosh is careful not to overstate his positions, but the implications of his concepts are evident: a fair evaluation of the economic impact of immigrants must include serious consideration of contributions by entrepreneurs. While his introductory data refers to Asian Pacific American-owned businesses, his theories are no less relevant to the numerous enterprises operated by natives of the Middle East and Latin America. In fact, although the 1992 uprising in South Central Los Angeles often highlighted the impact on Korean American businesses, a third of the businesses affected were Latino-owned.[2]

Sociologist Edward Park takes our inquiry on a more specific turn toward the impact of Asian Pacific American entrepreneurs. He first conducts a thorough review of the current literature that attempts to understand Asian Pacific American entrepreneurs, their role in the economy, their impact on the specific ethnic group and the larger community, and the models that have been fashioned by researchers to describe the phenomenon. As he moves to the focal point of his paper—Asian Pacific immigrants and the high tech industry of Silicon Valley—Park quickly establishes, however, that the Silicon Valley illustration does not fit neatly into prototypes constructed by even the most thoughtful modern commentators.

The Silicon Valley cluster is clearly not the laundry or grocery store that many Asian Pacific immigrants have turned to in response to discrimination, language barriers, limitations on capital, or cultural boundaries. Certainly analogies can be found: glass ceiling issues have prompted many Asian Pacific Americans to turn to their own Silicon Valley enterprises the way discrimination and other barriers pushed the smaller business owners; and the availability of venture capital from Asia for the high tech start-ups may be reminiscent of the pooling of money among friends and relatives for smaller scale businesses. High tech entrepreneurs, though, have positioned themselves in a subcontracting role that has played an instrumental role in the success of Silicon Valley. Unlike other Asian Pacific business endeavors, this one represents a path into the mainstream labor market via ethnic entrepreneurship. And the path toward high tech businesses relying on special educational and work backgrounds is also unique for this group of Asian Pacific Americans.

The case studies by Melanie Erasmus, Craig Huynh, and Gen Lee provide some modern, real life illustrations to our consideration of immigrant entrepreneurs. Erasmus follows Park's piece with a series of examples of high-tech ventures in which immigrants and refugees have played critical roles. Huynh and Lee focus on new waves of smaller financed businesses. Huynh considers the question of how and why Vietnamese refugees have come to operate a staggering 80 percent of all nail salons in Los Angeles, and 30 percent nationwide. And Lee, who has worked in doughnut shops herself, provides vivid examples of a handful of Cambodian refugees who are part of the community that has come to dominate the doughnut shop industry in California.

The Asian Pacific immigrant entrepreneur examples discussed by this group of researchers seem to be only the tip of the iceberg. Ghosh cites examples from across the country: Seattle, New York, Dallas, and Washington, D.C. Erasmus and Park add California and Massachusetts. But so many others are impressive. Consider Josie Natori, the founder and president of New York's Natori Company who was originally from the Philippines. Her fashion company does $30 million in annual sales. Japan-born Shoji Tabuchi, packs them in daily in his 2,000-seat Shoji Tabuchi Theater in Branson, Missouri, where he presents country and western family entertainment and occasionally brings down the house with his own violin playing. His company brings in $12 million a year. James Kim, from Korea, is the majority shareholder of two companies, including the Electronics Boutique stores located in busy shopping malls everywhere. His companies' sales are $400 million annually, and his headquarters are in Gladyne, Pennsylvania. China-born Bernard Chiu is the founder and CEO of Duracraft, Inc., of Whitinsville, Massachusetts. The company is the leading manufacturer of fans, space heaters, and humidifiers, and has annual sales of $140 million.[3]

The fact that Asian Pacific immigrants can make a go of it in troubled industries or in small stores and shops in poor neighborhoods across the country is also impressive. Consider the extensive firm development and growth among Chinese immigrants in the declining garment manufacturing industry in New York City. Or the fact that Korean-owned businesses in Los Angeles have established a major presence in low income Latino and African American communities, particularly in small scale retailing.[4] Surely contributions of the high and low profile immigrant entrepreneur in terms of capital investments, jobs, taxes, property values, civic pride, innovation, and vitality are inspiring and healthy for the entire nation.

As evidenced in the passage of Proposition 187, much of the backlash against immigrants is related to the belief that the education of immigrant children and the children of immigrants is too costly.[5] In Part III of our report, Paul Ong and Linda Wing provide a forthright appraisal of this difficult issue. Between 1970 and 1990, the number of first and second generation Asian Pacific American children increased by more than a million. Ong and Wing acknowledge the "additional costs" that many of these children may bring to bear on the educational system, such as in programs for limited-English speakers and the poor; after all, most Southeast Asian refugees and recent Asian Pacific immigrants speak little English and many live in poverty.

Ong and Wing, however, provide an enlightening context. They inform us that many adult Asian Pacific immigrants have already been educated abroad and therefore transfer those human capital qualities to the United States at no charge. Those workers immediately contribute tax revenues and boost the economy. More importantly, Ong and Wing remind us of the multi-purposes behind our society's social contract to educate our children: to transmit knowledge, culture, and skills from one generation to the next, to enable children to care for the future. Only a foolish country would not do its best to educate all of its children. Even the most cynical should realize that the payoff comes in terms of productivity and tax contributions. The fair way to view the so-called "cost of education" is as an investment in human capital. Only after considering the person's entire life—including the working years when the education pays off—is it fair to judge whether the educational expense was too costly. In order to begin an inquiry into the payoff, Ong and Wing cite the higher than average earnings of Asian Pacific Americans (which is tied to educational attainment). The implications are clear: educating the children of immigrants and immigrant children pays off in the long run.

Interviews of individuals who entered the United States as children follow the Ong and Wing article. Khanh Phan was eight years old when his family entered as refugees from Vietnam in 1975. He attended California public elementary and secondary schools, as well as state university. Today he is a social worker, earning $3,200 a month. He is buying a home and lives with his mother and brother. David Mao's family immigrated from Taiwan when he was age eleven. He attended public schools in Washington, D.C., served in the U.S. Army in Vietnam, went to college on the G.I. bill, and today he is a criminal investigator making $53,000 a year. Katherine Chan's family also fled Vietnam when she was a child. She attended public schools in New Jersey and eventually served in the Peace Corps. She also turned to social work and now earns about $42,000 a year. These individuals verify the strength of Ong and Wing's argument: the educational investments in these individuals have truly paid off for the nation.

A concern that many Americans have about today's immigrants is the extent to which they desire to become Americans. As nebulous as the concept of Americanization may be, in Part IV, Paul Ong and Don Nakanishi look at two measures that most people would regard as strong indications of Americanization: naturalization and voting. When it comes to naturalization, Asian Pacific immigrants have maintained high rates for three decades. In fact, Vietnamese, Chinese, and Filipinos are the ethnic groups with the highest naturalization rates, while Canadians, Italians, and British nationals are among the lowest. Voter registration and voting rates are more complex. Although recent Asian Pacific immigrants and refugees have lower voter registration rates than native-born citizens, naturalized Asian Pacific Americans who have resided here for more than 20 years have comparable or higher rates than the native-born. The voter registration rates for native-born Asian Pacific Americans are even higher. And when actual voting is considered, registered Asian Pacific American voters have among the highest electoral participation rates of any group.

The results of Parts III and IV should not be read to mean that Asian Pacific immigrants are somehow more inclined to pay back the investment in public education or more willing to Americanize than other immigrant groups. These case studies have focused on Asian Pacific Americans because we believe that such studies have seldom entered into public policy discussions, in spite of the substantial numbers of Asian Pacific immigrants and refugees entering today. Similar serious attention should be paid to other immigrant groups. Consider education. Ong and Wing's recognition of the authoritarian parenting style of Asian Pacific American parents in the context of good academic performance certainly should not be read to suggest that other immigrant families do not value education. Every immigrant group has its successes and failures; indeed, that fact encourages us to examine students' successes as the possible affirmation of identity and culture.[6] As for Americanization, naturalization rates certainly are not the only (nor necessarily most accurate) measure of intent to commit to the nation. Detailed surveys of Latino immigrants indicate that contrary to popular beliefs and despite low naturalization rates, the vast majority intend to reside in the United States permanently.[7] And given recent reports of increased naturalization applications across the country, new studies of naturalization rates are likely to demonstrate increasing rates for all nationalities.

The Context

Economic complaints about immigrants essentially fall into two broad categories: those dealing with the labor market and those relating to costs. Labor market complaints advance the popular image of immigrants competing with native workers for jobs or depressing their wages. Complaints concerning costs argue that immigrants are a burden on our public coffers, especially in terms of public education and public assistance.

But there is substantial evidence that should make us a little skeptical about whether these complaints are even partially, much less totally, valid. Consider jobs. The fear that immigrants take away jobs from native workers rests on the theory that the number of jobs is static, or fixed. Under this theory, when immigrants get jobs, fewer jobs are left for native workers—thereby causing increases in unemployment among native laborers. The idea of a fixed workforce has a certain common sense appeal but is inaccurate. Economists agree that the number of jobs is dynamic rather than fixed: as more persons begin working and spending their earnings, demand for more goods follows, and generally more labor is needed.

Immigrants are not simply workers—they are also consumers. Like everyone else, immigrants need basic goods such as food, shelter, and clothing. Immigrant workers spend their earnings on these goods as well as (to the extent they can afford them) on other nonessential items. Immigrants therefore increase the total demand for goods. In response, businesses increase their production. To do this, they must increase their labor force and hire more workers. Thus, the entry of immigrants into the labor market ultimately creates jobs by pressuring businesses to expand their production. In fact, the mere presence of a new immigrant—even one who is not working—can increase consumption or the demand for goods and services, and cause the same result. Thus, all native workers—including minorities and women—would find better job opportunities due to overall economic growth.[8]

If immigrants actually create jobs for native workers, why do so many people believe that immigrants pose a threat to native workers' jobs? This may be a matter of what we think we see. While the average person may actually see an immigrant working in a job once held by a native worker, the "more indirect and diffuse" job-creation process attributable to immigrants is not as easily perceived.[9] This may help account for much of the public suspicion about immigrants and jobs.

While far from perfect, apparently many economists offer theories supporting the rhetoric often offered by pro-immigrant advocates that "immigrants take jobs that native workers don't want." The argument is that the labor market is divided into primary "good" jobs and secondary "bad" jobs. The first group is largely populated by native workers; the latter, by migrants.[10] Primary sector jobs are situated in so called "core" industries, where investments and financing of production are relatively high, and mainly large-scaled and unionized, and where instability has been minimized by such market features as little effective competition. Workers who fill such jobs must have relatively high skills. They are paid well and work under generally desirable conditions. By contrast, secondary jobs are found in smaller firms where production is not as highly financed and products face highly competitive markets. Positions tend to be unstable, low or unskilled, relatively low paying, and generally marked by undesirable working conditions.

Migrants are more suited for these low-paying, low-skill jobs due to (1) the flexibility of the migrant work force; (2) the lasting nature of the migrant labor supply; and (3) their susceptibility to manipulation and control. Migrants thus dominate low-paying, low-skill jobs.[11] The question then is whether, on account of immigrant domination of secondary jobs, native workers are pushed into primary jobs, or whether they are unemployed. President Ronald Reagan's Council of Economic Advisors, agreeing with the principle that immigrants generally do not displace native workers, emphasized the job and occupational mobility of native workers. Native workers can move from one sector of the labor market to another, while immigrants generally cannot.

Given differences in English ability, education, and job experience between what economist George Borjas labels the "typical" Mexican undocumented alien and a native worker, the immigrant seems ill-equipped to fill many of the jobs open to native workers. Thus, many low-skilled immigrant workers and more skilled native workers may fulfill mutual needs (complementary rather than competitive) and result in increased productivity. Things are likely, however, more complicated. Borjas argues that "various combinations of complementary and substitutability among many immigrant and native groups are possible." To the extent that some immigrants serve as real or potential substitutes of native workers, their presence increases the supply of workers and, at the very least, can depress wage rates. And when wages are lowered, some natives no longer find it worthwhile to remain in the labor force and therefore drop out.[12]

Economist Julian Simon responds to Borjas' point about the possibility of native worker drop-out by suggesting that while many low-wage jobs filled by immigrants might otherwise go to teenagers and retirees (*e.g.*, at fast food chains), it may not be appropriate to consider such a phenomenon in the same light as displacement of an typical native worker. He urges us to look at the "long run" "positive general effect" of immigrants on the job market, even though in the "short run" "some particular groups may be injured by a particular group of immigrants."[13] Additionally, absent immigrants, some advertised jobs which currently go to immigrants would remain unfilled and therefore eventually be withdrawn "because employers can make other arrangements either by using machines or cutting back."[14] Immigrants who fill such positions pose no direct harm to native workers.

Recent studies on effects of immigrants on the labor market shed light on the debate. They suggest that a serious evaluation of the impact must consider regional (geographic) as well as sectoral (particular industry) variations. For example, a comprehensive study by the Alexis de Tocqueville Institution yields striking results on the relationship between immigration and unemployment. The researchers took a statistical look at each state comparing unemployment figures and foreign-born populations from 1900 to 1989.[15] Their findings were unequivocal: the median unemployment rate was higher in states with relatively little immigrant presence. If anything, unemployment seemed negatively associated with immigration—the more immigrants, the less unemployment. Researchers were confident in rejecting the view that immigration causes unemployment.[16]

That study paid particular attention to the effects of recent immigrants and concluded that even recent waves of immigration have reduced joblessness. In response to the current debate over immigration, researchers performed an analysis that looked exclusively at the 1980s. They looked at the ten states with the highest unemployment, compared them with the ten states with the lowest unemployment, and found that the immigrant (defined as foreign born) population in the high unemployment states was much lower than in the low unemployment states. Then they looked at the ten states with the largest proportion of immigrants, compared their unemployment rates with the ten states with the smallest immigrant population, and found that the typical unemployment rate in the states with low immigration was nearly one-third higher than in the states with relatively high immigration.[17]

One might wonder, of course, if the causal relationship between high immigration and low unemployment could work in the other direction — namely, whether high unemployment states simply attract fewer immigrants. Other researchers, however, have discounted that relationship, finding that areas of high immigrant concentrations are larger in cities where a low rate of labor participation among unskilled native workers is related to reasons other than immigration.[18]

Although researchers acknowledge anecdotal evidence of individuals who are perceived to have lost jobs due to immigration, they argue that these "occasional adverse employment effects are *completely* (and perhaps even more than completely) offset by the less visible but nonetheless equally real positive employment effects that immigration provides." Their data refuted the notion that immigration is associated with higher unemployment, suggesting instead that immigrants actually create more jobs than they take, thereby reducing the overall rate of unemployment.[19] These and similar findings have led most observers to conclude that immigration ultimately creates jobs, thereby producing increased employment opportunities for immigrants and native workers alike.[20]

Economist Robert Topel's research on less-skilled workers in the West provides a better understanding of the effect of less-skilled immigrants on wages.[21] By comparing wages among less-skilled workers in other parts of the country, he concludes that the increase of less-skilled Latino and Asian immigrants in the West has "adversely affected the wages of natives."[22] But it is important to keep in mind that through immigration, the West has maintained a steady supply of low-wage workers, which helps to explain why wages will not rise as much. In New England, for example, rising schooling levels has reduced the supply of unskilled workers over the past 20 years, which in turn raises wages among unskilled workers. Furthermore, Topel's conclusion that unskilled immigrants from Asia and Latin America result in wages among unskilled workers that are 10 percent lower than in other parts of the country is distorted. His data was taken from the Current Population Survey, which records broad ethnic categories rather than immigration status. To make his calculations on the impact of immigrants, he excluded all "Hispanics and Asians."[23] The problem of course is that not all "Hispanics and Asians" are immigrants, so the 10 percent effect is clearly overstated.

Examples of sectoral studies also show the complexity of immigrant impact on the labor market. For example, hiring low-wage immigrant workers has been used as a survival technique in some manufacturing industries such as the automotive parts industry. Economist Rebecca Morales' study of the use of undocumented workers in that industry in Los Angeles raises this and other questions about the role of immigrant labor.[24] Morales looked at the use of undocumented workers at 21 businesses, focusing principally on 8 automobile parts companies.[25] She found that undocumented workers were used to facilitate structural transitions in reaction to changing economic circumstances.[26]

The context of this study is important. In 1979, automobile manufacturers and parts suppliers employed over a million workers in Los Angeles. As a consequence of the 1979 to 1980 stage of the recession, the automobile industry lost about 5,500 jobs at the same time a sizable influx of low-skilled immigrants (including many undocumented aliens from El Salvador and Guatemala) began to arrive. Major automakers responded to the economic situation by consolidating some operations, shifting some production to foreign affiliates or to the Midwest, automating, and subcontracting some product lines. The 2,000 auto parts suppliers, mostly not unionized, did not have the same capacity to react and were more vulnerable to shifting market forces (*e.g.*, demand for original equipment, product aftermarkets, and local labor markets). Since assembly plants were closing, only suppliers who could shift to the aftermarket could survive.[27]

Survival strategies were influenced by several factors. Those companies that were subsidiaries of larger corporations could tap into the wealth of the parent for finance capital; many independent firms that were less likely to have reliable resources considered merging. Whether workers were unionized was important as a union meant that employers had to bargain over wages, job classifications, benefits, and the like. In order to survive, suppliers needed a more flexible work force, and many turned to undocumented workers as one solution.[28]

Morales has several noteworthy findings. Firms that were facing difficult market conditions turned to undocumented workers out of a need for a cheap labor force that could contract and expand easily. While unionization and the size of the enterprise were not significant indicators of likely employment of undocumented workers, subsidiaries were more likely than independent firms to hire undocumented aliens.[29] In conclusion, Morales states:

During expansionary periods, legal immigrants are absorbed into the economy, but during decline, they become redundant. In this way, undocumented workers are ideal since they are easily replaced. Lacking legal protection, they unwittingly benefit employers seeking union and wage erosion. Ironically, they may actually be preferable to legalized guestworkers from the point of view of assisting the transition, if guestworkers temper the momentum toward automation. From this perspective, the market found an alternate solution to guestworkers.[30]

Morales' study raises the question whether undocumented workers—whose labor allows some manufacturers to delay automation and remain competitive—do cause some union and wage erosion. They may also make it possible, however, for some industries to survive in the United States, thereby protecting some jobs for natives. Immigration restrictions would not necessarily make it possible for unions to maintain jobs and wages at high levels because the threat of industry relocation to countries with cheaper labor would remain a threat.

Other economists have considered furniture manufacturing. More than two-thirds of furniture production employment continue to be found in Southern states (especially North Carolina), where African Americans comprise much of the workforce. California is home to the other third of the jobs—mostly in Southern California where most of the workers are Mexican. Even in San Francisco, immigrants comprise much of the furniture workforce: one-third are Latino, one-sixth Asian.[31]

In a study of California furniture manufacturers, Richard Mines looked for trends related to immigrant workers and unions. He found that as unionized firms in San Francisco closed and relocated to Southern California, the new firms were clearly anti-union.[32] Most firms in Los Angeles were nonunion, and many consciously turned over the workforce regularly in order to control wages. Mines argues that new immigrants have come to dominate this low-wage, nonunion workforce because they are willing to tolerate these conditions. Even in the unionized workforce with more settled immigrants, however, new immigrants pose a displacement threat to the workers because the industry is so labor intensive and competitive.[33]

Low-wage, low-skilled immigrants have enabled many furniture manufacturers in Southern California to survive. The competition in much of the industry is between U.S. firms, and thus between various regions of the country. Low-wage immigrant workers give Southern California firms an advantage because they are able to keep labor costs down. In the process, though, the firms with settled immigrants get underbid by those using new low-wage workers, and settled immigrants can lose ground.[34]

The immigrant entrepreneur papers in Part III of this LEAP report contribute important new considerations to the labor market analysis. They highlight employment creation conditions that are directly attributable to immigrants (*e.g.*, in high-tech and other investment-type situations) as well as self-employment situations (smaller capitalized firms such as doughnut and manicure shops). The latter examples also raise the tension that may be created with respect to competition on a different level: head-to-head competition in small business operations as opposed to competition for jobs.

As for the alleged burden that immigrants place on public coffers, one literature survey conducted through 1991 found that national studies that took into account all levels of government reveal that immigrants are not a financial burden on the native population. State studies were mixed, because some states take on more responsibilities than others. Analyses at the local level found that immigrants were a net fiscal burden—but so were native residents.[35]

Economist Donald Huddle's report and his op-ed pieces based on the report have received extensive national attention.[36] With a good deal of fanfare, the report has been touted as the "first comprehensive study of the public sector costs of legal and illegal immigration."[37] His main conclusions are: (1) the poverty rate of immigrants is 42.8 percent higher than for natives; (2) immigrants as a group are 13.5 percent more likely to receive public assistance, and their households receive 44.2 percent more public assistance dollars than do native households; and (3) net immigrant costs in 1992 at the county, state, and national levels were $42.5 billion for the 19.3 million legal and undocumented immigrants who have settled in the United States since 1970, compared to $20.20 billion in taxes contributed. The biggest expense was for primary and secondary public education, followed by Medicaid and county social and health services.[38] Concluding that taxes contributed by immigrants were small, he claims that both legal and undocumented immigrants cost Texans more than $4 billion in 1992 for education, health care, and other services beyond what taxes they paid in Texas.[39]

The Urban Institute has issued a separate report responding to Huddle's findings.[40] In this report, economist Jeffrey Passel (1) uses more widely-accepted numbers of immigrants (*e.g.*, he uses the Immigration and Naturalization Service estimates of the undocumented population), (2) finds that Huddle grossly understates the taxes paid by immigrants, (3) argues that Huddle overstates the government benefits received by immigrants, and (4) disagrees with Huddle's hypothesis that immigrants displace native workers. As a result, Passel finds a that immigrants are net *contributors* to public coffers.

Passel points out four major flaws in Huddle's estimates of immigrant tax contributions. First, Huddle relies on faulty data that understated tax collections for immigrants by 30 percent. Huddle further used contributions of 1980-1990 legal immigrants to estimate taxes paid by 1970-1992 immigrants, even though those entering in the 1970s are known to have higher incomes than those entering a decade later.[41]

Second, Huddle estimates national immigrant income by erroneously assuming that since natives in Los Angeles earn more than average natives nationally, immigrants in Los Angeles must do the same.[42]

Third, Huddle tries to adjust for levels of taxation in Los Angeles different than those found in the rest of the country by taking the ratio of national per capita taxes to per capita taxes paid in the county by natives and immigrants combined, but fails to recognize that per capita taxes paid depends on income levels as well as taxation levels, further underestimating taxes paid by immigrants.[43]

Finally, in calculating revenue, Huddle leaves out 5 of the 13 taxes included in other studies—FICA (Social Security and Medicare taxes), unemployment insurance, vehicle license and registration fees, and federal and state gasoline taxes—which account for 44 percent of the revenues from immigrants in other studies. Huddle also omits corporate income tax, local income tax, commercial property tax and utility taxes. Thus, using a corrected version of Huddle's revenue framework, Passel finds that immigrants contribute an additional $50 billion.[44]

Passel finds that Huddle overstates immigrant costs by relying on overestimates of per capita service costs for recent legal immigrants;[45] using inflated participation rates in such programs as Headstart;[46] applying a school attendance rate based on 5-17 year olds for immigrants aged 5-19;[47] and using the national average for Medicaid payments (usually made to the elderly) as a measure for immigrants who tend to be younger than the average population.[48]

Parts II and III of this LEAP report on immigrant entrepreneurs and education also address many concerns related to the complaint about the cost of immigrants. The collection of papers on immigrant entrepreneurs addresses the problem in reports, such as Huddle's, when they leave out consideration of these important contributions to the economy. And Ong and Wing's education paper give the more complete, long-term view of educational costs as an investment in human capital.

Current debates over welfare reform have intersected with a concern that immigrants access public assistance at higher-than-average rates. Researchers at the Urban Institute also have looked at public assistance usage among immigrants. They have found that while immigrants use welfare at slightly higher rates than natives, non-native use is concentrated among two groups: elderly immigrants and refugees. The higher rate among refugees is understandable since they are fleeing persecution and have fewer economic or family ties in the United States than other immigrants. There is also substantial overlap between elderly and refugee benefits use, as refugees account for 27 percent of immigrants over 65 who receive public benefits. Welfare use among working-age immigrants (18-64) who did not enter as refugees is about the same as for natives.[49]

When it comes to Asian Pacific immigrants in particular, we are reminded by papers in this volume by Shinagawa, Jiobu, Ong and Nakanishi of the long history of immigration exclusion. Could that history partially explain the high welfare rate of elderly Asian Pacific immigrants? Might vestiges of exclusion laws have prevented them from entering at an age that would have allowed them to earn enough credits to qualify for social security retirement funds today? What other economic contributions can be attributed to their families? Indeed, several of Shinagawa's findings address these questions. For example, although he finds a higher than average welfare rate among elderly Asian Pacific Americans, they have an extremely lower than average rate of social security use.

With this understanding, recent findings by George Borjas of higher-than-average welfare use among immigrants can be placed into context. When his data were broken down by country of origin, those from Vietnam had a high rate, but the rates for immigrants from the Philippines, China, and India were about the same as that for natives. The welfare rate for Korean immigrants was only half that of natives.[50] Furthermore, there may be some concern with his data source: the Survey of Income and Program Participation (SIPP). The SIPP surveys only 50,000 persons in 20,000 households, with an emphasis on program participation. The sample size is relatively small and its Southeast Asian category includes only Vietnamese. In fairness, another data source such as the Current Population Survey (CPS) ought to be reviewed as well. The CPS survey includes Cambodians, Laotians, Thais, and Vietnamese in its Southeast Asian category and contains a question about parent's country of birth, which would allow an examination of the second generation as well. From the Borjas and Urban Institute findings, one can already infer that the second generation Asian Pacific Americans use welfare at a rate much lower than the general population. This suggests that their parents used welfare only as a transition, and high use among parents might be less of a policy concern since it did not become a way of life for the next generation of citizens.

Of course advocates calling for greater restrictions on immigration in this country do not limit their arguments to economic themes. For some, the millions of newcomers to this country in recent decades represent a challenge to their concept of what America itself is. For these critics, such as Republican presidential candidate Patrick Buchanan and journalist Peter Brimelow, cultural and racial issues may be more important. Senator Alan Simpson, a chief architect of U.S. immigration policy, argues, "[i]mmigration to the United States is out of control."[51] "[A]ssimilation to fundamental American public values and institutions may be of far more importance to the future of the United States. . . . [A] community with a large number of immigrants who do not assimilate will to some degree seem unfamiliar to longtime residents."[52] In Simpson's view, immigrants must accept the "public culture of the country — as opposed to private ethnic culture."[53]

Similarly, consider the Federation of Americans for Immigration Reform (FAIR). Touted as the nation's "main restrictionist lobbying group,"[54] one member of FAIR calls for restricted immigration so that Americans may give themselves some "breathing space" to perform the "task of assimilation."[55] Richard Lamm, former Colorado governor and chair of FAIR's advisory board, adds, "[America] can accept additional immigrants, but we must make sure they become Americans. We can be a Joseph's coat of many nations, but we must be unified."[56] Even some self-described liberals insist that immigrants demonstrate their desire to join other Americans and become "one of us."[57]

While high naturalization or voting rates may not fully satisfy those with cultural or racial complaints about immigration, the paper by Ong and Nakanishi in Part V of this report responds to some of the assimilationist concerns. For those who want something more from immigrants, however, the basic definition of what an American is seems to be in question.

Study after study demonstrates, however, that the vast majority of immigrants take on cultural traits of the host community. Some traits replace old ones, but most are simply added.[58] For example, immigrants entering the United States today learn English *at the same rate* as other immigrant groups before them. Immigrants want and encourage their children to learn English. First generation immigrants tend to learn English and pass it along to their children, who become bilingual. By the third generation, the original language is often lost.[59] Throughout the United States, the demand for English as a Second Language (ESL) training far outstrips supply, leading adult newcomers to encounter long lines and waiting lists before gaining access to classes.[60]

Cultural assimilationists frequently accuse the Latino community in particular of not assimilating or learning English. Yet Spanish-speaking immigrants residing in the country for fifteen years regularly speak English. They usually read English fluently within ten years. In addition, about 93 percent of all Mexican immigrants agree that U.S. residents should learn English.[61]

Although complete acculturation of all immigrants is impossible, immigrants and refugees of all ages become acculturated to some extent. Even before coming to the United States, some adult immigrants and refugees have been exposed to American culture due to its persuasiveness in the global media. Upon arriving in the United States, most adult immigrants and refugees work, learn English, and often strive to pick up U.S. cultural habits and customs. Many young Asian and Latino immigrants, in particular, aggressively strive to be "American." They are eager to learn English, get a job, and work hard; in short, they seek to achieve a part of the American dream. Their aspirations are similar to those of the Jewish, Irish, and southern and eastern European immigrants who came in earlier years. Due to school attendance, peer interaction, and media exposure, the children of immigrants, even those who are foreign born, generally become fully acculturated. These children speak English; and their customs, habits, and values are nearly indistinguishable from those of their native-born peers.

Besides complaining that new immigrants fail to adopt our society's cultural traits, cultural assimilationists also contend that immigrants threaten to dilute our Western cultural heritage. In truth, immigrants do *affect* our culture, perhaps as much as our culture affects them, but to describe this process as a dilution shows an ignorance of how culture in America has developed throughout our history: not as some monolith unmoved by the waves of immigration in the 18th, 19th, and 20th centuries, but as a dynamic understanding of what it means to be American. As immigrants acculturate, U.S. society in general has absorbed their customs, cuisine, interests, and values. Our culture and our definition of what it means to be American is ever-evolving. Immigrants play an integral role in helping to create that definition.

Changes in U.S. culture are, of course, not solely nor even mainly attributable to the influence of immigrants. Improved technologies, social movements, and economic developments are also crucial. A melting pot of sorts, however, does exist. Immigrants do not displace American culture; they help develop a distinctively new, constantly changing, and expanding U.S. culture.

The qualities of many new immigrants are also likely to help the United States compete in the world marketplace today. Papers by Ghosh, Park, and Erasmus on entrepreneurs in Part III remind us that a multicultural United States provides many advantages in the increasingly interdependent global economy.

Even casual attention to current events of the last decade has taught us that political and economic developments all over the world—in Europe, Latin America, Africa, Asia, and the Middle East—affect the United States economy. The Dow Jones, interest rates, production, the dollar's value, and economic growth all reacted to democracy movements in Asia and Eastern Europe, the Persian Gulf War, South Africa, NAFTA, and economic problems in Brazil and Mexico. Certainly the United States will remain economically linked to Europe, but Europe is only one of many regions that are vital to our economy. The blinders of a Euro-centric view of America limit our vision and viability in the international economic community. There are simply too many cultural differences that have to be considered for the United States to be effective globally. The economy increasingly demands expertise in more than just American or Euro-centric ways and customs.

Since Asia and the industrializing nations of Latin America are new areas of economic power, bicultural and multicultural U.S. residents will prove invaluable as American companies develop private trade agreements and cooperative business ventures with the nations and corporations of these regions. Many businesses, advertising agencies, and law firms already have recognized benefits of taking a multicultural approach in their Latin American and Asian endeavors. Some have established branches abroad, most have invested in culture and language training for employees, and even more have hired bicultural employees. In the age of jet travel, E-mail, tele-conferencing, cell phones, and fax machines, multicultural businesses are engaged in daily transactions in Tokyo, Singapore, Hong Kong, Manila, Beijing, Mexico City, Brasilia, and Caracas, as well as London, Paris, and Frankfurt.

A diverse work force is a domestic advantage as well. As the ethnic makeup and demographics of the country change, smart business managers make changes and innovations in response to needs of the changing population. In short, responding to demographic changes can help increase profits. However, producing commercials with slogans like "se habla espanol" and advertising in the *Asian Yellow Pages* in order to attract new business must be coupled with the cultivation of a staff that can develop a rapport with the new customers. Thus, more and more employers are coming to view diversity as good business as well as good public relations.

For example, the success of an AT&T service called Language Line, which allows U.S. companies to communicate with their non-English speaking customers and business contacts, illustrates the benefits of a diverse work force. Through a staff of interpreters on conference calls, Language Line allows businesses such as Whirlpool, Lands' End, Pepsi, and Gerber to communicate with U.S. and foreign customers who do not speak English. As the director of communications for the service explains, "Business is beginning to appreciate there are over 30 million people in this country who prefer to use a language other than English . . . . The U.S. business community is becoming increasingly attuned to the fact that not every customer speaks English."[62]

Moreover, gains from a diverse work place are also independent of changing demographics. A diverse work place is also a more innovative work place. For example, Burger King has implemented diversity and multicultural training seminars for its employees while increasing the percentage of people of color in its work force from 12 percent in 1986 to 28 percent in 1991. At Burger King and other businesses that have sought diversity, there is "a growing sentiment that diverse employee teams tend to outperform homogeneous teams of any composition . . . . [H]omogeneous groups may reach consensus more quickly, but often they are not as successful in generating new ideas or solving problems, because their collective perspective is narrower."[63] Thus, the old adage that "two heads are better than one" holds true, except that the more appropriate phrase might be "multiple ethnic perspectives are better than one."

Cultural pluralists rightly argue that the country continues to benefit from new immigrants. Although some may question the economic benefit of immigrants, new immigrants, like their predecessors, have the drive and willingness to make a better life for themselves and their families. As a class, immigrants and refugees could very well represent the most determined class of people from their countries of origin. Many have had to survive treacherous journeys and overcome severe obstacles. All have had to demonstrate the courage and fortitude needed to follow through on the difficult decision of uprooting themselves and often their families, by winding their way through immigration mazes and facing the logistical facets of relocation. With our native work force often charged with laziness and lack of drive, we stand to learn and to benefit from the hard work ethic of the immigrants and refugees who continue to enter.

More generally, immigrants represent a potential resource for adding to, rather than diluting, American culture. While the United States continues to be an innovative leader in many business, political, scientific, and social fronts, it is not the sole innovative leader in all these realms. We should be open to new ideas from people of different cultures who may have better ways of approaching the gamut of issues facing us, including business operations, protection of the environment, stress, interpersonal relations, and education.

The ultimate benefit from interaction with those of different cultures does not necessarily flow from learning about new innovations, however. Rather, by learning about other cultures through social interaction with people of other cultures, we begin to learn more about other people. We begin to understand their customs, attitudes, and values, as well as to share information about our own cultures. In that process, we begin to develop tolerance and respect for other cultures and backgrounds. This type of education provides the foundation for a peaceful, productive pluralism that must be fostered throughout the world.

Toward the Future

The research papers presented in this project provide us with context and information regarding the current state of research on the immigration controversy. They also remind us, though, that we should gather more information about how our society and the economy work before we can evaluate the actual effects—positive or negative—of immigrants on our lives.

For example, in California where much of the anti-immigrant sentiment has been fomented, shouldn't we be interested in knowing whether the taxpayer revolt of the 1970s has had a more fundamental impact on public services and schools than immigrants? Should we be troubled that because of Proposition 13, county property tax and general purpose revenues were lower in fiscal year 1988-89 than in fiscal year 1977-78, after adjusting for inflation, even though the state's population rose 27 percent during that period. The growth of sales tax revenue has lagged significantly behind the growth in personal income; during the 1980s, personal income in the state grew at 8.6 percent per year, but sales tax revenue grew only 7.4 percent per year—a full percentage point behind personal income growth. This is a significant gap and is explained largely because the sales tax applies only to a narrow—and declining—segment of total consumption, namely, tangible goods, and excludes most services (this is important because of the state's evolution from a production to a service economy). California, which was once one of the five highest states in spending per pupil, with high student performance, now ranks fortieth in spending per pupil, and student performance has dropped. California taxpayers pay only half the amount that New York and New Jersey pays per pupil.[64]

What about jobs? For whatever reason—global competition, mechanization, specialization, consumer attitudes, marketing techniques, military spending, or inventive management styles—the United States work force has undergone substantial change even in the last two decades. Although the economy is growing and American companies are prospering, job cuts are more numerous than ever. In sum, "[i]t is not that foreigners are stealing our jobs, it is that we are facing one another's competition, and we are doing so in a panic." Many American companies have become as efficient and modern as those in Japan and Germany, but several forces have emerged that continue to push corporations to shed workers. Advances in technology enable companies to produce much more with fewer employees. Price increases are hard to secure, and corporate America increasingly maintains profits by slicing labor costs. Finally, work force reduction has become fashionable—the mark of a good manager.[65] A typical headline reads, "Sara Lee to trim work force by 6%," in a story highlighting the layoffs of some 8,000 to 9,000 employees in the corporation's worldwide work force. The layoffs for this food and personal products conglomerate occurred despite "record annual sales and earnings." The Wall Street response? Sara Lee's stock was up.[66]

At the same time, more jobs are actually being added; recent headlines even cheer the increase in jobs.[67] Until about 1950, the migration was from the farms to the new "job multiplier" industries: railroads, automobiles, highway construction, aircraft manufacturing, and airlines. Now, the migration is to the service sector — retailing, health care, restaurants, finance, security, and other similar jobs. These are the job-multiplier industries in late twentieth-century America and they have, in fact, created enough jobs during the last decade or so to more than offset job cutbacks. In 1993, despite the cutbacks, two million people were added to the nation's total work force. So to some, layoffs and downsizing are not job cutbacks, but job "dislocation"—the dislocation being the time it takes a worker laid off from AT&T, for example, to find a new job, quite likely at lower pay.[68]

The increases in job opportunities are deceiving, however. Despite lower unemployment, the dramatic restructuring of U.S. business has made for major changes in the job market. Work is more specialized, information is harder to come by, employers are smaller and exceedingly cautious about hiring. It remains true that in most places outside California, home builders cannot find carpenters, trucking lines scramble for drivers, mortgage bankers scrape to hire loan processors. This, though, is misleading. Although total employment has been seen to increase by more than 200,000 in a single month, many of these new jobs are temporary; moreover, 8 million people are out of work, and many more can expect pink slips in the near future. Specialized training requirements and hard-to-find occupational niches complicate the job search. For example, three-quarters of new jobs in the late 1980s were at plants with fewer than 500 workers. New service jobs are widely dispersed as well. Those midsize employers are more likely to occupy obscure suburban business parks than to blaze their names atop skyscrapers. Divining exactly what niche a company fills means watching trade magazines, reading the business section of the local paper and, most of all, asking around.[69]

In sum, the nation's economy is producing two million new jobs a year, but they come with wages typically below $8 an hour, or about $16,000 a year, and offer no health benefits, no opportunity for promotion, and few promises that the jobs will last.[70]

We should also consider whether global competition and trade policies have implications for the movement of peoples across borders and to other jobs far beyond the control of immigration policy. For example, the completion of the Uruguay round of the General Agreement on Tariffs and Trade (GATT) in December 1993 extended free trade principles to services, meaning more access to foreign markets for U.S. banks and telecommunications countries.[71] Those changes, though, may come at a price. Just as NAFTA is likely to chip away at low-paying U.S. manufacturing jobs, so, too, GATT is expected to hurt industries like apparel, where U.S. goods will be forced to compete with a growing flood of cheap imports. Thus, the AFL-CIO has concerns about GATT that are quite similar to its concerns about NAFTA.[72] This may mean, however, that jobs in the exporting countries may expand and fewer emigrants may be driven to migrate.

The go-go 1980s once masked unease over America's changed economic position, but now, in a time of massive layoffs that threaten to continue even as the overall economy improves, trade has become the focus of a debate on whether the United States is turning into a society of economic haves and have-nots,[73] which translates into concern about immigration policy.

Consider international copyright agreements. In return for agreeing to tough copyright protection and a more open climate for services, Asian countries have successfully pushed for concessions in another agreement, the multi-fiber agreement, which restricts U.S. imports of textiles and clothing from developing countries. Labor believes that the phaseout of these restrictions is also likely to cost American jobs.[74]

Beyond the economic context, we need to realize that immigration reminds us that we may need a new way of looking at America. We need to look at the impact of immigrants on our lives, but, as the case studies by Erasmus, Lee, and Huynh suggest, we ought to also consider the impact that immigration has on the immigrants and refugees themselves. We all share to varying extents the blame for a culture that gives rise to protests epitomized by the uprising in South Central Los Angeles. Every time we engage in even subtle racism or the fostering of stereotypes, we perpetuate that culture. As much as each of us shares the blame, each of us also has the opportunity to be part of the solution. Every time we reach out to others whom we have been conditioned to distrust, fear, or subordinate because of race or class, we begin to chip away at the wicked culture that gives rise to irrational hatred, animosity, and violence.

Make no mistake. Immigrants *do* acculturate. Assimilation is a fluid and evolving process rather than a static one. Furthermore, immigrants' presence also influences the ongoing evolution of American culture. As a result, the definition of what an American is must be expanded. The concept must be one of addition rather than omission. It must embrace differences rather than attack them. It must respect diversity rather than disregard it. It must appeal to a sense of unity that incorporates multiculturalism rather than the illusion of Euro-centric unity, which often serves as a pretext or mask for ostracizing other cultures.[75]

Our task for the future is a difficult but not impossible one. We need a commitment to race relations and multiculturalism. We must reach a new level of consciousness, strive to develop a new, inclusive vocabulary, explore new ways of being American, and recognize the variety of racial and ethnic issues that face our society. We must urge one another to judge people by the content of their character rather than by skin color.[76] Our consideration of immigration policy reminds us that we must strive for a more inclusive sense of America for the entire community.

We also have learned much about how to regard certain institutions from the research presented. Consider the effectiveness of student loans and grants used by Vietnamese manicure students described by Huynh and the generally high educational, occupational, and income achievements highlighted by Shinagawa, Jiobu, Erasmus, Chang, Ong and Wing. The programs and education available to Asian Pacific Americans have been put to good use. Viewed as transitional programs or investments in human capital, these institutions have accomplished their purposes of getting new Americans and their children on the road to becoming productive members of society. We would do better as a nation if we focused on what makes these institutions work.

Even more noteworthy is that these accomplishments have been attained within the framework of the current immigration and refugee system.[77] Current proposals to severely reduce family immigration categories strike at the heart of Asian Pacific America. Until 1965, immigration from the Asia Pacific was stifled by exclusionary rules and quotas. Throughout this period, a sense of family stood out. For all their hardships Asian Pacific Americans demonstrated a remarkable resourcefulness, perhaps best revealed through an extraordinary drive to reunite their families. Early on, Chinese women were kept out, so to have a conventional family, Chinese and other Asian men had to reunite with relatives from abroad because of anti-miscegenation and expatriation laws. They were forced to imagine their past family as their future family. When the 1965 amendments favored reunification, Asians gradually expanded their communities. Koreans and Asian Indians expanded first through investor and employment categories, then by taking full advantage of the family categories. Asians' drive to reunify was important to their growth and their progress toward gender balance. Since the mid-1970s, the vast majority of Asian Pacific immigrants have entered in the family reunification categories.[78]

Certainly this volume leaves us with many remaining questions about immigrants and immigration, as well as about ourselves. Hopefully, however, the research that we offer provides important information and added context to the debate.

Notes

1   U.S. Department of Commerce, "Bureau of the Census Statistical Brief: The Nation's Asian and Pacific Islander Population—1994, November 1995.

2   Robert J. Lopez, "Group Battles for Latino Businessmen," Los Angeles Times, 13 June 1993, part B, p. 1; Bob Baker, "Latinos Shortchanged in Riot Aid, Group Says," Los Angeles Times, 14 September 1992, part B, p. 3.

3   "Transpacific 100 Great Asian American Entrepreneurs," *Transpacific*, December 1994. This *Transpacific* survey was confined to entrepreneurs of Chinese, Korean, Japanese, Vietnamese, and Filipino descent. The vast majority were foreign-born.

4   Roger Waldinger, *Through the Eye of the Needle: Immigrants and Enterprise in New York's Garment Trades*, (New York: New York University Press, 1986); Edna Bonacich and Ivan Light, *Immigrant Entrepreneurs: Koreans in Los Angeles*, (Berkeley: University of California Press, 1988).

5   A central provision of the California initiative passed by voters in 1994 would bar undocumented children and the children of undocumented parents from attending public schools. Other sections of Proposition 187 rendered undocumented aliens ineligible for all, but emergency, medical care. The law is currently blocked while federal courts are deciding its constitutionality.

6   Bill Ong Hing, *Making and Remaking Asian America Through Immigration Policy 1850-1990* (Stanford: Stanford University Press, 1993), 140-53.

7   Harry Pachon and Louis DeSipio, *New Americans By Choice* (Boulder, Colo.: Westview Press, 1994), 89-90.

8   Julian Simon, *The Economic Consequences of Immigration* (Cambridge: Cato Institute, 1989), 214-218; George Borjas, *Friends or Strangers* (New York: Basic Books, 1990), 82; Thomas Muller, *Immigrants and the American City* (New York: NYU Press, 1993), 10.

9   Simon, *Economic Consequences of Immigration*, 225.

10   Michael J. Piore, *Birds of Passage* (New York: Cambridge University Press, 1979), ch. 2. According to Piore, the division into two sectors results from two economic facts: some sectors are more capital intensive than others, and some sectors have a greater variation in demand.

11   Piore, *Birds of Passage*, ch. 4.

12   Borjas, *Friends or Strangers*, 82, 84-85.

13   Simon, *Economic Consequences of Immigration*, 249, 347-48.

14   *Ibid.*, 255.

15   Richard Vedder, Lowell Gallaway, and Stephen Moore, *Immigration and Unemployment: New Evidence* (Alexis de Tocqueville Institution 1994). To test for the relationship between immigrant presence and unemployment, the researchers incorporated into their model a variable measuring the estimated percent of the total U.S. resident population that was foreign born for each year. Then using an ordinary regression procedure, they ascertained the relationship between immigration (and other control variables) and unemployment. After running regressions from several perspectives, they could not find "any statistically meaningful positive relationship between immigration and unemployment." *Ibid.*, 14.

    Details of their basic labor market model are contained in Richard K. Vedder and Lowell E. Gallaway, *Out of Work: Unemployment and Government in Twentieth-Century America* (1993), ch. 3.

16   Vedder, *et al, Immigration and Unemployment*, 7-10.

17   The ten states with the highest unemployment were West Virginia, Michigan, Louisiana, Alabama, Mississippi, Alaska, Kentucky, Ohio, Arkansas, and Illinois. The ten states with the lowest unemployment were New Hampshire, Nebraska, South Dakota, Hawaii, Connecticut, Kansas, Vermont, Virginia, North Dakota, and Massachusetts.

The ten states with the largest proportion of immigrants were California, Florida, New Jersey, New York, Hawaii, Massachusetts, Rhode Island, Connecticut, District of Columbia, and Illinois. The ten states with the lowest proportion of immigrants were Mississippi, Kentucky, West Virginia, Alabama, Arkansas, Tennessee, South Dakota, South Carolina, Iowa, and Missouri. *Ibid.*, 11-13.

[18] *See* Joseph G. Altonji and David Card, "The Effects of Immigration on the Labor Market Outcomes of Less-skilled Natives," in John M. Aboud and Richard B. Freeman, eds., *Immigration, Trade, and the Labor Market* (1991); Robert J. LaLonde and Robert H. Topel, "Economic Impact of International Migration and the Economic Performance of Migrants," (Aug. 1994), p. 53 (Center for the Study of the Economy and the State, Univ. of Chicago, Working Paper No. 96).

[19] Vedder, *et al*, "Immigration and Unemployment," 15.

[20] Thomas Muller describes the situation like this:

> Some of the jobs that immigrants help to create—notably in retail trade and personal services—are taken by other immigrants. But in many other areas—utilities, banking, finance, real estate, and communications—new jobs tend to be filled by natives. Similarly, added economic activity creates new demand for non-technical professionals—lawyers, accountants, and bankers—primarily natives because language and licensing requirements make it difficult for immigrants to enter these fields (Muller, *Immigrants and the American City*, 142).

[21] See Robert H. Topel, "Regional Labor Markets and the Determinants of Wage Inequality," *American Econ. Rev.* 84 (1994): 17.

[22] *Ibid.*, 17.

[23] Topel, "Regional Labor Markets," 21.

[24] Rebecca Morales, "Transitional Labor: Undocumented Workers in the Los Angeles Automobile Industry," *International Migration Rev.* 17 (1983): 570. While the study was completed more than a decade ago, its findings appear quite relevant to the way businesses and industries are currently evolving in a more global environment.

[25] *Ibid.*, 586. Morales conducted case studies on the auto parts companies in order to observe hiring practices. She then looked at additional companies in the Los Angeles area to complement the data in order to perform a statistical analysis of the practice of hiring undocumented workers and differentiating various workers in terms of wages. *Ibid.*, 571.

[26] *Ibid.*, 571.

[27] *Ibid.*, 572-75.

[28] *Ibid.*, 575, 579-81.

[29] *Ibid.*, 587-88.

[30] *Ibid.*, 593-94?

[31] U.S. Department of Labor, *The Effects of Immigration on the U.S. Economy and Labor Market*, (GAO, 1989), 107-108.

[32] *Ibid.*, 108. Some managers even attended training seminars on how to circumvent unionization.

[33] *Ibid.*

[34] *Ibid.*, 109.

35 Eric S. Rothman and Thomas J. Espenshade, "Fiscal Impacts of Immigration to the United States," *Population Index*, 58 (1992).

36 For example, his data is even cited authoritatively and he is labeled an "immigration expert at Rice University" in a children's book I came across in the public library by Meish Goldish, *Immigration: How Should it be Controlled?* (New York: Twenty-First Century Books, A division of Henry Holt and Co., 1994).

37 Donald Huddle, *The Cost of Immigration* (Carrying Capacity, July 1993), 1.

38 Huddle calculated that public education (K-12) was 25.9 percent of all outlays on immigrants. Medicaid consumed 16.8 percent; while county social and health services, including medical care, accounted for 15.3 percent of costs. These three programs, together with AFDC, unemployment compensation, public higher education, and bilingual and English-deficient instruction comprised over 80 percent of total public outlays for immigrants. *Ibid.*, 9.

39 Richard L. Berke, "Politicians Discovering an Issue: Immigration," *New York Times*, 6 March 1994, sec. A, p. 14.

40 Jeffrey S. Passel, "Immigrants and Taxes: A Reappraisal of Huddle's 'The Cost of Immigrants'," Program for Research on Immigration Policy, The Urban Institute, January 1994.

41 *Ibid.*, 4. Legal immigrants to L.A. County entering between 1980-90 have a per capita income of about $9,700 according to the assumptions underlying the figures used by Huddle. But the Urban Institute's estimates show that legal immigrants to the U.S. entering between 1970-90 have an average per capita income exceeding $14,000.

42 The average income of immigrants nationally is 45 percent greater than Huddle's assumption of 10 percent less. *Ibid.*, 4-5.

43 *Ibid.*, 5.

44 *Ibid.*, 6.

45 Huddle's costs are overstated by $2.5 billion.

46 Huddle's costs for programs such as Headstart is thus overstated by $1 billion.

47 *Ibid.*, 7. Huddle's estimate for schooling costs is thus wrong by over $2 billion.

48 Huddle's estimated costs are off by $5 billion.

49 Michael Fix, Jeffrey S. Passel, and Wendy Zimmermann, "The Use of SSI and Other Welfare Programs by Immigrants," Testimony before the U.S. Senate Subcommittee on Immigration, 6 February 1996, pp. 2-3.

50 Jonathan Marshall, "Study Backs Fears About Immigrants, Report Shows Higher Welfare Dependence," *San Francisco Chronicle*, 26 February 1996, sec. D, p. 1.

51 Alan K. Simpson, "Forward," *San Diego Law Rev.* 20 (1982): 1.

52 Select Commission Immigration & Refugee Policy, *U.S. Immigration Policy and the National Interest*, (1981) (statement of Commissioner Alan K. Simpson, United States Senator), 412-13

53 Steven A. Chin, "Asian American Power Tested," *San Francisco Examiner*, 26 May 1992, sec. A, p. 6 (quoting Dick Day, Simpson's chief counsel on the Senate Judiciary Committee).

54 Morton M. Kondracke, "Borderline Cases," *New Republic*, 18 April 1989, p. 8, 9. FAIR describes itself as a "centrist" organization with a membership that includes environmentalists and people with a wide range of political philosophies, including Eugene

McCarthy. Telephone Interview with Anna Weinroth, lobbyist for FAIR, 4 November 1991,

55 Hearings Before the Subcomm. on Economic Resources, Competitiveness, and Security Economics of the Joint Economic Comm., 99th Cong., 2d Sess. 397 (1986) (statement of Otis L. Graham, Jr., Professor, Center for Advanced Studies, Stanford University).

56 Ibid., 359 (statement of Governor Richard D. Lamm).

57 Leon F. Bouvier, *Peaceful Invasions: Immigration and Changing America*, (New York: University Press of America, 1992), 184-86. In his acknowledgments, Bouvier states, "It has been a rewarding and challenging experience, and in one sense, troublesome as well. Here I am, a self-proclaimed and proud Liberal advocating reduced levels of immigration!" *Ibid.*, iii.

58 See, e.g., Won Moo Hurh and Kwang Chung Kim, "Adhesive Sociocultural Adaptation of Korean Immigrants in the U.S.: An Alternative Strategy of Minority Adaptation, *International Migration Rev.* 18 (1984): 188, 205; Eric Rosenthal, "Acculturation Without Assimilation? The Jewish Community of Chicago, Illinois," *American Journal of Sociology* 66 (1960): 275, 282-88; Paul J. Strand and Woodrow Jones, Jr., *Indochinese Refugees in America: Problems of Adaptation and Assimilation* (1985).

59 Frank Sharry, "Why Immigrants are good for America," *Orlando Sentinel*, 22 September, 1991, sec. G, pp. 1, 5; Lawrence Kutner, "Parent & Child," *New York Times*, 19 November 1992, sec. C, p. 12.

60 Ashley Dunn, "Immigrants Protest English Class Cuts," *Los Angeles Times*, 19 June 1991, sec. B, p. 3.

61 Sharry, "Why Immigrants are good for America"; Linda Chavez, "Tequila Sunrise: The Slow But Steady Progress of Hispanic Immigrants," *Heritage Foundation Policy Rev.* (Spring 1989): 64; Robert Suro, "Hispanic Pragmatism Seen In Survey," *New York Times*, 15 December 1992, sec. A, p. 20.

62 See Jim Cole, "Breaking the Language Barrier," *San Francisco Examiner*, 18 April 1993, sec. E, pp. 1, 7.

63 See Lena Williams, "Companies Capitalizing on Worker Diversity," *New York Times*, 15 December 1992, sec. A, p. 1, sec. D, p. 20.

64 Richard Reeves, "The Tax Revolt That Ruined California," *San Francisco Chronicle*, 23 January 1994, This World section, p. 5; Paul Ben-Itzak, "Budget Squeeze Hits Once-Wealthy California Schools," *Reuters*, 28 September 1992.

65 Louis Uchitelle, "Job Losses Don't Let Up Even as Hard Times Ease," *New York Times*, 22 March 1994, sec. A, p. 1 and sec. C, p. 4.

66 David Dishneau, "Sara Lee to Trim Work Force by 6 %," *San Francisco Examiner*, 6 June 1994, sec. D, p. 1, 5.

67 See, e.g., Patricia Commins, "Job Survey Shows Upturn," *San Francisco Examiner*, 31 May 1994, sec. D, p. 10.

68 Uchitelle, "Job Losses."

69 Marc Levinson, "Help Wanted—Reluctantly," *Newsweek*, 14 March 1994, 36.

70 Peter T. Kilborn, "For High School Graduates, A Job Market of Dead Ends," *New York Times*, 30 May 1994, 1, 29. In the first quarter of 1994, California had a net gain of 29,000 jobs. But that "is pittance compared with the 600,000 to 800,000 jobs lost during the long recession, and most of it comes in low-paying service and construction

jobs." Jane Gross, "California Shows Signs of Recovery as Jobs Increase," *New York Times*, 11 April 1994, sec. A, p. 1, 12.

71   Karen Rothmyer, "Everyone's Talking About It . . . . But Why? From NAFTA to GATT, free trade becomes a dinner-table issue," *Newsday*, 12 December 1993, 96.

72   *Ibid.*

73   *Ibid.*

74   Ravi Batra, a professor at Southern Methodist University and author of *The Myth of Free Trade* puts it this way: "If the U.S. had a 50 percent tariff on manufacturing imports, all foreign companies would have to produce here using American labor." Rothmyer, "Everyone's Talking About It."

75   The demographic data presented by Shinagawa on the increasing rate of intermarriage among Asian Pacific Americans raises new considerations of the evolution of what an American is.

76   This phrase comes from Martin Luther King's famous "I have a Dream" speech: "I have a dream my four little children will one day live in a nation where they will not be judged by the color of their skin but by content of their character. I have a dream today!" Martin Luther King, Jr., *A Testament of Hope: The Essential Writings and Speeches of Martin Luther King, Jr.* (James M. Washington ed., 1986): 219.

77   A recent study by Empower America, an organization co-directed by Jack Kemp and William J. Bennett, recognizes that key employees and even founders of high-tech companies enter the country as refugees and family-sponsored immigrants, as well as employment-based immigrants. See "Study Disputes Arguments for Caps on Employment-based Immigration," *Daily Labor Report*, 29 February 1996.

78   Hing, *Making and Remaking Asian American Through Immigration Policy,* 15, 79-105, 186.

Part I.
Demographics

Recent Asian Pacific Immigrants
The Demographic Background

by Robert M. Jiobu[*]

As is well known, the passage of the Immigration Act of 1965 reformed the immigration policies of the United States. Under that act, racial quotas were abolished and an emphasis was placed on family unification and occupational skills. Ironically, in passing the act, neither Congress nor the President wished to alter the racial and ethnic composition of the nation, yet the act has done exactly that (Kitano and Daniels, 1988, Hing, 1993).

As the number of immigrants has increased, so too has the controversy over them increased. Immigration is now a salient political issue. Yet as with many issues, a controversy rages in the absence of much scientifically based data. To help rectify that situation, this analysis examines the demography of Asian Pacific immigrants. More specifically, it focuses on: (1) the background characteristics of immigrants, (2) their human capital, and (3) their economic status. In each case, immigrants are contrasted to the native born, and in some cases, a contrast is drawn between immigrants and the nation as a whole.

The analysis is based on data drawn from the 1990 Census of Population, five percent Public Use Microdata Sample (PUMS). These data are for individuals and are a sample of the United States population. Because they are a sample, the data presented here might not precisely match figures found in other publications based on other samples from the 1990 Census. The differences, however, should be within random sampling error.

In the Census, race is a matter of self identification. The Census questionnaire presents a list of racial categories and the person who fills out the questionnaire selects a category for everyone in the household. Using these categories, eleven groups were selected for analysis. The groups are as follows:

---

[*]   Robert Jiobu is an Associate Professor in the Department of Sociology at The Ohio State University.

1   Asian Indian
2   Cambodian
3   Chinese
4   Filipino
5   Hmong
6   Japanese
7   Korean
8   Laotian
9   Pacific Islander
10 Thai
11 Vietnamese

To some extent, group size played a role in the decision to analyze these particular groups and not others. The principle was simple: there had to be a sufficient number of people in a given group to warrant statistical analysis. Although what constitutes "sufficient" might be debated, the smallest group, the Thai, numbered 90,000 people. While this figure might seem large, the following tables will show that for many statistical purposes the number is rather small. Also for reasons of size, various Pacific Island groups were combined into a generic group called "Pacific Islander." In doing so, the distinctiveness of each Pacific group is lost, yet the aggregated information is better than no information at all.

Throughout, the terms *native born* and *immigrant* are used. Note, however, that the PUMS data do not contain a direct measure of immigrant status, nor do the data address the question of "what is an immigrant?" Instead, the PUMS data indicate where people were born. Operationally, this means that an immigrant is a person residing in the United States but who was born in a foreign place.

Background Characteristics

In this section, several demographic characteristics of the eleven groups are examined. Taken collectively, these characteristics help to form an overall picture of Asian Pacific immigrants, especially in contrast to the native born.

Immigrant Population

Probably the most basic question one can ask about Asian Pacific immigrants being studied is "how many are there?" Table 1 addresses this question (see Table 1. Tables and figures located at the end of this essay. All tables and figures based on 1990 Census data).

The table shows the number of native born and immigrants for each group. The largest number of immigrants is found among the Chinese (about 1.2 million) while the smallest number is among the Hmong (62,000). Of course, the absolute number of immigrants should vary as group size varies: larger groups will contain, all else equal, more immigrants than smaller groups. This effect is easily controlled by taking the number of immigrants in a group as a percentage of the group's total size. These data are shown on Figure 1.

Except for Japanese and Pacific Islanders, the figure shows that immigrants constitute over half of the population of each group being studied, and in some instances equal or exceed 80 percent. The percentage of immigrants among the Japanese is low, but that is not too surprising. Japan is a wealthy nation, and there are few negative factors pushing the Japanese to emigrate. Indeed, the most important push factor might be Japanese firms operating in the United States. Employees of these firms, especially higher ranking managers and technical personnel, may immigrate to work in the firm's United States division. This results in a comparatively small immigration stream. Japanese immigrants intend to stay for short periods and then return home. In effect, these immigrants are a contemporary version of the old sojourners (Siu, 1952).

Before the 1965 act, Asian Pacific immigrants were minuscule in number, and the Chinese and Japanese were the largest Asian groups in the United States. Because of Asian exclusion laws, the population of these two groups could not be replenished by newcomers and native-born segments became proportionately larger than the immigrant segment. Asian exclusion, in other words, was forcing these groups to become overwhelming native born (Jiobu, 1988). Except for Japanese Americans, this is no longer the case today: the majority of Asian Pacific people are now immigrants, and their diversity is expanding dramatically.

Region of Residence

In the past, Asian Pacific immigrants overwhelmingly settled on the West Coast, especially in California. The same is true today, as the data in Table 2 indicate. In general, Asian Indians are the most geographically dispersed, while Pacific Islanders are the most concentrated. Interestingly, the native born tend to concentrate on the West Coast more than immigrants. This might be due to selective re-migration. Asian Pacific young people born outside of the Pacific Coast might, when they mature, selectively migrate to the Pacific Coast. Anecdotal evidence suggests that many

Asian Pacific youths who were reared in the Midwest move to California after graduating from college. Their specific motives may vary, but typically reasons center around the desire to experience life in a place where Asian Pacific people are more numerous (Jiobu, 1994).

Gender

Gender and age are two fundamental demographic characteristics. The sex ratio has implications for the growth of the group. A group with relatively few women cannot establish many traditional family units. If fertility is channeled through the traditional family, then the scarcity of women means that few families can be formed and few children will be born. Accordingly, Figure 2 shows the percentage of each group's population which is female.

The image of a mostly male immigrant stream is no longer applicable. In fact, the majority of groups studied here are fifty percent female or higher. Even among groups which are less than fifty percent female, the male predominance varies only from two to four percentage points—hardly overwhelming.

The number of females in this current immigration stream reflects a sharp break with past trends. The break may be due to employment opportunities, which have increased for women but decreased for men. Moreover, the 1965 act's emphasis on family unification, absent in past legislation, has meant an increase in the relative number of immigrant women (Gill, Glazer, and Thernstrom, 1992; Hing, 1993).

Age Composition

Age is a primary demographic consideration. A young group, for example, has many people in the child bearing ages, a factor that increases the group's fertility. With high fertility, the group must then devote considerable resources to child support, leaving relatively less for elders or for investment in economic endeavors. At the same time, a young group has many people who are in the early stages of their careers and are not likely to have reached their full earnings potential (Jiobu, 1988).

In order to examine the age composition of the Asian Pacific groups being studied here, age categories were divided beginning with 0-9 and ending with 80 or older. Although these categories are somewhat arbitrary, they do render a reasonably clear picture of age structure. The data are shown on Table 3.

Based on these figures, one pattern stands out: the predominance of youth, especially among the native born. About half of the native born population is under twenty, while some 90 percent of native born Cambodians, Hmong, and Laotians are nine or younger. Even though immigrants are older than the native born, immigrants are still fairly young too.

Marital Status

A major value in American culture concerns the family unit. Whether one approaches this concern from the viewpoint of traditional values or from the viewpoint of new age values, the family (or family-like unit) plays a central role in forging community cohesion and socializing children. With regard to immigration, this role underlies the family unification provisions of the 1965 act.

Precisely what constitutes a family, however, may be debated. Most people in the United States would agree that a wife and husband unit constitutes one type. The PUMS data contain an item that asks respondents their marital status. These responses are shown on Table 4 for people who are 18 years or older, an age cut-off that excludes children and young teenagers from the results.

The table shows that immigrants are more likely to be married than the native born, sometimes by substantial margins. For instance, 74 percent of immigrant Asian Indians are married as contrasted to 26 percent of the native born. Consistent with these differences, the native born are more likely to never have been married than immigrants.

One explanation for these results is age. Even though the data are limited to people 18 and older, marriage is often discouraged for youths, especially if they are in school or have not established themselves in a career. Moreover, the age of marriage is rising throughout the United States, and there is no reason to believe that Asian Pacific people are exempt from this trend.

The data in Table 4 also speak to social disorganization. The divorce rate is sometimes used to index individual and community stability. This rate varies from three to eight percent among the native born and from 2 to 7 percent among immigrants. All of these rates are low compared to the 1990 national divorce rate of 15 percent (U. S. Bureau of the Census, 1994). According to this indicator, then, Asian Pacific groups being studied are characterized by cohesive family units, which contributes to community cohesion.

Human Capital

Human capital is the investment people make in themselves to enhance their earnings (Becker, 1975). This concept rests on the assumption that human capital investments are costly but that over time, the amount of earnings generated by these investments will pay for themselves and then accrue a profit. Examples of human capital are education, job experience, and English proficiency.

Education

Of all the forms of human capital people might acquire, education is undoubtedly the one that comes to mind most readily. Education, which has been called America's secular religion, constitutes a ladder of upward social mobility. Some claim that education is also a strong cultural value among many Asian Pacific groups (Daniels and Kitano, 1988; Hing, 1993).

Table 5 shows the educational attainment of each group. Note that data have been calculated only for persons 25 or older. The standard assumption is that by age 25, people will have attained all of the education, including any graduate-level work, that they are likely to attain. This cut-off is somewhat arbitrary, of course, but some cut-off is necessary.

The breakdown of educational attainment begins with those with less than high school and goes through those who have attained a doctorate or professional degree. The attainment of at least a bachelor's degree is a key to upward mobility. Figure 3 contains a single educational category: attainment of a bachelor's degree or higher.

The figure suggests that no clear pattern exists, either among immigrants or in contrasting immigrants and native born. Some immigrant groups, notably Asian Indians, have considerable college attainment while others, notably the Hmong, have relatively little. In some cases, the native born have more college education than their immigrant counterparts, and in other cases the opposite is true. Although the data do not indicate where immigrants attended school, we might suspect that some groups bring a large endowment of educational capital with them when they immigrate and others do not.[1]

English Proficiency

Proficiency in English is an important dimension of human capital, enabling people to interact with the dominant culture and thereby enhancing their earning potential. Ability to speak English is also politically controversial. An English-only movement, seeking to make English the official language, has emerged, especially in states with large ethnic populations. Even in places that have relatively few immigrants, sentiment exists to make English the official language.

Before examining the data, note that the Census Bureau uses a rating system, not a test, to measure English proficiency. The person who fills out the Census questionnaire rates everyone in the household as to English-speaking ability. This procedure leaves many questions unanswered, such as how respondents define the categories of "very well," "well," and so forth. And what reference group do they have in mind: other immigrants, the native born, the media, or some other standard? Because of these problems, the proficiency ratings need to be interpreted with some reservation. Consider also the rating category, "speaks only English." Taken literally, of course, few people speak only English (virtually everyone knows a few words of another language). The common meaning of the phrase, however, indicates a person who does not have command of another language. Rating this aspect of English proficiency requires a dichotomous choice of yes or no, but this is likely more reliable than the multiple choices regarding how well a person speaks English. The data are shown on Table 6.

Although one would expect the native born to be more proficient in English than immigrants, this is not always the case. For example, among Asian Indians, Filipinos, Japanese, and Pacific Islanders, a larger proportion of immigrants rate their English as "very well" than do the native born. A partial explanation for these results is that Asian Indians, Filipinos, and Pacific Islanders come from cultures where English is a common language. That fact, of course, does not explain ratings of the Japanese.

A popular stereotype of Asian Pacific immigrants portrays them as inarticulate in English, but the majority of every group (except the Hmong) rates itself as speaking English well or very well. If these data are believed, a lack of English proficiency should neither impede acculturation nor constitute a costly lack of human capital.

With reference to speaking only English, no group had more than a quarter of its population fall into that category. This fact may be interpreted in two ways: (1) Most immigrants are not well assimilated because relatively few speak only English; or (2) *A priori*, one would anticipate that virtually no Asian Pacific immigrants would speak only English; the fact some do indicates a drive toward assimilation.

Economic Status

Although some instances of hostility toward immigrants are difficult to explain in terms other than private attitudes based on conscious and unconscious emotional processes, some hostility is rooted in economic fear. For instance, the media is replete with stories about the declining competitiveness of American industry and the threat that foreigners pose to American jobs. Even academic authors have implicitly incorporated this theme into their works, as illustrated by titles such as *Clamor at the Gates* (Glazer 1985), *Have We Decided to Control our Borders?* (Gill, et al., 1992: title to chapter 20), and *Mass Immigration and the National Interest* (Briggs 1992). These titles project the image of a beleaguered people desperately defending their nation from hordes of foreigners with different cultures and different skin color. The "Yellow Peril," as it were, has reappeared in a more politically correct guise of protecting America.

Although Census data do not directly tap discrimination, the data can indicate the economic status of immigrants and non-immigrants. Table 7 shows several such indicators.

One of the most basic determinants of economic attainment is employment. The larger the percentage of a group's population that participates in the labor force, the more workers the group has to generate earnings. Nationwide, about two-thirds of the population over 16 in 1990 was in the labor force (U. S. Bureau of the Census, 1991).

The data on Table 7 show that the participation rates for the immigrant groups being studied are, for the most part (except for the Hmong), close to the national figure. In general, immigrants participate in the labor force to a greater extent than the native born, but recall that the native born are very youthful.

Participating in the labor force is one type of economic behavior; another is unemployment. This measure is also shown in Table 7. Bearing in mind that the unemployment rate was about five percent in 1990 (U. S. Bureau of the Census, 1991), the unemployment rates among the groups being studied are, like the labor force participation rates, not unique. An exception to this conclusion are Cambodians, whose high unemployment rates are difficult to explain with the data at hand.

Another indicator of economic status is poverty. Approximately 13 percent of the nation in 1989 was defined as poor, that is, an individual earned less than $6,451 per year, (U. S. Bureau of the Census, 1994; U. S. Bureau of the Census, 1990). Table 7 shows that the poverty rates among immigrants are about the same or somewhat higher than the rates among the native born. In absolute terms, the rates are higher than average (above 20 percent) for almost half of the groups being studied here: Cambodians, Hmong, Laotians, Pacific Islanders, and Vietnamese.

We often hear the argument that immigrants take advantage of the welfare system and thus are a burden to the government and the taxpayer. While the census data used here do not contain a direct measure of welfare, they do report income from public assistance such as Supplemental Security Income (SSI) and Aid to Families with Dependent Children (AFDC). This type of income can be used as a proxy for "being on welfare," but one should understand that the outcomes will not necessarily match outcomes based on other data sources (for example, Ong and Blumenberg, 1994a).

According to this measure, immigrants tend to have a higher public assistance rate than the native born. Nevertheless, the differences are, with some exceptions, rather modest. In absolute terms, the rates are fairly low, but they reach a very high level among certain refugee groups: Cambodians, Hmong, and Laotians.

Another indirect index of welfare usage can be calculated from the percentage of poor people within a group who receive income from public assistance. This index is based on the assumption that even though poor people are most likely to receive welfare, not all poor people do. The culture of Asian Pacific Americans contains many stories of poor people who steadfastly refused to go on welfare (Kitano, 1976).

For the most part, Table 7 indicates that Asian Pacific immigrants are not likely to burden the welfare system. In no case is the majority of impoverished immigrants receiving public assistance payments, although in the case of the Cambodians, Hmong, Laotians, and Vietnamese a substantial percentage do. With an occasional and minor exception, the percentage of poor people with public assistance income is lower among immigrants than among the native born.

Perhaps the most important indicator of economic well-being is money. Accordingly, Table 7 shows total mean income for each group. This mean, it should be noted, is calculated only for persons 25 years or older who are employed in the civilian labor force. The reason for restricting the analysis to this age group is to control the extreme youthfulness of many Asian-Pacific groups (see Table 3). Interestingly, the mean income of Asian Indians and Japanese immigrants are the highest on the table. In the main, however, the data suggest that immigrants do about as well as the native born. Although immigrants surely have more difficulty adapting to American culture than the native born, immigrants somehow manage to overcome the difficulty with respect to income attainment.

Occupational Attainment

In the past, immigrants tended to be largely blue collar workers and laborers. Today they are much more diversified, as shown in Table 8.

The data are fairly detailed but attention usually focuses on the upper and lower extremes of the occupational rankings. In general, relatively few immigrants are in professional occupations compared to the native born. Conversely, a relatively large percentage of immigrants, especially Cambodians, Hmong, and Laotians, are in the laborer/operative category. Finally, among both the native born and immigrants, the largest percentage of workers is usually found in the technical/sales category.

Conclusions

In summary, the data indicate the following:
- Demographically, the Asian Pacific immigration stream contains relatively more females than males. The native born are extremely youthful while immigrants are older.
- Immigrants marry at a fairly high rate and divorce at a fairly low rate, suggesting a substantial degree of family and community cohesion.
- The data on education both support and contradict the popular image of Asian Pacific immigrants as a highly educated minority.
- A small proportion of immigrants speak only English, but a majority speak English well or very well.
- Economically, immigrants participate in the labor force to a greater extent than native born but unemployment is about the same for both groups.
- Among immigrants, the rates of poverty and welfare assistance are mostly low, with the exception of Southeast Asian groups.
- Immigrants tend to have as much or more income than the native born.

Given these findings and what is already known, three overall conclusions are warranted. *First*, no simple generalizations can be made about Asian Pacific immigrants as a whole. For instance, Asian Indians and the Hmong are clearly different from each other and from the other groups being studied here. These differences include historical backgrounds, culture, demography, and economic characteristics.

Second, the various Asian Pacific groups form two distinct clusters: those who are doing well economically and those who are not. In the latter cluster fall the Hmong, Laotians, Cambodians, and to a lesser extent, the Vietnamese. Given the war-induced circumstances of their arrival, we should not be surprised to find that they are not doing as well as, say, many Japanese and Filipino immigrants who have come voluntarily with good jobs in hand.

Third, Asian Pacific immigrants embody the best of American values. Their levels of education, English proficiency, rates of marriage, rates of divorce, levels of poverty, and percentage receiving public assistance payments all point to high levels of family cohesion, self sufficiency, and a drive to interact with the broader society. This does not mean, of course, that all Asian Pacific immigrants do not have problems. Some do fall into low income categories of poverty, welfare, and low occupational attainment.

Historically, Asian Pacific immigrants have made important contributions to American society. They have worked hard and paid taxes; they have developed businesses and established entire industries; they have created stable family units and cohesive communities; and they have participated in civic society and have fought in America's wars. In all these ways, and in others, they have continually moved from being marginal sojourners to the mainstream of American life (Okihiro 1994). The current data do not suggest a different outcome for today's immigrants from Asia and the Pacific.

Notes

1   Editor's Note: see the essay on education in this report by Paul Ong and Linda Wing.

Table 1
Immigration Status among Asian Pacific Americans

Immigration Status	Asian Indian	Cambodian	Chinese	Filipino	Hmong	Japanese	Korean	Laotian	Pacific Islander	Thai	Vietnamese
Native Born (x1,000)	180	31	488	447	31	560	142	30	260	18	107
Immigrants (x1000)	601	120	1160	970	62	305	654	122	92	72	480
Total (x1000)	781	151	1648	1417	93	865	796	152	352	90	587

Source: Information generated from 1990 Census of Population, five percent Public Use Microdata Sample (PUMS)

Table 2
Region of Residence among Asian Pacific Americans

NATIVE BORN

Region	Asian Indian	Cambodian	Chinese	Filipino	Hmong	Japanese	Korean	Laotian	Pacific Islander	Thai	Vietnamese
New England	4%	10%	4%	1%	1%	1%	3%	5%	1%	2%	3%
Mid Atlantic	27%	5%	19%	7%	*	3%	18%	4%	2%	9%	5%
East North Central	17%	3%	6%	6%	18%	4%	11%	8%	2%	12%	4%
West North Central	2%	4%	1%	1%	17%	1%	3%	8%	1%	3%	5%
South Atlantic	15%	7%	6%	7%	1%	2%	11%	5%	3%	13%	8%
East South Central	2%	1%	1%	1%	*	*	1%	2%	1%	1%	2%
West South Central	9%	5%	4%	3%	*	*	4%	8%	2%	10%	18%
Mountain	2%	3%	3%	2%	2%	4%	3%	5%	5%	5%	3%
Pacific	22%	62%	56%	72%	61%	84%	46%	55%	83%	45%	52%
Total Percent	100%	100%	100%	100%	100%	100%	100%	100%	100%	100%	100%

IMMIGRANT

Region	Asian Indian	Cambodian	Chinese	Filipino	Hmong	Japanese	Korean	Laotian	Pacific Islander	Thai	Vietnamese
New England	4%	14%	4%	1%	2%	4%	2%	6%	1%	2%	3%
Mid Atlantic	32%	3%	25%	10%	*	15%	21%	4%	3%	11%	7%
East North Central	14%	4%	6%	8%	22%	10%	10%	9%	2%	10%	4%
West North Central	3%	4%	2%	1%	20%	3%	4%	9%	2%	4%	4%
South Atlantic	14%	8%	7%	8%	2%	9%	13%	8%	6%	16%	10%
East South Central	2%	1%	1%	1%	*	2%	2%	3%	1%	2%	2%
West South Central	8%	6%	5%	3%	*	4%	5%	10%	5%	9%	15%
Mountain	2%	2%	2%	2%	2%	4%	3%	4%	8%	6%	3%
Pacific	21%	55%	48%	66%	52%	49%	40%	47%	72%	40%	52%
Total Percent	100%	97%	100%	100%	100%	100%	100%	100%	100%	100%	100%

Source: Information generated from 1990 Census of the Population, five percent Public Use Microdata Sample (PUMS)
* Less than one percent

Table 3
Age Composition of Asian Pacific Americans

NATIVE BORN

Years of Age	Asian Indian	Cambodian	Chinese	Filipino	Hmong	Japanese	Korean	Laotian	Pacific Islander	Thai	Vietnamese
0 - 9	57%	91%	38%	39%	90%	13%	55%	90%	26%	48%	76%
10 - 19	31%	7%	21%	28%	8%	11%	27%	7%	20%	44%	20%
20 - 29	7%	1%	14%	15%	1%	15%	8%	1%	18%	5%	2%
30 - 39	2%	*	12%	8%	*	17%	3%	1%	14%	1%	1%
40 - 49	1%	*	6%	5%	*	12%	2%	*	9%	1%	*
50 - 59	1%	*	3%	3%	*	10%	1%	*	6%	*	*
60 - 69	*	*	3%	2%	*	13%	2%	*	4%	*	*
70 - 79	*	*	2%	*	*	7%	1%	*	2%	*	*
80 +	*	*	1%	*	*	2%	1%	*	1%	*	*
Total Percent	100%	200%	100%	100%	100%	100%	100%	100%	100%	100%	100%

IMMIGRANT

Years of Age	Asian Indian	Cambodian	Chinese	Filipino	Hmong	Japanese	Korean	Laotian	Pacific Islander	Thai	Vietnamese
0 - 9	5%	15%	3%	3%	19%	7%	10%	10%	7%	3%	4%
10 - 19	11%	23%	11%	11%	27%	7%	15%	27%	16%	10%	23%
20 - 29	22%	19%	20%	18%	21%	18%	19%	22%	26%	20%	25%
30 - 39	26%	20%	25%	23%	14%	24%	22%	21%	23%	27%	24%
40 - 49	21%	12%	17%	20%	8%	17%	17%	11%	13%	30%	14%
50 - 59	9%	6%	11%	11%	5%	15%	10%	5%	8%	7%	7%
60 - 69	4%	3%	8%	7%	3%	8%	4%	2%	4%	2%	3%
70 - 79	*	1%	4%	5%	2%	1%	2%	1%	2%	*	*
80 +	*	1%	1%	2%	1%	3%	1%	1%	1%	*	*
Total Percent	100%	100%	100%	100%	100%	100%	100%	100%	100%	100%	100%

Source: Information generated from 1990 Census of the Population, five percent Public Use Microdata Sample (PUMS)
* Less than one percent

Table 4
Marital Status of Asian Pacific Americans
Percent of Persons 18 Years or Older

NATIVE BORN

Marital Status	Asian Indian	Cambodian	Chinese	Filipino	Hmong	Japanese	Korean	Laotian	Pacific Islander	Thai	Vietnamese
Married	26%	32%	44%	43%	56%	57%	33%	36%	51%	20%	30%
Widowed	3%	2%	3%	2%	9%	6%	3%	0%	4%	2%	3%
Divorced	4%	5%	5%	7%	2%	6%	6%	5%	9%	4%	5%
Separated	2%	5%	1%	2%	5%	1%	1%	6%	30%	2%	0%
Never Married	65%	56%	47%	46%	28%	30%	57%	53%	33%	72%	62%
Total	100%	100%	100%	100%	100%	100%	100%	100%	127%	100%	100%

IMMIGRANT

Marital Status	Asian Indian	Cambodian	Chinese	Filipino	Hmong	Japanese	Korean	Laotian	Pacific Islander	Thai	Vietnamese
Married	74%	58%	67%	66%	70%	65%	68%	65%	63%	64%	54%
Widowed	3%	8%	5%	6%	7%	7%	5%	4%	3%	2%	3%
Divorced	3%	3%	3%	4%	2%	5%	4%	3%	6%	7%	3%
Separated	1%	4%	1%	2%	2%	1%	2%	2%	3%	2%	3%
Never Married	20%	27%	24%	22%	19%	22%	21%	26%	25%	3%	37%
Total	100%	100%	100%	100%	100%	100%	100%	100%	100%	78%	100%

Source: Information generated from 1990 Census of the Population, five percent Public Use Microdata Sample (PUMS)

Table 5
Educational Attainment among Asian Pacific Americans
Persons 25 Years or Older

NATIVE BORN

Educational Attainment	Asian Indian	Cambodian	Chinese	Filipino	Hmong	Japanese	Korean	Laotian	Pacific Islander	Thai	Vietnamese
Less than High School	19%	46%	8%	16%	58%	12%	12%	48%	22%	23%	30%
High School Diploma	17%	13%	16%	28%	15%	26%	24%	16%	38%	13%	29%
Some College	19%	32%	25%	35%	23%	28%	27%	11%	29%	9%	23%
Bachelors Degree	24%	9%	33%	16%	4%	24%	22%	12%	8%	38%	11%
Masters Degree	11%	0%	11%	3%	0%	6%	9%	5%	2%	14%	5%
Doctorate or Professional	10%	0%	7%	2%	0%	4%	6%	8%	1%	3%	2%
Total	100%	100%	100%	100%	100%	100%	100%	100%	100%	100%	100%

IMMIGRANT

Educational Attainment	Asian Indian	Cambodian	Chinese	Filipino	Hmong	Japanese	Korean	Laotian	Pacific Islander	Thai	Vietnamese
Less than High School	15%	64%	29%	18%	13%	13%	20%	60%	32%	26%	39%
High School Diploma	12%	12%	15%	14%	27%	27%	25%	19%	31%	16%	18%
Some College	14%	17%	17%	26%	24%	24%	20%	14%	29%	25%	26%
Bachelors Degree	25%	5%	20%	34%	25%	25%	22%	5%	6%	20%	12%
Masters Degree	20%	1%	13%	3%	7%	7%	8%	1%	1%	9%	3%
Doctorate or Professional	14%	1%	6%	5%	4%	4%	5%	1%	1%	4%	2%
Total	100%	100%	100%	100%	100%	100%	100%	100%	100%	100%	100%

Source: Information generated from 1990 Census of the Population, five percent Public Use Microdata Sample (PUMS)

Table 6
English Proficiency among Asian Pacific Americans

NATIVE BORN

English Proficiency	Asian Indian	Cambodian	Chinese	Filipino	Hmong	Japanese	Korean	Laotian	Pacific Islander	Thai	Vietnamese
Very Well	43%	33%	37%	15%	22%	13%	39%	35%	11%	40%	45%
Well	7%	27%	10%	3%	34%	6%	9%	31%	2%	7%	24%
Not Well	3%	25%	4%	1%	35%	3%	6%	23%	1%	4%	12%
Not at All	1%	3%	1%	1%	6%	0%	1%	3%	1%	1%	1%
Speak only English	46%	12%	48%	80%	3%	78%	45%	8%	85%	48%	18%
Total	100%	100%	100%	100%	100%	100%	100%	100%	100%	100%	100%

IMMIGRANT

English Proficiency	Asian Indian	Cambodian	Chinese	Filipino	Hmong	Japanese	Korean	Laotian	Pacific Islander	Thai	Vietnamese
Very Well	57%	24%	32%	55%	20%	28%	29%	28%	43%	32%	31%
Well	18%	31%	32%	24%	29%	31%	28%	30%	20%	38%	35%
Not Well	7%	32%	22%	6%	32%	21%	23%	31%	10%	13%	24%
Not at All	2%	10%	9%	1%	17%	3%	5%	9%	2%	2%	5%
Speak only English	16%	3%	5%	14%	2%	17%	15%	2%	25%	15%	5%
Total	100%	100%	100%	100%	100%	100%	100%	100%	100%	100%	100%

Source: Information generated from 1990 Census of the Population, five percent Public Use Microdata Sample (PUMS)

Table 7
Economic Status of Asian Pacific Americans
Labor Force Participation, Unemployment, Poverty, Public Assistance Payments & Income

NATIVE BORN

Economic Status Variable	Asian Indian	Cambodian	Chinese	Filipino	Hmong	Japanese	Korean	Laotian	Pacific Islander	Thai	Vietnamese
In the Labor Force (%)*	48%	63%	68%	72%	20%	69%	56%	51%	70%	48%	58%
Unemployed (%)**	4%	16%	3%	4%	--	2%	3%	2%	5%	6%	6%
In Poverty (%)*	8%	43%	8%	7%	63%	4%	12%	40%	16%	7%	6%
Receiving Public Assistance Payments	2%	8%	2%	3%	25%	2%	2%	15%	6%	1%	14%
Poor Receiving Public Assistance Payments	6%	9%	4%	12%	38%	6%	4%	25%	21%	--	14%
Mean Total Income, 1989 (x $1,000)***	30	12	36	25	13	33	30	19	23	24	21

IMMIGRANT

Economic Status Variable	Asian Indian	Cambodian	Chinese	Filipino	Hmong	Japanese	Korean	Laotian	Pacific Islander	Thai	Vietnamese
In the Labor Force (%)*	74%	48%	65%	76%	29%	55%	64%	58%	69%	74%	65%
Unemployed (%)**	4%	4%	3%	4%	5%	2%	3%	5%	6%	4%	5%
In Poverty (%)*	10%	40%	16%	6%	63%	12%	14%	33%	22%	12%	25%
Receiving Public Assistance Payments	2%	27%	5%	4%	36%	1%	4%	19%	5%	2%	11%
Poor Receiving Public Assistance Payments	6%	40%	9%	8%	40%	2%	7%	32%	11%	2%	23%
Mean Total Income, 1989 (x $1,000)***	35	17	27	25	14	36	25	16	20	23	21

Source: Information generated from 1990 Census of the Population, five percent Public Use Microdata Sample (PUMS)
* Percent of population
** Percent of labor force
*** Persons 25 or older in the civilian labor force

TABLE 8
Occupational Attainment of Asian Pacific Americans

NATIVE BORN

Occupational Category	Asian Indian	Cambodian	Chinese	Filipino	Hmong	Japanese	Korean	Laotian	Pacific Islander	Thai	Vietnamese
Professional	19%	8%	23%	9%	0%	19%	15%	12%	9%	17%	10%
Executive/Management	9%	0%	16%	10%	3%	15%	11%	0%	10%	8%	9%
Technical/Sales	44%	40%	40%	40%	10%	37%	45%	22%	32%	33%	35%
Craft	5%	30%	6%	11%	50%	12%	6%	24%	14%	4%	11%
Service	14%	10%	9%	17%	9%	9%	15%	8%	20%	28%	21%
Operative/Laborer	9%	12%	6%	12%	28%	8%	8%	34%	15%	10%	14%
Total	100%	100%	100%	100%	100%	100%	100%	100%	100%	100%	100%

IMMIGRANT

Occupational Category	Asian Indian	Cambodian	Chinese	Filipino	Hmong	Japanese	Korean	Laotian	Pacific Islander	Thai	Vietnamese
Professional	28%	5%	19%	16%	7%	19%	13%	4%	6%	13%	10%
Executive/Management	13%	4%	13%	10%	4%	18%	11%	1%	7%	10%	6%
Technical/Sales	35%	23%	31%	36%	17%	30%	37%	16%	31%	27%	29%
Craft	6%	18%	6%	9%	18%	7%	9%	21%	16%	8%	17%
Service	8%	18%	19%	18%	24%	18%	17%	17%	22%	26%	16%
Operative/Laborer	10%	32%	12%	11%	30%	8%	13%	41%	18%	16%	22%
Total	100%	100%	100%	100%	100%	100%	100%	100%	100%	100%	100%

Source: Information generated from 1990 Census of the Population, five percent Public Use Microdata Sample (PUMS).
* Persons 16 years or older who last worked 1985 or later.

Figure 1
Asian Pacific American Immigrant Population by Ethnicity

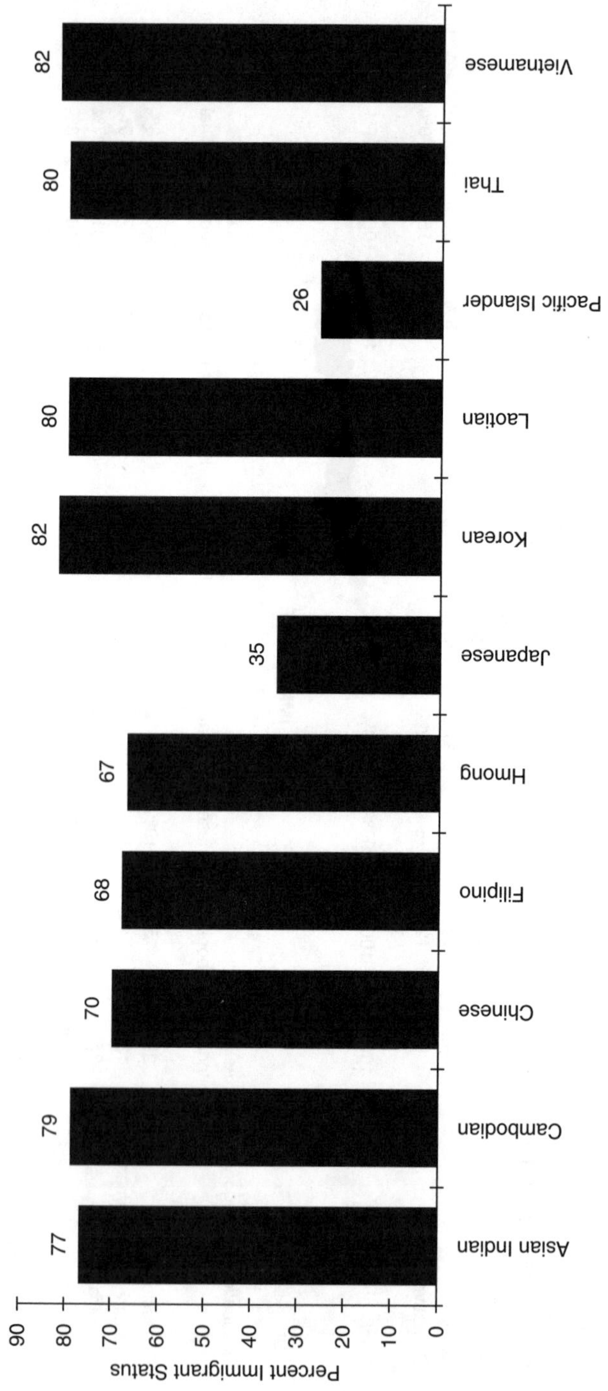

(Bar chart showing Percent Immigrant Status by ethnicity)

Asian Indian: 77
Cambodian: 79
Chinese: 70
Filipino: 68
Hmong: 67
Japanese: 35
Korean: 82
Laotian: 80
Pacific Islander: 26
Thai: 80
Vietnamese: 82

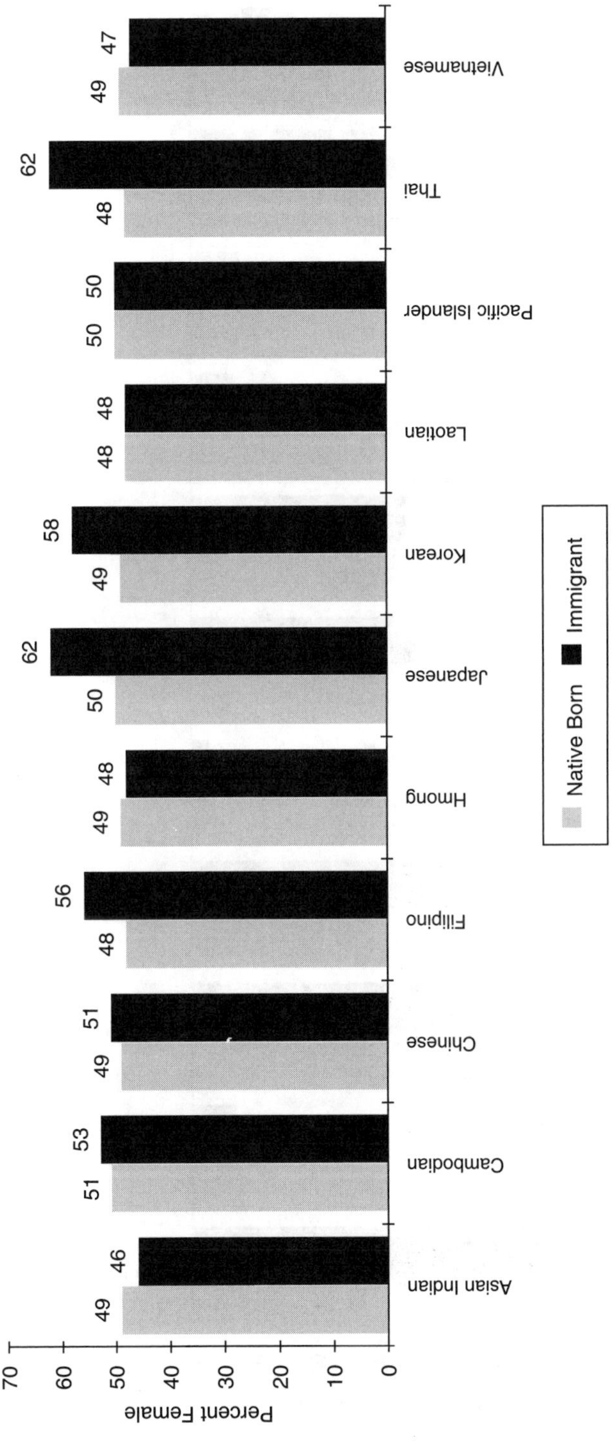

Figure 2
Female Asian Pacific Americans by Ethnicity and Immigrant Status

Figure 3

Asian Pacific Americans with a Bachelors Degree or Higher by Ethnicity and Immigrant Status

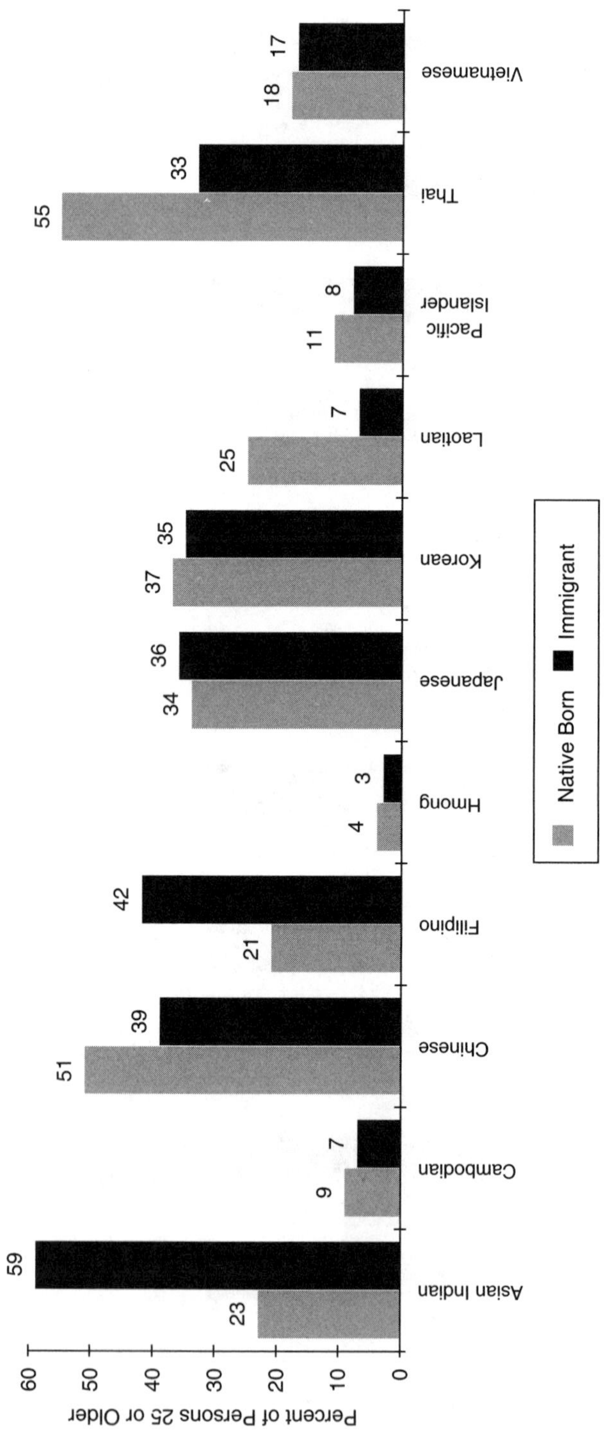

Legend: Native Born, Immigrant

Percent of Persons 25 or Older

Ethnicity	Native Born	Immigrant
Asian Indian	23	59
Cambodian	9	7
Chinese	51	39
Filipino	21	42
Hmong	4	3
Japanese	34	36
Korean	37	35
Laotian	25	7
Pacific Islander	11	8
Thai	55	33
Vietnamese	18	17

References

Becker, Gary S. (1975). *Human Capital: A Theoretical and Empirical Analysis with Special Reference to Education*, second edition. New York: National Bureau of Economic Research.

Briggs, Vernon M., Jr. (1992). *Mass Immigration and the National Interest*. Armonk New York: M. E. Sharpe, Inc.

Gill, Richard T., Glazer, Nathan, and Thernstrom, Stephan A. (1992). *Our Changing Population*. Englewood Cliffs, New Jersey: Prentice-Hall.

Glazer, Nathan (ed.). (1985). *Clamor at the Gates: The New American Immigration*. San Francisco: Institute for Contemporary Studies Press.

Haberman, Shelby, J. (1978). *Analysis of Qualitative Data: Volume 1: Introductory Topics*. New York: Academic Press.

Hing, Bill Ong. (1993). *Making and Remaking Asian America Through Immigration Policy, 1850-1990*. Stanford: Stanford Univeristy Press.

Jiobu, Robert M. (1994). Personal communication with Asian Pacific students at the Ohio State University, Columbus, Ohio.

Jiobu, Robert M. (1988). *Ethnicity and Assimilation*. Albany, State University of New York Press.

Kitano, Harry H. L., and Daniels, Roger. (1988). *Asian Americans: Emerging Minorities*. Englewood Cliffs, New Jersey: Prentice-Hall, Inc.

Kitano, Harry H. L. (1976). *Japanese Americans: The Evolution of a Subculture*, Second Edition. Englewood Cliffs, New Jersey: Prentice-Hall, Inc.

Mar, Don, and Kim, Marlene. (1994). "Historical Trends." Pp. 13 - 56 in Ong, Paul (ed.), *The State of Asian Pacific America: Economic Diversity, Issues & Policies*. Los Angeles, California: Leadership Education for Asian Pacifics (LEAP).

Ong, Paul, and Blumenberg, Evelyn. (1994a). "Scientists and Engineers." Pp. 165 - 189 in Ong, Paul (ed.), *The State of Asian Pacific America: Economic Diversity, Issues & Policies*. Los Angeles, California: Leadership Education for Asian Pacifics (LEAP).

Ong, Paul, and Blumenberg, Evelyn. (1994b). "Welfare and Work Among Southeast Asians," Pp. 113 - 138 in Ong, Paul (ed.), *The State of Asian Pacific America: Economic Diversity, Issues & Policies*. Los Angeles, California: Leadership Education for Asian Pacifics (LEAP).

Okihiro, Gary Y. (1994). *Margin and Mainstream: Asians in American History and Culture*. Seattle: University of Washington Press.

Siu, Paul C. (1952). "The Sojourner," *American Journal of Sociology* 58:34-44.

U. S. Bureau of the Census (1992). *Census of Population and Housing, Public Use Microdata Samples, 1990*. Prepared by the Bureau of the Census, Washington. D. C.

U. S. Bureau of the Census. (1994). *Statistical Abstract of the United States, 1994*. Washington, D. C.: U. S. Government Printing Office.

The Impact of Immigration on the Demography of Asian Pacific Americans

by Larry Hajime Shinagawa[*]

This article focuses on social and demographic characteristics of Asian Pacific Americans and discusses the impact of immigration on the demography of Asian Pacific Americans. The study is divided into five sections. The first section describes the data sources and the methodology used in collecting information about the immigration and demography of Asian Pacific Americans and other groups. The second section examines the growth of the Asian Pacific American population and discusses the racial composition of the United States and the ethnic composition of Asian Pacific Americans. The third section provides an historical overview of Asian Pacific American immigration. The fourth section provides demographic information about general patterns of immigration to the United States, the past and current composition of Asian ethnic immigrant groups, and their regional dispersion and occupational distribution.

The fifth section paints a portrait of the social demography of Asian Pacific Americans, with an emphasis on immigrants where information is available. An overview of the following characteristics is provided: age and gender composition, regional dispersion, educational attainment, household and family structure related to income, income distribution, occupational profile, workforce participation, percentage in poverty, relative rates of crime perpetration, and language usage within households.

Methodology

Data for this study are based on information gathered by the U.S. Immigration and Naturalization Service (INS) and the U.S. Bureau of the Census and were analyzed according to standard statistical procedures.[1]

Most of the analysis for the 1990s is conducted for the aggregate Asian Pacific American population, since information about specific ethnic groups is either unavailable or is statistically unreliable. In addition, much of the

---

[*] Larry Shinagawa is Associate Professor in the Department of Sociology, Sonoma State University, Sonoma, California.

Shinagawa, The Impact of Immigration on Demography   59

ethnic-specific information is for the aggregate ethnic category, rather than by nativity. Since the majority of the Asian Pacific American population is foreign-born and immigrant (66.8 percent in 1990), aggregate figures of specific Asian Pacific American ethnic groups are usually descriptive of the immigrant populations. Japanese Americans, Chinese Americans, and Filipino Americans represent exceptions to this generalization because these groups include statistically significant U.S.-born populations. Information by nativity is provided where available (a subsequent report will break down ethnic groups by nativity into more detail).

The term Asian Pacific American is used throughout the article to refer to persons of Asian descent. Depending upon the source of data, however, operational definitions may be different. When using INS data, information about Asian Pacific Americans refers to immigrants from Asia, with specific emphasis on Chinese, Japanese, Asian Indian, Korean, Filipino, and Vietnamese background. When referring to Census data, persons included are those who reported as a member of one of the Asian or Pacific Islander groups listed on the Census questionnaire or who provided write-in responses. Specific Asian Pacific American ethnic groups highlighted in the report include Chinese, Filipino, Japanese, Asian Indian, Korean, Vietnamese, Hawaiian, Laotian, Cambodian, Thai, Hmong, Samoan, Guamanian, Tongan, and the residual category of other "Asian Pacific Americans."

Asian Pacific American Population Growth

The racial group currently most affected by immigration is Asian Pacific Americans. Historically, the ebb and flow of Asian and Pacific Islander immigration have been primarily responsible for the size and diversity of Asian Pacific American populations. While immigration came in spurts— and virtually stopped between 1850 and 1965—the majority of Asian and Pacific Islander immigration occurred after the passage of the Immigration and Nationality Act Amendments of 1965.[2] This law and its successors have been chiefly responsible for the amazing growth of the Asian Pacific American population. Between 1960 and 1990, the Asian Pacific American population increased from 1 million to over 7 million, reflecting a 700 percent growth. Between 1970 and 1990, the Asian Pacific American population more than tripled (3.62 times); more recently, the population almost doubled in size between 1980 and 1990 (1.96 times). In 1990, there were 7,273,662 Asian Pacific American individuals, representing 31 diverse groups and constituting 2.9 percent of all Americans (see Table 1).

According to the 1994 Current Population Survey, the Asian Pacific American population was estimated at 8.8 million. In 1994, as in 1990, Asian Pacific Americans made up roughly 3 percent of America's population. Since 1990, their population has grown by an average of 4.5 percent annually. Eighty-six percent of this growth is attributable to immigration, the remainder to natural increase.[3]

By the year 2000, Asian Pacific Americans are projected to reach 12.1 million and to represent 4.3 percent of America's population. Until the year 2000, 75 percent of the Asian Pacific American population growth will be attributable to immigration. By the year 2050, the Asian Pacific American population will have increased five times its size from 1995,[4] and will comprise 10 percent of the total U.S. population.

Regionally, the western states, and California in particular, will continue to be the favorite locations of Asian Pacific Americans. Between 1993 and 2020, the western Asian Pacific American population of 8 million persons is expected to increase considerably. By the year 2000, 40.5 percent of all Asian Pacific Americans (almost 10 million) will live in California, compared to 40.0 percent in 1995 and 39.1 percent in 1990. By 2020, Texas and New York will each have more than 1 million Asian Pacific Americans.[5]

Major Asian Pacific American Groups

In 1990, Chinese Americans constituted the largest Asian Pacific American population, with 1,645,472 individuals. They made up 22.6 percent of all Asian Pacific Americans and represented about 0.7 percent of all Americans. Following closely were Filipino Americans, with a population of 1,406,770, which represented 19.3 percent of Asian Pacific Americans and 0.6 percent of all Americans. Smaller in size, in descending order were Japanese Americans (847,562), Asian Indian Americans (815,447), Korean Americans (798,849), Vietnamese Americans (614,547), Hawaiian Americans (211,014), Laotian Americans (149,014), Cambodian Americans (147,411), Thai Americans (91,275), Hmong Americans (90,082), Samoan Americans (62,964), Guamanian Americans (49,345), and Tongan Americans (17,606). The remainder of other Asian Pacific Americans numbered 326,304 (see Table 2).

The overall Asian Pacific American population increased 95.2 percent between 1980 and 1990. In comparison, the non-Hispanic White population grew 4.2 percent. Among Asian Pacific American ethnic groups, Japanese Americans increased by 18.3 percent, Filipino Americans by 79.9 percent, Chinese Americans by 102.6 percent, Asian Indian Americans by 110.6 percent, Korean Americans by 123.5 percent, and Vietnamese Americans by 150.8 percent. The most amazing growth was among Southeast Asian Americans.[6] Laotian Americans grew by 212.5 percent, Cambodian Americans by 818.8 percent, and Hmong Americans by 1,631 percent. Among Pacific Islander Americans, growth was moderate, ranging from Hawaiian Americans with 22.4 percent to Samoan Americans with 60.8 percent.[7]

Asian Pacific American Immigration

The examination of Asian Pacific American immigration must begin with an overview of general immigration to the United States. This provides a context for viewing the scope and degree of Asian Pacific American immigration.

Overview of General Immigration to the United States

With the exception of indigenous Hawaiian Americans and Native Americans, the United States is truly a nation of immigrants. Since the U.S. government started collecting immigration data in 1820, over 60 million legal immigrants have arrived. This land of immigrants now has a total population of 261,638,00 (as of 1 January 1995).[8]

Immigration totals have varied. Between 1880 and 1920, 23.5 million immigrants entered the United States. From 1921 to 1930, due to the passage of restrictive and discriminatory immigration laws, immigration dropped off down to 4.1 million. During the 1930s, these laws would slow immigration flow to just one million, the bulk of whom came from Europe. During the 1940s, immigration increased to just over a million and was comprised mainly of refugees and wives of U.S. servicemen. During the height of the Cold War, between 1951 and 1960, 2.5 million individuals entered. Most were European immigrants or political refugees fleeing communism.

The liberalization of immigration laws in the 1960s resulted in the resumption of large-scale immigration and remarkable changes in the racial composition of immigrants. Between 1961 and 1970, 5.3 million immigrants arrived, during the following decade, 7 million admissions were recorded. By the 1980s, the number was 9.9 million; and another 2.9 million immigrants entered between 1990 and 1993. By 1994, net international immigration accounted for 30 percent of the total increase the country's population for the year. Among immigrants, 40 percent came from Asia, and approximately 43 percent were from Latin America.[9]

Altogether, immigration to the United States has increased the indigenous population by over 120 million. Put another way, had it not been for immigration since 1790, the U.S. population would be an estimated 122 million, roughly the size of the population of current-day Japan.[10]

On average, about 800,000 legal immigrants arrive annually to the United States. In addition, depending upon the source, an estimated 200,000 to 300,000 undocumented aliens enter the United States every year.[11]

The percent of foreign-born individuals within the United States has risen and fallen with the changes in immigrations flows. In 1910, 13.5 percent were foreign-born; but by 1940, after decades of exclusionary immigration laws, the percentage dipped to 8.8 percent. Since then, despite major increases in immigration, the percentage of foreign-born in the United States remains low. In 1980, only 6.2 percent of the total U.S. population were foreign-born. Despite record-setting immigration in the 1980s, by 1990 the percent of foreign-born in the United States had only increased to 7.9 percent.

Map 1 illustrates the percent of foreign-born persons in the United States in 1990. Foreign-born populations are concentrated along the southern borders of the United States and along the Pacific Rim, Florida, and the Eastern seaboard. In Hawaii, California, Washington, Texas, Florida, and Massachusetts, the foreign-born constitute over 5 percent of the total populations in the majority of counties.

Table 3 depicts the overall immigration to the United States by decade since 1850 and in recent years (1991-1994). The table shows that between 1901 and 1910, new immigrants represented a substantial proportion of the total U.S. population—9.56 percent. Since then, the proportion has continually decreased. Even as late as 1990, immigrants who had entered in the previous decade represented less than 3 percent of the population.

The composition has changed as well. Between 1851 and 1860, about 89 percent of all immigrants were from northwestern Europe. Since then, the proportion from that region, however, steadily declined until by 1994, they comprised only 3.4 percent of immigrants to the United States.

In contrast, Latino and Asian immigration has risen dramatically. In 1851, only 1.6 percent of all immigrants were from Asia, but by 1990, Asian immigrants comprised over 38 percent of all immigrants, an all-time high. Similarly, Latinos were less than 0.1 percent of all immigrants between 1901 and 1910, and by 1990, they had reached an unprecedented high of 37.2 percent of all immigrants, roughly matching the immigration of Asians. More recent INS information indicates that between 1991 and

1994, the proportion of all immigrants of Latino origin increased to 42.7 percent!

A Brief Overview of Asian Immigration and Laws Affecting Asian Immigration

Despite record high percentages of immigration during the 1980s—including several waves of immigration from Asian and Pacific countries—Asian Pacific Americans never reached more than one-quarter of one percent of the total U.S. population before 1940. Racist legislation minimizing Asian immigration was repeatedly passed and amended, Asians of various nationalities and classes were barred from entering for a variety of reasons, including concern over economic competition with white workers.

The Chinese were the first to be affected by these discriminatory laws. Shortly after 20,000 Chinese immigrants arrived in response to news about the California Gold Rush, a foreign miners' tax was imposed in 1853. As a result, Chinese immigration dropped to less than 5,000 that year. In 1870 Congress amended the 1790 Naturalization Act (that had limited citizenship through naturalization to "free white persons") to extend citizenship benefits to aliens of African ancestry.[12] A similar attempt on behalf of the Chinese, however, failed. Their status as "aliens ineligible for citizenship" would eventually preclude Asian and Pacific immigrants from entering in substantial numbers.[13] Alarmed by the number of Chinese in California in 1882, Congress passed the Chinese Exclusion Act, which excluded most Chinese from entering the United States. The law suspended the immigration of Chinese laborers for ten years, but eventually the law was extended indefinitely. The Exclusion Act was the first immigration law directed at a specific ethnic or nationality group.[14]

The exclusion of the Chinese did not end Asian immigration. Shortly after the passage of the Chinese Exclusion Act, Japanese immigrants began arriving in the United States, and in time, they became the major agricultural labor force on Hawaii's plantations and California's fields. By 1908, 55,000 Japanese Americans lived on the mainland, primarily in California, and about 150,000 in Hawaii. Between 1908 and 1924, despite the 1907 Gentleman's Agreement between the United States and Japan, which limited the number of Japanese laborers who could immigrate, another 168,000 Japanese immigrants arrived in the United States.[15] Many were students and picture brides of Japanese immigrants.

In 1917, Congress created a "barred zone," which excluded natives of China, South and Southeast Asia, the Asian part of Russia, Afghanistan, Iran, part of Arabia, and the Pacific and Southeast Asian Islands not owned by the United States. Japan was left out of the barred zone because it was already excluded by the 1907 Gentlemen's Agreement. Filipinos and some Samoans were allowed entry as U.S. nationals, although they could not be naturalized.[16]

The Johnson-Reed Act of 1924, codified racial discrimination and exclusion on a broader basis. An annual limit of 150,000 visas was established for those outside the Western Hemisphere, and that number was divided into quotas based on nationality proportions of the U.S. population in 1920 (later the quota base was pushed back to 1890, to exclude more eastern and southern Europeans). Immigration for each nationality group was limited to only 2 percent of the U.S. residents of that nationality in the United States in 1890. The system favored Great Britain and the rest of northwestern Europe, since those nationalities constituted the bulk of the U.S. population. Since the 1924 law excluded aliens ineligible for citizenship, the Japanese became permanently barred from immigration pursuant to the law.[17]

By 1934, the Tydings-McDuffie Act closed the small door of immigration available to Filipino nationals of the United States. The act set a 1946 independence date for the Philippines, and in the process, upon independence, Filipinos would lose their status as U.S. nationals and became subject to a token quota of 50 immigrants each year. Filipino "deportation" was also encouraged by the passage of laws providing public funds for Filipinos returning permanently to the Philippines.[18]

Beginning with World War II, immigration policy directed toward Asian Pacific Americans change markedly. In 1943, Congress repealed Chinese exclusion laws, and, in 1946, the privilege of naturalization was extended to Filipinos and Asian Indians. That same year, President Truman raised the Filipino quota to 100, and Congress approved a law that allowed Chinese wives of American citizens to enter on a non-quota basis. By 1950, the law was liberalized and extended to give spouses and minor children of members of the armed forces the same rights, and in 1952, these rights were extended to Japanese Americans and other Asian Americans.[19]

The McCarran-Walter Immigration and Nationality Act of 1952 eliminated racial barriers to naturalization and thereby to immigration. The law, however, retained most quota preferences of the 1924 law. While the 1917 Act's Asiatic barred zone was abolished, the law created a new restrictive zone called "the Asia-Pacific triangle," which consisted of countries from India to Japan, and all Pacific islands north of Australia and New Zealand. An annual maximum of 2,000 people from this region were allowed to immigrate. For the 19 nations within the triangle, each was given a percentage of the 2,000-person quota. Asians were now eligible to enter America as immigrants, but their numbers, like those of southern and eastern Europeans, were kept low.

The Immigration and Nationality Act Amendments of 1965 changed this pattern. Passed during a period of optimism and the Civil Rights movement, the law went far to undo many of the racial biases of the 1924 Immigration Act. Race-based immigration restrictions were abandoned in favor of the dominating principle of family reunification. Eighty percent of numerically limited visas were for close relatives of U.S. citizens or residents.[20] In addition, immediate relatives of U.S. citizens and special immigrants were no longer subject to the numerical cap.[21]

Testifying in favor the 1965 amendments, Attorney General Robert Kennedy said that the number of Asian and Pacific Islander immigrants "to be expected from the Asia-Pacific triangle would be approximately 5,000."[22] What he did not realize, however, was that Asian Pacific Americans would make extensive use of the unlimited immediate relative category to bring in parents, spouses, and minor children of U.S. citizens.

As a result of this legal opportunity, many immigrants subsequently entered the United States without being subject to the numerical limitations of a preference system that determined eligibility for admission.[23] In the 1990s, immediate relatives have remained a substantial proportion of immigration. For example, in 1993, among the 708,394 immigrants who were admitted into the United States, 251,647 (35 percent of total immigrants) were immediate relatives of U.S. citizens.[24]

The Immigration Act of 1990 increased the opportunity for legal immigration even further. Designed to counter-balance the 1965 law's emphasis on family reunification, the 1990 law was drafted with the idea of supplying the country with skilled workers and also attracting needed capital. To help reach the latter objective, 10,000 visas have been set aside each year for those willing to invest $1 million in a new business that employs at least ten workers. The law almost tripled to 140,000 the number of visas distributed on the basis of skills. The law also provides an annual lottery that allows entry to 40,000 persons a year; about 1.4 million applicants have been received annually. In anticipation of the 1997 changeover in government control of Hong Kong, the 1990 changes also increased the quota for natives of Hong Kong to 20,000.

Since the 1940s, refugees from Asia have been able to take advantage of refugee provisions shaped mainly by Cold War policy. In 1948, the first of two Displaced Persons Acts was passed. Displaced persons were defined as those who had been victims of fascist and totalitarian regimes; who were considered refugees, persecuted for reasons of race, religion, nationality, or political opinion; who have been deported from, or obliged to leave, their country of nationality or place of former habitual residence. Many individuals from China and Korea entered through this provision. The 1965 amendments provided special preference for those fleeing communist-dominated countries. Other Asians, including thousands of Southeast Asians after 1975, were paroled into the United States through special authority of the Attorney General. In 1980, the Refugee Act of 1980 purported to change this Cold War bias. A refugee was now more broadly defined as someone who was unable or unwilling to return to his country because of a well-founded fear of persecution on account of race, religion, nationality, membership in a particular social group, or political opinion.[25] As a result of these various policies, many refugees have come to the United States from Southeast Asia and China. Between 1980 and 1991, 327,183 Vietnamese entered the United States as refugees, while more recently, after the passage of the Chinese Student Protection Act of 1992, 48,212 students from the People's Republic of China have become legal immigrants between 1992 and 1993.

As a result of changes brought about by immigration laws beginning in the 1960s, a dramatic rise in the number of Asian immigrants and a concurrent downward trend of European immigration has ensued. In the 1950s, 53 percent of immigrants came from Europe and just 6 percent from Asia. By contrast, in the 1980s, only 11 percent came from Europe, and most of the remaining immigrants were evenly split between Asians and Latinos.

Immigration of
Asian Pacific American Ethnic Groups

This section provides demographic information about general patterns of immigration to the United States, the past and current composition of Asian ethnic immigrant groups, Asian Pacific American immigrant regional dispersion, and finally, the occupational distribution of these immigrants.

The effect of changes in immigration policies directed at Asian Pacifics is readily apparent from a review of immigration figures. Table 4 shows immigration by decade between 1820 and 1990 and in recent years (1991-

1994) for selected Asian ethnic groups. Pacific Islander groups are not shown, since most are either numerically small or indigenous to the United States, as in the case of Samoan Americans and Hawaiian Americans. In 1820, six Asian immigrants to the United States were recorded. Between 1851 and 1860, with the news of gold in California, immigration increased substantially as over 41,000 Chinese arrived in the United States. But even with this sizable number, Asian immigrants constituted only 1.6 percent of the overall immigration during that decade. Prior to World War II, the period between 1871 and 1880 had the greatest flow of Chinese immigrants (123,201); and the period between 1901 and 1910 saw the peak years of Korean immigration (7,697), Asian Indian immigration (4,713), and Japanese immigration (129,797). The entry of Filipinos, arriving as U.S. nationals, peaked between 1921 and 1930 (54,747).

Between 1930 and 1960, few Asian immigrants entered the United States, but after the 1965 immigration amendments went into effect in the late 1960s, this changed. By the 1970s, Asian Pacific immigration totaled 1,586,140; in the 1980s the total reached 2,817,391. More recently, between 1991 and 1994, 1,356,447 Asian Pacific immigrants entered. In the 1980s, immigrants from China, India, Korea, the Philippines and Vietnam all numbered over a quarter million.

Table 5 shows a more detailed, year-by-year summary of Asian Pacific immigration from the 1960s to 1994. Chinese immigration hit a peak of 65,552 in 1993. Japanese immigration since 1960 has generally totaled below 6,000 annually, but in more recent years (1992 through 1994), the figure has reached more than 10,000. In 1960, only 2,954 Filipino immigrants were admitted, but immigration increased steadily until by 1990, Filipino immigration reached an all-time high of 64,756 admissions. The number has experienced a small decline since then. For Koreans, large scale immigration began in the late 1970s, peaking at 35,849 in 1987, and declining to 15,985 in 1994. Since the 1992 South Central Los Angeles uprising, immigration has declined by over 10,000 per year. Asian Indian immigration gradually rose from 1970 to 1990. In 1991, Asian Indian immigration increased dramatically to 45,064, but since that time, has declined somewhat (34,873 in 1994). Among Vietnamese entrants, peaks in flows coincided with forced departures from Vietnam. In 1978, 88,543 Vietnamese, primarily refugee boat people, arrived in the United States. Subsequently, in 1982, after further crackdowns on ethnic Chinese Vietnamese, another 72,553 arrived. Since that time, another peak occurred in 1992 (77,726), partly due to the wholesale immigration of Amerasian children from Vietnam. Since then, Vietnamese entries have declined somewhat (41,344 in 1994).

By 1990, the foreign-born constituted 68.2 percent of Asian Pacific America. Since only 6.2 percent of the general population was foreign-born in 1990, Asian Pacific Americans were eleven times more likely to be foreign-born than the general population. In descending order, the percentage of foreign-born among Asian Pacific American ethnic groups were: Laotian (93.9 percent), Cambodian (93.7 percent), Vietnamese (90.4 percent), Thai (82.1 percent), Korean (81.9 percent), Tongan (74.7 percent), Asian Indian (70.4 percent), Filipino (64.7 percent), Chinese (63.3 percent), Samoan (35.5 percent), and Japanese (28.4 percent).[26]

Regional Dispersion

Recent Asian Pacific immigrants have continued the long-term pattern of bi-coastal immigration and immigration to metropolitan areas. Selected Asian Pacific groups by number and percent of immigration are shown in Table 6 for the top five states of intended residence between the years 1990-1993. For every major group, the top-ranked state of intended residence is California. In five of six groups, with the exception of Vietnamese Americans (who chose Texas), New York ranks second. For immigrants from China, Korea, and India, New Jersey is the third choice. Hawaii is the third choice for Japanese Americans and Filipino Americans.

Recent Asian Pacific immigrants are heavily concentrated in California, New York, Washington, DC and other metropolitan areas. Table 7 shows the top five metropolitan areas of intended residence in 1991 for selected Asian Pacific immigrants. For Chinese Americans, three of the top five metropolitan areas are located in California. Although their number one area of intended residence is New York, for Chinese from Taiwan, New York is the second choice. For Asian Indians, New York is also the principal destination, followed by Chicago, Los Angeles, San Jose, and Washington, DC. Among Pakistanis, New York is by far the principal location (32.8 percent), followed by Washington, DC, Chicago, Los Angeles, and Houston. Korean immigrants are about evenly split between New York (17.3) and Los Angeles (16.7), with substantial populations in Washington, DC, Chicago, and the Anaheim-Santa Ana, Calif., area. Among Filipino immigrants, the top three locations are in California (Los Angeles, San Francisco, and San Diego), followed by New York and Honolulu. Finally, among Vietnamese, four of the top five metropolitan areas of intended residence are in California, with Washington, DC, as the fourth choice.

Occupational Distribution

The occupational distribution of recent immigrants from Asia varies widely. Table 8 shows the occupational distribution of selected Asian ethnic groups for immigrants admitted between 1990 and 1993. Overall, 11.2 percent held managerial positions, 13.3 percent professional, 16.9 percent technical, 17.1 percent service, 14.5 percent craft, with 27.1 percent indicating laborer or not specifying. Among the various groups, Vietnamese Americans had the highest percentage of laborers (42.6 percent), followed by Chinese Americans (21.6 percent) and Korean Americans (20.0 percent). In managerial and professional occupations, Asian Indian Americans had the highest percentage (51.2 percent), followed by Japanese Americans (41.1 percent) and Chinese Americans (38 percent). Vietnamese Americans were the least likely to be within the managerial and professional ranks (2.6 percent).

Disparities by ethnicity and gender were also apparent when occupations were assessed for socio-economic prestige.[27] In this assessment, managerial and professional occupations are given high scores, while jobs as laborers are assigned low scores. Table 9 delineates the mean socioeconomic prestige scores for select Asian groups for 1993, by gender, for those over age 25.

The table demonstrates that immigrants from Asia have roughly the same socio-economic prestige as immigrants from Europe. Mean scores for immigrants from China, Japan, Korea, and India were higher than those of European immigrants. Lowest scores were among Vietnamese immigrants (50.4); highest scores were among Asian Indian immigrants (66.9). Except among Filipino and Vietnamese immigrants, males had higher occupational prestige than females.

Asian Pacific American Social Demography

Residential Dispersion

Asian Pacific Americans are heavily concentrated on the Western and Eastern seaboards of the United States, and they also live in metropolitan areas, with greater proportions living in central cities, compared to non-Hispanic whites. Map 2 focuses on various counties of the United States in 1990, and emphasizes the fact that most Asian Pacific Americans reside in the West or the Northeast. The map also shows that Asian Pacific Americans are heavily concentrated in major metropolitan areas throughout the United States. The Western region, including Hawaii, accounted for 58.5

percent of all Asian Pacific Americans, while the Northeast region accounted for 17.3 percent. Only 10.3 percent and 13.8 percent of Asian Pacific Americans settled in the Midwest and South, respectively. Over 94 percent resided in metropolitan areas. In contrast, only 76.4 percent of non-Hispanic whites lived in metropolitan areas.[28]

The ten states with the largest 1990 Asian Pacific American populations, in descending order, were: California, New York, Hawaii, Texas, Illinois, New Jersey, Washington, Virginia, Florida, and Massachusetts (see Table 10). These states were home to 5,769,651 Asian Pacific Americans, and accounted for close to 80 percent of the total Asian Pacific American population. With the exception of Illinois and Washington, Asian Pacific American populations in these states more than doubled between 1980 and 1990, with most of this increase attributable to immigration.[29] Among the top ten states, immigration accounted for 79.2 percent of the total Asian Pacific American population.

In each state, the distribution of each ethnic group differed. In California, Filipino Americans were the most numerous (731,685), followed closely by Chinese Americans (704,850). In New York, Chinese Americans were first in size (284,144), followed by Asian Indian Americans (140,985). In Hawaii, a state with tremendous Asian Pacific American ethnic diversity, Japanese Americans numbered 247,486 (22.3 percent of the state population), with Filipino Americans coming in second with 168,682 (15.2 percent). In Texas, Vietnamese Americans were the largest population (69,634), followed by Chinese Americans (63,232). In Illinois, the largest Asian Pacific American group was Filipino Americans (64,224), closely followed by Asian Indian Americans (64,200). In New Jersey, Asian Indian Americans were the largest population (79,440), representing 1 percent of the state's population; Chinese Americans were second (59,084). In Washington, Virginia, and Florida, Filipino Americans were the largest population, with Japanese Americans being the second largest in Washington, Korean Americans in Virginia, and Asian Indian Americans in Florida. In Massachusetts, Chinese Americans were the largest population (53,792), followed by Asian Indian Americans (19,719) (see Table 11).

The ten cities with the largest Asian Pacific American populations showed the typical bi-coastal pattern and a regional concentration in Chicago and in Houston. In 1990, Asian Pacific Americans represented 28 percent of San Francisco's population, 19 percent of San Jose, 11 percent of San Diego, 9 percent of Los Angeles, 7 percent of New York City, and 5 percent of Boston. All these cities were among the 20 largest in the United States (see Table 12).

Los Angeles County had the largest Asian Pacific American population (954,485), followed by Honolulu County, Hawaii; Queens County, New York; Santa Clara, Orange, San Francisco, San Diego, and Alameda Counties in California; Cook County, Illinois; and Kings County, New York (see Table 13). Among these counties, the three with the largest Asian Pacific American percentage concentration were Honolulu, Hawaii (63 percent); San Francisco, California (29.1 percent); and Santa Clara, California (17.5 percent). Among the top ten counties, six were in California, and seven were in the West.

The *counties* and *cities* with the largest population of a specific Asian Pacific American ethnic group were as follows: Chinese Americans (Los Angeles County; New York); Filipino Americans (Los Angeles County; Los Angeles); Japanese Americans (Honolulu County; Honolulu); Asian Indian American (Queens County; New York); Korean American (Los Angeles County; Los Angeles); Vietnamese Americans (Orange County; San Jose); Hawaiian Americans (Honolulu County; Honolulu); Laotian American (Fresno County; Fresno); Cambodian American (Los Angeles County; Long Beach); Thai American (Los Angeles County; Los Angeles); Hmong American (Fresno County; Fresno); Guamanian American (Los Angeles County; San Diego); Samoan American (Honolulu County; Honolulu); Tongan American (Salt Lake County; Salt Lake City).[30]

Asian Pacific American Age and Gender

The median age of Asian Pacific Americans in 1991 was 30.4 years,[31] compared to 33.9 for non-Hispanic whites. In terms of gender, 48.7 percent were male, and 51.3 percent were female.[32]

Asian Pacific Americans had the highest proportion of persons of working age: 65 percent were between the ages of 18 and 64, compared to 61 percent of non-Hispanic whites, 59 percent of African Americans, 60 percent of Latinos, and 58 percent of Native Americans.[33] Tables 14 through 20 show the age and sex profile of certain Asian Pacific American ethnic groups in the United States for 1990.

According to Table 14, the median age of the general American population is about 33. Among males, the median is 33 and among females, the figure is 31.8. In comparison, Asian Pacific Americans tend to be slightly younger than the general populations. As an aggregate, Asian Pacific Americans had an median age of 30.1, with females at 31.1 years of age and males 29 years of age. Overall, proportions of male to female are as expected for each population: 51.3 percent of the general population is female, while 48.7 percent are male. In comparison, Asian Pacific Americans are 51.2 percent female and 48.8 percent male.

Great disparities in the median age appear when the native-born general population and the native-born Asian Pacific American population are compared. While the general population has a median age of 32.5 among native-born, Asian Pacific Americans have a median age of only 15.8 among the native-born. As seen in the tables, with the exception of Japanese Americans, the median age of native-born among most Asian Pacific American groups is markedly lower than among the general population. These lower figures reflect the youthful population structure of immigrant Asian Pacific American populations. For example, among the native-born Asian Indian Americans, the median was 8.8 years, and among Korean Americans, it was 9.0. The lowest median age among native-born Asian Pacific Americans was among Cambodian Americans: 4.7 years.

Other significant details emerge from the age and gender distributions set forth in the tables. Most Asian Pacific Americans—even the foreign-born—are youthful, with a median age lower than that of the general population. Moreover, the tables indicate that many of the immigrants have arrived since 1980, and among that population, they tend to be more youthful than their pre-1980 counterparts. The tables also show that the majority (59 percent) of foreign-born are not citizens.[34] Those not naturalized tend to be slightly older (35.7 years of age) than those who are (35). The Hmong American population has the highest proportion of persons not naturalized (90 percent).

Gender ratio imbalances among Asian Pacific American groups were highest among Pakistani, Thai, Korean, and Japanese Americans. The Thai and Pakistani American communities have more males than females, while the opposite was the case for the Korean and Japanese American communities. The greater number of male Pakistani Americans may be due to the large influx of professionals from Pakistan. The larger number of female Korean and Japanese Americans may be attributable to the longer life expectancy of females compared to males, more elderly immigrants females arriving among Korean Americans, and the presence of wives of U.S. servicemen among Korean Americans and Japanese Americans.

Households and Family Structure

According to 1991 figures, marital status for persons 15 years and older was as follows: 31.1 percent never married, 56.4 percent married with spouse present, 3.4 percent married with spouse absent, 5.1 percent widowed, and 4 percent divorced. Comparable statistics for non-Hispanic whites are 22 percent never married, 58.1 percent married with spouse present, 2.6 percent married with spouse absent, 7 percent widowed, and 8 percent divorced.[35]

In 1994, the average number of persons per family for Asian Pacific Americans and Non-Hispanic whites were 3.8 and 3.1, respectively. About 73 percent of Asian Pacific American families had three or more persons in 1994, compared to only 55 percent of non-Hispanic white families. Another 22 percent of all Asian Pacific American families had five or more persons, compared to 12 percent of non-Hispanic White families. Six in ten Asian and Pacific American families had related children under 18 years old, compared with almost half (49 percent) of non-Hispanic white families. In each group, about 80 percent of related children under 18 years old lived with two parents.

In 1990, among Asian Pacific Americans, 31.2 percent of all Asian Pacific American husbands and 40.4 percent of all Asian Pacific American wives were intermarried. About 19 percent of Asian Pacific American husbands were interethnically married and 12.3 percent were interracially married. Among the interracially married, 9.9 percent of these husbands married non-Hispanic whites. Among Asian Pacific American wives, 16.2 percent were interethnically married, and 24.2 percent were interracially married. Among the interracially married, 20.8 percent of Asian Pacific American wives had married non-Hispanic whites. Japanese American wives and Filipino American wives had the highest proportion of intermarriages (51.9 percent and 40.2 percent, respectively).[36] The high proportion of intermarriage among Japanese Americans is partly attributable to the large number of wives of U.S. servicemen.

Table 21 shows the marriage patterns of California Asian Pacific American husbands and wives in 1990. Most Asian Pacific Americans in-marry either intraethnically or intraracially. Intermarriages have been on the increase, but recent trends show small increases in interracial marriages and dramatic increases in interethnic marriages. Among Asian Pacific American husbands, Cambodian Americans are the least likely to intermarry, while Hawaiian Americans are the most likely to intermarry. Among wives, Hmong Americans are least likely, while Hawaiian Americans were the most likely to intermarry.

Among foreign-born Asian Pacific American husbands, Cambodian American husbands were the least likely to intermarry, while Tongan Americans were the most likely. Among foreign-born wives, Hmong American wives were the least likely to intermarry, while Thai Americans were the most likely.

Among husbands of Asian Pacific American groups with substantial U.S.-born populations (Chinese, Filipino, and Japanese), Japanese Americans are the most likely to inmarry, while Filipino Americans are the most likely to intermarry. In California, by 1990, more U.S.-born Filipino American husbands had intermarried than inmarried. Among Asian Pacific American wives born in the United States, Chinese Americans are the mostly likely to inmarry, while Filipino Americans are the most likely to intermarry. In California, by 1990, the three largest Asian Pacific American groups with substantial U.S.-born populations had close to 50 percent or more who had intermarried outside their ethnic group.

Household and Family Income

The 1993 median income of Asian and Pacific Islander families ($44,460) was similar to that of non-Hispanic white families ($41,110). The median income for Asian and Pacific Islander families maintained by women with no spouses present ($28,920) was higher than that for comparable non-Hispanic white families ($21,650). Male householder families with no spouse present had median family incomes that were not statistically different ($23,130 for Asian Pacific American and $30,170 for non-Hispanic whites).

Asian Pacific American married-couple families had a higher median income ($49,510) than comparable non-Hispanic white families ($45,240). Both the husband and wife worked in about 60 percent of all Asian Pacific American and non-Hispanic white married-couple families. The husband was the only earner, however, in 18 percent of Asian Pacific American and 15 percent of non-Hispanic white married-couple families. The 1990 census showed that 20 percent of Asian Pacific American families, compared to 13 percent of non-Hispanic white families, had three or more earners.

Of Asian Pacific American householders under the age of 25, 23.1 percent had an annual household income of less than $5,000. Compared to other age groups, this age category of householders had the largest percentage with an annual income of $5,000 or less. At the other end of the household income spectrum, Asian Pacific American householders in California between the ages 45 and 54 had the largest percentage (11.8 percent) of households with income of $100,000 or more.

Table 22 shows the median household income for Asian Pacific Americans between the ages of 18 and 64 by nativity, sex, and selected ethnic group. Nationally, Asian Pacific Americans in 1990 had an average household income of $53,104. U.S.-born Asian Pacific Americans had considerably higher household income than foreign-born ($58,723 compared to $51,643). Generally, Asian Indian Americans had the highest median household income ($60,903), while the lowest median income was evident among Hmong Americans ($20,648). Among foreign-born Asian Pacific Americans, Asian Indian Americans had the highest household income ($60,960), followed by Filipino Americans ($59,463) and Japanese Americans ($54,620). Among U.S.-born Asian Pacific Americans, Filipino Americans had the highest household income ($63,881), followed by Asian Indian Americans ($62,597), and Chinese Americans ($58,723).

Much of the high household median incomes of Asian Pacific American groups is attributable to the higher proportion of workers in households. Table 23 shows the percent of families with three or more workers in 1989 among selected Asian Pacific American groups. The table shows that while the general population has only 13.3 percent of all households with 3 or more workers, Asian Pacific Americans had a substantially higher percentage of workers contributing to the household wage (19.8 percent). This is especially evident among the group with some of the highest median household incomes (Chinese Americans, 19.0 percent; Filipino Americans 29.6 percent; and Asian Indian Americans, 17.6 percent). Even groups with low household median incomes have high workforce participation rates among family members. Vietnamese American families had 21.3 percent with three workers or more, while Laotian Americans and Pacific Islanders had similar high percentages (18.9 percent and 19.7).

Individual Incomes

In 1993, Asians and Pacific Islander males 25 years and older who worked full-time year round had median earnings ($31,560) higher than comparable females ($25,430). Asians and Pacific Islander and non-Hispanic white females with at least a bachelor's degree had similar earnings ($31,780 versus $32,920), while comparably educated Asian and Pacific Islander males ($41,220) earned about $87 for every $100 of non-Hispanic white males' earnings ($47,180).

In 1990, Asian Pacific American males who worked full-time year round had median incomes of $26,764, compared to $28,881 for non-Hispanic white males. Comparable Asian Pacific American females received a median income of $21,323, while the median income for non-Hispanic white females was $20,048.

According to Table 24, among Asian Pacific Americans between the ages of 18 and 64, foreign-born Japanese American, foreign-born Asian Indian American, U.S.-born Japanese American, and U.S.-born Chinese Americans had on average higher wage and salary incomes than non-Hispanic white men. However, the high figures for foreign-born Japanese American men ($46,783) includes Japanese corporate businessmen who had been counted by the U.S. census and were not actually residents of the United States. Among the other groups, their higher income may be due to their concentration in high cost-of-living areas compared to the more dispersed distribution of non-Hispanic white men.

In almost all instances, Asian Pacific American women made substantially less than both Asian Pacific American men and non-Hispanic white men. The highest individual wage and salary incomes among Asian Pacific American women were Japanese American ($20,959) and Chinese American ($20,908) women.

Per-capita income among Asian Pacific Americans in 1990 was $13,420, compared to $15,265 for non-Hispanic whites. In the West, per capita income among Asian Pacific Americans was $13,774, compared to $15,444 for non-Hispanic whites. In California, per-capita income among Asian Pacific Americans in 1990 was $13,733, compared to $19,028 for non-Hispanic whites. Thus, Asian Pacific American per capita income was 27.8 percent below the non-Hispanic white population.

A map of the ratio of Asian Pacific American to non-Hispanic white per-capita income dramatically shows that differences in where populations are concentrated affect income comparisons between Asian Pacific Americans and non-Hispanic whites. Map 3 shows that Asian Pacific Americans make more per-capita than the white population only in areas where Asian Pacific Americans are not heavily concentrated. Since most Asian Pacific Americans are located in urban areas, the counties showing higher per-capita income among Asian Pacific Americans represent a very small proportion of the overall population. Thus, when regional incomes of Asian Pacific Americans are compared with those of non-Hispanic whites, Asian Pacific Americans in metropolitan areas tend to have lower incomes in the same labor markets as non-Hispanic whites.

Asian Pacific American Occupational Distribution

Table 25 shows the occupational distribution of Asian Pacific American groups in 1990. Occupationally, Asian Pacific Americans had a higher concentration than the general U.S. population in managerial, professional, and technical fields. Nationally, in 1990, 12.6 percent were in managerial positions, 18.1 percent in professional positions, and 17.9 percent in technical positions. Japanese Americans (17.5 percent) and Chinese Americans (15.1 percent) had the highest proportion of workers in managerial positions. Asian Indian Americans (29.6 percent) and Chinese Americans (20.7 percent) were the most likely of Asian Pacific American groups to be in professional occupations. Korean Americans (26.8 percent) and Asian Indian Americans (20 percent) were highly concentrated in technical and sales occupations. Southeast Asian American groups were disproportionately represented in craft (over 15 percent) and operative occupations (over 20 percent — many of those specified as operatives are actually sewing machine operators). Almost 43.9 percent of Laotian Americans specified themselves as operatives and laborers.

Tables 26 and 27 disaggregate the Asian Pacific American populations by nativity. Table 26 shows the occupational distribution of U.S.-born Asian Pacific Americans while Table 27 shows those of foreign-born Asian Pacific Americans. Table 26 shows that among U.S.-born Asian Pacific Americans, Chinese Americans (18.2 percent) and Japanese Americans (16) percent are the most likely to be in managerial occupations; Chinese Americans (25 percent) and Asian Indian Americans (22.2 percent) are most likely in professional occupations; and Asian Indian Americans and Korean Americans have similar high percentages in technical and sales occupations (22.5 percent). U.S.-born Chinese American, Japanese American, Asian Indian American, and Korean American males and females are more likely than the general male population to be in managerial, professional, and technical ranks.

Table 26 showed that U.S.-born Asian Pacific Americans were generally more likely than the general U.S. population to be in managerial, professional, technical/sales, and administrative ranks. However, Table 27 indicates that foreign-born Asian Pacific Americans are less likely than the general population to be in such professions, with the exception of managerial/entrepreneurial occupation, and more likely to be in service, craft, and operative/laborer occupations. The lower occupational status of foreign-born Asian Pacific Americans was especially evident among Southeast Asian Americans.

Asian Pacific American Education

In the aggregate, Asian Pacific Americans have an impressive educational profile. In 1991, 83.8 percent of Asian Pacific American males and

80 percent of Asian Pacific American females had completed 4 years of high school or more. Among those between 25 and 34 years, the median school years completed for an Asian Pacific American was 14.6, compared to 12.9 for non-Hispanic whites.[37]

According to a separate study based on the March 1991 Current Population Survey, 49 percent of Asian Pacific Americans between ages 16 and 24 were only attending school, 19 percent were attending school and working, 21 percent were only working, and 11 percent were neither working nor going to school. In comparison, 26 percent of non-Hispanic whites were only attending school, 26 percent were going to school and working, 40 percent were only working, and 8 percent were neither working nor going to school.[38]

In 1994, two-fifths of Asian Pacific Americans 25 years and older had at least a bachelor's degree. Asian Pacific American males and females (46 and 37 percent, respectively) were more than 1-1/2 times as likely to have a bachelor's degree than comparable non-Hispanic white males and females (28 and 21 percent, respectively).[39] Among specific Asian groups in the 1990 census, Asian Indians had the highest proportion who earned at least a bachelor's degree (58 percent) and Tongans, Cambodians, Laotians, and Hmongs the lowest (6 percent or less).[40] Educational attainment continues to be high for the Asian Pacific American population as a whole. According the U.S. National Science Foundation, in 1993, 7 percent of all doctorates were awarded to Asian Pacific Americans.[41]

Nearly 9 out of 10 Asian Pacific American males 25 years and older, and 8 out of 10 females had at least a high school diploma in 1994. High school graduation rates vary widely among Asian Pacific American groups, from 31 percent for Hmongs—who are the most recent Asians to immigrate—to 88 percent for Japanese—who have been in the country for several generations. Within the Pacific American group, the proportion with at least a high school diploma ranged from 64 percent for Tongans to 80 percent for Hawaiians.[42]

Table 28 shows the detailed educational attainment of select Asian Pacific American groups in 1990, with an emphasis on higher education. More than half of the Asian Indian American population over the age of 25 had attained at least a bachelor's degree. Chinese American, Filipino American, Japanese American, Asian Indian American, and Korean Americans also attained relatively high levels of educational achievement. Among these groups, more than a third had a bachelor's degree or higher. Among Southeast Asian Americans and Pacific Islander Americans, educational achievement was considerably lower. On average, among these groups, less than 10 percent had a bachelor's degree or higher. Asian Pacific American women, with the major exception of Filipino Americans, tended to have lower educational attainment than that of Asian Pacific American men. Educational attainment by nativity did not substantially change the portrait, with the exception of Filipino Americans. While more than half of the foreign-born Filipino American population had a bachelor's degree or higher, only slightly more than 20 percent of Filipino Americans had attained such levels.

Market Power

According to the Asian and Pacific Islander Center for Census Information and Services (ACCIS), in 1993, Asian Pacific Americans represented a $94 billion consumer market. In 1987, businesses owned by Asian Pacific Americans had gross receipts of over $33 billion. Asian Pacific Americans earned a total of $79 billion of wage and salary income in 1990.[43]

Poverty

Despite higher educational attainments and high median family income, the poverty rate for Asian Pacific American families (14 percent) was higher than that for non-Hispanic white families (8 percent) in 1993. Only 16 percent of both poor Asian Pacific American and non-Hispanic white families had a householder who worked full-time year round. Twelve percent of Asian and Pacific Islander and 5 percent of non-Hispanic white married-couple families lived in poverty.

In 1993, 15 percent of Asian Pacific Americans were poor, compared to 10 percent of non-Hispanic whites. Of poor Asian and Pacific Islanders at least 15 years old, 28 percent worked, compared to 42 percent of poor non-Hispanic whites.

Asian Pacific American families and Asian Pacific American individuals on average are more likely to be in poverty. Between 1990 and 1994, poverty among Asian Pacific American families rose from 11.9 in 1990 to 13.5 percent in 1994. Among individuals, the figure rose from 14.1 percent in 1990 to 15.3 percent in 1994.

Table 29 shows that Asian Pacific Americans over the age of 65 were more likely to use public assistance than the general population. While 11.4 percent of all Americans over the age of 65 used public assistance, 22.6 percent of Asian Pacific Americans used some form of public assistance. U.S.-born Asian Pacific Americans were very unlikely to use public assistance (5.1 percent), while foreign-born Asian Pacific Americans were substantially more likely to use public assistance (29.9 percent).

Among Asian Pacific American ethnic groups, the top five groups to use public assistance were Hmong Americans (64.7 percent), Laotian Americans (57.3 percent), Cambodian Americans (52.5 percent), Vietnamese Americans (50.7 percent), and Korean Americans (39.3 percent).

The higher than average poverty among these groups likely contributes to the high participation in public assistance. In addition, lack of eligibility for social security during the initial years of immigration may lead the elderly to seek other sources of social support, such as public assistance. This argument is plausible, given that Asian Pacific Americans are much less likely to use social security benefits than the general population. While 79 percent of the general population in 1990 used social security benefits among the elderly, a far smaller percentage of elderly Asian Pacific Americans received social security benefits. The low use of social security benefits among the elderly was especially present among Asian Pacific American groups with high proportions of immigrants who disproportionately used public assistance.

Asian Pacific American Crime

According to the Justice Department, only 1 percent of all persons arrested in 1993 were Asian Pacific Americans. Categories of offenses with highest percentages of Asian Pacific Americans perpetrators were motor vehicle theft (1.7 percent), curfew and loitering (2.0 percent), runaways (3.4 percent), and gambling (4.6 percent). Overall, Asian Pacific Americans were three times less likely to be arrested for a crime than what would have been expected given their population proportion.

Asian Pacific Languages

In California in 1990, of those who speak an Asian Pacific American language, 18.2 percent of those 5 to 17 years, 24 percent of those 18 to 64 years, and 51.3 percent of those 65 years and over, responded they spoke English "not well" or "not at all." Of the persons age 5 to 17 who speak an Asian Pacific American language, 43.3 percent are in a household where no one speaks English "well" or "very well." Forty-one percent of persons age 65 and over are in a household where no one speaks English "well" or "very well."

In California in 1990, 665,605 households spoke an Asian Pacific American language. Among these households, 32.8 percent were classified as linguistically isolated, *i.e.*, no one in the household over the age of 13 spoke English "well" or "very well."

In 1990, languages spoken in California homes by persons 5 years and over included Chinese (575,447), Tagalog (464,644), Korean (215,845), Vietnamese (233,074), Japanese (147,451), Indic (119,318), and Mon-Khmer (59,622).

Closing Remarks

Since the mid-1800s, immigration policies have influenced the development of Asian Pacific America. Virtually every measurable characteristic of the various ethnic groups that make up Asian Pacific America is substantially effected by the traits of immigrants. And given current levels of Asian Pacific immigrants and refugees, the effect will continue well into the next millennium.

Notes

[1] Data for this study are based on annual reports and statistical yearbooks of the U.S. Immigration and Naturalization Service (INS) for 1820 to 1993; INS Public Use Tapes (PUS) for 1990 through 1993; and documents, tape, and CD-ROM datasets of the U.S. Bureau of the Census. Among census datasets used are the 1994 Current Population Survey; the 1 and 5 percent 1990 Public Use Microdata Sample (PUMS); Summary Tape Files (STF) 1A and 3A for states, counties, and census tracts; and specially constructed Geographic Information Systems (GIS) datasets in ARCVIEW format using 1990 STF 1A and 3A data and 1990 TIGER (Topologically Integrated Geographically Encoded Reference) census line files.

Statistical procedures used include frequencies, cross-tabulations, and means analyses. The statistical significance of all cross-classification tables are at the .01 level, with a 95 percent confidence interval. Following Tukey's recommendation to emphasize either general characteristics or controlled detail, I have elected to exclude multivariate analysis. John W. Tukey, *Exploratory Data Analysis* (Reading, Massachusetts: Addison-Wesley Publishing Company, 1977), 51.

[2] Bill Ong Hing, *Making and Remaking Asian America Through Immigration Policy, 1850-1990* (Stanford, California: Stanford University Press, 1993), 38-44.

[3] U.S. Bureau of the Census, *Population Profile of the United States, 1995* (Washington, D.C.: U.S. Government Printing Office, 1995), 48.

[4] U.S. Bureau of the Census, *Population Projections for States, by Age, sex, Race, and Hispanic Origin: 1993 to 2020*, P25-1111 (Washington, D.C.: U.S. Government Printing Office, 1994), table 3. U.S. Bureau of the Census, *Population Profile*, 7.

[5] Ibid. , 13.

[6] Though the percentage of growth was great, the population base in 1980 was small.

[7] U.S. Bureau of the Census, Summary Tape File 1A.

[8] U.S. Immigration and Naturalization Service, *Statistical Yearbooks, 1820-1993*. U.S. Bureau of the Census, *Population Profile*, 2.

[9] INS PUS tape, 1990 to 1993. U.S. Bureau of the Census, *Population Profile*, 7.

10   Campbell Gibson, "The Contribution of Immigration to the Growth and Ethnic Diversity of the American Population," *Proceedings of the American Philosophical Society* 136, no. 2 (1992): 165.

11   See Nicolaus Mills, ed., *Arguing Immigration: The Debate Over the Changing Face of America* (New York: Simon and Schuster, 1994), for several estimates of undocumented aliens from a variety of political perspectives. In particular, read the articles written by Linda Chavez, Richard Rothstein, George Borjas, and Robert Kuttner. The Center for Immigration Studies estimates that by 1992, 4.8 million undocumented aliens lived in the United States, and that this core population was growing by about 200,000 to 300,000 every year. See also Center for Immigration Studies, "Immigration-Related Statistics, 1993" *Backgrounder*, no. 4-93 (June 1993).

12   Hing, *Immigration Policy*, 23.

13   The Naturalization Act of 1790 would also be the basis for many laws directed against Asian Pacific Americans from owning land or businesses, attending particular schools, and residing in particular areas. By using the language of "aliens ineligible for citizenship," local, state, and federal governments could discriminate specifically against Asian Pacific Americans without naming them directly, which would otherwise subject them to prosecution under the 14th Amendment. See Frank F. Chuman, *The Bamboo People: The Law and Japanese Americans* (Del Mar, California: Publishers Incorporated, 1976), chapters 1-3 for an extended discussion of laws directed against Asians based in part on the 1790 Naturalization Act.

14   Victor G. Nee and Brett de Bary Nee, *Longtime Californ': A Documentary Study of an American Chinatown* (Boston: Houghton Mifflin Company, 1973), 38-43. See also Hing, 23-25.

15   Sucheng Chan, *Asian Americans: An Interpretive History* (Boston, Massachusetts: Twayne Publishers, 1991), 25-42.

16   Harry H. L. Kitano, *Asian Americans: Emerging Minorities* (Englewood Cliffs, N.J.: Prentice-Hall, 1988), 12.

17   Ibid., 12; Hing, *Immigration Policy*, 32-33.

18   Kitano, *Emerging Minorities*, 13. Hing, *Immigration Policy*, 35-38.

19   Kitano, *Emerging Minorities*, 14-15.

20   Hing, *Immigration Policy*, 38-40. *U.S. Code*, vol. 8: section 1152(a) (1969).

21   Three major groups would not be subject to numerical caps: (1) immediate relatives of U.S. citizens, (2) refugees, and (3) special immigrants. Immediate relatives include spouses, unmarried sons and daughters under the age of 21, and parents. In the case of parents, the sponsoring U.S. citizen (the child) must be over the age of 21. Special immigrants include certain former U.S. citizens and U.S. government employees, ministers of recognized religions who have two years of experience, Amerasians, and lawfully admitted, permanent residents returning from a temporary trip abroad.

22   House Subcommittee 1 of the Committee on the Judiciary, *Immigration Hearings*, 88th Congress., 2d Session., 1964, 418.

23   Until 1990, the basic system consisted of six preferences. First preference referred to unmarried sons and daughters of U.S. citizens over the age of 21. Second preference referred to unmarried sons and daughters of permanent residents over the age of 21, and spouses of permanent residents. Third preference was for aliens of exceptional ability in the arts and sciences, or members of the professions, such as engineers, lawyers, or architects. Business executives could also qualify. Fourth preference re-

ferred to married sons and daughters of U.S. citizens. Fifth preference was for brothers and sisters of U.S. citizens. Finally, sixth preference referred to any alien who had a permanent job offer in the United States, regardless of whether it involved skilled or unskilled work, and who was not displacing an available U.S. worker.

24 Immigration and Naturalization Service, WWW data, 1995, Table 2.

25 Hing, *Immigration Policy*, 123-28.

26 Computations based on the 5 percent 1990 Public Use Microdata Sample (PUMS).

27 The National Opinion Research Center standardized occupational scores representing socio-economic prestige were used. Using a scale from 0 to 100, occupations were given rank scores by the level of prestige associated with them.

28 U.S. Bureau of the Census, *The Asian and Pacific Islander Population in the United States: March 1991 and 1990*, Current Population Reports, Population Characteristics, P20-459 (Washington, DC: U.S. Government Printing Office, 1992), table 1.

29 Examination of the PUMS for 1980 and 1990 indicate that the majority of the growth can be attributed to the presence of foreign-born immigrants.

30 Figures from special tabulations of the 1990 STF1C.

31 According to the 1991 March Current Population Survey.

32 U.S. Bureau of the Census, *Asian and Pacific Islander Population*, 4.

33 O'Hare, *America's Minorities*, 18.

34 Editor's note: see also the article below by Paul Ong and Don Nakanishi.

35 U.S. Bureau of the Census, *Asian and Pacific Islander Population*, 13.

36 Larry Hajime Shinagawa and Gin Yong Pang, "Asian American Pan-Ethnicity and Intermarriage," *Amerasia Journal* (Spring 1996), (forthcoming).

37 Editor's note: also see the article below by Paul Ong and Linda Wing. Figures from March 1991 CPS.

38 William P. O'Hare, *America's Minorities B The Demographics of Diversity* (Washington, DC: Population Reference Bureau, 1992), 31.

39 U.S. Bureau of the Census, *Population Profile. . .* , p. 48.

40 U.S. Bureau of the Census, *Population Profile*, 48. Special tabulations of the 5 percent 1990 PUMS.

41 National Science Foundation, *Science and Engineering Doctorate Awards: 1993* (Washington, DC: National Science Foundation, 1993), table 3, 19.

42 U.S. Bureau of the Census, *Population Profile*, 49. Special tabulations of the 5 percent 1990 PUMS.

43 Glass Ceiling Commission, *Good for Business: Making Full Use of the Nation's Human Capital. The Environmental Scan* (Washington, DC: U.S. Government Printing Office, 1995), 10. U.S. Bureau of the Census, *Survey of Minority-Owned Business Enterprises: Asian Americans, American Indians, and Other Minorities* (Washington, DC: Government Printing Office, 1991), table A, 3. Special tabulations of the 5 percent 1990 PUMS.

Table 1
Population by Percent Distribution
By Race and Hispanic Origin
Years 1980, 1990 and 2000*

Race/Hispanic Origin	1980	1990	2000
Non-Hispanic White	79.7	75.3	71.2
African American	11.7	12.0	12.6
American Indian	0.6	0.8	0.8
Asian Pacific American	1.5	2.9	4.3
Hispanic American	6.5	9.0	11.1

Source: Department of Commerce -- Economics and
Statistics Administration 1980 and 1990 Census Counts
on Specific Racial Groups, Year 2000 -- Bureau of the
Census, Population Branch.
*Year 2000 represents a population estimate.

Table 2
The Asian Pacific American Population
Of the United States, 1990

Ethnicity	1990 Population	Percent of A/PI Population	Percent of Total U.S. Population
Chinese	1,645,472	22.6	0.7
Filipino	1,406,770	19.3	0.6
Japanese	847,562	11.7	0.3
Asian Indian	815,447	11.2	0.3
Korean	798,849	11.0	0.3
Vietnamese	614,547	8.4	0.2
Hawaiian	211,014	2.9	0.1
Laotian	149,014	2.0	0.1
Cambodian	147,411	2.0	0.1
Thai	91,275	1.3	*
Hmong	90,082	1.2	*
Samoan	62,964	0.9	*
Guamanian	49,345	0.7	*
Tongan	17,606	0.2	*
Other A/PI	326,304	4.5	0.1
TOTAL	7,273,662	100.0	2.9

*Less than one tenth of one percent.
Source: U.S. Bureau of the Census, 1990 Summary Tape File 1C.

Table 3

Immigration to the United States by Decade and in Recent Years, 1850-1994

Period	Total Immigration	Total as % of U.S. Population	% from Northwestern Europe	% from Southern and Eastern Europe	% from Asia	% of Hispanic Origin
1851-1860	2,598,214	8.26	89.11	0.42	1.60	NA
1861-1870	2,314,824	5.81	84.53	1.04	2.80	NA
1871-1880	2,812,191	5.61	69.20	6.44	4.42	NA
1881-1890	5,246,613	8.33	68.08	17.82	1.33	NA
1891-1900	3,687,564	4.85	41.66	50.85	2.03	NA
1901-1910	8,795,386	9.56	19.47	68.76	3.68	0.10
1911-1920	6,735,811	5.43	14.57	55.02	4.31	4.10
1921-1930	4,107,209	3.35	28.68	26.32	2.73	12.60
1931-1940	528,431	0.40	32.17	25.71	3.04	6.80
1941-1950	1,035,039	0.69	39.91	11.19	6.76	10.10
1951-1960	2,515,479	1.40	31.28	13.99	5.97	20.50
1961-1970	3,321,677	1.63	14.57	12.35	12.88	32.20
1971-1980	4,493,314	1.98	5.12	8.23	35.35	30.00
1981-1990	7,338,124	2.95	3.65	5.96	38.39	37.20
1991-1994	4,479,508	1.72	3.41	9.96	30.50	42.70

Sources: U.S. Immigration and Naturalization Service. Beginning in 1952, Asia includes the Philippines.
"Hispanic Origin" includes persons from Central America, South America, and Mexico from 1851-1950, after which time Cuban immigrants are added to the original three categories.

Table 4
Immigration by Decade and In Recent Years of Asian Groups, 1820-1994

Period	From Asia	Total Immigration	Asian % of Total Immigration	Chinese	Japanese	Asian Indian	Korean	Filipino	Vietnamese
1820	6	8,385	0.1	1	—	1	—	—	—
1821-30	30	143,439	0.0	2	—	8	—	—	—
1831-1840	55	599,125	0.0	8	—	39	—	—	—
1841-1850	141	1,713,251	0.0	35	—	36	—	—	—
1851-1860	41,571	2,598,214	1.6	41,397	—	43	—	—	—
1861-1870	64,815	2,314,824	2.8	64,301	186	69	—	—	—
1871-1880	123,736	2,812,191	4.4	123,201	149	163	—	—	—
1881-1890	68,206	5,246,613	1.3	61,711	2,270	269	—	—	—
1891-1900	73,751	3,687,564	2.0	14,799	25,942	68	—	—	—
1901-1910	325,430	8,795,386	3.7	20,605	129,797	4,713	7,697	—	—
1911-1920	246,640	5,735,811	4.3	21,278	83,837	2,082	1,049	869	—
1921-1930	110,895	4,107,209	2.7	29,907	33,462	1,886	598	54,747	—
1931-1940	15,853	528,431	3.0	4,928	1,948	496	60	6,159	—
1941-1950	32,086	1,035,039	3.1	16,709	1,555	1,761	—	4,691	—
1951-1960	153,444	2,515,479	6.1	25,201	46,250	1,973	6,231	19,307	—
1961-1970	428,496	3,321,677	12.9	109,771	39,988	27,189	34,526	98,376	3,788
1971-1980	1,586,140	4,493,314	35.3	237,793	49,775	164,134	271,956	360,216	179,681
1981-1990	2,817,391	7,338,062	38.4	446,000	44,800	261,900	338,800	495,300	401,400
1991-1994	1,356,447	4,316,210	31.4	282,900	28,995	154,587	79,435	239,465	233,992

Sources: All data derived from U.S. Immigration and Naturalization Service and its predecessors. Figures for 1981-1990 are rounded to the nearest hundredth. According to INS definition, Asia includes Southwest Asia, e.g., Iraq, Israel, Syria, Turkey, etc.

Table 5
Asian Immigrants by Country of Birth, 1960, 1965-1994

Year	All Countries (A)	All Asian Countries (B)	(B) as % of (A)	China*	Japan	Philippines	Korea	India	Vietnam
1960	265,398	23,864	9.0	3,681	5,471	2,954	1,507	391	-
1965	296,697	19,788	6.7	4,057	3,180	3,130	2,165	582	-
1966	323,040	39,878	12.3	13,736	3,394	6,093	2,492	2,458	275
1967	361,972	59,233	16.4	19,741	3,946	10,865	3,956	4,642	490
1968	454,448	57,229	12.6	12,738	3,613	16,731	3,811	4,682	590
1969	358,579	73,621	20.5	15,440	3,957	20,744	6,045	5,963	983
1970	373,326	92,816	24.9	14,093	4,485	31,203	9,314	10,114	1,450
1971	370,478	103,461	27.9	14,417	4,357	28,471	14,297	14,310	2,038
1972	384,685	121,058	31.5	17,339	4,757	29,376	18,876	16,926	3,412
1973	400,063	124,160	31.0	17,297	5,461	30,799	22,930	13,124	4,569
1974	394,861	130,662	33.1	18,056	4,860	32,857	28,028	12,779	3,192
1975	386,194	132,469	34.3	18,536	4,274	31,751	28,362	15,733	3,039
1976	398,613	149,881	37.6	18,823	4,285	37,281	30,803	17,487	3,048
1977	462,315	157,759	34.1	19,764	4,178	39,111	30,917	18,613	4,629
1978	601,442	249,776	41.5	21,315	4,010	37,216	29,288	20,753	88,543
1979	460,348	189,293	41.1	24,264	4,048	41,300	29,248	19,708	22,546
1980	530,639	236,097	44.5	27,651	4,225	42,316	32,320	22,607	43,483
1981	596,600	264,343	44.3	25,803	3,896	43,772	32,663	21,522	55,631
1982	594,131	313,291	52.7	36,984	3,903	45,102	31,724	21,738	72,553
1983	559,763	277,701	49.6	25,777	4,092	41,546	33,339	25,451	37,560
1984	543,903	256,273	47.1	23,363	4,043	42,768	33,042	24,964	37,236
1985	570,009	264,691	46.4	24,789	4,086	47,978	35,253	26,026	31,895
1986	601,708	268,248	44.6	25,106	3,956	52,558	35,776	26,227	29,993
1987	601,516	257,684	42.8	25,841	4,174	50,060	35,849	27,803	24,231
1988	643,025	264,465	41.1	28,717	4,512	50,697	34,703	26,268	25,789
1989	1,090,924	312,149	28.6	32,272	4,849	57,034	34,222	31,175	37,739
1990	1,536,438	338,581	22.0	31,815	5,734	63,756	32,301	30,667	48,792
1991	1,827,167	358,533	19.6	33,025	5,049	63,596	26,518	45,064	55,307
1992	973,977	348,553	35.8	38,735	10,975	59,179	18,983	34,629	77,728
1993	880,014	357,041	40.6	65,552	6,883	63,189	17,949	40,021	59,613
1994	798,394	292,320	36.6	53,976	6,088	53,501	15,985	34,873	41,344

Source: U.S. Immigration and Naturalization Service, 1960-1978, 1979-1994.

*Up to 1981 immigrants from China included both immigrants from mainland China and those from Taiwan. Since 1982, immigrants from mainland China have been tabulated separately from those from Taiwan.

Table 6
Top Five States of Intended Residence, 1990-1993
For Selected Asian Groups by Number and Percent of Immigration

Chinese

	State	Number	Percent
1st	California	87,053	34.2
2nd	New York	55,367	21.8
3rd	New Jersey	10,697	4.2
4th	Massachusetts	9,367	3.7
5th	Illinois	8,793	3.5

Japanese

	State	Number	Percent
1st	California	9,332	35.1
2nd	New York	3,893	14.6
3rd	Hawaii	1,791	6.7
4th	New Jersey	1,488	5.6
5th	Washington	996	3.7

Filipino

	State	Number	Percent
1st	California	96,298	43.8
2nd	New York	18,151	8.3
3rd	Hawaii	16,251	7.4
4th	New Jersey	13,617	6.2
5th	Illinois	9,883	4.5

Korean

	State	Number	Percent
1st	California	25,630	30.2
2nd	New York	9,798	11.5
3rd	New Jersey	4,764	5.6
4th	Illinois	3,941	4.6
5th	Virginia	3,909	4.6

Asian Indian

	State	Number	Percent
1st	California	25,313	19.3
2nd	New York	18,744	14.3
3rd	New Jersey	16,340	12.5
4th	Illinois	13,041	10.0
5th	Texas	8,890	6.8

Vietnamese

	State	Number	Percent
1st	California	90,008	40.9
2nd	Texas	19,266	9.8
3rd	Washington	9,381	4.3
4th	New York	8,544	3.9
5th	Massachusetts	6,973	3.2

Source: U.S. Immigration and Naturalization Service, Public Use Tape, 1990-1993.
Copyright (c) 1996, Larry Hajime Shinagawa, Ph.D., Department of American Multi-Cultural Studies, Sonoma State University.

Table 7

Top Five Metropolitan Areas of Intended Residence, 1991
By Country of Asian Origin by Number and Percent of Immigration

Mainland China

	Metropolitan Area	Number	Percent
1st	New York, NY	8,964	27.1
2nd	San Francisco, CA	4,068	12.3
3rd	Los Angeles, CA	3,626	11.0
4th	Oakland, CA	1,667	5.1
5th	Boston, MA	1,083	3.3

Hong Kong

	Metropolitan Area	Number	Percent
1st	New York, NY	2,131	20.4
2nd	San Francisco, CA	1,352	13.0
3rd	Los Angeles, CA	1,302	12.5
4th	Oakland, CA	710	6.8
5th	San Jose, CA	390	3.7

Taiwan

	Metropolitan Area	Number	Percent
1st	Los Angeles, CA	2,748	20.7
2nd	New York, NY	1,200	9.0
3rd	San Jose, CA	848	6.4
4th	Anaheim-Santa Ana, CA	745	5.6
5th	Oakland, CA	432	3.3

India

	Metropolitan Area	Number	Percent
1st	New York, NY	7,368	16.4
2nd	Chicago, IL	3,409	7.6
3rd	Los Angeles, CA	2,565	5.7
4th	San Jose, CA	1,774	3.9
5th	Washington, DC	1,653	3.7

Pakistan

	Metropolitan Area	Number	Percent
1st	New York, NY	6,676	32.8
2nd	Washington, DC	1,432	7.0
3rd	Chicago, IL	1,348	6.6
4th	Los Angeles, CA	1,203	5.9
5th	Houston, TX	1,089	5.4

Korea

	Metropolitan Area	Number	Percent
1st	New York, NY	4,579	17.3
2nd	Los Angeles, CA	4,419	16.7
3rd	Washington, DC	1,441	5.4
4th	Chicago, IL	960	3.6
5th	Anaheim-Santa Ana, CA	946	3.6

Philippines

	Metropolitan Area	Number	Percent
1st	Los Angeles, CA	12,147	19.1
2nd	San Francisco, CA	3,702	5.8
3rd	San Diego, CA	3,548	5.6
4th	New York, NY	3,421	5.4
5th	Honolulu, HI	3,022	4.8

Vietnam

	Metropolitan Area	Number	Percent
1st	Anaheim-Santa Ana, CA	5,366	9.7
2nd	Los Angeles, CA	5,156	9.3
3rd	San Jose, CA	4,640	8.4
4th	Washington, DC	2,611	4.7
5th	San Diego, CA	1,683	3.0

Source: U.S. Immigration and Naturalization Service, Statistical Yearbook 1991.

Table 8
Immigration of Selected Asian Ethnic Groups by Occupational Percent Distribution*
United States of America, 1990-1993

	From Asia	Chinese**	Japanese	Filipino	Korean	Asian Indian	Vietnamese	Other Asians
Managerial	11.2	18.3	27.6	15.8	16.6	17.8	1.3	15.5
Professional	13.3	19.7	13.5	7.3	16.3	33.4	1.3	15.1
Technical	16.9	15.8	16.1	30.6	22.2	14.8	2.1	11.6
Service	17.1	18.0	24.1	22.3	16.8	16.7	29.7	21.0
Craft	14.5	6.7	7.4	7.7	8.1	4.3	23.1	13.1
Laborer	27.1	21.6	11.3	16.3	20.0	13.1	42.6	23.6
Count	231,020	130,357	11,981	86,871	20,237	51,116	92,578	45,392
Total	100	100	100	100	100	100	100	100

Source: U.S. Immigration and Naturalization Service (INS), Public Use Tapes.
Copyright (c) 1996, Larry Hajime Shinagawa, Ph.D., Department of American Multi-Cultural Studies, Sonoma State University.
*Figures are for those reporting occupations.
**Comprised of persons whose country of birth are Mainland China, Hong Kong, and Taiwan.

Table 9

Socio-Economic Prestige Scores of Select Asian Ethnic Groups by Gender
United States of America, Persons Over Age 25, 1990-1993

	Male	Female	Total
From Europe	59.9	58.7	59.4
From Asia	60.8	58.6	59.9
Chinese*	64.0	60.5	62.5
Japanese	64.9	60.5	63.2
Filipino	59.7	60.6	60.2
Korean	63.3	60.2	62.2
Asian Indian	67.6	64.4	66.9
Vietnamese	50.2	50.7	50.4
Other Asians	60.7	58.8	60.1

Source: U.S. Immigration and Naturalization Service (INS), Public Use Tapes, 1990-93.

Copyright (c) 1996, Larry Hajime Shinagawa, Ph.D., Department of American Multi-Cultural Studies, Sonoma State University.

*Comprised of persons whose country of birth are Mainland China, Hong Kong, and Taiwan.

Table 10
Top Ten States with the Largest 1990
Asian Pacific American Population

Rank	State	APA Population	Percent of State Population	Percent of National APA Population	Cumulative APA Percentage
1	California	2,845,659	9.6	39.1	39.1
2	New York	603,760	3.9	9.5	48.7
3	Hawaii	685,236	61.8	9.4	58.1
4	Texas	319,459	1.9	4.4	62.5
5	Illinois	285,311	2.5	3.9	66.4
6	New Jersey	272,521	3.5	3.7	70.1
7	Washington	210,958	4.3	2.9	73.0
8	Virginia	159,053	2.6	2.2	75.2
9	Florida	154,302	1.2	2.1	77.4
10	Massachusetts	143,392	2.4	2.0	79.3
TOTAL		5,769,651		79.2	79.3

Source: U.S. Bureau of the Census, 1990 Summary Tape File 1C.

Table 11
Top Ten States with Large Asian Pacific American Populations
State by State Breakdowns of Asian Pacific American Population
1990 Population, Percent Increase Since 1980, and Percent of State Population

CALIFORNIA: APA Population - 2,845,659; 116.7% Increase since 1980; and 9.6% of 1990 State Population.

Group	Population	% Increase	% State
Filipino	731,685	104.2%	2.5%
Chinese	704,850	116.3%	2.4%
Japanese	312,989	16.4%	1.1%
Vietnamese	280,223	228.8%	0.9%
Korean	251,981	153.4%	0.9%
As. Indian	159,973	167.6%	2.5%
Cambodian	68,190	1120.7%	0.2%
Laotian	58,058	386.0%	0.2%
Hmong	46,892	6297.3%	0.2%
Hawaiian	34,447	42.1%	0.1%
Thai	32,064	139.1%	0.1%
Samoan	31,917	76.5%	0.1%
Guamanian	25,059	47.3%	0.1%
Tongan	7,919	236.1%	*
Oth. APA	91,452	383.1%	0.3%

NEW YORK: APA Population - 693,760; 109.6% Increase since 1980; and 3.9% of 1990 State Population.

Group	Population	% Increase	% State
Chinese	284,144	93.0%	1.6%
As. Indian	140,985	108.4%	0.8%
Korean	95,648	187.6%	0.5%
Filipino	62,259	74.7%	0.3%
Japanese	35,281	42.5%	0.2%
Vietnamese	15,555	165.9%	0.1%
Thai	6,230	54.7%	*
Cambodian	3,646	635.1%	*
Laotian	3,253	139.7%	*
Guamanian	1,803	77.3%	*
Hawaiian	1,496	-23.3%	*
Samoan	586	288.1%	*
Hmong	165	1550.0%	*
Tongan	30	3.4%	*
Oth. APA	42,679	464.9%	0.2%

HAWAII: APA Population - 685,236; 16.0% Increase since 1980; and 61.8% of 1990 State Population.

Group	Population	% Increase	% State
Japanese	247,486	3.2%	22.3%
Filipino	168,682	27.7%	15.2%
Hawaiian	138,742	17.3%	12.5%
Chinese	68,804	23.0%	6.2%
Korean	24,454	40.1%	2.2%
Samoan	15,034	4.8%	1.4%
Vietnamese	5,468	60.7%	0.5%
Tongan	3,088	108.4%	0.3%
Guamanian	2,120	30.1%	0.2%
Laotian	1,677	22.5%	0.2%
Thai	1,220	59.5%	0.1%
As. Indian	1,015	43.4%	0.1%
Cambodian	119	105.2%	*
Hmong	6	-88.5%	*
Oth. APA	7,321	114.4%	0.7%

TEXAS: APA Population - 319,459; 137.6% Increase since 1980; and 1.9% of 1990 State Population.

Group	Population	% Increase	% State
Vietnamese	69,634	150.6%	0.4%
Chinese	63,232	136.7%	0.4%
As. Indian	55,795	138.5%	0.3%
Filipino	34,350	115.3%	0.2%
Korean	31,775	130.7%	0.2%
Japanese	14,795	22.4%	0.1%
Laotian	9,332	224.9%	0.1%
Cambodian	5,887	474.3%	*
Thai	5,816	72.4%	*
Hawaiian	2,979	25.4%	*
Guamanian	2,209	79.7%	*
Samoan	916	128.4%	*
Tongan	630	1868.8%	*
Hmong	176	2414.3%	*
Oth. APA	7,321	544.0%	0.7%

ILLINOIS: APA Population - 285,311; 65.7% Increase since 1980; and 2.5% of 1990 State Population.

Group	Population	% Increase	% State
Filipino	64,224	44.9%	0.6%
As. Indian	64,200	71.5%	0.6%
Chinese	49,936	73.1%	0.4%
Korean	41,506	70.4%	0.4%
Japanese	21,831	18.4%	0.2%
Vietnamese	10,309	64.0%	0.1%
Thai	5,180	58.7%	*
Laotian	4,985	61.5%	*
Cambodian	3,026	446.2%	*
Guamanian	1,105	201.1%	*
Hawaiian	1,000	3.7%	*
Hmong	433	0.0%	*
Samoan	367	317.0%	*
Tongan	15	1500.0%	*
Oth. APA	17,194	354.4%	0.2%

Table 11
Top Ten States with Large Asian Pacific American Populations
State by State Breakdowns of Asian Pacific American Population
1990 Population, Percent Increase Since 1980, and Percent of State Population

NEW JERSEY: APA Population - 272,521; 149.1% Increase since 1980; and 3.5% of State Population.

Group	Pop	%	%	Group	Pop	%	%	Group	Pop	%	%
As. Indian	79,440	158.9%	1.0%	Vietnamese	7,330	157.6%	0.1%	Cambodian	475	813.5%	*
Chinese	59,084	151.5%	0.8%	Thai	1,758	90.9%	*	Samoan	217	93.8%	*
Filipino	53,146	117.2%	0.7%	Guamanian	644	223.6%	*	Hmong	25	2500.0%	*
Korean	38,540	192.6%	0.5%	Hawaiian	638	10.2%	*	Tongan	9	900.0%	*
Japanese	17,253	68.1%	0.2%	Laotian	478	107.8%	*	Oth. APA	13,484	470.9%	0.2%

WASHINGTON: APA Population - 210,958; 89.0% Increase since 1980; and 4.3% of 1990 State Population.

Group	Pop	%	%	Group	Pop	%	%	Group	Pop	%	%
Filipino	43,799	70.7%	0.9%	Cambodian	11,096	533.3%	0.2%	Guamanian	3,779	117.3%	0.1%
Japanese	34,366	25.5%	0.7%	As. Indian	8,205	92.3%	0.2%	Thai	2,386	79.5%	*
Chinese	33,962	88.8%	0.7%	Laotian	6,191	150.6%	0.1%	Hmong	741	732.6%	*
Korean	29,697	120.9%	0.6%	Hawaiian	5,423	91.0%	0.1%	Tongan	448	409.1%	*
Vietnamese	18,696	109.3%	0.4%	Samoan	4,130	124.8%	0.1%	Oth. APA	8,039	349.9%	0.2%

VIRGINIA: APA Population - 159,053; 125.4% Increase since 1980; and 2.6% of 1990 State Population.

Group	Pop	%	%	Group	Pop	%	%	Group	Pop	%	%
Filipino	35,067	83.5%	0.6%	Japanese	7,931	53.3%	0.1%	Guamanian	923	68.4%	*
Korean	30,164	135.7%	0.5%	Cambodian	3,889	764.2%	0.1%	Samoan	440	126.8%	*
Chinese	21,238	123.7%	0.3%	Thai	3,312	262.8%	0.1%	Hmong	7	-63.2%	*
Vietnamese	20,693	119.0%	0.3%	Laotian	2,589	333.7%	*	Tongan	6	-68.4%	*
As. Indian	20,494	126.6%	0.3%	Hawaiian	1,384	34.0%	*	Oth. APA	10,916	533.5%	0.2%

FLORIDA: APA Population - 154,302; 146.8% Increase since 1980; and 1.2% of 1990 State Population.

Group	Pop	%	%	Group	Pop	%	%	Group	Pop	%	%
Filipino	31,945	109.4%	0.2%	Japanese	8,505	50.1%	0.1%	Guamanian	1,241	180.8%	*
As. Indian	31,457	185.0%	0.2%	Thai	4,457	209.3%	*	Samoan	577	159.9%	*
Chinese	30,737	137.7%	0.2%	Laotian	2,423	347.0%	*	Tongan	122	1255.6%	*
Vietnamese	16,346	131.0%	0.1%	Hawaiian	2,049	38.1%	*	Hmong	7	16.7%	*
Korean	12,404	150.7%	0.1%	Cambodian	1,617	352.9%	*	Oth. APA	10,415	848.5%	0.1%

MASSACHUSETTS: APA Population - 143,392; 172.5% Increase since 1980; and 2.4% of 1990 State Population.

Group	Pop	%	%	Group	Pop	%	%	Group	Pop	%	%
Chinese	53,792	116.2%	0.9%	Japanese	8,784	104.8%	0.1%	Guamanian	364	45.0%	*
As. Indian	19,719	120.5%	0.3%	Filipino	6,212	95.3%	0.1%	Hmong	248	439.1%	*
Vietnamese	15,449	442.6%	0.3%	Laotian	3,985	599.1%	0.1%	Samoan	204	119.4%	*
Cambodian	14,050	6996.0%	0.2%	Thai	1,424	159.4%	*	Tongan	15	1500.0%	*
Korean	11,744	118.7%	0.2%	Hawaiian	505	43.5%	*	Oth. APA	6,897	560.0%	0.1%

Source: U.S. Bureau of the Census, 1990 Summary Tape File (STF) 1C, and tabulations from the 1990 5 percent Public Use Microdata Sample (PUMS).
Copyright (c) 1996, Larry Hajime Shinagawa, Ph.D., Department of American Multi-Cultural Studies, Sonoma State University.
*Less than one tenth of one percent.

Table 12

Top Ten Cities with the Largest 1990
Asian Pacific American Populations

Rank	City	State	1990 APA Population	Percent of Total County Population	Percent of State APA Population
1	New York	New York	512,719	7.0	73.9
2	Los Angeles	California	341,807	9.8	12.0
3	Honolulu	Hawaii	257,552	70.5	37.6
4	San Francisco	California	210,876	29.1	7.4
5	San Jose	California	152,815	19.5	5.4
6	San Diego	California	130,945	11.8	4.6
7	Chicago	Illinois	104,118	3.7	36.5
8	Houston	Texas	67,113	4.1	21.0
9	Seattle	Washington	60,819	11.8	28.8
10	Long Beach	California	58,266	13.6	2.0

Source: U.S. Bureau of the Census, 1994 City and County Book.

Table 13
Top Ten Counties with the Largest 1990
Asian Pacific American Populations

Rank	State	County	1990 APA Population	Percent of Total County Population	Percent of State APA Population
1	California	Los Angeles	954,485	10.8	33.5
2	Hawaii	Honolulu	526,459	63.0	76.8
3	New York	Queens	238,336	12.2	34.8
4	California	Santa Clara	261,466	17.5	9.2
5	California	Orange	249,192	10.3	8.8
6	California	San Francisco	210,876	29.1	7.4
7	California	San Diego	198,311	7.9	7.0
8	California	Alameda	192,554	15.1	6.8
9	Illinois	Cook	188,565	3.7	66.1
10	New York	Kings	111,251	4.8	16.0

Source: U.S. Bureau of the Census, special tabulations of the 1990 Summary Tape File 3A.

Table 14
Age and Sex Characteristics of Total and Asian Pacific Americans
By Nativity, Citizenship, and Year of Entry
United States of America, 1990

Ethnicity, Age, and Sex	All Persons	Native-Born	Foreign Born: Total	Foreign Born: 1980 to 1990	Foreign Born: Before 1980	Naturalized: Total	Naturalized: 1980 to 1990	Naturalized: Before 1980	Not a Citizen: Total	Not a Citizen: 1980 to 1990	Not a Citizen: Before 1980
Total											
General											
Count	248,709,873	228,942,557	19,767,316	8,663,627	11,103,689	7,996,998	1,350,647	6,746,351	11,770,318	7,412,980	4,357,338
Percent of All Persons	100.0	92.1	7.9	3.5	4.5	3.2	0.5	2.7	4.7	3.0	1.8
Median Age	33.0	32.5	37.3	28.0	46.5	36.3	29.5	45.3	38.0	27.8	51.2
Female											
Count	127,537,494	117,441,039	10,096,455	4,120,094	5,976,361	4,277,022	590,312	3,686,710	5,819,433	3,529,782	2,289,651
Percent of All Persons	100.0	92.1	7.9	3.2	4.7	3.4	0.5	2.9	4.6	2.8	1.8
Median Age	33.0	32.5	37.3	28.0	46.5	36.3	29.5	45.3	38.0	27.8	51.2
Male											
Count	121,172,379	111,501,518	9,670,861	4,543,533	5,127,328	3,719,976	760,335	3,059,641	5,950,885	3,883,198	2,067,687
Percent of All Persons	100.0	92.0	8.0	3.7	4.2	3.1	0.6	2.5	4.9	3.2	1.7
Median Age	31.8	31.4	35.3	27.5	44.3	34.6	28.9	43.5	36.0	27.3	48.0
Percent Female	51.3	51.3	51.1	47.6	53.8	53.5	43.7	54.6	49.4	47.6	52.5
Percent Male	48.7	48.7	48.9	52.4	46.2	46.5	56.3	45.4	50.6	52.4	47.5
Asian Pacific Americans											
General											
Count	7,226,986	2,668,242	4,558,744	2,622,059	1,936,685	1,830,508	460,593	1,349,915	2,728,236	2,161,466	566,770
Percent of All Persons	100.0	36.9	63.1	36.3	26.8	25.3	6.4	18.7	37.8	29.9	7.8
Median Age	30.1	15.6	35.2	30.5	42.1	35.0	32.1	41.8	35.7	30.1	46.3
Female											
Count	3,701,295	1,320,445	2,380,850	1,335,497	1,045,353	968,082	236,800	731,282	1,412,768	1,098,697	314,071
Percent of All Persons	100.0	35.7	64.3	36.1	28.2	26.2	6.4	19.8	38.2	29.7	8.5
Median Age	31.1	15.8	36.0	31.0	42.5	35.8	32.4	42.1	36.7	30.7	47.6
Male											
Count	3,525,691	1,347,797	2,177,894	1,286,562	891,332	862,426	223,793	618,633	1,315,468	1,062,769	252,699
Percent of All Persons	100.0	38.2	61.8	36.5	25.3	24.5	6.3	17.5	37.3	30.1	7.2
Median Age	29.0	15.5	34.2	29.9	41.7	34.1	31.7	41.4	34.6	29.5	44.8
Percent Female	51.2	49.5	52.2	50.9	54.0	52.9	51.4	54.2	51.8	50.8	55.4
Percent Male	48.8	50.5	47.8	49.1	46.0	47.1	48.6	45.8	48.2	49.2	44.6

Source: 1990 Census of Population, Asians and Pacific Islander in the United States, 1990 CP-3-5, Table 1 and special tabulations of the 1990 Census data.

Table 15
Age and Sex Characteristics of Chinese Americans and Filipino Americans
By Nativity, Citizenship, and Year of Entry
United States of America, 1990

Ethnicity, Age, and Sex	All Persons	Native-Born	Foreign Born Total	Foreign Born: Year of Entry 1980 to 1990	Foreign Born: Year of Entry Before 1980	Naturalized Total	Naturalized 1980 to 1990	Naturalized Before 1980	Not a Citizen Total	Not a Citizen 1980 to 1990	Not a Citizen Before 1980
Chinese American											
General											
Count	1,648,696	506,116	1,142,580	649,214	493,366	496,209	116,683	379,526	646,371	532,531	113,840
Percent of All Persons	100.0	30.7	69.3	39.4	29.9	36.3	7.1	45.3	39.2	32.3	6.9
Median Age	32.3	16.3	36.7	31.7	43.3	36.5	32.7	43.1	37.3	31.5	52.6
Female											
Count	827,154	245,539	581,615	329,522	252,093	254,335	62,037	192,298	327,280	267,485	59,795
Percent of All Persons	100.0	29.7	70.3	39.8	30.5	30.7	7.5	23.2	39.6	32.3	7.2
Median Age	32.9	16.4	37.1	32.2	43.3	36.9	32.9	43.0	37.9	32.0	53.8
Male											
Count	821,542	260,577	560,965	319,692	241,273	241,874	54,646	187,228	319,091	265,046	54,045
Percent of All Persons	100.0	31.7	68.3	38.9	29.4	29.4	6.7	22.8	38.8	32.3	6.6
Median Age	31.7	16.1	36.2	31.2	43.3	36.1	32.5	43.1	36.7	31.0	51.6
Percent Female	50.2	48.5	50.9	50.8	51.1	51.3	53.2	50.7	50.6	50.2	52.5
Percent Male	49.8	51.5	49.1	49.2	48.9	48.7	46.8	49.3	49.4	49.8	47.5
Filipino American											
General											
Count	1,419,711	505,988	913,723	448,365	465,358	491,646	116,584	375,062	422,077	331,781	90,296
Percent of All Persons	100.0	35.6	64.4	31.6	32.8	34.6	8.2	26.4	29.7	23.4	6.4
Median Age	31.3	14.3	38.7	32.8	43.9	38.5	34.2	43.6	39.6	32.3	50.2
Female											
Count	762,946	245,991	516,955	259,659	257,296	269,130	66,330	202,800	247,825	193,329	54,496
Percent of All Persons	100.0	32.2	67.8	34.0	33.7	35.3	8.7	26.6	32.5	25.3	7.1
Median Age	32.8	14.4	38.9	33.4	43.6	38.8	34.5	43.4	39.8	33.0	48.3
Male											
Count	656,765	259,997	396,768	188,706	208,062	222,516	50,254	172,262	174,252	138,452	35,800
Percent of All Persons	100.0	39.6	60.4	28.7	31.7	33.9	7.7	26.2	26.5	21.1	5.5
Median Age	29.0	14.0	38.4	31.8	44.3	38.1	33.7	43.9	39.2	31.1	52.3
Percent Female	53.7	48.6	56.6	57.9	55.3	54.7	56.9	54.1	58.7	58.3	60.4
Percent Male	46.3	51.4	43.4	42.1	44.7	45.3	43.1	45.9	41.3	41.7	39.6

Source: 1990 Census of Population, Asians and Pacific Islander in the United States, 1990 CP-3-5, Table 1 and special tabulations of the 1990 Census data.

Table 16
Age and Sex Characteristics of Japanese Americans and Asian Indian Americans
By Nativity, Citizenship, and Year of Entry
United States of America, 1990

Ethnicity, Age, and Sex	All Persons	Native-Born	Foreign Born Total	Foreign Born — Year of Entry 1980 to 1990	Foreign Born — Year of Entry Before 1980	Naturalized Total	Naturalized — Year of Entry 1980 to 1990	Naturalized — Year of Entry Before 1980	Not a Citizen Total	Not a Citizen — Year of Entry 1980 to 1990	Not a Citizen — Year of Entry Before 1980
Japanese Americans											
General											
Count	866,160	585,474	280,686	153,371	127,315	72,194	4,325	67,869	208,492	149,846	59,496
Percent of All Persons	100.0	67.6	32.4	17.7	14.7	36.3	295.0	45.3	24.1	17.3	6.9
Median Age	36.5	35.3	38.5	29.7	53.3	37.1	32.2	51.3	38.6	29.6	55.1
Female											
Count	468,521	291,439	177,082	79,749	97,333	58,834	2,673	56,161	118,248	77,076	41,172
Percent of All Persons	100.0	62.2	37.8	17.0	20.8	12.6	0.6	12.0	25.2	16.5	8.8
Median Age	38.5	36.0	42.5	29.2	55.6	40.4	35.0	54.3	42.6	29.1	56.6
Male											
Count	397,639	294,035	103,604	73,622	29,982	13,360	1,652	11,708	90,244	72,770	18,324
Percent of All Persons	100.0	73.9	26.1	18.5	7.5	3.4	0.4	2.9	22.7	18.3	4.6
Median Age	34.5	34.7	42.5	29.2	55.6	40.4	35.0	54.3	42.6	29.1	56.6
Percent Female	54.1	49.8	63.1	52.0	76.5	81.5	61.8	82.7	56.7	51.4	69.2
Percent Male	45.9	50.2	36.9	48.0	23.5	18.5	38.2	17.3	43.3	48.6	30.8
Asian Indian Americans											
General											
Count	786,694	193,271	593,433	345,622	247,801	203,614	49,498	154,116	389,809	296,124	93,685
Percent of All Persons	100.0	24.6	75.4	43.9	31.5	25.9	6.3	19.6	49.6	37.6	11.9
Median Age	29.4	8.8	34.8	30.3	41.6	34.7	32.0	41.4	35.1	30.0	41.7
Female											
Count	362,764	94,115	268,649	158,515	110,134	87,920	23,497	64,423	180,729	135,018	45,711
Percent of All Persons	100.0	25.9	74.1	43.7	30.4	24.2	6.5	17.8	49.8	37.2	12.6
Median Age	28.6	8.9	34.3	30.1	40.2	34.2	31.1	40.1	34.8	29.9	40.5
Male											
Count	423,930	99,156	324,784	187,107	137,667	115,694	26,001	89,693	209,080	161,106	47,974
Percent of All Persons	100.0	23.4	76.6	44.1	32.5	27.3	6.1	21.2	49.3	38.0	11.3
Median Age	30.1	8.8	35.2	30.4	42.7	35.0	32.9	42.5	35.5	30.0	42.8
Percent Female	46.1	48.7	45.3	45.9	44.4	43.2	47.5	41.8	46.4	45.6	48.8
Percent Male	53.9	51.3	54.7	54.1	55.6	56.8	52.5	58.2	53.6	54.4	51.2

Source: 1990 Census of Population, Asians and Pacific Islander in the United States, 1990 CP-3-5, Table 1 and special tabulations of the 1990 Census data.

Table 17
Age and Sex Characteristics of Korean Americans and Vietnamese Americans
By Nativity, Citizenship, and Year of Entry
United States of America, 1990

Ethnicity, Age, and Sex	All Persons	Native-Born	Foreign Born — Total	Year of Entry 1980 to 1990	Year of Entry Before 1980	Naturalized — Total	Year of Entry 1980 to 1990	Year of Entry Before 1980	Not a Citizen — Total	Year of Entry 1980 to 1990	Year of Entry Before 1980
Korean Americans											
General											
Count	797,304	218,031	579,273	326,842	252,431	232,488	48,004	184,484	346,785	278,838	67,947
Percent of All Persons	100.0	27.3	72.7	41.0	31.7	36.3	295.0	45.3	43.5	35.0	8.5
Median Age	29.1	9.0	35.1	31.9	41.0	35.0	32.3	40.9	35.6	31.8	43.8
Female											
Count	447,573	116,840	330,733	178,043	152,690	140,620	28,210	112,410	190,113	149,833	40,280
Percent of All Persons	100.0	26.1	73.9	39.8	34.1	31.4	6.3	25.1	42.5	33.5	9.0
Median Age	30.4	9.1	36.0	32.1	41.1	35.9	32.5	41.0	36.6	31.9	44.6
Male											
Count	349,731	101,191	248,540	148,799	99,741	91,868	19,794	72,074	156,672	129,005	27,667
Percent of All Persons	100.0	28.9	71.1	42.5	28.5	26.3	5.7	20.6	44.8	36.9	7.9
Median Age	27.0	8.8	34.0	31.8	40.7	33.9	31.9	40.6	34.2	31.8	42.6
Percent Female	56.1	53.6	57.1	54.5	60.5	60.5	58.8	60.9	54.8	53.7	59.3
Percent Male	43.9	46.4	42.9	45.5	39.5	39.5	41.2	39.1	45.2	46.3	40.7
Vietnamese Americans											
General											
Count	593,213	119,360	473,853	292,717	181,136	200,069	74,897	125,172	273,784	217,820	55,964
Percent of All Persons	100.0	20.1	79.9	49.3	30.5	33.7	12.6	21.1	46.2	36.7	9.4
Median Age	25.6	6.7	30.1	27.7	34.2	30.1	29.9	34.1	30.2	26.4	33.7
Female											
Count	281,355	58,628	222,727	133,924	88,803	91,375	30,833	60,542	131,352	103,091	28,261
Percent of All Persons	100.0	20.8	79.2	47.6	31.6	32.5	11.0	21.5	46.7	36.6	10.0
Median Age	26.2	6.6	31.5	28.8	35.5	31.5	29.6	35.5	31.9	28.4	35.9
Male											
Count	311,858	60,732	251,126	158,793	92,333	108,694	44,064	64,630	142,432	114,729	27,703
Percent of All Persons	100.0	19.5	80.5	50.9	29.6	34.9	14.1	20.7	45.7	36.8	8.9
Median Age	25.1	6.8	29.1	27.0	33.0	29.1	30.0	33.0	28.8	25.0	31.7
Percent Female	47.4	49.1	47.0	45.8	49.0	45.7	41.2	48.4	48.0	47.3	50.5
Percent Male	52.6	50.9	53.0	54.2	51.0	54.3	58.8	51.6	52.0	52.7	49.5

Source: 1990 Census of Population, Asians and Pacific Islander in the United States, 1990 CP-3-5, Table 1 and special tabulations of the 1990 Census data.

Table 18
Age and Sex Characteristics of Cambodian Americans and Hmong Americans
By Nativity, Citizenship, and Year of Entry
United States of America, 1990

Ethnicity, Age, and Sex	All Persons	Native-Born	Foreign Born — Total	Foreign Born — Year of Entry: 1980 to 1990	Foreign Born — Year of Entry: Before 1980	Naturalized — Total	Naturalized — Year of Entry: 1980 to 1990	Naturalized — Year of Entry: Before 1980	Not a Citizen — Total	Not a Citizen — Year of Entry: 1980 to 1990	Not a Citizen — Year of Entry: Before 1980
Cambodian Americans											
General											
Count	149,047	31,190	117,857	103,796	14,061	20,181	13,847	6,334	97,676	89,949	7,727
Percent of All Persons	100.0	20.9	79.1	69.6	9.4	13.5	9.3	4.2	65.5	60.3	5.2
Median Age	19.7	4.7	25.8	24.4	34.8	28.4	26.9	34.6	25.4	23.7	33.5
Percent Female	51.8	49.7	52.4	52.9	48.5	47.7	49.4	43.9	53.4	53.5	52.2
Percent Male	48.2	50.3	47.6	47.1	51.5	52.3	50.6	56.1	46.6	46.5	47.8
Female											
Count	77,250	15,504	61,746	54,932	6,814	9,626	6,847	2,779	52,120	48,083	4,035
Percent of All Persons	100.0	20.1	79.9	71.1	8.8	12.5	8.9	3.6	67.5	62.2	5.2
Median Age	20.9	4.8	26.8	25.8	32.9	27.3	26.9	32.7	26.7	25.5	33.4
Male											
Count	71,797	15,686	56,111	48,864	7,247	10,555	7,000	3,555	45,556	41,866	3,692
Percent of All Persons	100.0	21.8	78.2	68.1	10.1	14.7	9.7	5.0	63.4	58.3	5.1
Median Age	18.5	4.7	24.6	22.8	36.3	28.6	27.3	36.3	24.1	22.4	33.6
Hmong Americans											
General											
Count	94,439	32,865	61,574	46,739	14,835	5,668	2,610	3,058	55,906	44,129	11,777
Percent of All Persons	100.0	34.8	65.2	49.5	15.7	6.0	2.8	3.2	59.2	46.7	12.5
Median Age	12.7	5.2	22.0	20.1	27.2	22.0	23.4	27.1	21.9	19.8	26.0
Percent Female	48.8	49.2	48.6	48.6	48.5	43.6	42.7	44.5	49.1	49.0	49.5
Percent Male	51.2	50.8	51.4	51.4	51.5	56.4	57.3	55.5	50.9	51.0	50.5
Female											
Count	46,105	16,181	29,924	22,733	7,191	2,474	1,114	1,360	27,450	21,619	5,831
Percent of All Persons	100.0	35.1	64.9	49.3	15.6	5.4	2.4	2.9	59.5	46.9	12.6
Median Age	13.0	5.2	23.2	21.6	28.8	23.1	22.6	28.6	23.2	21.5	29.5
Male											
Count	48,334	16,684	31,650	24,006	7,644	3,194	1,496	1,698	28,456	22,510	5,946
Percent of All Persons	100.0	34.5	65.5	49.7	15.8	6.6	3.1	3.5	58.9	46.6	12.3
Median Age	12.4	5.2	23.2	21.6	28.8	23.1	22.6	28.6	23.1	21.5	29.5

Source: 1990 Census of Population, Asians and Pacific Islander in the United States, 1990 CP-3-5, Table 1 and special tabulations of the 1990 Census data.

Table 19
Age and Sex Characteristics of Laotian Americans and Thai Americans
By Nativity, Citizenship, and Year of Entry
United States of America, 1990

Ethnicity, Age, and Sex	All Persons	Native-Born	Foreign Born — Total			Naturalized			Not a Citizen		
			Total	Year of Entry 1980 to 1990	Before 1980	Total	Year of Entry 1980 to 1990	Before 1980	Total	Year of Entry 1980 to 1990	Before 1980
Laotian Americans											
General											
Count	147,375	30,394	116,981	93,010	23,971	20,279	11,805	8,474	96,702	81,205	15,497
Percent of All Persons	100.0	20.6	79.4	63.1	16.3	36.3	295.0	45.3	65.6	55.1	10.5
Median Age	20.5	5.4	26.2	25.2	29.8	26.1	27.1	29.6	26.0	24.8	29.2
Female											
Count	71,014	14,592	56,512	45,138	11,374	9,097	5,272	3,825	47,415	39,866	7,549
Percent of All Persons	100.0	20.5	79.6	63.6	16.0	12.8	7.4	5.4	66.8	56.1	10.6
Median Age	20.4	5.3	25.9	24.9	29.5	25.9	25.8	29.3	25.9	24.7	29.4
Male											
Count	76,361	15,802	60,469	47,872	12,597	11,182	6,533	4,649	49,287	41,339	7,948
Percent of All Persons	100.0	20.7	79.2	62.7	16.5	14.6	8.6	6.1	64.5	54.1	10.4
Median Age	20.6	5.4	26.5	25.5	30.0	26.4	28.2	30.0	26.2	24.8	28.8
Percent Female	48.2	48.0	48.3	48.5	47.4	44.9	44.7	45.1	49.0	49.1	48.7
Percent Male	51.8	52.0	51.7	51.5	52.6	55.1	55.3	54.9	51.0	50.9	51.3
Thai Americans											
General											
Count	91,360	22,385	68,973	29,379	39,596	21,405	2,944	18,461	47,570	26,435	21,135
Percent of All Persons	100.0	24.5	75.5	32.2	43.3	23.4	3.2	20.2	52.1	28.9	23.1
Median Age	32.3	11.7	37.4	30.5	41.3	37.4	31.9	41.3	37.7	30.3	41.5
Female											
Count	54,404	11,133	43,271	17,108	26,163	14,917	1,890	13,027	28,354	15,218	13,136
Percent of All Persons	100.0	20.5	79.5	31.4	48.1	27.4	3.5	23.9	52.1	28.0	24.1
Median Age	35.4	11.8	38.6	31.8	41.6	38.5	33.0	41.5	38.8	31.7	41.8
Male											
Count	36,956	11,252	25,702	12,271	13,433	6,488	1,054	5,434	19,216	11,217	7,999
Percent of All Persons	100.0	30.4	69.5	33.2	36.3	17.6	2.9	14.7	52.0	30.4	21.6
Median Age	27.3	11.6	34.9	28.7	40.7	34.8	29.9	40.7	35.1	28.6	41.1
Percent Female	59.5	49.7	62.7	58.2	66.1	69.7	64.2	70.6	59.6	57.6	62.2
Percent Male	40.5	50.3	37.3	41.8	33.9	30.3	35.8	29.4	40.4	42.4	37.8

Source: 1990 Census of Population, Asians and Pacific Islander in the United States, 1990 CP-3-5, Table 1 and special tabulations of the 1990 Census data.

Table 20

Age and Sex Characteristics of Pakistani Americans and Pacific Islander Americans
By Nativity, Citizenship, and Year of Entry
United States of America, 1990

			Foreign Born								
						Naturalized			Not a Citizen		
				Year of Entry			Year of Entry			Year of Entry	
Ethnicity, Age, and Sex	All Persons	Native-Born	Total	1980 to 1990	Before 1980	Total	1980 to 1990	Before 1980	Total	1980 to 1990	Before 1980
Pakistani Americans											
General											
Count	81,691	18,537	63,154	42,376	20,778	23,122	7,226	14,896	41,032	35,150	5,882
Percent of All Persons	100.0	22.7	77.3	51.9	25.4	36.3	295.0	45.3	50.2	43.0	7.2
Median Age	28.4	6.7	32.7	29.8	39.4	32.7	30.9	39.4	33.0	29.5	38.8
Female											
Count	32,289	9,051	23,238	15,522	7,716	8,304	2,854	5,450	14,934	12,668	2,266
Percent of All Persons	100.0	28.0	72.0	48.1	23.9	25.7	8.8	16.9	46.3	39.2	7.0
Median Age	25.7	6.7	31.9	29.2	37.6	31.9	30.1	37.5	32.3	29.0	37.3
Male											
Count	49,402	9,486	39,916	26,854	13,062	14,818	4,372	9,446	26,098	22,482	3,616
Percent of All Persons	100.0	19.2	80.8	54.4	26.4	30.0	8.8	19.1	52.8	45.5	7.3
Median Age	29.9	6.6	33.2	30.1	40.6	33.1	31.5	40.5	33.4	29.8	39.4
Percent Female	39.5	48.8	36.8	36.6	37.1	35.9	39.5	36.6	36.4	36.0	38.5
Percent Male	60.5	51.2	63.2	63.4	62.9	64.1	60.5	63.4	63.6	64.0	61.5
Pacific Islander Americans											
General											
Count	350,592	305,195	45,397	24,612	20,785	16,461	5,426	11,035	28,936	19,186	9,750
Percent of All Persons	100.0	87.1	12.9	7.0	5.9	4.7	1.5	3.1	8.3	5.5	2.8
Median Age	25.1	23.5	31.6	26.9	37.9	31.3	27.1	37.4	32.3	26.9	38.8
Female											
Count	173,757	151,330	22,427	11,825	10,602	8,173	2,325	5,848	14,254	9,500	4,754
Percent of All Persons	100.0	87.1	12.9	6.8	6.1	4.7	1.3	3.4	8.2	5.5	2.7
Median Age	24.7	23.0	31.5	27.0	37.9	31.2	26.8	37.5	32.2	27.0	38.3
Male											
Count	176,835	153,865	22,970	12,787	10,183	8,288	3,101	5,187	14,682	9,686	4,996
Percent of All Persons	100.0	87.0	13.0	7.2	5.8	4.7	1.8	2.9	8.3	5.5	2.8
Median Age	25.1	23.0	29.1	27.0	33.0	29.1	30.0	33.0	28.8	25.0	31.7
Percent Female	49.6	49.6	49.4	48.0	51.0	49.7	42.8	53.0	49.3	49.5	48.8
Percent Male	50.4	50.4	50.6	52.0	49.0	50.3	57.2	47.0	50.7	50.5	51.2

Source: 1990 Census of Population, Asians and Pacific Islander in the United States, 1990 CP-3-5, Table 1 and special tabulations of the 1990 Census data.

Table 21
Marriage Patterns of Asian Pacific American Husbands and Wives
General and by Nativity, State of California, 1990

Husband's Ethnicity	General Marriage Count	Percent of General APA* Marriages				FB Marriages Count	Percent of Foreign-Born APA Marriages				US-Born Marriage Count	Percent of U.S.-Born APA Marriages			
		IT	IE	MM	MJ		IT	IE	MM	MJ		IT	IE	MM	MJ
Chinese American	183,567	75.8	16.7	1.5	6.0	150,686	79.8	15.1	1.0	4.0	32,881	57.1	23.9	3.6	15.4
Filipino American	149,256	73.8	13.9	4.3	8.0	127,943	78.9	12.9	3.2	5.0	21,313	43.3	19.4	10.9	26.4
Japanese American	89,187	62.1	21.2	3.6	13.1	27,487	65.7	22.5	2.1	9.7	61,700	60.5	20.6	4.2	14.6
South Asian American	46,456	65.3	23.7	3.3	7.8	45,482	66.3	23.5	2.8	7.4	974	18.9	31.5	22.5	27.1
Korean American	65,360	78.1	18.3	0.5	3.1	63,550	79.6	17.8	0.4	2.2	1,810	25.9	35.9	3.3	34.9
Vietnamese American	48,786	75.5	19.9	1.3	3.3	48,436	75.6	19.9	1.3	3.3	350	71.1	18.6	2.3	8.0
Cambodian American	11,224	80.4	17.2	0.7	1.7	11,159	80.6	17.0	0.7	1.7	65	40.0	60.0	0.0	0.0
Hmong American	7,587	79.8	16.7	0.9	2.7	7,550	79.7	16.8	0.9	2.7	37	100.0	0.0	0.0	0.0
Laotian American	11,051	76.9	18.8	2.3	2.0	10,987	76.9	18.8	2.3	2.0	64	75.0	25.0	0.0	0.0
Thai American	6,481	54.0	35.2	3.2	7.6	6,391	54.3	34.7	3.3	7.7	93	31.2	68.8	0.0	0.0
Other Asian American	9,614	44.3	30.8	6.7	18.2	7,704	47.2	30.7	6.5	15.6	1,910	32.6	31.2	7.4	28.8
Hawaiian American	7,809	15.6	31.6	13.5	39.3	145	69.7	30.3	0.0	0.0	7,664	14.5	31.6	13.8	40.1
Samoan American	5,019	54.5	28.8	5.2	11.6	2,035	62.5	27.0	4.4	6.1	2,984	49.1	30.0	5.7	15.3
Tongan American	963	68.3	20.6	3.0	8.1	906	69.2	19.0	3.2	8.6	57	54.4	45.6	0.0	0.0
Chamorran American	5,035	39.7	28.1	9.9	22.3	745	41.7	39.9	13.8	4.6	4,290	39.3	26.1	9.2	25.4
Other Pacific American	2,470	56.8	29.5	3.4	10.3	2,257	60.3	27.8	3.3	8.5	213	19.7	47.4	3.8	29.1
Total	649,968	71.1	18.4	2.8	7.7	513,463	76.1	17.3	1.9	4.7	136,405	52.3	22.7	6.0	18.9

Table 21
Marriage Patterns of Asian Pacific American Husbands and Wives
General and by Nativity, State of California, 1990

Wife's Ethnicity	General Marriage Count	Percent of General APA* Marriages				FB Marriage Count	Percent of Foreign-Born APA Marriages				US-Born Marriage Count	Percent of U.S.-Born APA Marriages			
		IT	IE	MM	MJ		IT	IE	MM	MJ		IT	IE	MM	MJ
Chinese American	186,967	74.3	13.9	1.4	10.4	153,542	79.2	11.6	1.1	8.2	33,425	51.7	24.4	3.0	20.9
Filipino American	184,114	59.9	15.0	5.5	19.7	159,624	63.7	13.7	4.5	18.2	24,490	35.2	23.2	12.0	29.6
Japanese American	115,099	48.1	20.0	4.4	27.5	48,220	44.9	16.7	4.8	33.7	66,879	50.4	22.4	4.2	23.1
South Asian American	37,852	80.1	12.0	1.4	6.4	36,608	80.8	11.5	1.4	6.3	1,244	58.4	29.1	2.9	9.6
Korean American	74,622	68.5	16.1	2.5	12.9	71,802	70.3	14.9	2.4	12.4	2,820	22.2	46.6	6.5	24.6
Vietnamese American	52,383	70.7	19.4	1.6	8.3	51,735	71.1	19.4	1.4	8.2	648	45.4	21.3	18.7	14.7
Cambodian American	12,115	74.8	19.8	1.3	4.2	12,115	74.8	19.8	1.3	4.2	-	-	-	-	-
Hmong American	6,900	89.2	8.6	0.9	1.4	6,850	89.5	8.2	0.9	1.4	50	42.0	58.0	0.0	0.0
Laotian American	10,686	80.6	14.9	1.7	2.9	10,612	80.4	15.0	1.7	2.9	74	100.0	0.0	0.0	0.0
Thai American	9,016	38.7	26.7	5.3	29.3	8,912	39.1	26.4	5.1	29.4	104	0.0	56.7	20.2	23.1
Other Asian American	11,460	35.6	28.4	4.0	31.9	8,513	41.6	26.2	2.6	29.6	2,947	18.2	35.0	8.1	38.7
Hawaiian American	7,474	15.7	29.9	12.0	42.5	242	44.6	41.7	8.3	5.4	7,232	14.7	29.5	12.1	43.7
Samoan American	4,709	54.7	21.4	10.8	13.0	2,258	58.9	18.6	9.0	13.6	2,451	50.8	24.1	12.5	12.6
Tongan American	1,340	55.5	25.0	6.0	13.4	1,265	58.8	22.4	6.4	12.4	75	0.0	69.3	0.0	30.7
Chamorran American	5,153	38.8	25.2	12.2	23.8	572	46.7	25.3	12.4	15.6	4,581	37.8	25.2	12.2	24.9
Other Pacific American	2,453	57.3	14.7	4.5	23.5	2,185	63.1	12.3	2.7	21.8	268	9.7	34.3	19.0	36.9
Total	722,343	64.0	16.4	3.4	16.2	575,055	68.9	14.4	2.7	14.0	147,288	44.8	24.3	6.2	24.8

Source: Calculations by Larry Hajime Shinagawa, Ph.D., based upon the 5 percent Public Use Microdata Sample (PUMS), U.S. Bureau of the Census, 1990.
Copyright (c) 1996, Larry Hajime Shinagawa, Ph.D., Assistant Professor, Department of American Multi-Cultural Studies, Sonoma State University.
* APA = "Asian Pacific American"   IT = "Intraethnic Marriage"   IE = "Interethnic Marriage"   MM = "Minority-Minority Marriage"   MJ = "Minority-Majority Marriage"
FB = Foreign-Born

Table 22
Household Income
Asian Pacific Americans Between the Ages of 18 and 64
By Nativity, Sex, and Selected Ethnic Group
United States of America, 1990

	Total Count	Total Income	Foreign-Born Count	Foreign-Born Income	U.S.-Born Count	U.S.-Born Income
Total	4,499,583	$53,104	3,598,965	$51,643	901,558	$58,723
Chinese Americans	1,071,906	$52,774	883,124	$50,400	188,782	$63,881
Filipino Americans	903,490	$58,718	746,680	$59,463	156,810	$55,167
Japanese Americans	570,450	$59,689	227,247	$54,620	343,203	$62,597
Asian Indian Americans	509,239	$60,903	487,058	$60,960	22,181	$59,648
Korean Americans	481,888	$47,958	458,199	$47,558	23,629	$55,715
Vietnamese Americans	361,278	$44,040	355,983	$43,965	5,295	$49,074
Cambodian Americans	74,069	$32,518	73,291	$32,471	778	$37,008
Hmong Americans	33,320	$20,648	32,863	$20,604	457	$23,789
Laotian Americans	77,896	$33,110	77,065	$33,126	831	$31,638
Thai Americans	62,762	$49,124	60,936	$48,931	1,826	$55,573
Other Asian Americans	155,777	$47,218	130,522	$46,975	25,255	$48,477
Hawaiian Americans	117,836	$49,636	3,690	$47,690	114,146	$49,699
Samoan Americans	27,794	$39,223	19,387	$36,948	9,407	$41,448
Tongan Americans	8,145	$42,996	7,539	$42,304	606	$51,606
Guamanian Americans	28,573	$43,504	22,189	$43,162	6,384	$44,691
Other Pacific Islander American‡	15,160	$39,158	13,192	$39,107	1,968	$39,501
Male	2,140,404	$53,766	1,690,183	$52,216	451,089	$59,146
Chinese Americans	523,786	$52,693	428,264	$50,137	95,522	$64,149
Filipino Americans	392,513	$60,521	313,502	$61,669	79,011	$55,964
Japanese Americans	252,059	$61,756	81,005	$58,531	171,054	$62,383
Asian Indian Americans	279,780	$60,290	268,335	$60,230	11,373	$61,698
Korean Americans	202,777	$49,733	191,006	$49,218	11,711	$58,132

Table 22

Household Income

Asian Pacific Americans Between the Ages of 18 and 64

By Nativity, Sex, and Selected Ethnic Group

United States of America, 1990

	Total Count	Total Income	Foreign-Born Count	Foreign-Born Income	U.S.-Born Count	U.S.-Born Income
Vietnamese Americans	190,018	$44,988	187,356	$44,902	2,662	$51,054
Cambodian Americans	34,247	$34,066	33,893	$34,070	354	$33,760
Hmong Americans	17,212	$21,372	16,975	$21,354	237	$22,631
Laotian Americans	40,595	$34,179	40,173	$34,168	422	$35,210
Thai Americans	23,119	$50,353	22,247	$50,100	872	$56,805
Other Asian Americans	87,285	$46,184	75,193	$45,594	12,092	$49,849
Hawaiian Americans	58,305	$50,478	1,889	$44,024	56,416	$50,694
Samoan Americans	13,256	$40,800	9,200	$38,110	5,056	$40,800
Tongan Americans	4,057	$43,680	3,702	$42,785	355	$53,006
Guamanian Americans	13,919	$44,220	10,951	$43,567	2,968	$46,627
Other Pacific Islander American:	7,476	$35,317	6,492	$35,515	984	$34,012
Female						
Chinese Americans	2,359,251	$52,504	1,908,782	$51,136	450,469	$58,299
Filipino Americans	548,120	$52,853	454,860	$50,648	93,260	$63,606
Japanese Americans	510,977	$57,333	433,178	$57,867	77,799	$54,358
Asian Indian Americans	318,391	$58,053	146,242	$52,454	172,149	$62,809
Korean Americans	229,531	$61,651	218,723	$61,856	10,808	$57,490
Vietnamese Americans	279,111	$46,669	267,193	$46,371	11,918	$53,341
Cambodian Americans	171,260	$42,988	168,627	$42,925	2,633	$47,073
Hmong Americans	39,822	$31,187	39,398	$31,095	424	$39,720
Laotian Americans	16,108	$19,874	15,888	$19,802	220	$25,036
Thai Americans	37,301	$31,948	36,892	$31,992	409	$27,953
Other Asian Americans	68,492	$48,537	55,329	$48,851	13,163	$47,216
Hawaiian Americans	59,531	$48,812	1,801	$51,536	57,730	$48,727
Samoan Americans	14,538	$37,785	10,187	$35,899	4,351	$42,202
Tongan Americans	4,088	$42,317	3,837	$41,839	251	$49,627
Guamanian Americans	14,654	$42,823	11,238	$42,767	3,416	$43,009
Other Pacific Islander American:	7,684	$42,896	6,700	$42,588	984	$44,991

Source: U.S. Bureau of the Census, 5 percent 1990 Public Use Microdata Sample.

Table 23
Percent of Families with 3 or More Workers in 1989
Among Selected Asian and Pacific Islander Groups
By Nativity and Citizenship
United States of America, 1990

Percent of Families with 3 or more workers	All Persons	Native-Born	Foreign Born Total	Foreign Born Naturalized Total	Foreign Born Not a Citizen Total
General	13.3	12.8	18.5	18.5	18.6
Asian or Pacific Islander	19.8	18.0	20.2	24.2	16.1
Chinese American	19.0	14.4	19.9	21.4	18.0
Filipino American	29.6	21.8	31.1	32.9	26.8
Japanese American	15.2	18.7	6.8	14.5	4.9
Asian Indian American	17.6	12.3	17.9	21.0	15.2
Korean American	15.8	13.9	16.0	18.1	14.3
Vietnamese American	21.3	16.7	21.4	25.0	17.2
Cambodian American	13.5	15.2	13.5	25.1	10.3
Hmong American	6.7	8.3	6.7	16.8	5.2
Laotian American	18.9	13.1	18.9	30.3	15.8
Thai American	15.5	3.4	15.7	17.0	15.0
Pakistani American	15.0	20.3	15.0	17.5	12.5
Pacific Islander	19.7	19.8	19.4	20.6	18.4

Source: 1990 Census of Population, Asians and Pacific Islander in the United States, 1990 CP-3-5, Table 4 and special tabulations of the 1990 Census data.

Table 24
Mean Wage & Salary Income
Asian Pacific Americans Between the Ages of 18 and 64
By Nativity, Sex, and Selected Ethnic Group
United States of America, 1990

	Total Count	Total Income	Foreign-Born Count	Foreign-Born Income	U.S.-Born Count	U.S.-Born Income
Total	3,429,929	$22,579	2,651,297	$22,520	778,635	$22,779
Chinese Americans	825,494	$22,908	658,515	$22,308	166,979	$25,275
Filipino Americans	779,490	$21,416	641,754	$22,160	137,736	$17,947
Japanese Americans	442,393	$28,257	147,603	$31,290	294,790	$26,738
Asian Indian Americans	397,243	$27,815	377,557	$28,512	19,686	$14,455
Korean Americans	312,794	$20,079	291,590	$20,332	21,204	$16,605
Vietnamese Americans	249,515	$17,590	245,457	$17,638	4,058	$14,655
Cambodian Americans	38,226	$14,364	37,639	$14,444	587	$9,223
Hmong Americans	11,526	$9,923	11,318	$9,938	211	$9,093
Laotian Americans	48,901	$13,634	48,341	$13,610	560	$15,741
Thai Americans	47,570	$19,738	46,113	$19,941	1,457	$13,305
Other Asian Americans	117,744	$21,104	95,440	$22,006	22,304	$17,247
Hawaiian Americans	96,778	$19,225	3,055	$16,231	93,723	$19,322
Samoan Americans	21,208	$16,112	13,911	$16,473	7,297	$15,424
Tongan Americans	5,477	$14,772	4,980	$14,517	497	$17,379
Guamanian Americans	23,513	$17,680	17,804	$18,504	5,709	$15,110
Other Pacific Islander American:	12,057	$13,880	10,220	$13,707	1,837	$14,844
Male	1,807,397	$27,023	1,400,643	$27,099	406,754	$26,763
Chinese Americans	439,916	$27,118	352,878	$26,583	87,038	$29,286
Filipino Americans	358,019	$23,687	285,745	$24,522	72,274	$20,388
Japanese Americans	224,436	$36,820	71,883	$46,783	152,553	$32,126
Asian Indian Americans	249,569	$33,635	238,891	$34,366	10,678	$17,273
Korean Americans	150,188	$25,527	139,598	$25,985	10,590	$19,489

Table 24
Mean Wage & Salary Income
Asian Pacific Americans Between the Ages of 18 and 64
By Nativity, Sex, and Selected Ethnic Group
United States of America, 1990

	Total Count	Total Income	Foreign-Born Count	Foreign-Born Income	U.S.-Born Count	U.S.-Born Income
Vietnamese Americans	147,750	$19,884	145,576	$19,938	2,174	$16,300
Cambodian Americans	21,313	$16,579	20,999	$16,672	314	$10,334
Hmong Americans	7,670	$10,479	7,516	$10,548	154	$7,109
Laotian Americans	28,537	$15,014	28,161	$15,000	376	$16,070
Thai Americans	19,746	$25,346	19,062	$25,597	684	$18,346
Other Asian Americans	73,813	$24,628	62,439	$25,520	11,374	$19,728
Hawaiian Americans	52,068	$22,653	1,654	$19,247	50,414	$22,765
Samoan Americans	11,866	$18,476	7,849	$18,771	4,017	$17,899
Tongan Americans	2,873	$17,884	2,576	$17,380	297	$22,342
Guamanian Americans	13,029	$20,777	10,083	$21,995	2,946	$16,609
Other Pacific Islander American:	6,604	$15,304	5,733	$15,222	871	$15,849
Female	1,622,535	$17,628	1,250,654	$17,392	371,881	$18,421
Chinese Americans	385,578	$18,105	305,637	$17,372	79,941	$20,908
Filipino Americans	421,471	$19,486	356,009	$20,265	65,462	$15,251
Japanese Americans	217,957	$19,439	75,720	$16,583	142,237	$20,959
Asian Indian Americans	147,674	$17,981	138,666	$18,426	9,008	$11,116
Korean Americans	162,606	$15,048	151,992	$15,140	10,614	$13,727
Vietnamese Americans	101,765	$14,259	99,881	$14,287	1,884	$12,758
Cambodian Americans	16,913	$11,573	16,640	$11,632	273	$7,946
Hmong Americans	3,859	$8,817	3,802	$8,732	57	$14,453
Laotian Americans	20,364	$11,701	20,180	$11,670	184	$15,067
Thai Americans	27,824	$15,757	27,051	$15,955	773	$8,844
Other Asian Americans	43,931	$15,184	33,001	$15,356	10,930	$14,665
Hawaiian Americans	44,710	$15,232	1,401	$12,670	43,309	$15,315
Samoan Americans	9,342	$13,110	6,062	$13,497	3,280	$12,394
Tongan Americans	2,604	$11,339	2,404	$11,450	200	$10,009
Guamanian Americans	10,484	$13,831	7,721	$13,945	2,763	$13,512
Other Pacific Islander American:	5,453	$12,155	4,487	$11,771	966	$13,938

Source: U.S. Bureau of the Census, 5 percent 1990 Public Use Microdata Sample (PUMS).
Copyright (c) 1996, Larry Hajime Shinagawa, Ph.D., Department of American Multi-Cultural Studies, Sonoma State University.

Table 25
Occupational Distribution of the General Population and Selected Asian Pacific American Groups By Sex, United States of America, 1990

	Total Count	Total Percent	Managerial	Professional	Technical & Sales	Administrative Support	Service	Farming, Forestry & Fishing	Precision Prod., Craft, & Repair	Operative & Laborers
Total										
General Population	115,681,202	100.0	12.3	14.1	15.5	16.3	13.2	2.5	11.3	14.9
Asian Pacific Americans	3,411,586	100.0	12.6	18.1	17.9	15.4	14.8	1.2	8.0	12.1
Chinese Americans	819,932	100.0	15.1	20.7	17.6	13.5	16.5	0.4	5.6	10.6
Filipino Americans	750,613	100.0	10.3	16.4	15.6	21.0	16.8	1.5	7.4	11.0
Japanese Americans	452,005	100.0	17.5	19.4	16.6	17.8	11.1	2.7	7.8	6.9
Asian Indian Americans	391,949	100.0	14.0	29.6	20.0	13.2	8.1	0.6	5.2	9.4
Korean Americans	345,655	100.0	12.0	13.5	26.8	10.3	15.1	0.7	8.9	12.8
Vietnamese Americans	248,881	100.0	6.1	11.5	17.7	11.8	15.0	1.4	15.7	20.9
Cambodian Americans	35,623	100.0	4.0	5.8	12.6	10.7	17.9	1.7	17.2	30.0
Hmong Americans	9,756	100.0	3.4	9.4	7.3	11.6	20.0	2.3	13.9	32.1
Laotian Americans	46,010	100.0	1.8	3.3	6.9	8.2	14.6	1.5	19.8	43.9
Thai Americans	48,028	100.0	9.6	14.0	15.1	11.4	26.8	0.7	7.5	15.0
Pacific Islander Americans	147,318	100.0	9.7	8.3	13.0	19.0	19.2	2.5	11.9	16.3
Male										
General Population	62,704,579	100.0	14.6	13.4	16.6	7.5	11.3	4.2	21.0	22.5
Asian Pacific Americans	1,820,689	100.0	0.2	0.3	0.3	0.1	0.2	0.0	0.2	0.2
Chinese Americans	446,767	100.0	17.5	27.2	20.3	8.7	21.6	0.6	8.7	9.8
Filipino Americans	339,220	100.0	11.7	13.4	16.4	17.4	17.6	2.6	13.7	16.8
Japanese Americans	236,686	100.0	24.2	22.8	20.3	10.0	10.2	5.1	14.2	9.8
Asian Indian Americans	250,921	100.0	18.9	38.5	23.7	9.8	7.3	0.9	7.8	11.6
Korean Americans	172,233	100.0	16.9	18.3	33.2	7.1	11.3	1.1	14.3	13.9

Table 25
Occupational Distribution of the General Population and Selected Asian Pacific American Groups By Sex, United States of America, 1990

	Total Count	Total Percent	Managerial	Professional	Technical & Sales	Administrative Support	Service	Farming, Forestry & Fishing	Precision Prod., Craft, & Repair	Operative & Laborers
Vietnamese Americans	147,577	100.0	5.7	14.1	19.2	8.0	12.9	2.3	20.5	22.9
Cambodian Americans	20,232	100.0	4.9	6.8	12.0	8.1	18.9	2.2	21.5	30.8
Hmong Americans	6,483	100.0	3.9	10.5	7.6	9.8	21.5	3.4	16.5	31.1
Laotian Americans	27,163	100.0	2.0	3.4	6.2	6.2	14.6	1.8	22.7	45.2
Thai Americans	19,689	100.0	13.8	17.1	18.6	9.9	23.8	0.5	12.5	17.2
Pacific Islander Americans	79,189	100.0	9.5	7.5	10.4	9.1	18.1	4.1	20.9	24.4
Female										
General Population	52,976,623	100.0	10.1	14.8	14.4	24.6	15.1	0.8	2.1	7.6
Asian Pacific Americans	1,590,897	100.0	10.0	14.9	15.6	19.8	14.4	0.5	3.6	9.6
Chinese Americans	373,165	100.0	12.9	14.8	15.2	18.0	11.9	0.2	2.8	11.3
Filipino Americans	411,393	100.0	9.3	18.5	15.0	23.6	16.2	0.7	3.0	7.0
Japanese Americans	215,319	100.0	12.1	16.7	13.5	24.2	11.9	0.7	2.7	4.6
Asian Indian Americans	141,028	100.0	8.1	19.3	15.7	17.2	9.0	0.2	2.1	6.8
Korean Americans	173,422	100.0	8.3	9.8	21.9	12.7	18.0	0.4	4.9	12.0
Vietnamese Americans	101,304	100.0	6.7	8.1	15.8	16.6	17.7	0.3	9.4	18.2
Cambodian Americans	15,391	100.0	3.0	4.7	13.3	13.8	16.7	1.2	12.3	29.0
Hmong Americans	3,273	100.0	2.6	7.4	6.8	14.8	17.4	0.4	9.3	33.9
Laotian Americans	18,847	100.0	1.5	3.1	7.9	11.0	14.8	1.1	15.9	41.9
Thai Americans	28,339	100.0	7.3	12.2	13.1	12.3	28.5	0.8	4.7	13.7
Pacific Islander Americans	68,129	100.0	10.0	9.2	15.9	29.7	20.3	0.7	2.3	7.6

Source: U.S. Bureau of the Census, 1990 CP-3-5, Asians and Pacific Islanders in the United States, Table 3.

Table 26
Occupational Distribution of the General Population and Selected Asian Pacific American Groups
U.S.-Born
By Sex, United States of America, 1990

	Total Count	Total Percent	Managerial	Professional	Technical & Sales	Administrative Support	Service	Farming, Forestry & Fishing	Precision Prod., Craft, & Repair	Operative & Laborers
Total										
General Population	105,016,223	100.0	12.5	14.3	15.7	16.7	12.7	2.3	11.3	14.5
Asian Pacific Americans	849,922	100.0	14.2	17.3	17.3	19.9	12.1	1.9	8.3	9.1
Chinese Americans	167,712	100.0	18.2	25.0	18.7	18.3	8.6	0.6	5.0	5.6
Filipino Americans	151,012	100.0	10.7	10.7	18.2	22.5	15.6	1.4	9.3	11.6
Japanese Americans	322,486	100.0	16.0	20.1	16.5	20.2	8.6	3.0	8.6	6.9
Asian Indian Americans	18,692	100.0	10.8	22.2	22.5	17.9	12.1	0.8	5.3	8.5
Korean Americans	28,511	100.0	11.3	14.3	22.5	17.3	20.1	1.0	4.3	9.1
Vietnamese Americans	7,745	100.0	5.7	7.5	19.9	16.3	22.5	1.3	9.1	17.7
Cambodian Americans	667	100.0	4.5	6.6	21.0	16.6	15.6	6.6	13.2	15.9
Hmong Americans	330	100.0	-	0.9	7.0	16.1	21.2	5.5	17.9	31.5
Laotian Americans	772	100.0	4.4	7.3	12.8	8.0	18.9	1.4	18.1	29.0
Thai Americans	3,076	100.0	4.9	10.4	24.2	16.9	26.2	1.4	3.8	12.1
Pacific Islander Americans	122,938	100.0	10.6	8.7	13.5	19.9	18.0	2.1	11.9	15.3

Table 26
Occupational Distribution of the General Population and Selected Asian Pacific American Groups
U.S.-Born
By Sex, United States of America, 1990

	Total Count	Total Percent	Managerial	Professional	Technical & Sales	Administrative Support	Service	Farming, Forestry & Fishing	Precision Prod., Craft, & Repair	Operative & Laborers
Male										
General Population	68,778,580	100.0	13.4	12.1	15.2	28.7	9.7	3.6	19.1	20.1
Asian Pacific Americans	447,451	100.0	0.1	0.1	0.1	0.0	0.1	0.0	0.1	0.1
Chinese Americans	89,200	100.0	18.8	27.3	20.8	11.3	9.5	0.8	8.6	8.6
Filipino Americans	78,421	100.0	9.8	10.2	16.7	13.5	16.8	2.4	16.6	18.1
Japanese Americans	170,859	100.0	16.3	19.0	17.3	9.6	8.3	4.8	14.6	10.1
Asian Indian Americans	10,334	100.0	14.7	31.5	30.0	15.8	16.2	1.9	11.2	15.5
Korean Americans	13,875	100.0	13.9	17.4	23.5	11.7	23.1	1.8	8.8	16.9
Vietnamese Americans	4,122	100.0	5.2	9.8	27.6	14.6	31.7	2.9	21.3	30.7
Cambodian Americans	372	100.0	3.1	10.5	22.8	32.7	35.8	27.2	39.5	58.0
Hmong Americans	220	100.0	-	1.4	10.8	1.4	23.9	8.5	17.4	39.9
Laotian Americans	472	100.0	6.6	9.7	5.1	8.9	26.5	1.3	30.6	31.6
Thai Americans	1,575	100.0	4.2	14.9	19.3	10.2	29.3	1.7	5.7	20.2
Pacific Islander Americans	65,318	100.0	9.9	7.4	10.5	8.9	16.9	3.5	20.4	22.7
Female										
General Population	36,237,643	100.0	11.5	16.8	16.3	2.8	16.3	0.8	2.2	7.9
Asian Pacific Americans	402,471	100.0	14.0	17.3	17.2	29.5	11.8	0.6	1.8	4.2
Chinese Americans	78,512	100.0	17.7	22.6	16.6	25.3	7.6	0.3	1.4	2.6
Filipino Americans	72,591	100.0	11.7	11.3	19.7	31.5	14.3	0.5	2.0	5.1
Japanese Americans	151,627	100.0	15.7	21.3	15.7	32.2	9.0	0.9	1.9	3.3
Asian Indian Americans	8,358	100.0	8.1	15.9	17.3	19.4	9.3	0.0	1.2	3.7
Korean Americans	14,636	100.0	9.5	12.2	21.8	21.4	17.9	0.5	1.1	3.5
Vietnamese Americans	3,623	100.0	6.1	6.1	15.4	17.2	17.2	0.4	1.8	10.0
Cambodian Americans	295	100.0	5.0	5.3	20.4	11.5	9.1	-	4.8	2.4
Hmong Americans	110	100.0	-	-	-	42.7	16.2	-	18.8	16.2
Laotian Americans	300	100.0	2.1	4.7	20.8	7.1	11.1	1.6	5.3	26.3
Thai Americans	1,501	100.0	5.7	6.2	28.9	23.2	23.2	1.1	2.1	4.4
Pacific Islander Americans	57,620	100.0	11.3	10.3	16.9	32.2	19.3	0.7	2.2	6.9

Source: U.S. Bureau of the Census, 1990 CP-3-5, Asians and Pacific Islanders in the United States, Table 3.

Table 27
Occupational Distribution, General Population and Selected Asian Pacific American Groups by Sex
Foreign-Born
United States of America, 1990

	Total Count	Total Percent	Managerial	Professional	Technical & Sales	Administrative Support	Service	Farming, Forestry & Fishing	Precision Prod., Craft, & Repair	Operative & Laborers
Total										
General Population	10,664,979	100.0	9.9	12.3	13.3	12.0	18.1	3.8	12.0	18.6
Asian Pacific Americans	5,148,664	100.0	59.8	9.1	9.0	6.9	7.8	0.5	3.9	6.5
Chinese Americans	652,220	100.0	14.3	19.6	17.3	12.3	18.5	0.3	5.8	11.8
Filipino Americans	599,601	100.0	10.2	17.8	15.0	20.7	17.1	1.5	7.0	10.9
Japanese Americans	129,519	100.0	21.3	17.8	16.7	11.9	17.5	1.9	5.9	7.1
Asian Indian Americans	373,257	100.0	14.1	30.0	19.9	13.0	7.9	0.6	5.2	9.4
Korean Americans	317,144	100.0	12.1	13.4	27.1	9.7	14.6	0.6	9.3	13.2
Vietnamese Americans	241,136	100.0	6.1	11.6	17.7	11.6	14.7	1.4	15.9	21.0
Cambodian Americans	34,956	100.0	4.0	5.8	12.4	10.6	17.9	1.6	17.3	30.2
Hmong Americans	9,426	100.0	3.5	9.7	7.4	11.4	20.0	2.2	13.7	32.1
Laotian Americans	45,238	100.0	1.7	3.2	6.8	8.2	14.6	1.5	19.8	44.1
Thai Americans	44,952	100.0	9.9	14.2	14.5	11.0	26.8	0.6	7.8	15.2
Pacific Islander Americans	24,380	100.0	5.5	6.3	10.7	14.7	25.0	4.2	12.1	21.4

Table 27
Occupational Distribution, General Population and Selected Asian Pacific American Groups by Sex
Foreign-Born
United States of America, 1990

	Total Count	Total Percent	Managerial	Professional	Technical & Sales	Administrative Support	Service	Farming, Forestry & Fishing	Precision Prod., Craft, & Repair	Operative & Laborers
Male.										
General Population	6,233,999	100.0	10.6	11.7	12.5	6.2	14.5	5.5	17.6	21.4
Asian Pacific Americans	3,960,238	100.0	27.7	2.6	2.4	1.2	1.8	0.2	1.4	1.7
Chinese Americans	357,567	100.0	14.7	23.3	17.3	6.8	21.3	0.4	7.5	8.7
Filipino Americans	260,808	100.0	11.1	12.9	14.6	16.7	16.0	2.4	11.5	14.7
Japanese Americans	65,827	100.0	32.2	21.0	17.8	5.9	10.0	3.1	6.0	4.0
Asian Indian Americans	240,584	100.0	16.2	32.9	19.9	8.2	5.9	0.7	6.5	9.7
Korean Americans	158,631	100.0	14.8	15.8	29.3	5.8	8.8	0.9	12.7	11.9
Vietnamese Americans	143,455	100.0	5.4	13.5	18.2	7.5	11.9	2.2	19.6	21.7
Cambodian Americans	23,153	100.0	4.7	6.4	12.9	9.3	18.0	1.7	19.0	27.9
Hmong Americans	6,263	100.0	3.8	10.4	7.2	9.7	20.5	3.1	15.8	29.5
Laotian Americans	26,691	100.0	1.9	3.2	6.1	6.1	14.1	1.8	22.2	44.7
Thai Americans	18,114	100.0	12.9	15.2	16.2	8.6	20.4	0.4	11.5	14.8
Pacific Islander Americans	13,873	100.0	5.5	6.4	7.6	7.7	20.1	6.4	18.7	27.4
Female										
General Population	4,430,980	100.0	8.9	13.1	14.5	20.2	23.2	1.3	4.1	14.6
Asian Pacific Americans	1,188,426	100.0	10.2	16.5	17.6	19.6	17.7	0.5	4.8	13.1
Chinese Americans	294,653	100.0	13.8	15.1	17.5	19.0	15.1	0.2	3.7	15.7
Filipino Americans	338,793	100.0	9.4	21.5	15.2	23.7	17.9	0.8	3.5	8.0
Japanese Americans	63,692	100.0	10.0	14.5	15.5	18.0	25.2	0.7	5.8	10.2
Asian Indian Americans	132,673	100.0	10.4	24.8	19.8	21.7	11.4	0.3	2.7	8.9
Korean Americans	158,513	100.0	9.3	10.9	25.0	13.6	20.5	0.4	5.9	14.4
Vietnamese Americans	97,681	100.0	7.2	8.7	16.9	17.7	18.9	0.3	10.5	19.9
Cambodian Americans	11,803	100.0	2.6	4.7	11.6	13.2	17.8	1.5	13.9	34.8
Hmong Americans	3,163	100.0	2.9	8.3	7.7	15.0	18.8	0.4	9.7	37.3
Laotian Americans	18,547	100.0	1.6	3.1	7.9	11.3	15.2	1.1	16.5	43.3
Thai Americans	26,838	100.0	8.0	13.5	13.2	12.6	31.2	0.8	5.2	15.4
Pacific Islander Americans	10,507	100.0	5.5	6.2	14.7	24.0	31.5	1.3	3.4	13.5

Source: U.S. Bureau of the Census, 1990 CP-3-5, Asians and Pacific Islanders in the United States, Table 3.

Table 28

Educational Attainment of the General Asian Pacific American Population Over 25, by sex, and by selected Asian Pacific American Groups United States of America, 1990

	Total Count	Total Percent	Less Than Bachelor's	Bachelor's Degree	Master's Degree	Doctorate
Total						
Chinese Americans	1,074,009	100.0	59.3	21.7	15.6	3.5
Filipino Americans	866,022	100.0	60.3	31.9	7.3	0.5
Japanese Americans	623,511	100.0	65.6	24.4	8.8	1.3
Asian Indian Americans	461,631	100.0	41.6	25.3	27.3	5.8
Korean Americans	452,333	100.0	65.6	21.9	10.6	1.9
Vietnamese Americans	300,999	100.0	83.2	12.4	3.9	0.5
Cambodian Americans	62,367	100.0	93.6	4.8	1.2	0.4
Hmong Americans	27,114	100.0	96.8	2.2	0.7	0.3
Laotian Americans	65,002	100.0	93.4	4.6	1.8	0.2
Thai Americans	57,443	100.0	66.8	19.9	12.3	1.0
Other Asian Americans	136,082	100.0	58.3	21.9	17.4	2.4
Hawaiian Americans	107,185	100.0	88.7	8.0	2.9	0.3
Samoan Americans	23,977	100.0	91.8	5.4	2.3	0.5
Tongan Americans	7,467	100.0	95.1	3.6	1.2	0.1
Guamanian Americans	25,512	100.0	89.9	7.1	2.5	0.5
Other Pacific Islander American:	12,303	100.0	89.5	7.7	2.4	0.4
Male						
Chinese Americans	524,160	100.0	53.2	21.3	19.8	5.7
Filipino Americans	373,386	100.0	64.1	27.5	7.8	0.6
Japanese Americans	270,911	100.0	57.2	28.5	12.0	2.2
Asian Indian Americans	254,995	100.0	33.7	24.1	33.5	8.8
Korean Americans	185,053	100.0	53.3	25.5	17.1	4.1

Table 28
Educational Attainment of the General Asian Pacific American Population Over 25, by sex, and by selected Asian Pacific American Groups
United States of America, 1990

	Total Count	Total Percent	Less Than Bachelor's	Bachelor's Degree	Master's Degree	Doctorate
Vietnamese Americans	155,403	100.0	78.1	15.7	5.5	0.8
Cambodian Americans	28,585	100.0	90.0	7.3	2.0	0.8
Hmong Americans	13,055	100.0	95.6	2.9	1.0	0.5
Laotian Americans	33,831	100.0	91.3	5.8	2.6	0.3
Thai Americans	20,594	100.0	50.1	28.8	19.3	1.8
Other Asian Americans	75,901	100.0	52.0	23.2	21.3	3.5
Hawaiian Americans	52,632	100.0	87.8	8.9	3.0	0.3
Samoan Americans	12,277	100.0	90.4	5.5	3.7	0.4
Tongan Americans	3,784	100.0	96.1	2.6	1.1	0.2
Guamanian Americans	12,666	100.0	87.7	9.3	2.2	0.9
Other Pacific Islander American:	5,873	100.0	90.1	5.2	4.3	0.4
Female						
Chinese Americans	549,849	100.0	65.0	22.1	11.5	1.3
Filipino Americans	492,636	100.0	57.5	35.3	6.9	0.3
Japanese Americans	351,600	100.0	72.0	21.3	6.2	0.5
Asian Indian Americans	206,636	100.0	51.4	26.8	19.7	2.1
Korean Americans	267,280	100.0	74.1	19.5	6.0	0.5
Vietnamese Americans	145,596	100.0	88.7	8.9	2.3	0.1
Cambodian Americans	33,782	100.0	96.7	2.7	0.5	0.0
Hmong Americans	14,059	100.0	97.9	1.7	0.5	0.0
Laotian Americans	31,171	100.0	95.7	3.4	0.8	0.1
Thai Americans	36,849	100.0	76.1	14.9	8.3	0.6
Other Asian Americans	60,181	100.0	66.3	20.3	12.4	1.0
Hawaiian Americans	54,553	100.0	89.6	7.2	2.8	0.4
Samoan Americans	11,700	100.0	93.3	5.2	0.9	0.5
Tongan Americans	3,683	100.0	94.1	4.6	1.4	0.0
Guamanian Americans	12,846	100.0	92.0	5.0	2.9	0.1
Other Pacific Islander American:	6,430	100.0	89.0	9.9	0.7	0.4

Source: U.S. Bureau of the Census, 1990 5 percent Public Use Microdata Sample (PUMS).
Copyright (c) 1996, Larry Hajime Shinagawa, Ph.D., Department of American Multi-Cultural Studies, Sonoma State University.

Table 29
Asian Pacific Americans Over 65
Percent Using Public Assistance, Percent Using Social Security, and Percent in Poverty
By Nativity and Sex, for Selected Asian Pacific American Groups

	Count Total Over 65	Percent U.S.-Born Over 65	Percent Foreign Born Over 65	Total			U.S. Born			Foreign Born		
				Public Assistance	Social Security	Below Poverty	Public Assistance	Social Security	Below Poverty	Public Assistance	Social Security	Below Poverty
Total	439,224	29.2	70.8	22.6	51.8	13.7	5.1	79.3	8.5	29.9	40.5	15.8
Chinese Americans	130,269	15.2	84.8	23.0	50.8	16.4	6.4	76.0	8.7	25.9	46.3	17.8
Filipino Americans	101,923	5.0	95.0	28.4	43.1	9.9	11.3	66.7	16.0	29.3	41.9	9.6
Japanese Americans	104,526	82.7	17.3	4.1	80.5	7.8	3.2	82.2	5.9	8.0	72.6	16.9
Asian Indian Americans	20,862	5.4	94.6	27.7	25.6	10.9	15.1	46.9	43.2	28.4	24.4	9.0
Korean Americans	33,469	7.9	92.1	39.3	26.8	22.4	7.0	75.7	8.7	42.1	22.6	23.5
Vietnamese Americans	15,325	1.7	98.3	50.7	22.1	20.1	26.5	51.5	38.8	51.1	21.6	19.7
Cambodian Americans	3,426	1.2	98.8	52.5	21.5	30.7	0.0	32.5	67.5	53.2	21.4	30.3
Hmong Americans	2,697	4.6	95.4	64.7	12.5	40.6	26.0	23.6	29.3	66.6	11.9	41.1
Laotian Americans	3,365	0.8	99.2	57.3	21.7	31.6	0.0	0.0	57.1	57.8	21.8	31.3
Thai Americans	1,410	2.9	97.1	36.5	14.0	17.8	0.0	0.0	58.5	37.5	14.4	16.6
Other Asian Americans	6,911	25.3	74.7	21.5	49.8	20.0	10.6	78.4	29.1	25.2	40.2	17.0
Hawaiian Americans	10,027	98.4	1.6	11.6	74.3	13.0	11.2	75.2	12.9	31.7	20.1	18.9
Samoan Americans	1,550	22.1	77.9	21.7	58.1	49.5	14.0	75.4	95.6	23.9	53.3	36.5
Tongan Americans	753	1.7	98.3	7.6	42.4	24.0	0.0	100.0	0.0	7.7	41.4	24.5
Guamanian Americans	2,226	20.2	79.8	18.9	61.8	16.2	8.9	67.7	26.7	21.4	60.3	13.6
Other Pacific Islander Americans	485	9.3	90.7	25.8	48.9	33.6	0.0	42.2	100.0	28.4	49.5	26.8

Table 29

Asian Pacific Americans Over 65
Percent Using Public Assistance, Percent Using Social Security, and Percent in Poverty By Nativity and Sex, for Selected Asian Pacific American Groups

	Count Total Over 65	Percent U.S.-Born Over 65	Percent Foreign Born Over 65	Total Public Assistance	Total Social Security	Total Below Poverty	U.S. Born Public Assistance	U.S. Born Social Security	U.S. Born Below Poverty	Foreign Born Public Assistance	Foreign Born Social Security	Foreign Born Below Poverty
Male	196,662	30.3	69.7	18.5	55.7	12.3	4.7	79.2	6.2	24.4	45.5	14.9
Chinese Americans	60,938	14.7	85.3	18.3	53.4	15.4	5.6	76.7	5.8	20.5	49.4	17.1
Filipino Americans	49,042	5.0	95.0	22.4	52.4	10.3	10.5	69.2	17.9	23.0	51.5	9.9
Japanese Americans	45,168	90.6	9.4	3.0	81.1	3.9	3.0	81.4	3.1	3.1	78.0	12.0
Asian Indian Americans	9,476	4.8	95.2	23.6	28.0	12.0	28.4	48.6	45.9	23.3	26.9	10.3
Korean Americans	11,661	10.3	89.7	33.2	29.6	20.7	9.9	76.9	10.1	35.9	24.1	22.0
Vietnamese Americans	6,667	1.3	98.7	46.5	24.2	21.2	29.1	46.5	46.5	46.7	23.9	20.8
Cambodian Americans	1,290	3.1	96.9	54.0	19.1	25.0	0.0	32.5	67.5	55.7	18.7	23.7
Hmong Americans	743	2.0	98.0	75.8	12.0	38.2	100.0	0.0	100.0	75.3	12.2	37.0
Laotian Americans	1,426	1.1	98.9	53.3	23.4	33.1	0.0	0.0	100.0	53.9	23.7	32.3
Thai Americans	429	4.0	96.0	43.6	10.0	13.8	6.4	0.0	0.0	45.4	10.4	14.3
Other Asian Americans	3,123	24.9	75.1	17.5	55.5	20.3	8.9	84.5	35.0	21.2	45.9	15.4
Hawaiian Americans	4,279	97.1	2.9	9.5	72.7	12.2	24.4	74.3	12.2	32.0	15.6	13.1
Samoan Americans	824	23.9	76.0	22.0	57.4	49.2	0.0	69.0	94.9	21.2	53.8	34.8
Tongan Americans	399	0.0	100.0	0.0	37.8	24.6	18.4	0.0	0.0	0.0	37.8	24.6
Guamanian Americans	984	18.2	81.8	18.0	71.1	9.3	0.0	81.6	18.4	17.9	68.8	7.3
Other Pacific Islander American:	213	21.1	78.9	28.6	43.7	27.7	18.4	42.2	100.0	36.3	44.0	8.3
Female	242,562	28.2	71.8	26.0	48.7	14.8	5.4	79.4	10.4	34.1	36.6	16.6
Chinese Americans	69,331	15.5	84.5	27.1	48.6	17.3	7.1	75.5	11.0	30.7	43.6	18.4
Filipino Americans	52,881	5.1	94.9	33.9	34.5	9.6	12.0	64.5	14.3	35.1	32.9	9.3
Japanese Americans	59,358	76.7	23.3	4.8	80.1	10.8	3.4	82.8	8.4	9.6	71.0	18.4
Asian Indian Americans	11,386	6.0	94.0	31.1	23.6	10.0	6.3	45.8	41.4	32.7	22.2	8.0
Korean Americans	21,808	6.6	93.4	42.6	25.3	23.2	4.5	74.8	7.6	45.3	21.8	24.3
Vietnamese Americans	8,658	2.0	98.0	54.0	20.4	19.2	25.3	54.0	35.1	54.6	19.7	18.9
Cambodian Americans	2,136	0.0	100.0	51.7	22.9	34.1	0.0	0.0	0.0	51.7	22.9	34.1
Hmong Americans	1,954	5.5	94.5	60.5	12.6	41.5	15.7	26.9	19.4	63.2	11.8	42.8
Laotian Americans	1,939	0.6	99.4	60.3	20.4	30.4	0.0	0.0	0.0	60.7	20.5	30.6
Thai Americans	981	2.4	97.6	33.3	15.7	19.6	0.0	0.0	100.0	34.2	16.1	17.6
Other Asian Americans	3,788	25.6	74.4	24.8	45.2	19.8	13.9	73.6	24.3	28.5	35.5	18.3
Hawaiian Americans	5,748	99.3	0.7	13.1	75.5	13.6	13.0	75.8	13.5	31.0	33.3	35.7
Samoan Americans	726	20.0	80.0	21.5	59.0	49.9	0.0	84.1	96.6	26.9	52.7	38.2
Tongan Americans	354	3.7	96.3	16.1	47.5	23.4	0.0	100.0	0.0	16.7	45.5	24.3
Guamanian Americans	1,242	21.7	78.3	19.6	54.4	21.7	2.6	58.5	32.2	24.3	53.3	18.7
Other Pacific Islander American:	272	0.0	100.0	23.5	52.9	38.2	0.0	0.0	0.0	23.5	52.9	38.2

Source: U.S. Bureau of the Census, special tabulations of the 5 percent 1990 Public Use Microdata Sample (PUMS).
Copyright (c) 1996, Larry Hajime Shinagawa, Ph.D. Department of American Multi-Cultural Studies, Sonoma State University.

Table 30
Demographic Characteristics
Of Adults on Probation
By Gender and Race
1988

Characteristics	Number of adults on probation from State or Federal courts	Percent of those persons with a known status
Sex	2,064,966	100.0
Male	1,714,114	83.0
Female	350,852	17.0
Race	1,740,553	100.0
White	1,200,720	69.0
African American	523,574	30.1
American Indian	12,061	0.7
Asian Pacific American	4,198	0.2
Ethnicity*	1,268,709	100.0
Hispanic	155,694	12.3
Non-Hispanic	1,113,015	87.7

Source: U.S. Department of Justice, 1989 Statistical Yearbook.
Note: Data are for June 30 of each year. Sex of all inmates were reported in both years. Race and ethnicity were reported for 91% of the parolees in 1988. Percentages may not add to total.

*Jurisdictions failed to report ethnicity for 46% of the probation population. Caution must be used in interpreting this category.

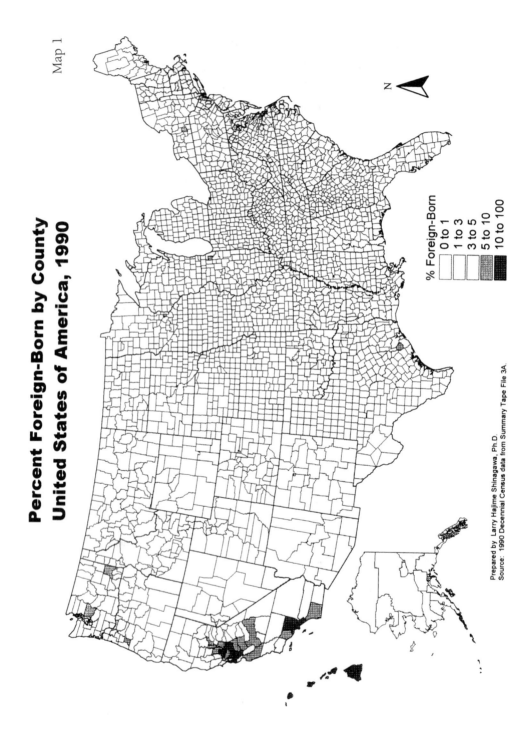

Map 1

Percent Foreign-Born by County
United States of America, 1990

N

% Foreign-Born

0 to 1
1 to 3
3 to 5
5 to 10
10 to 100

Prepared by Larry Hajime Shinagawa, Ph.D.
Source: 1990 Decennial Census data from Summary Tape File 3A.

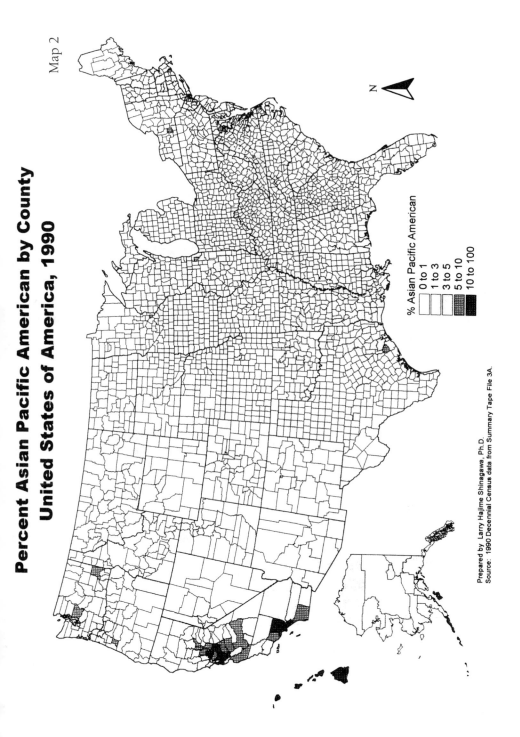

Map 2

Percent Asian Pacific American by County
United States of America, 1990

N

% Asian Pacific American

- 0 to 1
- 1 to 3
- 3 to 5
- 5 to 10
- 10 to 100

Prepared by Larry Hajime Shinagawa, Ph.D.
Source: 1990 Decennial Census data from Summary Tape File 3A.

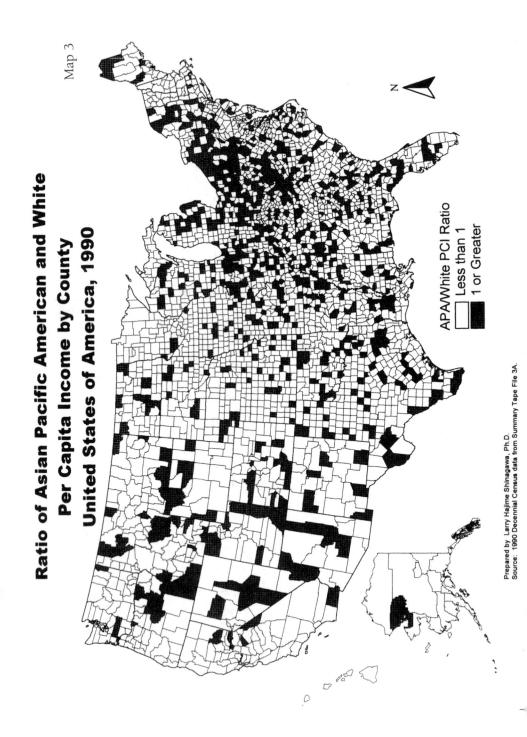

Ratio of Asian Pacific American and White
Per Capita Income by County
United States of America, 1990

Map 3

N

APA/White PCI Ratio

Less than 1

1 or Greater

Prepared by Larry Hajime Shinagawa, Ph.D.
Source: 1990 Decennial Census data from Summary Tape File 3A.

Part II.
Immigrant
Entrepreneurs

Understanding Immigrant Entrepreneurs: Theoretical and Empirical Issues

by Shubha Ghosh[*]

What are the benefits of immigration? What are the costs? The focus of recent debate on immigration policy has been on these two questions. Of course the answers depend upon the subsidiary question of benefits and costs to whom. Although several scholars have proffered answers to these questions — answers intended as policy recommendations — one element that often has been overlooked is entrepreneurship among immigrants, and the benefits they confer.

Although current immigration law creates a special category for entrepreneurs,[1] our concern is not with the big investor but with the small immigrant business owner, the vast majority of whom entered in immigrant categories for relatives or as refugees. What we know for sure is that the small immigrant business owner exists. There was an 89.3 percent increase in Asian American owned businesses between 1982 and 1987; of the firms in 1987 that were established since 1979, 80 percent were immigrant owned.[2] Recent census statistics show that 2.7 percent of all businesses in the United States were owned by Asian Pacific Islanders, with the largest percentage in Hawaii (51.4 percent) and the lowest in Vermont, South Dakota, and Maine (each at 0.2 percent).[3] In 1987 total sales and receipts generated by Asian Pacific Islander businesses were a little over $33 billion, with an annual payroll of over $3 billion in total and over 351,000 employees. In 1987 businesses run by Asian Pacific Islanders ranged across sectors, with per firm receipts across all sectors averaging $93,000. The highest average receipts per firm came from "Wholesale Trade" ($393,000). Other sectors where Asian presence is strong include "Construction" ($38,000), "Finance, Insurance and Real Estate" ($40,000), and "Manufacturing" ($144,000).[4] Despite the availability of these Census fig-

---

[*] Shubha Ghosh has a Ph.D. in Economics from the University of Michigan and a J.D. from Stanford Law School. The author has benefitted from conversations with Masao Suzuki and Bill Ong Hing.

ures, benefits created by immigrant entrepreneurship has never been fully measured by most researchers.

The entrepreneurial diversity represented by Asian Pacific immigrant businesses is remarkable. In addition to the conventional "mom and pop" grocery stores, laundries, restaurants, and liquor stores, Asian Pacific immigrant entrepreneurs are involved in clothing manufacturing, publishing, banking, jewelry, fast foods, medical equipment designing and manufacturing, herbal extracts, entertainment, fashion designing, and of course the high-tech industry. And their businesses and headquarters are located all across the United States, in virtually every state of the union.[5] In downtown Flushing, Queens, New York, Asian immigrant businesses make up many of the bustling "greengrocers, butchers, bakeries, beauty parlors, restaurants and video, fish and jewelry stores, . . . [and now the area seems] light-years away from the deterioration and vacancies that characterized it in the 1970s." Korean American merchants have flourished and become "synonymous with small business in New York City."[6] Asian Pacific Americans own over half of all small businesses in Washington, D.C. In nearby northern Virginia, a thriving Koreatown has developed with an estimated 200 Korean American-owned businesses.[7] In Seattle's busy Rainier Avenue South, hundreds of Asian Pacific American-owned shops dot the street with "restaurants, dry cleaners, discount stores, export shops, and manicure shops." In the Puget Sound area, Koreans own 70 percent of the more than 500 dry cleaning businesses and 15 beauty-supply stores.[8] Korean American entrepreneurs who own restaurants, import shops, and professional offices have also revitalized neighborhoods in Dallas. In fact, immigrants from India, as well as Pakistan, Ethiopia, Eritrea, and Ghana have become small-business owners in Dallas.[9]

The principal thesis of this paper is that the existence of a sizeable number of immigrant entrepreneurs introduces important and previously overlooked factors into the theoretical and policy discussion of immigration. For purposes of this discussion, theories of immigration can be divided into two camps: (1) free market advocates who hold that the unfettered mobility of goods and people maximizes global welfare and the welfare of individual nations and (2) interventionist advocates who propose limitations on the global mobility through either strict controls or by targeted controls in order to protect against transfers of wealth across nations or within nations. The existence of immigrant entrepreneurs — as a theoretical category, previously overlooked, and as an empirical fact, understudied — provides a common ground between these two prongs of the immigration debate. Immigrant entrepreneurs coordinate and expand markets, under the free market world view, by injecting capital into the domestic economy, although with the risk that the returns on capital may be repatriated. Immigrant entrepreneurs also can provide employment and external benefits in a way that is overlooked by the interventionist world view. If the focus is on the benefits and costs of immigration, then the role of immigrant entrepreneurs must be considered.

This paper should be read with two caveats. First, the conclusions of this paper are impartial ones; this is not an advocacy piece for a particular policy agenda. Instead, the purpose is to address one area generally overlooked in the immigration debate: the existence and impact of immigrant entrepreneurs. This piece is intended to provoke thought and discussion, and although several policy conclusions can be imagined, including providing preferences for certain entrepreneurial groups or expanding current categories for entrepreneurship, the advocacy of particular reform is not intended. Indeed, the impressive figures on Asian Pacific entrepreneurs set forth above have resulted from the current, mostly family-based, immigration system. Many connections could be made between the theory and the application, but those discussions are for future debate.

The second caveat relates to the limitation of examples presented in this paper just to Asian immigrants. The choice of this group is dictated by the purpose of this project. There is no presumption that Asian immigrants are somehow particularly more fit for entrepreneurship or are different from other immigrants. Therefore, any attempt to use this research to favor Asian immigrants would be a misuse of this paper. By focusing on the Asian subpopulation of immigrants, this paper addresses several open hypotheses about immigrant entrepreneurs, such as the "protected market" hypothesis, which states that immigrant business success results in part from providing services to immigrants of the same ethnicity.[10] As argued below, the protected market hypothesis is not as successful at explaining the success of Asian entrepreneurs as the "capital endowment hypothesis."[11] This result may mitigate the role of purely ethnic or cultural factors in explaining entrepreneurial success. The next logical step is to expand the analysis to other ethnic groups and conduct cross-ethnic group comparisons, this paper's focus on Asian entrepreneurs is intended to serve as a model for future researchers rather than as a model for policy makers or advocates seeking to single out the Asian population for different treatment.

The next section places the immigrant entrepreneur in the context of various theoretical models of immigration and trade. The following section moves from the theoretical to the empirical and focuses on actual determinants of the success of Asian entrepreneurs in the United States. The final section ties the theoretical and empirical work together as a critique of various immigration reform proposals, particularly those of Huddle and Borjas.

The Immigrant Entrepreneur, Free Trade, And Protectionism

As shown by the statistics cited above and discussed below, immigrant entrepreneurs are a real phenomenon. This section of the paper, however, approaches the existence of immigrant entrepreneurs from a purely theoretical perspective. The basic question is, what does the existence of immigrant entrepreneurs imply about the various possible theoretical constructs used to explain trade and immigration. Put another way, do immigrant entrepreneurs support or destroy a particular theoretical construction? This section focuses on two principal theories: the free trade theory and the various theories that I collectively call the interventionist theory.

The economic theory of free trade is common knowledge: countries under conditions of perfect competition will trade in goods according to the principle of comparative advantage. Comparative advantage means that a country will export those goods that it can produce more cheaply in relative terms than other countries.[12] To take a simple example, assuming goods can be produced with a combination of human labor and physical capital, then a country that has more labor relative to capital than other countries will tend to have a comparative advantage in those goods that use more labor relative to capital, i.e., "labor intensive goods." Although several factors, such as differences in consumption patterns and tastes across countries and imperfect markets like monopolies, may cause actual trade to deviate from this theoretical prediction, the economic theory of free trade stands firmly on the principle of comparative advantage. The corollary to this theory is that comparative advantage will generate a surplus that will increase world income, that is, the sum of incomes of all countries. Because of gains from trade, free trade is said to be more efficient than an autarkic policy of national self-sufficiency and nonreliance on imports or economic aid.

The free trade theory described above is textbook material. Variants appear in many debates about trade policy. Less often emphasized is the subtle effect of free trade: factor price equalization, which theoretically describes the tendency of factor prices, including wages and returns to capital, to equalize under free trade conditions. Analytically, factor price equalization result depends on many assumptions about the underlying technology by which goods are produced. Conceptually, the principle captures an important aspect of free trade in goods: integration of disparate and isolated regions through exchange. In a world of autarky, workers in region A may be earning considerably less than those in region B.[13] In contrast, a world of perfect factor price equaliation would result eventually in equal wages throughout each region. Similarly the returns to capital may differ widely between the regions in an autarky. One way to equalize factor payments under the free trade theory is to have interregional mobility of labor and capital; the principle of arbitrage or the law of one price would guarantee equalization of factor prices. Under the factor price equalization proposition, equality of factor returns could also result by free exchange of goods that are produced with factors of production. Put another way, factor price equalization means that trade in goods substitutes for the global mobility of factors of production.

Free trade theory taken to its limits means that it would be redundant to advocate for both free trade in goods and free migration because the former would simply be a substitute for the latter. A stronger implication is that the goal of free migration may work against goals of free trade. Free trade in goods and free migration, however, may not be redundant positions if, for instance, political factors prevented trade from being completely free. Trade, for example, could be used as a strategic weapon for geopolitical or security reasons. In such a world, where trade plays the role both of integrating markets and protecting national security, a free migration policy might be necessary to guarantee economic benefits of free markets without losing the use of free trade as a strategic weapon.

So far we have spoken very abstractly about factors of production, trade, and mobility of factors. What does this analysis have to do with immigrant entrepreneurs? The role that immigrant entrepreneurs play in the theory of free trade rests specifically on which factors of productions they embody. While immigrant entrepreneurs certainly constitute labor and their mobility is very likely in response to differences in wages, entrepreneurs also constitute capital since many bring financial capital with them to invest in the United States. Furthermore immigrant entrepreneurs embody certain skills or human capital. Explaining immigrant entrepreneurs within the context of free trade theory entails explaining first, why free trade fails to equalize differences in wage rates, returns to financial capital or returns to human capital globally and second, how immigrant entrepreneurs substitute for the missing global market in goods.[14]

On the surface, encouraging immigrant entrepreneurs is arguably a strong free trade position, but a closer consideration of the free trade theory suggests certain deficiencies in explaining why immigrant entrepreneurship occurs in the first place. Would, for example, free trade theory predict that immigrant entrepreneurship should decline as markets open up? This prediction is not wholly consistent with the ethnic pattern of Asian immigrant entrepreneurs who originate from India (protectionist vis-a-vis the world), South Korea (less protectionist than India) and Southeast Asia (more recently the least protectionist of the three).[15] The problem with the free trade position is that it cannot wholly explain where differences in comparative advantage arise. In support of the free trade theory, we should add that for the purposes of realizing gains from trade the question of the origins of comparative advantage is irrelevant. Understanding the differences can, however, uncover previously unexplored benefits of immigrant entrepreneurs. Interventionist theories can better aid this exploration.

What we refer to as the interventionist theory actually encompasses a range of theories, including economist Paul Krugman's models of trade under increasing returns and economist George Borjas' theory of immigration and human capital.[16] The main theme of the interventionist theory is that differences across nations result from the existence of "external economies," benefits or costs that arise from an exchange that affects those who are not party to the exchange. For example, the existence of one or two educated individuals in an economy may not have much of an impact on output. Increasing the number, though, may result in external economies: not only does the economy benefit from the individual contributions but also from the network of educated individuals who can work together. External economies can also be negative, such as those that arise from having too many individuals taking advantage of a government entitlement program: participants beyond a certain number may increase the costs of the program above the additional direct costs of their participation.[17]

The presence of external economies alters the free trade theory in two ways. Free trade by itself may not be enough to generate all the potential gains from trade. The United States may need more scientists, for example. Individuals may not, however, have the full incentive to become scientists if they cannot capture the full additional benefits generated by entering the field. In this case, financial incentives or quotas may be needed to correct the problem. The question of what institution should implement these incentives is left to others. The initial inclination may be to designate this role to "the government," even though the question of how large a role government should play is still unsettled. Another alternative is the business sector, which may be able to exploit external economies because of size and access to financial markets. Leaving this point aside, this type of argument is what essentially buttresses government intervention programs that target the class of immigrants permitted into the country.

The concept of external economies also fills in the missing element of the free trade theory: the origins of comparative advantage. According to the interventionist view, comparative advantage arises from that combination of accident and planning which we call history.[18] Some regions, for instance, gain a comparative advantage in computer technology because at some point in time a critical mass of entrepreneurs came together to generate external economies in the production of computers. Other regions became well endowed in certain types of human capital because of decisions by individuals to invest in human capital and in the creation of institutions to support its development. Thus, external economies can explain the paradox within free trade theory of why countries that vary in protectionist policies, such as India and Southeast Asia, do not vary as much in immigration. While free trade theory would tend to argue that immigration substitutes for trade in goods, interventionist theory would look at factors that promote and sustain immigration from one country, such as the Vietnam War that resulted in Southeast Asian refugees entering the country or the liberal U.S. immigration policy toward India after 1965. Historical events coupled with the presence of external economies, can explain why immigration occurs from countries that are otherwise different under free trade theory.

Furthermore, not only can external economies help us understand the origins of comparative advantage, the concept is useful in explaining a trade phenomenon that would otherwise be unexplainable by free trade theory: intra-industry trade, or trade between different countries in the same commodity, such as the global automobile market. In some ways, immigrant entrepreneurs also represent a species of intra-industry trade: U.S. investors take their capital overseas to invest in business at the same time that immigrants bring their capital to the United States. To the extent that immigrant entrepreneurship is an example of intra-industry trade, it can be explained by external economies.

Just as comparative advantage had its corollary in the theory of gains from trade, so external economies has a corollary in the phenomenon of rent seeking. As discussed above, the reason that external economies do not lead necessarily to the realization of the full gains from trade is that an individual may not be able personally to capture all additional benefits the concept of external economies provides for the economy. The existence of these additional benefits, however, creates incentives for entry into markets that have external economies. Of course these incentives also exist under free trade, but the chief difference is that under free trade all rents are dissipated. Such is not the case when there are external economies: Being the first to enter a market with external economies allows an entrepreneur to capture much of the rents, and provide incentives to keep others out of the market even though society may gain from having more entrepreneurs enter. This tension between individual and societal interests arises from the presence of external economies and rent seeking.

To fully understand tensions created by immigration, we need also to consider negative external economies. A system of government entitlement can create negative external economies since the program beneficiaries often do not bear program costs. Negative external economies can be exacerbated by fraud and corruption. These phenomena all result from rent seeking behavior. Draconian measures like Proposition 187, as well as more moderate immigration reforms, are motivated in part by the problems of negative external economies generated by entitlement programs. By defining which individuals are entitled to the programs — documented and undocumented immigrants, for instance — policy makers seek to mitigate the negative external economies. Proposals to do so, however, often ignore, or at least fail to balance, potentially positive external economies that motivate immigration.

Mainstream economic research is lacking in focused and detailed research on the phenomenon of entrepreneurship.[19] Consequently, immigrant entrepreneurship poses problems for both the free trade and the interventionist theories. Immigrant entrepreneurship is consistent with free trade theory but cannot be fully explained by it. Immigrant entrepreneurship potentially plays a role in interventionist theory, but it is not clear *a priori* whether external economies are a net positive or a net negative. While free market theory has no explanation, it would advocate unrestricted entry as immigration policy. Intervention theory has an explanation but it cannot provide a specific policy recommendation to either encourage or limit immigration.[20]

Immigrant entrepreneurship poses challenges to many elements of free trade and interventionist theories of trade and migration. An empirical analysis of the role of immigrant entrepreneurs, presented in the next section, outlines further challenges.

The Effects Of Immigrant Entrepreneurs On Labor Markets, Fiscal Finance, And Regional Economies

Some empirical information can be presented on the economic effects of immigrant entrepreneurs but the topic is open for future research. The purpose of this section is not to offer a complete empirical analysis. This section has two goals. The first is to demonstrate that empirical findings that appear to be robust provide even more challenges to the theoretical positions described in the previous section and to any related policy prescriptions. The second is to highlight impediments, both theoretical and empirical, to the pursuit of empirical research on immigrant entrepreneurship and to provide some skepticism about various empirical claims made in the media. Although the focus is on immigrant entrepreneurship, immigration is addressed broadly. Implications for immigrant entrepreneurship are developed in each subsequent section.

Immigrant Entrepreneurs and Labor Markets

The free trade theory has a definite prediction about effects of immigrants on domestic wages and employment: Immigration will increase the supply of domestic workers, thereby lowering wages and raising employment. The prediction of interventionist theorists, on the other hand, is not so clear. Although many interventionist theorists would accept the basic free trade supply-and-demand model, they would consider other factors as well. For example, interventionists who emphasize positive externalities associated with immigrants would emphasize higher skill level of immigrants, which according to this view, may increase wages in the long run by improving the quality of the workforce. In addition, highly skilled immigrant workers may not substitute for domestic workers so that job competition may be minimal. Some may even predict a positive effect on employment because skilled workers and unskilled workers may actually complement the native force.[21] In contrast, interventionist theorists focusing on negative externalities generated by immigrants would predict that employment may worsen with immigration because of increased public assistance utilization by immigrants and by domestic workers who now face competition in labor markets and lower wages.

Empirical findings support both theories. The fundamental problem with assessing the effects of immigrants on labor markets is isolating immigration from other variables, such as macroeconomic trends and regional effects. In 1980, the influx of Mariel Cubans into Miami provided economist David Card with a subject for study.[22] The arrival was an external change in the economic environment of Miami, which allowed Professor Card to isolate the effects of migration from other changes. Interestingly he found that the increase in migration had no effect on unemployment rates or wages of low-skilled native workers. While the earnings dropped for Latinos in the early 1980s, earnings for African Americans remained constant up to 1981, dropped from 1982-83, and then rose in 1984. Professor Card attributed the phenomena to the ability of Miami's strong textile and clothing industries to absorb unskilled workers.

Professor Card's results are consistent with those reported in a recent study from the Alexis de Tocqueville Institution.[23] That study looked at the correlation between state level unemployment and immigration and found a negative correlation. The implication is that serious causation problems arise in interpreting the data. While Professor Card was able to treat the arrival of Cubans into Miami as an external event and could thus interpret resulting changes causally, authors of the de Tocqueville study, however, could not conclude that immigration reduces unemployment or that lower unemployment attracts immigration. The de Tocqueville study's finding of negative correlation is also not completely consistent with the view that immigration tends to increase unemployment either. A more complete study and analysis must include the relationships between local wages and immigration.

Several principal lessons can be drawn from studies of the impact of immigration on labor markets. First, the effect of immigration on labor markets varies regionally.[24] One pattern is that immigrants occupy a niche in the low wage, unskilled segment of the labor market. This pattern tends to create an empirical bias toward the finding that immigration lowers wages since regions with a higher proportion of immigrants will tend to have lower wages. Therefore, empirical studies of the effects of immigration on wages should be careful in separating out the sorting effect (i.e., immigrants tend to be found in the low wage sector) from the market effect (i.e., immigrants do in fact depress wages). Some studies that have attempted to disentangle these two effects have found that immigrants tend to have the largest negative effect on wages of fellow immigrants and a lesser, or sometimes even negligible, effect on the wages of young African Americans and Latinos.[25] One researcher concluded from an international comparison that a 10 percent increase of immigration into a country would have less than a 1 percent depressing effect on wages.[26]

Second, the sorting effect of immigrants into the low wage sector tends to increase wages for some minority groups by shifting them into higher paid jobs, a pattern observed in New York and Los Angeles.[27] This upward push on wages for some non-immigrant minority groups is strengthened by the presence of immigrant entrepreneurs who provide employment in some formerly depressed regions. Not only are external benefits generated for minority groups but they are also generated from the rejuvenation of certain industries that would otherwise be in decline without the presence of immigrant labor. Studies of the automobile parts, textile, and garment industries support this finding.[28]

Whether these findings support the free trade or the interventionist theory is impossible to say. The empirical findings are consistent with both the view that immigration works to integrate disparate, regional markets and the view that immigration is in response to increasing returns to scale. The presence of immigrant entrepreneurs makes the situation even more complicated. While traditional analysis of immigration focuses squarely on changes in the supply of workers, immigrant entrepreneurs potentially affect the demand and the supply of labor since immigrant entrepreneurs not only demand additional labor for their business ventures but also supply labor to other sectors. The theoretical prediction of how wages are affected is ambiguous, because immigrant entrepreneurs could potentially increase, decrease, or have no effect on wages. The effect on employment, however, is unambiguous since immigrant entrepreneurs would increase employment by expanding both the demand for, and supply of, workers.

Sociologists Ivan Light and Carolyn Rosenstein recently published the first comprehensive study of the effect of immigrant entrepreneurs on regional economies, and their findings clarify the ambiguous theoretical predictions. Looking at data on self-employment as a measure of entrepreneurship, they found that during the '70s, "[h]igh rates of immigrant self-employment neither increase[d] nor reduce[d] self-employment of native whites."[29] During this period the self-employment rate was also higher among the foreign born than among native born African Americans, Asians, Latinos, and whites in the metropolitan areas studied. In addition, the authors found strong regional effects on entrepreneurship across all regions of the United States, with the strongest effects being in New York, New Jersey, Pennsylvania, the East Central United States, and the South Atlantic. They also found no depressing effects on the earnings of native whites or African Americans regionally.[30]

Measuring effects of immigrant entrepreneurs on labor markets is complicated by the entrepreneurship's hybrid production factor: part labor, part capital. The impact can best be seen within the free trade theory. To the extent that immigrant entrepreneurs are motivated by factor price differences, *i.e.*, returns to entrepreneurship are greater domestically than overseas, free trade theorists would predict that immigrant entrepreneurs would lead to a drop in the domestic factor price in order to equalize the differences. The issue, however, is the relevant factor price. Wages do not adequately measure the underlying factor price because wages earned by entrepreneurs could be measuring the revenues generated by their business ventures. Factor price equalization does not imply that revenues would be equalized across regions, only the returns to the mobile factor. Under the free trade theory, returns to the skill owned by entrepreneurs should equalize across regions with migration. The skill would be a hybrid of returns to capital and wages not readily available.

Furthermore, immigrant entrepreneurs affect capital markets, as well as labor markets. Under the assumption that capital markets are perfectly competitive, an increase in immigrant entrepreneurs would affect both the supply of financial capital and the demand for financial capital; once again the effect on the price, in this case, the interest rate would be ambiguous. Empirical work, so far non-existent, could clarify the ambiguity.

The analysis, whether under the free trade theory or under the interventionist theory, is riddled by what economists refer to as the "missing market problem."[31] Often immigrant entrepreneurs are leaving one vacuum to enter another. For example, several groups migrating from the Indian sub-Continent are not leaving behind entrepreneurial opportunities, they are leaving tight labor markets. Those who do become entrepreneurs in the United States do not necessarily do so in regions that are centers for entrepreneurial activity. Immigrant entrepreneurs act not only as market participants but also as market creators and, thus, do not necessarily cause factor prices to equalize across regions. Factor prices may instead rise domestically and not change at all in the foreign country. The domestic increase rises as entrepreneurs push up the demand for labor and other production factors in previously underdeveloped regions. While this possibility is often overlooked under the free trade theory, it is consistent with the interventionist theory. Entrepreneurs who create markets generate rents for themselves and external benefits for others. This prediction is consistent with much of the empirical research discussed below.

The difficult question is how capital markets affect, and are affected by, markets created by entrepreneurs. The access to capital markets may be a critical determinant of business survivability. Timothy Bates shows that among Asian immigrant entrepreneurs in 1979, 43.1 percent borrowed from financial institutions and 37.7 percent from family.[32] Among the ones who borrowed from institutions, 20.4 percent also borrowed from family.[33] The average loan from financial institutions was greater than that from family, and the resulting debt-equity ratio was higher as well among those who borrowed from financial institutions than those who borrowed from family. He also found that initial capitalization directly affected survivability of the businesses over the eight-year period of his study.[34] We do not know how immigrant entrepreneurs affect capital markets. For example, do they dominate loans that might otherwise have gone to native entrepreneurs? Do immigrant entrepreneurs face the same difficulties as native-born minority groups in credit markets? Finally, do immigrant entrepreneurs raise the cost of borrowing for native entrepreneurs? The relationship between immigrant entrepreneurs and credit markets is an open and crucial area for further inquiry.[35]

Immigrant Entrepreneurs And Fiscal Finance

Fiscal finance issues are matters of federal, state, and regional governments. Unfortunately many researchers who have commented on the impact of entrepreneurs on fiscal finance have ignored federalism issues. This section explicitly distinguishes between federal and local finance issues. Once again we begin with a discussion of the effects of immigrants in general on fiscal finance and then proceed to the special problems raised by immigrant entrepreneurs in particular.

The following fundamental concepts will facilitate analysis of the next point:

Y = gross national product
C = total consumption
S = total savings
I = total private investment
G = total government spending, including spending on entitlement and government investments
T = total federal taxes collected
X = total exports
M = total imports

The basic relationship among these concepts is as follows: $Y = C + I + G + (X - M)$. That is to say, in the aggregate, gross national product must be spent on consumption, private investment, government spending, and net exports. A similar relationship holds for the consumption side of the equation. Since gross national product represents the total income earned by all members of society, it must also be true that $Y = C + S + T$, which states that total income is consumed, saved, or paid in taxes. Combining and rearranging these equations allows us to derive the basic formula that provides a relationship among all the potential deficits in society: $0 = (I - S) + (G - T) + (X - M)$. This states that, in the aggregate, the budget deficit $(G - T)$ must be balanced by the trade surplus $(X - M)$ and the savings deficit $(I - S)$. The last equation summarizes the basic macroeconomic relationships in the economy and provides a basis for comparing various arguments concerning the effect of immigration on federal fiscal finance.

Under the free trade view, immigration substitutes for free trade. One of the effects of immigration would be to lower the amount of imports and correspondingly to raise the trade surplus $(X - M)$. Since all deficits must balance, the effect of increased immigration on the trade surplus must be balanced by either a decrease in the budget deficit or a decrease in the savings deficit. The premise that immigration substitutes for trade in goods, however, is suspect, as discussed above. Furthermore, which deficit is affected by immigration is largely an empirical matter. Immigration may have some counteracting effects as well, such as increasing savings or increasing taxes. Immigration may also raise the volume of exports if immigrant entrepreneurs produce and sell goods overseas or even raise the volume of imports if immigration increases the demand for goods from overseas. What matters is not the direction of the effects on these elements of the GNP, that is, whether the effects are positive or negative, but the magnitude of the effects. Isolating the role immigration plays in affecting these individual variables is difficult.

The presence of external costs and benefits makes predictions even harder. Interventionist theorists would have difficulty in isolating the effects of immigration on the GNP and its elements because, as discussed in this paper, external benefits and costs may largely be local phenomena from which extrapolating to the macro economy is complex. Given increasing returns, an immigration multiplier theoretically exists so that an increase in immigration stimulates local economies and increases gross national product. This effect is hard — if not impossible — to measure, but it contrasts with the free trade view, which implies that immigration substitutes for trade in goods. The effect contrasts also with "zero sum" views of immigration, which would suggest immigrants crowd out many of the benefits earned by natives. To the extent, however, that interventionist theorists posit negative externalities generated by immigrants — through use of entitlement programs, for example — immigration would increase the government deficit.

Immigrant entrepreneurs introduce several interesting factors into the analysis. In contrast to the free trade view, immigrant entrepreneurs do not substitute for markets in goods; they most likely create markets regionally. The creation of previously missing markets potentially increases gross national product through the effects on regional economies in much the same way as the "immigration multiplier" described in the previous paragraph. In this way, interventionist theorists would appreciate effects of immigrant entrepreneurs in a way that free trade theorists do not. Immigrant entrepreneurs can, however, generate the immigration multiplier without generating external benefits. In the framework of national income identity equations discussed above, activities of immigrant entrepreneurs would also affect the private investment component of the savings deficit equation and may also affect the import component to the extent they repatriate many of the goods produced domestically. Once again the magnitude of these effects is hard to measure.

Because of measurement problems on the federal level, researchers have tended to study the more manageable regional effects of immigration on fiscal finance, even though this regional focus is misleading for several reasons. Foremost is the disregard of the potential national effects of immigration discussed above. These ignored effects, however, undercut the finding that immigrants are a net burden to regional economies because they contribute less to the regional economy than they take. This fact, as others have pointed out, is true for all citizens.[36] As a result of local economies of scale and large fixed costs of infrastructure, most citizens provide less to their local governments than they receive in local services. Focusing solely on regional effects biases studies toward a finding that immigrants are a net burden. This criticism has been correctly leveled against the study of the Los Angeles County Board of Supervisors, which concluded that immigrants imposed an annual net cost of $808 million to the county.[37] This figure was determined by measuring costs imposed on various local public services — such as health, justice, and public social services — and the local tax revenue paid by immigrants. Although the study acknowledged an amount of aggregate taxes above local costs, the study also discounted the total amount of taxes paid because most of that revenue went to the federal government. The study was arguably correct to focus on local costs and local taxes paid, but this approach overlooks the fact that much of the federal tax revenues trickle back to state coffers in the form of block grants and subsidies. Completely ignoring federal taxes paid disregards some of the benefits generated by immigrants.

A similar error is made by economist Donald Huddle in calculating net costs of immigrants through gross measures of consumption of public services. His measurements overlook the federal structure of fiscal finance and do not take into account that immigrants contribute to the fisc in many ways other than just through payment of income taxes.[38] Specifically, immigrants pay local property taxes and sales taxes, the latter often regressive (where the tax rate decreases as income increases) and therefore placing a heavier burden on immigrants. More subtly, Huddle's study overlooks intergenerational transfers of money, goods, and services within immigrant social groups that may often substitute for dependence on public services. Thus, measuring present welfare dependence from a projection of past use would be wrong because these transfers would result in vast differences across generations in consumption of public services. This last point is underscored by a recent study, which found that compared to the native-born population, newer immigrants are concentrated in the youthful workforce age range, during which "people contribute more to the coffers than they draw out."[39]

Immigrant entrepreneurs, of course, add further complications to the analysis. Economists Rebecca Clark and Jeffrey Passell criticized the Los Angeles Internal Services study for ignoring revenues and taxes generated by immigrant-owned businesses and "multiplier effects" of job creation from immigrant businesses.[40] Problems with measuring these factors stem from the lack of data and the lack of a good conceptual framework to balance effects on the regional versus national economy. The latter difficulty also arises because of inherent tensions in fiscal federalism between regional and national powers. The data problem has been addressed in a promising way by recent research conducted by Light and Rosenstein and is discussed in the next sub-section.

Immigrant Entrepreneurs and Regional Economies

Understanding immigrant entrepreneurs, whether within the free trade view or the interventionist, entails recognizing that entrepreneurs provide a service. Much of the literature on the sociology of entrepreneurship is not helpful in this regard because the common prediction is that entrepreneurship declines over time as market economies mature and develop. This sociological argument has an interesting parallel in economics literature, which shows that as market economies mature and develop, the importance of the managerial class grows and that of the entrepreneurial class wanes.[41] Light and Rosenstein challenge many of sociological and economic arguments by demonstrating that, at least in regional economies, entrepreneurship has not waned and perhaps has increased, especially with the influx of immigrants. Their causal model attempts to explain the persistence of entrepreneurship by examining factors affecting the demand and supply of entrepreneurs.[42]

Light and Rosenstein focus on general demand factors, that is, those that are national in scope and work across all metropolitan areas, and on specific demand factors, which are purely local. These factors are measured for the most part by dummy variables to reflect the region, population ethnicity, and industrial structure. They also include measures of mean income by region. Not too surprisingly, they found that, on the demand side, specific factors were better able to explain statistically the rate of self-employment locally.[43] What is somewhat frustrating about their study is that determining exactly which specific factors affect the demand for entrepreneurs is impossible because of the lack of more detailed data on the economic and social characteristics of the regions studied in the sample. Bates' study of the survivability of Asian immigrant businesses fills in one gap in the puzzle. He found that one very important survivability factor was the entrepreneur's ability to service demands outside of the particular ethnic group. Those businesses that survived and were more profitable were those that served the African American community rather than the Asian community alone.[44]

Light and Rosenstein's stronger results come from measuring supply factors that affect immigrant entrepreneurship. On this point, they provide very cogent findings that challenge the conclusion of much of the sociological and economic literature that entrepreneurship wanes as market economies mature. Considering such supply factors as ethnicity and sectoral composition of local economies, once again measured with dummy variables, they conclude that these supply variables are very significant in explaining the rate of self-employment locally and that the supply factors make the effects of the demand factors larger.[45] These findings support the conclusion that supply factors can counter any tendency for entrepreneurship to wane as markets mature.

Also frustrating is discerning exactly what is being measured. For example, Light and Rosenstein find that rates of entrepreneurship are positively related with the percentage of population that is Asian and negatively related with the percentage of population that is African American. They offer little guidance as to how to interpret this result except to say that in some way culture matters.[46] What is especially confounding is that this result is not completely consistent with the hypothesis that entrepreneurship results in part from discrimination in labor markets. Fortunately, part of the puzzle once again is filled in by Bates' research on Asian immigrant-owned businesses, which found that initial capitalization was a key variable in explaining survivability.[47] This result suggests that while discrimination in labor markets may explain entrepreneurial success, access to capital markets may be an even more important explanatory variable. Access to capital markets may, in fact, explain Light and Rosenstein's results regarding the relative self-employment rates among Asians and African Americans.[48]

What is perhaps most frustrating is the impossibility of extrapolating from Light and Rosenstein's findings to make inferences or further findings about the many economic factors discussed above. Their research suggests one conclusion: immigrant entrepreneurs are linked to local economies. The unknowns are how these linkages occur, how large they are, and how they filter to, and affect, the national economy. Yet their research is stimulating despite some of the frustrations and offers challenges for future research.

Summary

The issue of immigration has created some unexpected political alignments. Progressives like the late Barbara Jordan ostensibly adopt the same position toward immigration as conservatives such as Patrick Buchanan. The rather odd constellation of political opinions reflects the varying interest groups affected by immigration.

In this paper we have neither attempted to disentangle the politics of immigration, nor to address social forces that have led to the current immigration debate. Instead we highlighted the hidden economic and social assumptions that affect how individuals, whether acting in the legislature or in the voting booth, weigh costs and benefits of immigration. The major lesson of this paper is that entrepreneurship has been an overlooked element in the immigration debate.

This conclusions summarizes why immigrant entrepreneurship matters and where future research energies should be directed. The "why" question can best be understood in the context of two proposals that have recently garnered policy attention. The first propagated by Huddle, is that immigrants are too large a drain on the public fisc and therefore should be limited. This analysis pays no attention to benefits provided by immigrant entrepreneurs. No claims are made here about the size of these benefits except to assert that the benefits are positive and should be considered before supporting policies. Similarly, the reality of immigrant entrepreneurs has implications for Borjas' pro-immigrant policies. While Huddle seeks limits on immigration, Borjas advocates targeting policy to promote immigration of highly skilled immigrants. Borjas' research provides much compelling evidence on the benefits provided by immigrants in terms of human capital, but his analysis overlooks the benefits of immigrant entrepreneurs. There is a strong reason to include entrepreneurship among the human capital skills targeted in promoting immigration. Recall however, that today's entrepreneurs have entered as relatives and refugees. Immigrant entrepreneurs, then, have implications for both conservative and progressive immigration policies.

Further research is needed to flesh out the details highlighted in this paper and to answer questions concerning immigration entrepreneurs. Some issues include the following:

Capital Markets. How is the success of immigrant entrepreneurs affected by access to capital markets? Do immigrant entrepreneurs have easier access to capital than native minorities? To what extent do immigrant entrepreneurs rely on, or contribute to, family and social networks through transfers?

Discrimination. Light and Rosenstein present compelling evidence that immigrant entrepreneurship is often a response to discrimination in labor markets. The question is: why has entrepreneurship not been a successful response for other groups that have suffered from discrimination? Our null hypothesis is that access to capital markets explains the difference.

Contributions of immigrant entrepreneurs to local taxes. Many studies of the economic impact of immigrants have focused on crude estimates of immigrant contributions to federal taxes. Some researchers have discussed the contribution to local sales and property taxes as well. What is missing is a study of the contributions that immigrant entrepreneurs make to local taxes by creating businesses that generate sales taxes, improving property values — thus raising property taxes, and creating employment — therefore increasing income taxes.

Externalities generated by immigrant entrepreneurs to regional economies.
Many of the case studies presented in this most current LEAP project contribute to the necessary research agenda. We need more detailed studies of
this kind, however, to understand better the range of businesses to which
immigrant entrepreneurs contribute. Along these lines, we need to know
how these various businesses affect employment, earnings, and development of local infrastructure. Vis-a-vis the last point, we would like to know
whether immigrant entrepreneurs have "agglomeration effects," that is, does
the creation of immigrant entrepreneur businesses help generate other businesses and investments?

Effects on the national economy. Light and Rosenstein suggest that "just
encouraging entrepreneurship can have a significant, cost-effective impact
upon the reduction of poverty, the promotion of economic growth, job
creation, and even the reduction of intergroup conflict in society."[49] Although proposed regional studies go a long way in answering some of these
questions, the subsequent question is: how do these regional effects trans-
late to the national economy? For example, if immigrant entrepreneurship
reduces poverty and unemployment, do these benefits affect federal spending
on poverty and unemployment? If so, how much? As discussed in this
paper, this question is perhaps the most difficult to answer.

This research agenda should be tempered by the reality that overemp-
hasizing the effects of immigrant entrepreneurship may be easy. In the
context of the global economy, or even the national economy, movement
away from entrepreneurship to managerial power militates against entrepreneurship benefits. Regional economies may, however, benefit substantially from entrepreneurship as the research discussed in this paper suggests. Nonetheless, effects should not prejudged in either direction. What
is important is that as the immigration debate moves toward a question of
benefits and costs, immigrant entrepreneurship should not be overlooked.

Notes

1   Federal immigration law creates a special category of "alien entrepreneur," defined as
    an alien intending to start employment-generating activity (10 jobs) in the United
    States with an initial capital investment of $1 million dollars. See 8 U.S.C. 1186b.

2   Timothy Bates, "Social Resources Generated by Group Support Networks May Not Be
    Beneficial to Asian Immigrant-Owned Small Businesses," *Social Forces* 72 no. 3 (March
    1994):671-89.

3   "Asians in America, 1990 Census," Bureau of Census, U.S. Dept. of Commerce, *Survey
    of Minority Owned Business Enterprises* (Washington, D.C., June 1991).

4   *Ibid.*

5   "Transpacific 100 Great Asian American Entrepreneurs," *Transpacific*, December 1994. Editor's note: see also the papers in this report by Edward Park and Melanie Erasmus.

6   Cara S. Trager, "Despite Market's Cooling, Flushing is Still Hot," 16 December 1994, *Newsday*, sec. E, p. 4; Lynette Holloway, "The Cost of Success; Superstores' Impact on Small Grocers Strains Koreans' traditional Spirit of Community," *The Dallas Morning News*, 29 January 1995, sec. A, p. 1.

7   Daniel Choi, *History of Korean-Americans in the Washington, D.C. Area 1883-1993* (Korean Association of Greater Washington, 1995); Lena H. Sun, "Videotape Explains Legal System to Asian Americans," *The Washington Post*, 17 December 1995, sec. B, p. 7.

8   Karen Ogden, "Korean Americans Find a Home in Federal Way; Community Thrives in Receptive City," *News Tribune*, 31 July 1995, sec. B, p. 1; Stanley Holmes, "Cosmetic Changes—Koreans are Moving Into a Beauty-Supply Market Once Dominated by African Americans," *The Seattle Times*, 24 September 1995, sec. F, p. 1.

9   Bill Marvel, "A Century of Newcomers; Immigrants from as Far Away as Milan, Moscow and Monterrey Have Helped Shape Dallas' History," *The Dallas Morning News*, 30 October 1995, sec. C, p. 1.

10   Timothy Bates, "Determinants of Survival and Profitability Among Asian Immigrant-Owned Small Businesses" paper presented at the Center for Economic Studies, U.S. Bureau of Census, Washington, D.C., Aug. 1993, 5-9.

11   *Ibid.*

12   For an excellent overview of trade theory, see Avinash Dixit, *Theory of International Trade* (1986).

13   In contrast, a world of perfect factor price equalization would result eventually in equal wages throughout the region.

14   *Ibid.* For another perspective that incorporates external economies see Elhanin Helpman and Paul Krugman, *Increasing Returns and The Theory of International Trade* (1985).

15   For a general discussion of these patterns, see Ivan Light *Ethnic Enterprises in America* (1972), Ivan Light and Edna Bonacich, *Immigrant Entrepreneurs: Koreans in Los Angeles* (1988), and Ivan Light and Carolyn Rosenstein, *Race, Ethnicity, and Entrepreneurship in Urban America* (1995).

16   See Paul Krugman, *Geography and International Trade* (1991) and Paul Krugman, *Peddling Prosperity* (1994). Also see George J. Borjas, "The Economic Benefits from Immigration," *Journal of Economic Perspectives* 9 (1995) 3-22.

17   Richard Cornes and Todd Sandler, *The Theory of Externalities, Public Goods, and Club Goods* (1986).

18   See Krugman, *Geography and International Trade*.

19   For a discussion of the paucity of research on entrepreneurship among economists, see Mark Blaug, *Economic Theory in Retrospect*, 4th ed. (1993) 458-65. Blaug discusses three theories about entrepreneurship: (1) Frank Knight's theory, which analyzed entrepreneurship as a response to business uncertainty, (2) Joseph Schumpeter's, which analyzed entrepreneurship as the basis for technical change and technological diffusion, and (3) the "Austrian School" theory that analyzed entrepreneurship as a response to arbitrage possibilities in financial and product markets. Each theory is deficient in predicting when entrepreneurship is likely to arise and when it is likely to be most successful. None of the theories helps to understand the role of the immigrant

entrepreneur in either integrating the global market or fostering development in regional economies.

20   This point is made by Paul Krugman in his criticisms of policy makers who attempt to apply some of his theoretical findings to real world problems. See Krugman, *Peddling Prosperity*.

21   See Borjas, "Economic Benefits."

22   David Card, "The Impact of the Mariel Boatlift on the Miami Labor Market," *Industrial and Labor Relations Review*, 40 (1990) 382-93.

23   Richard Vedder, Lowell Gallaway, and Stephen Moore, "Immgiration and Unemployment: New Evidence," Alexis de Tocqueville Institution (March 1994).

24   For a survey of these findings, see Bill Ong Hing, *To Be An American: Cultural Pluralism and the Rhetoric of Assimilation* (1996).

25   Rachel M. Friedberg and Jennifer Hunt, "The Impact of Immigrants on Host Country Wages, Employment and Growth," *Journal of Economic Perspectives* 9, (1995) 23-44.

26   *Ibid.*

27   See Hing, *Cultural Pluralism*.

28   *Ibid.*

29   Light and Rosenstein, *Race, Ethnicity, and Entrepreneurship*, 193. *Ibid.*

30   *Ibid.*, 98-103.

31   See Dixit, *International Trade*.

32   See Bates, "Social Resources," 11.

33   *Ibid.*

34   *Ibid.*, 34.

35   For an excellent discussion of discrimination in credit markets, see Peter Swire, "The Persistent Problem of Lending Discrimination: A Law and Economics Analysis," *Texas Law Review*, 73, (1995) 787.

36   See Hing, *Cultural Pluralism*.

37   Los Angeles County Internal Services Department, *Impact of Undocumented Persons and Other Immigrants on Costs, Revenues, and Services in Los Angeles County* (November 6, 1992).

38   Donald Huddle, "The Costs of Immigration" (July 20, 1993, manuscript).

39   "New Study says Immigrants Contribute More Than They Take," *San Jose Mercury News*, December 11, 1995.

40   Rebecca L. Clark and Jeffrey Passell, "How Much Do Immigrants Pay in Taxes? Evidence from Los Angeles County" (working paper, Urban Institute, August 1993).

41   See Light and Rosenstein, *Race, Ethnicity, and Entrepreneurship*, 24.

42   *Ibid.*

43   *Ibid.*, 109-110.

44   See Bates, "Determinants of Survival," 34.

45   See Light and Rosenstein, *Race, Ethnicity, and Entrepreneurship*, 139.

46   *Ibid.*

47   See Bates, "Determinants of Survival."

48 See Light and Rosenstein, *Race, Ethnicity, and Entrepreneurship,* 167, 197.
49 *Ibid.,* 208.

Asians Matter: Asian American Entrepreneurs in the Silicon Valley High Technology Industry

by Edward Jang-Woo Park[*]

Among the diverse topics concerning Asian Pacific Americans, one that has received systematic and sustained attention is immigrant entrepreneurship. This focus reflects the perception that entrepreneurship is the defining difference in the economic integration of many Asian Pacific Americans into the U.S. economy compared to other racial groups. This difference has profound economic, political, and social consequences.

While a high rate of entrepreneurship is widely acknowledged as the most important feature of Asian Pacific American economic participation, there remains a great deal of controversy regarding what immigrant entrepreneurship says about Asian Pacific Americans, or about the U.S. economy. This debate, from its inception, has taken on profoundly partisan tones: participants have often cited Asian immigrant entrepreneurship to support various political visions and sociological theories regarding race and the economy in contemporary American society. Today, as the nation reassesses immigration policy and reexamines economic contributions and the social status of various immigrant groups, the debate has become more important than ever.

This essay proceeds in three parts. The first critiques two common assessments of immigrant entrepreneurship and examines two relatively new contributions to the theoretical debate. The second examines the role of Asian Pacific Americans in the Silicon Valley high technology industry and provides a revealing look at the complexity of contemporary Asian immigrant entrepreneurship. That section also highlights some blind spots and limitations of the current debate. Finally, the third part outlines a number of issues derived from the case study to point out areas of further research and discussion that could lead to a more comprehensive understanding of Asian immigrant entrepreneurship.

---

[*] Edward Jang-Woo Park is an Associate Professor in the Department of Sociology at the University of Southern California.

Contemporary Debate Revisited

Two Shores of the Debate

The historical discussion of Asian immigrant entrepreneurship stemmed from efforts to understand Asian Pacific American economic adaptation to an uninviting and hostile society (Lyman 1974; Modell 1977; Choy 1979). More recently, mainstream social scientists have approached ethnic entrepreneurship to describe why Asian Pacific Americans might fare much better than any other racial group in the changing economic environment of the United States.

Sowell (1983, 1994) and Wilson (1987) represent political opposites in policy debates surrounding racial inequality. They both rely heavily, however, on Asian immigrant entrepreneurship and its "elevating" impact on the overall socioeconomic status of Asian Pacific Americans to attack racially-based policies such as affirmative action to aid African Americans and Latinos. Instead, they support policies to aid small business growth to raise the socioeconomic status of the latter two communities. Because of the centrality of Asian immigrant entrepreneurship in the broad debates regarding race and economy, this topic has received close attention, marked by intense divisions. In the more specific debate surrounding Asian immigrant entrepreneurship, divisions arise from the radically different assessments over its impacts on the broader U.S. society and on the Asian Pacific American community itself, and how best theoretically to frame its formation.

Portes (1985), Waldinger (1985), Light (1993), and Zhou (1992) have argued that Asian immigrant entrepreneurship has benefited both the broader society and Asian Pacific American communities. According to them, Asian immigrant entrepreneurship begins as an economic response by professional and middle-class Asian immigrants who face limited economic options in the mainstream labor market due to barriers such as limited English proficiency and professional licensing. Unable to recreate their class status through the mainstream labor market, they engage in entrepreneurship to take advantage of a growing Asian Pacific American population that can serve simultaneously as a ready-made and untapped market for goods and services and as a source of readily-available and inexpensive labor.

In this analysis, Asian immigrant entrepreneurship is seen as a creative and successful economic adaptation to overcome barriers in the mainstream economy. Professional and middle-class Asian immigrants are able to retain their class-status, while providing a robust labor market to their fellow co-ethnic, working-class immigrants, who might otherwise face even more profound barriers in the mainstream labor market. They point to generally low rates of unemployment in Asian Pacific American communities as an indication of the real benefit this "enclave economy" entrepreneurship brings.

In addition, Light (1993), Gold (1994), and Waldinger (1990) argue that Asian immigrant entrepreneurship, especially in ethnic enclave economies, has injected long-neglected inner-cities and sleepy suburban communities with much needed capital investment, neighborhood revitalization, and increased commercial activity. Readily identifiable Asian Pacific American commercial districts in California—such as Koreatown (Los Angeles), Little Saigon (Westminster), Little Taipei (Monterey Park), and Little Cambodia (Long Beach)—are seen as a new locus of urban growth and renewal. These sociologists point out that a substantial percentage of benefits, such as jobs creation, business services, linkages to international capital and markets, and generation of sales and property tax revenues, go beyond ethnic boundaries and enrich the broader public.

In contrast, other analysts such as Bonacich (1994), Ong (1993), Kwong (1987), and Nee (1994) argue that Asian immigrant entrepreneurship is detrimental to both the broader society and Asian Pacific American communities. In their analysis, Bonacich (1994) and Ong (1993) underscore the role of racial discrimination, in addition to other factors mentioned above, as one of the key reasons why Asian immigrants engage in entrepreneurship. They argue that discriminatory practices, such as barriers for promotions into management positions ("glass ceiling") and cultural biases in licensing of professionals, push professional and middle-class Asian immigrants into entrepreneurship. With limited availability of capital, language skills, and business ties, however, these entrepreneurs face severely curtailed opportunities and are forced into those industries or neighborhoods that "native" entrepreneurs find undesirable. Asian immigrant entrepreneurship, they say, is limited to "backward" and "declining" industries that are characterized by informal organization and hyper-exploitive working conditions. In the case of retail services, enterprises are largely concentrated in poor, inner-city neighborhoods. These businesses require cheap, and even unpaid (for the entrepreneur and family members) labor, to stay in business. To be competitive they often side-step safeguards regulating work place health and safety.

Indeed, Kwong (1987) and Bonacich (1994) argue that Asian immigrant entrepreneurship is the primary vehicle for the economic exploitation of the Asian Pacific American working class that benefits not only immigrant entrepreneurs but also the broader society in terms of providing inexpensive goods and services and exploiting undesirable markets.

In addition, Bonacich and Chang contend that Asian immigrant entrepreneurship contributes to the straining of urban race relations. These entrepreneurs exploit an increasingly racially diverse work force (for instance, Latinos represent the vast majority of workers in Korean American-owned garment factories), compete over urban space, and engage in exploitive retail trade (such as opening liquor stores in embattled inner-city communities).

In a different vain, Nee, Sanders, and Ong argue that Asian immigrant entrepreneurship levies a considerable "cost" to those who are integrated into the ethnic economy. Nee and Sanders (1987) find that immigrants working in the ethnic economy fare poorly since they receive fewer returns on their human capital than counterparts working in the mainstream economy. Similarly, Ong (1993) finds that Asian immigrant entrepreneurship creates few quality jobs, including for self-employment, that provide a living wage. While supporters of Asian immigrant entrepreneurship point to the low unemployment rates for Asian immigrants, opponents look at the high rate of "working poor." (Ong, 1993:16).

New Contributions

While much of the debate on Asian immigrant entrepreneurship has focused on evaluating its economic and social consequences, two relatively recent contributions have raised more conceptual and theoretical issues. These debates reflect conceptual ambiguities about the definition of ethnic entrepreneurship and about why ethnic entrepreneurship has become such a prominent feature in the contemporary U.S. economic landscape.

In a recent article, Nee, Sanders, and Sernau (1994:850) point out that various analysts have defined ethnic enclave economy by casually using a combination of factors, such as locational clustering, vertical and horizontal integration of firms, ethnicity of employer and employees, and types of industries. In the process, the Asian Pacific American ethnic economy has been defined without any proven set criteria that can be used to formulate a reliable definition. In addition, these factors tend to overstate the economic and social isolation of Asian immigrant entrepreneurship by drawing tight geographic, industrial, or ethnic boundaries around enclave economies.

Nee, Sanders, and Sernau argue that these conceptual problems must be addressed *before* any substantive analysis should occur. They propose a new definition in which Asian ethnic economy is conceptualized as an "integrated" part of the metropolitan economy with "porous boundaries," lying at an end of a continuum defined by high density of ethnic entrepreneurs and a relatively informal work environment for the employees (1994:851-4). This more flexible approach rejects the traditional approach that assumes fixed boundaries of geography (in ethnic residential districts) or ethnicity (of entrepreneurs and their "co-ethnic" workers) and treats Asian immigrant entrepreneurship as a set of relationships and conditions rather than as a fixed object. Most importantly, the argument that Asian immigrant entrepreneurship is enmeshed within the broader metropolitan economy, stresses the *integration* of Asian ethnic economy into, rather than its *isolation* from, broader economic and geographic surroundings. As the size and domain of Asian immigrant entrepreneurship expand, this reconceptualization paves a way to comprehend its increasing regional dispersion, industrial composition, work force diversity, and expanding markets for their products and services.

Similarly, Ong, Bonacich, and Cheng (1994) have recently offered a more theoretically rigorous discussion of contemporary Asian immigrant entrepreneurship. They argue that the tremendous growth in Asian immigrant entrepreneurship since the 1970s is a product of a global and national restructuring of capitalist development. In general terms, this restructuring has been defined by increasing capital and labor mobility at the global level and by the increasing organizational flexibility and the political power of capital in the U.S. economy. Under this framework, Asian immigrant entrepreneurship is a quintessential manifestation of these restructuring processes, because it (1) reconstitutes and reinvests capital (2) recruits and deploys politically marginal labor, and (3) increases the number of small firms crucial for more flexible modes of production and marketing (Ong, Bonacich, and Cheng 1994:14-29).

The linkage of Asian immigrant entrepreneurship to a broader theoretical debate on global and U.S. capitalism as well as to a set of structural processes such as capital and labor mobility is significant. By moving away from an approach which highlights only local factors, Ong, Bonacich, and Cheng have provided a broader understanding of contemporary Asian immigrant entrepreneurship—both as a general phenomena in contemporary global capitalism *and* a specific response to the conditions in U.S. urban economies.

Limits of Asian Immigrant Entrepreneurship

Despite differences and divisions in the debate, most participants view the impact of Asian immigrant entrepreneurship in a severely limited fashion. Those who confide Asian immigrant entrepreneurship largely within an ethnic boundary see it as an ethnic matter with little significance to the broader economy. While they have stressed the impact of Asian immigrant entrepreneurship to a host of broader *political* and *social* issues—ranging from race relations to urban renewal—they have ignored its *economic* impact on mainstream society. These theorists view this entrepreneurship as an ethnic "growth machine" (see Logan and Molotch 1989) that fuels economic development within Asian Pacific American communities. They have little to say, however, about how the Asian immigrant entrepreneurship is enmeshed into the larger U.S. economy and what functions it serves in different industries. By in large, their broader interest lies in a comparative study of economic integration of racial groups, and, depending on the orientation of the theorist, Asian immigrant entrepreneurship is seen as either the foundation of their success or mechanism of their exploitation (Modell 1977; Light 1972; Kwong 1987; Bonacich 1994).

Even models that argue a more relatively expansive theoretical formulation still either relegate Asian immigrant entrepreneurship to those areas of the economy that lie on the margins or deflate its broader significance. For instance, Nee, Sanders, and Sernau (1994:859-861) assert that Asian immigrant entrepreneurship and its labor market are a transitory phenomena that will tend to diminish over time, as immigrants become more assimilated. In particular, they argue that immigrant entrepreneurs and workers alike reduce barriers to the mainstream economy by learning English and becoming familiar with the mainstream society. As a result, they will move out of the ethnic economy and into the mainstream labor market where they can earn better returns on their human capital.

In contrast, Ong, Bonacich, and Cheng (1994) view Asian immigrant entrepreneurship as a *structurally*—not *culturally*—based phenomena, as a feature of global and national economic restructuring that shows no sign of decline. They reject the assimilationist assumption in the previous model by underscoring the role of racial discrimination in the mainstream labor market in the formation of Asian immigrant entrepreneurship. According to them, Asian immigrant entrepreneurship is largely concentrated in marginal economic activities because of limited access to capital and because of institutional ties Asian immigrant entrepreneurs have. Indeed, they view the major role of Asian immigrant entrepreneurship as keeping declining U.S. industries alive. These businesses serve marginal economic niches in the restructuring U.S. urban economies, with limited impact to the "core" sectors of the economy.

The Case of High Technology Industry in Silicon Valley

Silicon Valley High Technology Industry and Asian Immigration

The high technology industry in Silicon Valley serves as a useful case study to examine the economic possibilities of Asian immigrant entrepreneurship.[1] From the industry point of view, the high technology industry in Silicon Valley is unequivocally a core industry that represents a decisive economic sector for rebuilding the U.S. economic future. This economic and political significance was punctuated in 1992, when then Presidential candidate Bill Clinton made the support of CEO's of four of the largest high technology companies in Silicon Valley—Hewlett-Packard, Apple Computer, National Semiconductor, and Silicon Graphics—one of the keys to his political campaign (*Global Electronics* 1992:1). In addition, the inordinate amount of media and academic coverage the industry receives reaffirms daily the significance of the high technology industry in Silicon Valley.

From an economic point of view, why the high technology industry, in general, and the high technology industry in Silicon Valley, in particular, have achieved such a visible position is apparent. Nationwide, the high technology industry generated $466.2 billion dollars in 1991. It was one of the few manufacturing industries actually to experience growth since 1972 ($76 billion in 1991 dollars), growing at an astounding annual rate of 10.6 percent. In 1991, the high technology industry accounted for an astonishing 60 percent of the manufacturing employment in Silicon Valley, which translated to 9.7 percent of all high technology jobs in the country. In addition, nearly 800 high technology firms in Silicon Valley generated over $80 billion, accounting for over 17 percent of the nation's total industrial output. From 1988 to 1991, the area's high technology industry actually *gained* both its national shares of jobs and economic activities. Given the prediction that the Valley's grip would be waning in the face of increasing costs, aging infrastructure, and competition from other regions seeking to attract high technology firms, this was a suprising fact. Indeed, as Saxenian (1994:2) has demonstrated, Silicon Valley has recently *tightened* its grip on the high technology industry; by 1990, Silicon Valley accounted for one-third of the nation's electronics exports and claimed 39 of the 100 fastest growing electronics corporations. In 1992, the high technology industry in Silicon Valley posted record profits and number of initial public offerings, or creation of publicly-traded corporations. In that same year, the area's industry attracted a record $900 million in venture capital, suggesting more growth to come (CCSCE 1993:C24).

This industry is also a well-suited case study from the Asian immigrant entrepreneurship point of view. Much of the industry's transformation into its contemporary form coincided with massive Asian Pacific immigration into the United States and California. In the mid-1970s, the high technology industry underwent a revolutionary change caused by the 1971 invention of the microprocessor, which dramatically reduced computer prices and opened up massive markets for high technology industry. The PC (personal computer) revolution was ushered in, creating enormous intermediary markets that utilize high technology products. From 1975 to 1980, the employment base for the Silicon Valley high technology industry tripled from 50,000 to nearly 150,000.

At the same time, changes initiated by the 1965 Immigration Act which eliminated racial-preference in U.S. immigration policy for the first time since 1882, began to take hold. From 1970 to 1984, the number of immigrants from Asia grew from 83,000 to 240,000 per year. In addition, from 1975 to 1984, 761,000 political refugees from Vietnam, Laos, and Cambodia were admitted.

For both immigrants and refugees, California was the primary destination: in 1990, 2.8 million of the 7 million Asian Pacific Americans nationally lived in the state. From 1970 to 1990 in Silicon Valley, the number of Asian Pacific Americans grew six-fold, from 43,000 to 261,000, increasing their share of the population from 4 percent to 17 percent, a rate surpassed in California only by the San Francisco metropolitan area.

A New Social Equation for Industrial Growth

This parallel growth in high technology industry and Asian immigration in Silicon Valley has provided a unique economic environment in which to examine Asian immigrant economic integration. As an emerging industry whose growth came after the 1970s in the politically conservative north Santa Clara County, the high technology industry in the Valley had a strong pro-growth environment that actively catered to the economic and political needs of the industry. As Trounstein and Christensen (1982) have demonstrated, local political leaders took what was then unprecedented steps to assure the industry's success: public bonds were issued to build private industrial infrastructure, and industrial leaders were appointed to commissions through which they could exercise direct control over important public policies affecting high technology growth.

Most importantly, without established institutions—especially labor unions—that could mount a challenge to its industrial organization, the high technology industry in Silicon Valley essentially invented its own "social equation" for economic growth and competitiveness. To this day, *none* of the high technology firms in Silicon Valley has been successfully unionized. This is startling given the size of the industry and its location in the San Francisco Bay Area, the traditional center of California's labor movement (Robinson and McIlwee 1989; Abate 1993). Without the presence of labor unions, the industry has built its manufacturing competitiveness on two crucial strategies that have been unprecedented for a "core" industry: the integration of a "non-traditional" manufacturing labor force (Hossfeld 1990) and the development of an extensive subcontracting system (Saxenian 1994).

Asian immigrants have played the prominent role in both of these strategies. In 1990, within the traditional "blue collar" segment of the industry, 9,000 Asian Pacific Americans (57 percent of them women) accounted for 47 percent of the 19,000 workers. Their representation has grown over the last decade (18 percent in 1980 and 44 percent in 1988). In Silicon Valley in 1990, the traditional blue collar work force of white and African American men accounted for less than 12 percent of the workforce, while APAs and Latinos accounted for 69 percent.

Among the 9,000 Asian Pacific American workers, well-over 70 percent work for large, mainstream firms where they generally receive higher wages and more benefits. Over the years, Vietnamese workers have dominated the ranks of manufacturing workers at Hewlett-Packard and Intel while Filipinos have integrated the work force at National Semiconductor and Advanced Micro Devices (Rogers and Larsen 1984). These large, mainstream firms also provide a sense of employment stability rarely found in subcontracting firms where nearly all Asian Pacific American firms are concentrated. In this economic reality, Asian Pacific American manufacturing workers, as with all workers in the industry, prefer mainstream firms over Asian Pacific American ones.

Along with providing nearly half of the area's manufacturing labor force, Asian immigrants have made another crucial contribution: as entrepreneurs they make possible the system of contracting that lies at the heart of Silicon Valley's industrial competitiveness.[2] In her comparative study of industrial competitiveness in California's Silicon Valley and Route 128 in Massachusetts, Saxenian (1994) argues that flexibility allowed Silicon Valley to outpace its larger and more established competitor during the mid-1970s and late-1980s as the country's premier high technology region. While large Silicon Valley firms could turn to subcontractors, large firms in Route 128 had to rely on "in-house" manufacturing facilities. As waves of innovations changed the manufacturing technologies, large Silicon Valley firms kept pace by changing subcontractors, and these subcontractors, in turn, absorbed the cost of new capital investments in manufacturing facilities. Large firms in Route 128, however, were left with out-dated manufacturing plants that consumed enormous financial and human resources.

Large firms in Silicon Valley also could rely on the subcontractors system to absorb the notoriously violent economic changes in the industry. Since subcontractors were responsible for maintaining the industry's work force and inventory, they were the ones who were responsible for costly tasks: laying off workers during recessions, recruiting workers during recovery, and selling off excess inventory at deep discounts when the market turned soft. In this way, the contracting system increased the economic flexibility of large firms, and allowed them to concentrate on technological innovation and marketing, the two central elements in high technology economic competitiveness. In addition, the subcontractors *collectively* possessed an enormous industrial capacity that allowed larger firms to reduce the time-to-market for their products, another critical factor in the high technology industry. Saxenian (1994:150-2) concludes that within high technology-led regional economies, the development of this subcontracting system in such a large scale and so early on has provided the decisive difference for Silicon Valley.

One way to gauge this system of subcontracting in the Silicon Valley high technology industry is to examine its industrial structure. In 1990, of the 500 "electronic components and accessories" firms in Silicon Valley, only 95 firms had 100 or more workers, while 254 had fewer than 20 workers. Similarly, of the 215 "computer and office equipment" firms, 119 of 215 firms had fewer than 20 workers (SIC Codes 367, 357; U.S. Census 1990).

A study by the Asian Pacific American Manufacturing Association found more than 500 Asian Pacific American-owned high technology firms in the San Francisco Bay Area, generating over $1 billion in 1989 (Peterson 1989). Although this data is dated, especially given the pace of change in the high technology industry, it nonetheless offers a useful snapshot to assess the relative position of Asian Pacific American firms in the industry: while $1 billion is an impressive figure, it represented only 1 percent of the high technology output in the region. The average firm output, in 1989, for all high technology firms in Silicon Valley was close to $80 million, while the average firm size in the AAMA survey placed the figure for Asian Pacific American-owned firms at close to $2 million. In a detailed analysis of Chinese American-owned high technology firms in Los Angeles County, the high technology industry is placed well ahead of all other industries for Asian Pacific American entrepreneurs (Tseng 1994:139).

In Silicon Valley itself, an estimated 300 of the 800 high technology firms in 1990—including over half of all start-ups—were headed by Asian Pacific American entrepreneurs (Pollack 1992). The data suggest that the vast majority of Asian Pacific American-owned firms are small firms, integrated into the industry as subcontractors.

In their function, subcontracting firms in the high technology industry resemble their more extensively-researched garment industry counter-parts. Like garment industry subcontractors, high technology subcontractors work for larger firms—referred to in the industry as "original equipment manufacturers" (OEMs)—in the production of component parts ranging from printed circuit boards to graphics cards. More recently, an increasing number of software subcontractors who write component codes for large software companies have appeared. For a vast majority of subcontractors, their main "customers" consists of one or two OEMs or large software companies that provide almost all of a subcontractor's business under short-term renewable contracts.

As in the garment industry, high technology contractors are in a sense employees of the manufacturers—but without any of the economic or legal protections enjoyed by conventional employees. In Silicon Valley, individual contracts can last less than one month. Plus, more often than not, these "contracts" are based on informal understandings between production managers of the OEMs and owners of subcontracting firms, making the relationship even more flexible and unequal. Under this arrangement, subcontractors and their employees are wholly dependent on larger companies who exercise great control over their economic survival, and subcontractors effectively function as a manufacturing facility or a software division of the larger firms.

Despite these conditions, some Asian immigrant subcontractors have become very successful. For instance, Solectron Corporation (CEO, Winston Chen, 1977-1994) subcontracts circuit boards for some of the major OMEs in Silicon Valley, including Hewlett-Packard, IBM, and Apple, and generated $1.5 billion in sales in 1994. Other notable successes include DataExpert Corp (founder and CEO Bruce Yen, systems board and peripheral cards), Diamond Multimedia (founder and CEO Chong Moon Lee, graphics accelerator and digital video cards), and Fora Addonics (founder and CEO Victor Wu, component card and motherboard), firms that all generated sales of $130 million or higher in 1993.

While Asian Pacific American subcontractors in both the high technology and the garment industries serve similar functions, the monetary scale is quite different. Examples of spectacular success continue to fuel the already intense entrepreneurial environment in Silicon Valley for Asian immigrants and encourage them to take the subcontractor risk.

Paths to Entrepreneurship

Two important factors have emerged in the discussion about why Asian immigrants have chosen to enter entrepreneurship in the first place: glass ceiling problems and the availability of venture capital from Asian countries.

The glass ceiling. Like their white counterparts, Asian immigrant entrepreneurs in the high technology industry come primarily from the ranks of engineers or low-level managers. In their shift into entrepreneurship, however, immigrant entrepreneurs cite racial discrimination in their promotion to middle- and upper-level management—the so-called "glass ceiling"—as one of the primary reasons for leaving mainstream careers.

The most well known figure on this issue is David Lam, who left Hewlett-Packard in 1979 after repeatedly being passed over for promotion. He is credited with a series of successful start-ups and helped to organize other Asian Pacific Americans in the industry by starting the Asian Pacific American Manufacturers Association (Matsumoto 1994; Pollack 1992). Lam has become one of the strongest critics of the industry's glass ceiling and is often cited in the popular media.

Aggregate data tend to support the presence of the glass ceiling for Asian Pacific Americans in the industry. The 1990 ratio for white "professionals" to "officers and managers" was 0.54 (36,747 to 19,902), almost twice as high as the ratio for Asian Pacific Americans at 0.28 (3,084 to 11,066). While the number of Asian Pacific American executives and managers grew from 1988 to 1990 (from 2,766 to 3,084), the ratio did not. The absolute and relative difference in the Asian and white ratios has actually *increased* since 1988, when the ratios were 0.46 and 0.24, respectively. Aside from Ray Ocampo (vice president, Oracle), there are no high-profile Asian Pacific American executives in high technology firms in Silicon Valley (Viloria and Lai 1995).

Venture capital from abroad. While the prevailing image of glass ceiling has pushed some Asian immigrant entrepreneurs to start their own businesses, venture capital firms from Asian countries have provided some of the necessary capital to facilitate and even encourage start-ups. From 1985 to 1990, Eckhouse (1990) estimates that close to 60 Asian venture capital firms invested a staggering $1.7 billion to high technology start-ups. To place this figure in context, in 1992, all high technology firms in Silicon Valley attracted a record $900 million in venture capital.

In addition to earning a good return on their investment, most of these Asian venture capital firms invest with "secondary" hopes of accessing technology for their firms in Asia and as a way developing a "presence" in the Valley (Yoshihara 1990). In nearly all studies that have examined Asian venture capital firms, observers have underscored how these firms "target" Asian immigrant start-ups, hoping that their ethnically-based ties can facilitate their goals (Eckhouse 1990; Tseng 1994; Burkett 1994). In a detailed study of venture capital firms from Taiwan, Liu found that nearly *all* of the Taiwan venture capital firms that invested in the United States high technology industry invested in Chinese American-owned firms. Similarly, Tseng observes that Taiwanese venture capitalist, largely drawn from the ranks of scientists and engineers, target Taiwanese start-ups since they "mainly rely on existing human networks such as former colleges, classmates, and friends" (Tseng 1994:118).

Pollack (1992), in particular, argues that this access to capital has helped Asian immigrant entrepreneurs launch new start-ups even during the early 1990s, when a domestic credit crunch discouraged others from establishing new firms. This involvement of Asian venture capital firms in the formation of Asian immigrant entrepreneurship has renewed the "start-up fever" in Silicon Valley—this time, for Asian immigrants.

Organizing Asian Immigrant Entrepreneurs

In the Silicon Valley high technology industry, Asian Pacific American entrepreneurs have organized politically for two reasons: (1) to take advantage of the unique economic status of high technology industry, and (2) to advocate for racial equality in the promotion of Asian Pacific American professionals into executive and managerial positions in mainstream firms. While a number of ethnic specific organizations have been founded, including the Chinese Software Professionals Association and the Silicon Valley Indian Professionals Associations, the Asian American Manufacturers Association (AAMA) has been the most influential organization representing Asian Pacific American entrepreneurs.

Founded in 1980 and currently headed by Thinh Tran (chairman of Sigma Design), the association has urged federal and state governments to strengthen economic ties with Asian economies. Asian immigrant entrepreneurs feel that they can exploit their ethnic-based ties and open new markets in Asia (Rajendran 1994). The group played a prominent role in several fronts on this issue, including organizing numerous trade shows to bring together Asian and Asian Pacific American high technology firms and lobbying the federal government to relax regulations on high technology exports.

In addition to advancing its members' business interests, the association has also lobbied for racial equality in the promotion of Asian Pacific American professionals into management. When the organization was founded, this was their main role in Silicon Valley.

A striking political accomplishment of AAMA has been its ability to develop and support Asian Pacific American political leadership in the Valley. Co-founder David Lam[3] was one of the first to benefit from the group's political visibility: he received a coveted appointment to the Presidential Commission on Minority Business Development during the Bush Administration. Since then, AAMA has been credited with providing support for various Asian Pacific American community leaders, including a number of appointments to the Valley's educational districts and public commissions (Matsumoto 1994). In their efforts as an industrial association and as an advocate for Asian Pacific American political interests, AAMA's membership to the economically important and politically visible high technology industry has allowed it to achieve a measure of political success that would have been far more difficult in other industries.

Asian Pacific American
Entrepreneurship Reconsidered

From Sunset to Sunrise

As this case study of the high technology industry in Silicon Valley demonstrates, Asian immigrant entrepreneurship can have a defining impact on the core industries in the U.S. economy. Asian immigrant entrepreneurs in the Valley have played an instrumental role in developing a highly capitalized and technologically sophisticated subcontracting system—one that lies at the heart of industry's economic competitiveness and industrial organization. The high technology industry in Silicon Valley is not alone in this regard. Within the industry, other regions with high concentration of high technology firms have seen increasing integration of Asian Pacific Americans into the industry as both manufacturing workers and as entrepreneurs. Such regions include Research Triangle, North Carolina; Fairfax Country, Virginia; and Austin, Texas. Economic opportunities in these areas have actually triggered large-scale Asian Pacific American migration into these communities for the first time.

Similar processes have unfolded in other core industries as well, with notable examples in the biotechnology industry of San Francisco Bay Area and Boston, the multimedia industry in the "Multimedia Gulch" of San Francisco and Los Angeles, and the medical devices industry in Southern California. These examples from newly-emerging "sunrise" industries collectively signal a need to rethink the relationship between Asian immigrant entrepreneurship and core industries. Much of the previous debate has assumed that Asian immigrant entrepreneurship is largely limited to marginal or declining industries. Some have even argued that the very presence of Asian immigrant entrepreneurship indicates the decline of a "sunset" industry. Examples raised here, however, refute this position.

"Opting Out" of the Mainstream Labor Market

Another central assumption in the existing debate about immigrant entrepreneurs views the entry of Asian Pacific Americans into the mainstream labor market as a path out of the ethnic economy, including ethnic entrepreneurship, once and for all (Nee, Sanders, and Sernau 1994, Light, Light and Bonacich, Ong). Given their serious misgivings about Asian immigrant entrepreneurship and its economic and social costs, it is not surprising that some researchers have difficulty imagining an Asian Pacific

American who has entered the mainstream labor market only then to leave and enter ethnically-based entrepreneurship. Yet this is exactly the process that is taking place, however, in the high technology industry in Silicon Valley: ever-increasing large numbers of Asian Pacific Americans are leaving relatively well-paid engineer and middle-level manager jobs in mainstream firms to start their own subcontracting companies.

This "reverse flow" of Asian Pacific Americans suggests that the gate between Asian immigrant enterprises and the mainstream labor market is open both ways. This calls for a serious revision of the theoretical conceptualization Asian immigrant entrepreneurship. First, this "reverse flow" challenges the prevailing assumption that Asian immigrant entrepreneurship is a temporary phenomena that marks a transitory stage between the entry of Asian immigrants into a new economy and their eventual economic assimilation into the mainstream labor market. In the case of the Silicon Valley high technology industry, Asian immigrants have shown that they can "opt out" of the mainstream labor market and "go back" to ethnic entrepreneurship, suggesting that Asian immigrant entrepreneurship might be more durable than previously believed.

Second, the case study demonstrates that the entry of Asian Pacific Americans into the mainstream labor market does not make them immune from economic and social pressures to move "back" into ethnic entrepreneurship. In the narratives of Asian Pacific Americans who make this decision, the glass ceiling is cited as one of the most important factors.

Measuring the impact of racial discrimination in the formation of Asian immigrant entrepreneurship is difficult. Recognizing, however, that racial barriers to management is a real-world frustration for Asian immigrants in the mainstream labor market is essential. Regardless of social and educational backgrounds such as foreign-birth and limited-English status that might statistically explain away their relative disadvantage in obtaining promotion into management (Ong and Blumenberg 1994:181-182), discrimination is perceived as a major factor.[4] One frustrated Asian immigrant engineer who became an entrepreneur posed a basic question:

If Asian immigrant engineers did not have the capability of becoming managers, why do all these Asian-owned firms in Silicon Valley exist in the first place? If Asian immigrants aren't good enough to be trusted to manage a several hundred thousand dollar operations in white firms, how come they are good enough to run their own multi-million dollar businesses? (Park 1992:144-145).

From Family and Community to Transnational Ties

As an important core industry with a coveted technological base and economic future, the high technology industry in Silicon Valley has attracted the attention of Asian venture capital firms. In addition to seeking high returns for their investments, these firms also seek to facilitate technological transfers to Asia and to gain a foothold in the Valley's high technology industry. To facilitate these aims, they have invested in Asian immigrant enterprises hoping to take advantage of ethnic and national ties. The sheer number of these firms and their infusion of start-up capital in Silicon Valley have made it easier for Asian immigrant engineers and middle-level managers to "opt out" of the mainstream labor market. In the process, a new international relationship between Asian immigrant subcontractors and Asian venture capitalists has been built.

This dynamic is a departure from the previous theoretical understanding of Asian immigrant entrepreneurship that placed emphasis on family- and community-based resources behind its formation. In the Silicon Valley high technology industry, traditional sources for starting Asian immigrant entrepreneurship, such as family loans and rotating credit associations, are being supplemented—indeed overwhelmed—by Asian venture capital investments. In this context, Asian immigrant entrepreneurship has gone beyond an *ethnic* phenomena and has become an increasingly *transnational* one.

While the high technology industry clearly has economic characteristics that makes the industry an exceptionally attractive target for Asian investments, this phenomenon may be part of a greater trend. There has been a proliferation of Asian financial institutions, including venture capital firms and over-seas branches of Asian banks located in, and serving, predominantly their own ethnic communities. This development indicates that the financial basis of Asian immigrant entrepreneurship is shifting toward Asian financial institutions and away from traditional familial and ethnic networks. Within Asian Pacific American communities, this economic reality is most noticeable in their urban form which includes large shopping malls financed by Asian real estate syndicates.

Conclusion

The case study of the Silicon Valley high technology industry suggests that Asian immigrant entrepreneurship is becoming increasingly complex. This complexity reflects profound economic and social changes in both the

U.S. economy and the formation of Asian immigrant entrepreneurship. Within the U.S. economy, the industrial organization between core and marginal or declining industries has been blurred. Many new core industries require technological and scientific knowledge, as well as relatively heavy capital investments. Yet they rely heavily on a system of smaller and unregulated subcontractors to carry out many of their industrial activities. This is a characteristic that has been traditionally associated with marginal or declining industries that depended on this practice for their tenuous economic survival.

In the Valley, however, the subcontractors system was created from the beginning of its industrial development and has become a major reason for its economic success. As other core industries follow suit, a structural place for subcontractors in core industries is evident. Subcontracting firms in core and marginal industries share striking similarities, such as heightened vulnerability to the economic cycles and organizational flexibility, but dramatic differences are apparent as well.

One important difference stems from the economic backgrounds of the ethnic entrepreneurs themselves. Asian immigrant entrepreneurs in core industries are highly educated—some in the U.S., and their training is usually in technical and scientific fields relevant to their industry. In addition, most have had long work experience within the industry's mainstream labor market. This educational background and work experience set them apart from other Asian immigrant entrepreneurs, who generally do not have as high a level of familiarity with mainstream U.S. institutional and economic life.

Along with the background of Asian immigrant entrepreneurs, their integration into a core industry with economic and political prestige allows them to access resources that their counterparts in other types of industries do not possess. This includes political visibility in the United States and attention from Asian venture capitalists eager to gain access to U.S. technologies and markets.

All of these factors bring Asian immigrant entrepreneurship to another level. Asian immigrant entrepreneurs can no longer be viewed monolithically as newly-arrived immigrants who face structural barriers to the mainstream labor market and only have family- and ethnic-based resources. Rather, a new group of Asian immigrant entrepreneurs, equipped with professional background and access to Asian investment capital, are changing the role of Asian immigrants in the U.S. economy.

These changing realities point out the need to reassess other key elements in the current social science debate on Asian immigrant entrepreneurship. The assumption that Asian immigrant entrepreneurship is a transitory stage for the eventual incorporation into the mainstream labor market must be reassessed. This case study shows that Asian immigrants can and do "opt out" when they discern limits to their mobility in the mainstream labor market. Ethnic entrepreneurship may be a viable way to expand their economic opportunities. In the high technology industry, where subcontracting system is encouraged and a strong infrastructure to support entrepreneurship has developed, this decision is more easily made. In this way, Asian immigrant entrepreneurship might prove to be far more durable than predicted.

Notes

[1] As with most studies, high technology industry is defined here as a combination of three industries: computers and peripherals, electronic components, and non-defense related instruments. Also, Silicon Valley is defined as Santa Clara County, California.

[2] Editor's note: see also the survey of high-tech entrepreneurs by Melanie Erasmus contained in this volume.

[3] See comment on p. 24 re Lam.

[4] Ridell (1989) along with a host of other journalists have written countless articles, documenting the pervasive sentiment in the industry that Asian Pacific Americans make "good workers, not good leaders."

References

Abate, Tom 1993. "Heavy Load for Silicon Valley Workers." *San Francisco Examiner*, May 23, pp. E1.

Bluestone, Barry and Bennett Harrison. 1982. *The Deindustrialization of America*. New York: Basic Books.

Bonacich, Edna. 1973. "A Theory of Middleman Minorities." *American Sociological Review* 38:583-94.

Bonacich, Edna. 1994. "Asians in the Los Angeles Garment Industry." Pp. 137-163 in *The New Asian Immigration in Los Angeles and Global Restructuring*, edited by P. Ong, E. Bonacich, and L. Cheng. Philadelphia: Temple University Press.

Bonacich, Edna and John Modell. 1980. *The Economic Basis of Ethnic Solidarity: Small Business in the Japanese American Community*. Berkeley: University of California Press.

Burkett, Tom 1994. "Asian California: Asians Are Critical to Four Key Sectors of the Golden State's Economy." *Transpacific*, August, pp. 36.

Calandra, Thom 1993. "Gold Fever Infectious." *San Francisco Examiner*, May 23, pp. E1.

CCSCE. 1993. "California Economic Growth, 1993 Edition." Center for the Continuing Study of the California Economy, Palo Alto.

Choy, Bong-Youn. 1979. *Koreans in America*. Chicago: Nelson-Hall.

Eckhouse, J. 1990. "Silicon Valley Awash in Asian Venture Capital: Foreign Firms See Chance for Big Profits." *San Francisco Chronicle*, September.

Gold, Steve. 1994. "Chinese-Vietnamese Entrepreneurs in California." Pp. 196-226 in *The New Asian Immigration in Los Angeles and Global Restructuring*, edited by P. Ong, E. Bonacich, and L. Cheng. Philadelphia: Temple University Press.

Gordon, David M., Richard Edwards, and Michael Reich. 1982. *Segmented Work, Divided Workers*. New York: Cambridge University Press.

Hall, Peter and Ann Markusen. 1985. *Silicon Landscapes*. Boston: Allen and Unwin.

Henderson, J. 1989. *The Globalization of High Technology Production*. New York: Routledge.

Hing, Bill Ong. 1993. *Making and Remaking Asian America Through Immigration Policy, 1850-1990*. Stanford: Stanford University Press.

Hossfeld, Karen. 1988. "Division of Labor, Division of Lives." Ph.D. Thesis, Department of Sociology, University of California, Santa Cruz.

Hossfeld, Karen. 1990. "Their Logic Against Them." in *Women Workers and Global Restructuring*, edited by K. Ward. Ithaca: Cornell University Press.

Keller, John. 1981. "The Production Workers in Electronics." Ph.D. Thesis, Department of Anthropology, University of Michigan, Ann Arbor.

Kwong, Peter. 1987. *The New Chinatown*. New York: Noonday Press.

Light, Ivan. 1979. "Disadvantaged Minorities in Self-Employment." *International Journal of Comparative Sociology* 20:31-45.

Light, Ivan. 1980. "Asian Enterprise in America." Pp. 33-37 in *Self-Help in America: Patterns of Minority Economic Development*, edited by S. Commings. Port Washington, New York: Kennikat Press.

Light, Ivan and P. Bhachu. 1993. *Immigration and Entrepreneurship: Culture, Capital and Ethnic Networks*. New Brunswick: Transaction Publishers.

Light, Ivan H. 1972. *Ethnic Enterprise in America: Business and Welfare Among Chinese, Japanese, and Blacks*. Berkeley: University of California Press.

Light, Ivan H. and Edna Bonacich. 1988. *Immigrant Entrepreneurs: Koreans in Los Angeles 1965-1982*. Berkeley: University of California Press.

Liu, J. Harper 1994. "The Baron of Silicon Valley: Entrepreneur David K. Lam." *Transpacific*, April, pp. 50.

Logan, John R. and Harvey L. Molotch. 1987. *Urban Fortunes: The Political Economy of Place*. Berkeley: University of California Press.

Lyman, Stanford. 1974. *Chinese Americans*. New York: Random House.

Makusen, Ann, Peter Hall, and Amy Glasmeier. 1986. *High Tech America*. Boston: Allen and Unwin.

Markusen, Ann. 1985. *Profit Cycles, Oligopoly, and Regional Development*. Cambridge: MIT Press.

Matsumoto, Craig 1994. "David Lam: Asian Immigrant Presses Quest for Leadership Diversity." *Business Journal-San Jose*, August 8, pp. 12.

Min, Pyong Gap. 1984. "From White Collar Occupations to Small Business." *The Sociological Quarterly* 25:333-352.

Min, Pyong Gap. 1988. *Ethnic Business Enterprise*. New York: Center for Migration Studies.

Modell, John. 1977. *The Economics and Politics of Racial Accommodation: The Japanese of Los Angeles, 1900-1942*. Urbana: University of Illinois Press.

Nee, Victor and Jimy M. Sanders. 1987. "On Testing the Enclave Economy Thesis." *American Sociological Review* 52:771-73.

Nee, Victor, Jimy M. Sanders, and Scott Sernau. 1994. "Job Transitions in an Immigrant Metropolis: Ethnic Boundaries and the Mixed Economy." *American Sociological Review* 59:849-872.

Omi, Michael and Howard Winant. 1994. *Racial Formation in the United States: From the 1960s to the 1990s*. New York: Routledge.

Ong, Paul. 1993. *Beyond Asian American Poverty: Community Economic Development Policies and Strategies*. Los Angeles: LEAP Asian Pacific American Public policy Institute.

Ong, Paul and Evelyn Blumenberg. 1994. "Scientists and Engineers." Pp. 165-189 in *The State of Asian Pacific America: Economic Diversity, Issues and Policies*, edited by P. Ong. Los Angeles: Leadership Education for Asian Pacifics (LEAP) and UCLA Asian American Studies Center.

Ong, Paul, Edna Bonacich, and Lucie Cheng. 1994. "The Political Economy of Capitalist Restructuring and the New Asian Immigration." Pp. 3-35 in *The New Asian Immigration in Los Angeles and Global Restructuring*, edited by P. Ong, E. Bonacich, and L. Cheng. Philadelphia: Temple University Press.

Ong, Paul and John M. Liu. 1994. "U.S. Immigration Policies and Asian Migration." Pp. 45-73 in *The New Asian Immigration in Los Angeles and Global Restructuring*, edited by P. Ong, E. Bonacich, and L. Cheng. Philadelphia: Temple University Press.

Ong, Paul, Kye Young Park, and Yasmin Tong. 1994. "The Korean-Black Conflict and the State." Pp. 264-294 in *The New Asian Immigration in Los Angeles and Global Restructuring*, edited by P. Ong, E. Bonacich, and L. Cheng. Philadelphia: Temple University Press.

Park, Edward. 1992. "Asian Americans in Silicon Valley: Race and Ethnicity in the Postindustrial Economy." Ph.D. Thesis, Ethnic Studies, University of California at Berkeley.

Peterson, J. 1989. "Asian Entrepreneurs: An Influx of Immigrants, many Educated Here, Are Bringing Jobs and Innovation to the U.S. Market." *Los Angeles Times*, August 6, pp. D1.

Pollack, A. 1992. "It's Asians' Turn in Silicon Valley." *New York Times*, January 14, pp. A1.

Portes, Alejandro and Robert L. Bach. 1985. *Latin Journey: Cuban and Mexican Immigrants in the United States*. Berkeley: University of California Press.

Portes, Alejandro and Leif Jensen. 1987. "What's an Ethnic Enclave? The Case for Conceptual Clarity." *American Sociological Review* 52:768-71.

Portes, Alejandro and Leif Jensen. 1992. "Disproving the Enclave Hypothesis." *American Sociological Review* 57:418-20.

Rajendran, Joseph 1994. "Silicon Valley Groups Busy Building Links with Asia." *Business Times*, April 4, pp. 9.

Reimers, David. 1986. *Still the Golden Door*. New York: Columbia University Press.

Riddell, P. 1989. "East Makes Good in the West." *Financial Times*, September 23, pp. 1.

Robinson, J. Gregg and Judith McIlwee. 1989. "Obstacles to Unionization in High-Tech Industries." *Work and Occupations* 16:115-136.

Rogers, E. and J. Larsen. 1984. *Silicon Valley Fever*. New York: Basic books.

Sanders, Jimy and Victor Nee. 1987a. "The Road to Parity: Determinants of the Socio-economic Achievements of Asian Americans." *Ethnic and Racial Studies* 8:75-93.

Sanders, Jimy M. and Victor Nee. 1987b. "Limits of Ethnic Solidarity in the Enclave Economy." *American Sociological Review* 52:745-73.

Sanders, Jimy M. and Victor Nee. 1992. "Problems in Resolving the Enclave Economy Debate." *American Sociological Review* 57:415-18.

Sassen, Saskia. 1988. *The Mobility of Labor and Capital: A Study of International Investments and Labor Flow*. New York: Cambridge University Press.

Saxenian, AnnaLee. 1994. *Regional Advantage: Culture and Competition in Silicon Valley and Route 128*. Cambridge: Harvard University Press.

Siegel, Lenny. 1992. "Global Electronics." , vol. 116. Mountain View, California: Pacific Studies Center.

Sowell, Thomas. 1983. *The Economic and Politics of Race: An International Perspective*. New York: Quill.

Sowell, Thomas. 1994. *Race and Culture: A World View*. New York: Basic Books.

Transpacific 1994. "Transpacific 100 Great Asian American Entrepreneurs; 1994." *Transpacific*, December, pp. 49.

Trounstein, P. and T. Christensen. 1982. *Movers and Shakers*. New York: St. Martin's Press.

Tseng, Yen-Fen. 1994. "Suburban Ethnic Economy: Chinese Business Communities in Los Angeles." Ph.D. Thesis, Department of Sociology, University of California, Los Angeles, Los Angeles.

Tucker, E. 1988. "High Tech, High Hopes: Southeast Asians Find a Niche in Local Companies." *The Washington post*, February 22, pp. D1.

Viloria, Theresa C. and Eric Lai 1995. "Immigrant Job Machine." *San Jose Mercury News*, August 27, pp. D1.

Waldinger, Roger. 1985. "Immigrant Enterprise and the Structure of the Labor Market." Pp. 66-88 in *New Approaches to Economic Life*, edited by B. Roberts, R. Finnegan, and D. Gallie. Manchester: Manchester university Press.

Waldinger, Roger. 1994. "The Making of an Immigrant Niche." *International Migration Review* 28:3-30.

Waldinger, Roger, Howard Aldrich, and Robin Ward. 1990. *Ethnic Entrepreneurs: Immigrant Business in Industrial Societies*. Newbury Park, California: Sage publications.

Wilson, William Julius. 1978. *The Declining Significance of Race*. Chicago: University of Chicago Press.

Wilson, William Julius. 1987. *The Truly Disadvantaged: The Inner City, the Underclass, and Public*. Chicago: University of Chicago Press.

Xiong, X. 1990. "Asian American Entrepreneurs Enrich Silicon Valley Tradition." *Electronic Business*, November 12.

Yoshihara, N. 1990. "Taiwan Move in U.S.: Banking Is Just a Start." *Los Angeles Times*, May 14, pp. D1.

Zhou, Min. 1992. *Chinatown: The Socioeconomic Potential of an Urban Enclave*. Philadelphia: Temple University Press.

Zhou, Min and John Logan. 1989. "Returns on Human Capital in Ethnic Enclaves: New York City's Chinatown." *American Sociological Review* 54:809-20.

Immigrant Entrepreneurs
In The High-Tech Industry

by Melanie Erasmus[*]

Immigrant entrepreneurship has been an important part of the history of immigrants in the United States. For many, the topic conjures up images of small neighborhood grocery stores, and the like. Certainly many of today's immigrants have continued the tradition of engaging in these types of modest enterprises, but many immigrant entrepreneurs of recent vintage have developed businesses that are anything but small. This paper provides a sampling of companies in one area — the high-tech industry — in which immigrants have played key roles in developing.

Political Backdrop

Heated political debate has surrounded several bills moving through the Republican-dominated Congress that seek to clamp down on both undocumented and documented immigration.[1] Among the provisions being considered are: reducing the total number of legal immigrants from 800,000 to 535,000 per year; making political asylum more difficult to obtain; placing an annual ceiling of 50,000 on refugees; increasing financial requirements for a United States citizen to sponsor an immigrant; requiring employers to verify the legal status of job applicants through a new registry of social security and alien registration numbers; eliminating immigrant categories for siblings of U.S. citizens and adult children of lawful resident aliens; and making it more difficult for United States firms to recruit foreign workers.[2]

Senator Alan Simpson's bill is typical of these bills and focuses on limiting both family reunification categories and employment visas.[3] In addition to seeking to charge businesses a fee for hiring and bringing in highly-skilled foreign workers, the bill would reduce immigrant visas currently reserved mostly for skilled workers from 140,000 to 90,000.[4] This is despite the fact that the number was just raised to the 140,000 level in 1990, because of a two-year backlog of foreign workers that American companies

---

[*]   Melanie Erasmus has a J.D. from Stanford University Law School.

wanted to hire. To Simpson, the issue at stake is jobs; he asserts that immigrants, many of whom may be engineers and computer programmers in high-technology industries, are taking job opportunities away from native workers.[5] While he believes the United States needs to admit foreign skilled workers to keep American business at the forefront, this goal must be balanced with protecting American workers.[6]

The High-Tech Industry

The world-dominant computer industry in the United States depends on a workforce that is disproportionately composed of immigrants. An estimated 15,000 Asian immigrants are employed in Silicon Valley, about a quarter of the total workforce.[7] Some 20 percent of Intel Corporation's engineers are Chinese immigrants; and at Cadence Design Systems, a software company, foreign-born Chinese American engineers may represent as many as 80 percent of the technical staff.[8] At AT&T Bell Labs in New Jersey, 40 percent of researchers in the communications sciences department were born outside the United States. Similarly, a quarter of the researchers at IBM's Yorktown Heights facility in New York, are of Asian descent.[9] As one computer industry analyst put it, "The United States would not be remotely dominant in high-technology industries without immigrants. We are now utterly dominant in all key information technology domains. And at every important high-tech company in America, the crucial players, half of them or more, are immigrants."[10] Intel's Chief Executive Officer Andy Grove, who immigrated from Hungary in the 1950s, called his ranks of immigrant engineers "our secret weapon."[11]

According to industry officials, one reason for their reliance on foreign nationals is that the United States is not producing enough skilled workers in certain job categories to be globally competitive.[12] Leading software company Microsoft, for example, was unable to fill a quarter of its openings in technical positions in 1994 because of a scarcity of qualified candidates. According to Microsoft, the U.S. labor pool does not have enough graduates in technical fields to meet the demand.[13] The founder of RayDream, another software company, asserts that the company's goal of hiring native-born software engineers has not been very successful because too few applicants have the desired mathematical backgrounds.[14]

Foreign nationals in 1974 accounted for 33 percent of engineering master's degrees and 52 percent of engineering Ph.D.s in the United States. This makes them highly desirable in the high-technology and scientific fields, and a significant portion remains in the United States as employees in the high-tech industry. Indeed, close to 50 percent of the foreign born entrepreneurs surveyed in this project completed their studies in the United States.[15]

The industry also serves as a magnet for talented engineers and scientists from abroad. The concentration of computer, biotechnology, and other electronics companies in certain geographic areas of the United States draws foreign entrepreneurs to those areas. Founders of RayDream, ParaGraph, Genelabs Technologies, and Solectron, for example, all assert that they chose to locate their companies in Silicon Valley in order to be close to customers and suppliers.[16]

The high-tech industry reaps an enormous benefit from its multicultural workforce. Stephen Pachikov, the Russian-born founder of the software company ParaGraph, believes that diversity in education and culture of foreign workers contributes to the development of cutting edge technology.[17] Further, many immigrant entrepreneurs in the high-tech industry have connections throughout the world, enabling them to sell their products and services internationally. Eric Hautemont, the French founder of RayDream, is convinced that the mix of European and American cultures in his company has helped them do business abroad.[18]

In a field where an industry goal is to operate in the worldwide arena, the multicultural workforce seems to be a must. As one scholar put it, "This allows U.S. companies to relate more effectively with international markets [and] builds connections between the U.S. and international markets."[19] For example, Genelabs Technologies, a biotechnology company, was able to form a joint venture with Taiwan and received investment from the Taiwanese government because of its Chinese co-founder.

Little wonder that the high-technology industry is strongly opposed to proposals that would reduce the category for skilled immigrant workers. Its leaders argue that these changes would cripple their ability to recruit worldwide for highly specialized jobs and that the industry would therefore suffer. They maintain that immigrants not only fill critical engineering and scientific positions, but, as entrepreneurs, they also create jobs and push the boundaries of technology. Put differently, entrepreneur Daniel Kwoh, co-founder of VCR products company Gemstar, does not believe that legal immigration should be more restrictive because the United States is "reaping the benefits of brain drain from other countries."[20]

Immigrant Entrepreneurs And Their Companies

Computer Associates International Inc.

Computer Associates International Inc., located in Islandia, New York, was co-founded in 1976 by Charles B. Wang,[21] who is the company's chairman and chief executive officer. The enterprise started with no venture capital and only one product and is now the second largest software company in the world (after Microsoft). Computer Associates is the world's leading independent software company for multi-platform, business software computing; its software products have been installed in almost every Fortune 500 company.[22]

Computer Associates employs 9,000 people worldwide, with approximately 6,000 employees based in the United States. Its revenues for fiscal 1995 exceeded $2.6 billion, representing a 22 percent increase over 1994. The success of this Fortune 500 company is attributed to Wang who has a deep knowledge of computer technology and the challenges facing senior corporate management.[23]

In 1949, Wang fled mainland China at the time of the Communist Revolution and came to the United States with his family. He was eight years old and spoke no English. He subsequently majored in physics and mathematics at Queens College in New York before deciding that he would become a computer programmer. Wang learned programming at the Electronic Research Laboratory at Columbia University. When he founded Computer Associates, he was 32 years old and completely without resources. Today his software business is worth nearly $11 billion.[24]

Solectron Corporation

Solectron was co-founded by Winston Chen and Roy Kusumoto in 1977, in Milpitas, California. What began as a small assembly shop with annual revenues of several thousand dollars is now a company whose 1995 sales revenues were $2.06 billion. Solectron has enjoyed a growth rate of 60 percent per year since 1978, and employs 10,000 people worldwide, with 5,500 employees in the United States.[25]

The company operates one of the world's largest facilities for the assembly of complex printed circuit boards and subsystems for makers of computers and other electronics products. Solectron has won two prestigious awards: the Malcolm Baldridge National Quality Award in 1991 and the (California) Governor's Golden State Quality Award in 1994.[26]

Chen emigrated from Taiwan in 1965, and came to the United States where he obtained his M.S. and Ph.D. in applied mechanics from Harvard University. After working for IBM for eight years, he started Solectron with $300,000 and served as chairman and chief executive officer from 1978 to 1994. He now chairs the Paramitas Foundation and serves on the board of directors of several high technology companies. He was chosen Bay Area Entrepreneur of the Year in 1990, and was selected as a member of the business delegation for President Bush's Asia/Pacific visit in 1992. Chen is a member of the board of trustees of Santa Clara University and the Engineering Advisory Committee of the National Science Foundation.[27]

Intel Corporation

Intel, with its headquarters in Santa Clara, California, is the world's largest maker of computer chips. The company produced the world's first microprocessor and sparked a computer revolution that has changed the world. About 75 percent of the personal computers in use around the world today are based on Intel-architecture microprocessors. It employs 32,600 people worldwide, with approximately 23,000 based in the United States, and its revenues for 1994 exceeded $11.5 billion.[28]

Andrew Grove, president and chief executive officer of Intel, is a Hungarian immigrant who fled Soviet tanks and came to the United States in 1956. Although he could not speak a word of English when he entered, Grove graduated at the top of his engineering class at City College three years later.[29] Grove went on to earn his doctorate in chemical engineering from the University of California, Berkeley. After five years at Fairchild Semiconductor in California, he left to help form Intel. He was 31 years old.[30] Intel was founded in 1968 by Gordon Moore and Robert Noyce along with six others from Fairchild. Grove received the 1995 Heinz Award for his contribution to technology and the economy.[31]

Intel introduced the state-of-the-art Pentium microprocessor in 1994. The project was managed by Vinod Dham of India, and one of the chip's two principal architects is another Asian Indian American, Avtar Saini.[32]

LSI Logic

LSI Logic was founded in 1981 by Wilfred Corrigan in Milpitas, California. LSI Logic is the market share and technology leader in the custom, high-performance application-specific integrated circuits (ASICs) market. Its sales revenue for 1994 was $902 million and exceeded $1 billion in 1995.[33] The company has 3,700 employees, 2,400 of whom are employed in the United States. Currently the company is investing $4 billion in a new campus in Gresham, Oregon that is expected to employ nearly 500 employees. Interestingly, a company spokesperson has warned that "the rate at which the development group can grow will be limited by the small number of engineers qualified to work in this specialized field."[34]

Corrigan immigrated from England in 1960, after receiving a chemical engineering degree from London's Imperial College of Science and after deciding that his future lay in the United States.[35] Prior to starting LSI Logic, he worked for Motorola Semiconductor and then went onto Fairchild. He eventually became chairperson of Fairchild Camera and Instrument Corporation in Mountain View, California. Today he is chair and chief executive officer of LSI Logic.

Wang Laboratories

Wang Laboratories, based in Lowell, Massachusetts, was founded in 1951 by An Wang,[36] who invented magnetic computer memory. The company now produces workflow, integrated imaging, document management, and related office software for client/server systems.[37] Much of its designs are based on the perceived potential in software services that may reduce paperwork.[38]

The company was a major player in the high-tech industry but began slipping in the mid-1980s. The company's downfall came when the industry shifted away from the minicomputer and proprietary systems that Wang offered and moved toward smaller personal computers or open systems that accommodate varied vendor technologies. By the late 1980s, Wang began reporting heavy losses.[39] After a bankruptcy reorganization, however, the company emerged as a slimmer, more focused imaging software company. The company reported revenue for 1995 of $946.3 million, and employs 6,800 people worldwide. Further, software leader Microsoft recently invested $90 million in Wang.[40]

Wang, a Chinese immigrant, came to the United States in 1945. He was admitted to Harvard and in less than four years made a fundamental discovery about core memories. His work became the cornerstone of the computer industry's development for almost two decades. In 1988, Wang was inducted into the National Inventors Hall of Fame, where he joined an elite group of 68 past inventors with names like Edison, Marconi, Bell and the Wright brothers. Wang has 40 patents.[41]

AST Research Inc.

Three immigrants co-founded AST Research in 1980: Safi Qureshey, Albert Wong, and Tom Yuen. Located in Irvine, California, AST has grown from a tiny start-up into the seventh-largest personal computer manufacturer in the United States, with $2.5 billion in worldwide revenue. The company designs, manufactures, and markets IBM-compatible personal computers, including desktop, notebook, and network server systems. The company has been one of the premier systems manufacturers and consistently controls a 2.7 percent market share.[42] The company has 6,500 employees worldwide, with 2,500 in the United States. Although AST reported losses of $99.3 million in 1995, the company has restructured its domestic operations, changed management, and received a large infusion of cash from Samsung.[43]

Qureshey, originally from Pakistan, is chair of the AST board. His co-founders, Wong and Yuen, are both immigrants from Hong Kong. The three began business in Yuen's garage with $12,000 in cash and $28,000 in equipment. Qureshey came to the United States in 1971 in order to obtain a degree in engineering and chose to remain in the United States because "there was hardly anything going on in electronics (in Pakistan). So the skills that I had I could not really apply in my homeland.... California was really the state that was producing the components, the new companies, the excitement." Although he first worked as an engineer, he decided to "go out on his own" because he could not get marketing or sales experience working for others as an engineer.[44]

Lam Research

Based in Fremont, California, Lam Research was founded by David Lam in 1983. The company manufactures semiconductor processing equipment. In 1995, the company had revenues of $600.7 million. It employs over 3,000 employees worldwide, 2,650 of whom work in the United States. The company intends to actively increase jobs in order to keep up with the demand for their equipment from chip factories all over the world.[45]

Lam was born in China but fled with his family during World War II to Cholum, Vietnam. After finishing high school in Hong Kong,[46] Lam decided to complete his education in the West where he believed there were more opportunities. He completed his undergraduate studies in Canada before receiving his Ph.D. at MIT in chemical engineering. His thesis on plasma engineering later became the foundation of his work with Lam Research. He worked for Texas Instruments, Xerox, and Hewlett Packard before founding his own company.

Lam started his own business because he perceived a glass ceiling for immigrants in the high-tech industry. He felt that Asians were underrepresented in the management ranks and believed that programmers and engineers should take the initiative to develop basic managerial and interpersonal skills, which are not generally taught at engineering school.[47]

In addition to Lam Research, in 1988, Lam also co-founded software company Expert Edge, with Stanford University professor Erlison Tse.[48] Lam serves as president and chief executive officer of the Palo Alto company. Expert Edge employs 22 employees and writes software that controls manufacturing equipment for chipmakers and automakers.

Lam was appointed to President Bush's Presidential Commission on Minority Business Development in 1990.[49]

Borland International Inc.

Borland International, located in Scotts Valley, California, was founded in 1982 by Phillippe Kahn. The company has 900 employees worldwide, 700 of whom are located in the United States, and 1995 revenues were $254 million. In the late 1980s, Borland was the number three maker of personal computer software, boasting top-selling spreadsheet and database products, such as Quattro Pro and Paradox. Borland was one of the first companies to incorporate object-oriented technology in its products, and today the benefits of object-oriented technology are recognized throughout the industry. Since that time, however, Borland has suffered financial losses culminating in Kahn's resignation as board chair. The company's strategy to continue as a smaller operation and reposition itself as a maker of software development tools has made the company profitable again.[50]

Kahn was born in France and led Borland for 12 years as president and chief executive officer. A mathematician and self-taught programmer, he founded Borland by selling an inexpensive version of the Pascal computer language through the mail. At the time that he started Borland, he was an undocumented immigrant. Kahn also co-founded the software company Starfish, in 1994, based in Scotts Valley. Starfish, founded without venture capital, posted $8.5 million in sales in its first nine months and has 60 employees[51] working on producing a variety of internet and on-line products.

Komag Inc.

Komag is the world's largest supplier of thin-film media for computer hard disk drives. Based in Milpitas, California, Komag was co-founded by

Tu Chen. The company's sales revenue for 1994 was $392.4 million and posted record financial results for its 1995 third fiscal quarter. Komag employs 2,700 people worldwide, 1,803 of whom work in the United States.[52]

Chen was born in Taiwan. He has a Master's and Doctorate degree in metallurgical engineering from the University of Minnesota. Chen, two other Taiwan-born friends from IBM, and Stephen Johnson founded Komag with the assistance of venture capital. Chen had led the Xerox company's research efforts to adapt the thin-film technology used in the production of semiconductors to the production of magnetic disks for storing and retrieving data in computers. Komag's goal was to bring Chen's ideas into production after Xerox abandoned its thin-film technology efforts. Today, thin-film sputtering, the technology approach pioneered by Komag, has become the basic process used in all disk drive designs.[53]

Chen, currently Komag chair, has received the Arthur Young Entrepreneurial Success of a Business Founded by a Minority Award and the 1988 Entrepreneur of the Year Award from *Venture Magazine*. He has been credited with more than 15 patents.[54]

Cadence Design Systems

Headquartered in San Jose, California, Cadence provides Electronic Design Automation software and services that automate and enhance the design of integrated circuits and electronic systems. Cadence currently leads this market with an estimated 18 percent market share.[55] The company reported revenues of $429 million for fiscal year 1994, and has 2,600 employees worldwide with 1,600 based in the United States.

Yen-son (Paul) Huang, a native of Taiwan, co-founded ECAD, which merged with SDA Systems to form Cadence. He stepped down as executive vice president of research and development at Cadence in 1989, but remains a member of the board of directors and consultant to the company. Company president Joseph Costello considers Huang "one of Cadence's technical gurus since (its) inception and ECAD's primary technical officer since its founding." Huang has since co-founded another electronics company, PIE Design Systems.[56]

Kingston Technology Corp.

Kingston Technology was founded by immigrants John Tu and David Sun. Based in Fountain Valley, a town in Southern California, the company manufacturers upgrade memory, processor, networking and storage products for personal computers. Kingston started in 1987 with only two employees and $12,000 in annual sales and now has 450 employees. In 1992,

Inc. Magazine named Kingston the fastest growing, privately held company in America, and by 1995, sales revenues reached $1 billion. The company is the largest minority-owned business in Orange County.[57]

Kingston entered the industry in 1987 when the computer industry was suffering from a shortage in memory modules for personal computers. This shortage could have severely hampered the ability of computer manufacturers and users to acquire the memory necessary to upgrade their systems. Tu and Sun met this need by designing an industry standard Single in Line Memory Module (SLMM), using an alternate chip that was available.[58]

Tu, who served as president of Kingston Technology since its founding, had previously co-founded Camminton Corporation with Sun, Kingston's vice president; Cammington was sold to AST Research. Sun immigrated to the United States from Taiwan after obtaining an electrical engineering degree.

Advanced Logic Research

Advanced Logic Research was founded in 1984, in Irvine, California, and designs, manufactures, markets, and supports computer systems targeted at the client/server and desktop markets. In 1995 the company reported its best quarterly and fiscal year results in four years, with sales revenue of $192.4 million, compared to $183.4 million the year before. It has 500 employees worldwide and approximately 400 employees in the United States.

Founder Gene Lu immigrated from Taiwan at age 9, and now serves as chair, chief executive officer, and president of the company. He studied electronics at Cal Poly Pomona and worked as an engineer at Micro Data, National Semiconductor, and Advanced Systems prior to founding Advanced Logic Research.[59]

Gemstar Development Corporation

Gemstar Development was co-founded in 1986, by three immigrants: Daniel Kwoh, Wilson Cho, and Henry Yuen. It produces several consumer VCR products — including VCR++, a one-step solution to accurate VCR taping that has become the best selling consumer electronics product of the 1990s. The Pasadena-based enterprise employs 200 people; 100 are based in the United States. The company started with an initial investment of $100,000 and its 1995 revenue exceeded $40 million.[60]

Kwoh came to the United States in 1966 as a student, became a U.S. citizen and earned a Master's and Doctorate in physics. Yuen and Kwoh both graduated from the California Institute of Technology and worked as research scientists at TRW. Cho, a professor of physics at Hong Kong University, together with Yuen and Kwoh, developed the technology to make the VCR more user-friendly after Yuen had difficulty programming his own VCR. President Bush acknowledged the founders' achievement in a commencement address in 1991.[61]

Genelabs Technologies Inc.

Genelabs was established in 1984, in the Northern California town of Redwood City, California. The international biopharmaceutical and diagnostics company develops therapeutic and vaccine products for viral diseases, autoimmune disorders, and other life-threatening or -debilitating conditions. It also develops viral diagnostic products. The company reported revenues of $16.5 million for 1994, and recently announced a joint venture with the Taiwan government to build a Genelabs subsidiary in Taiwan.[62] Genelabs employs 150 people worldwide, with half based in the United States.

Co-founder and board chair Frank Kung was born in China and obtained his Master's and Doctoral degrees in molecular biology from the University of California, Berkeley. His postdoctoral training was in cell biology and immunology. Before co-founding Genelabs, Kung founded Clinical BioResearch and held positions in research planning and business development at Cetus Immune from 1979 to 1981. He sits on the boards of the Biotechnology Industry Organization and the National Biotechnology Policy Board of the National Institute of Health.[63]

Netmanage

Netmanage is an internet software company, based in Cupertino, California. Zvi Alon, an immigrant from Israel, founded Netmanage and now serves as board chair and chief executive officer. The company experienced 180 percent growth from 1993 to 1994 and reported revenues of $62 million. It employs 600 people worldwide, over 400 of whom work in the United States.[64]

Sigma Designs Inc.

Sigma Designs Inc. was co-founded in 1982, by Thinh Tran, Jimmy Chan, and Jasen Chen, immigrants from Vietnam, Hong Kong and Taiwan respectively. Tran is the chair and chief executive officer. The company, headquartered in Fremont, California, manufactures MPEG (Moving Picture Experts Group)-based multimedia products, including MPEG video and audio encoding and decoding devices, chip sets, and a full line of interactive MPEG software titles. Sigma's sales revenue for 1995 was $30 million. The enterprise has 75 employees worldwide with all but 5 people working in the United States.[65]

Qume Corporation/Wyse Technology

Qume Corporation was founded in 1973, by David Lee, an immigrant from Taiwan. Qume, which produced terminals, monitors and printers was purchased by Wyse Technology, headquartered in San Jose, California, in December 1993. Wyse Technology was also founded by an immigrant. The company is a supplier of advanced video display terminal technology and high resolution desktop monitors. It employs 1400 people worldwide and 450 in the United States.[66]

Action Instruments

James Pinto, a native of Bangalore, India, started Action Instruments in Kearny Mesa, California. Its core business is manufacturing instruments needed for the measurement and control of industrial processes. The privately-held company delivers its products throughout Europe, Asia, and North America. The company now employs 180 workers and has been recognized as one of the best employers in the United States by *Inc. Magazine* partly for its employee ownership program. The revenues for 1995 were $21 million.[67]

Pinto immigrated to the United States in the 1960s and brought with him a Master's degree in physics and several years experience working in the European electronics industry.[68]

Conclusion

This paper has presented examples of numerous immigrants who have founded companies and played key roles in the high-tech industry by developing technology and creating jobs. Contrary to the popular view of immigrants engaging in narrow self-employment or running mom-and-pop shops, immigrant entrepreneurs discussed in this paper have created dynamic, successful high-tech companies that are leaders in the industry. The United States remains the center of innovation in most fields of high technology and has benefited from the immigration of energetic, capable and highly-motivated immigrants.

Importantly, the individuals highlighted entered in a variety of capacities. While many entered as foreign students, others entered as members of an immigrant family or as refugees. What they seemed to have in common were creativeness, ingenuity, and an enterprising spirit.

Notes

1   "Stick to the Real Problem," *Los Angeles Times*, 30 November 1995, Home Edition.

2   Editorial, "Give Border Control, Refugee Cap and National Registry Top Priority," *Fort Lauderdale Sun-Sentinel*, 27 September 1995.

3   *Immigration Reform Act of 1995*, S. 1394.

4   "Real Problem."

5   "Congress Creates High-Tech Worries; Planned Immigration Reform Could Curtail Foreign Expertise," *The News Tribune*, 29 September 1995.

6   "High-Tech Worries."

7   "Newcomers Put Stamp on Silicon Valley," *San Francisco Chronicle*, 8 July 1991, Business Section. The Asian American Manufacturing Asociation and the Mount Jade Science and Technology Association, both based in Silicon Valley, were contacted for an updated estimate but none was available.

8   "The Golden Decade: In Pursuit of a Better Way of Life," *Los Angeles Times*, 15 January 1990, Special Section.

9   "Anti-immigration laws could damage high-tech industry; Intel, IBM, AT&T rely on immigrant expertise," *Business Wire*, 16 March 1995.

10   "George Gilder, author on the computer industry, Immigrants Keep America at its Best," *Tampa Tribune*, 23 March 1995, Final Edition.

11   "Stamp on Silicon Valley."

12   "Congress Plans Stiff New Curb on Immigration," *The New York Times*, 25 September 1995, Late Edition.

13   Up to 5 percent of Microsoft's 12,000-member workforce are foreign nationals on temporary visas. "High-Tech Worries."

14   Eric Hautemont interview by author, tape recording, Mountain View, Calif., 20 November 1995.

15   National engineering association results reported in *The News Tribune*, 29 September 1995. "Guest Workers Might Ease Immigration Flow," *USA Today*, 2 August 1995, Final Edition. "Anti-immigration laws." Over 50 percent of successful immigrant entrepreneurs highlighted in this paper have Ph.D.s.

16   Hautemont, interview. Also questionnaires completed by founders of Genelabs Technologies and Solectron.

17   Stepan Pachikov, interview by author, 21 November 1995.

18   Eric Hautemont interview.

19   "Many Immigrants Demonstrate Flair for Creating Jobs," *San Diego Union-Tribune*, 31 January 1995, Perspective. Ivan Light, interview by author, "Race, Ethnicity and Entrepreneurship in the United States."

20   "Panel's Hearing to Focus on Effects of Immigration—Spotlight May Fall on GOP Proposals," *The Seattle Times*, 28 September 1995, Final Edition. Daniel Kwoh questionnaire, 11 December 1995.

21   Wang launched the company with Russell Artzt and two others.

22 "Bootstrapping for Billions," *Inc. Magazine*, September 1994. Srikumar S. Rao, "Software Warrior, How Charles Wang is repositioning Computer Associates for the road ahead," Systems User, *Financial World*, 4 July 1995. *Id.* Computer Associates International, *Online*, 1995.

23 "The House that Wang Built," *Newsday*, 15 August 1995. Biographical information provided by Computer Associates International, Public Relations, December 1995.

24 New Book about Computer Associates founder explores business mastery; Software Dragon: Charles Wang and His CA Empire Debuts in China, *Business Wire*, 10 October 1995.

25 Winston Chen, questionnaire, 7 December 1995. *Id.*

26 Solectron Online, December 1995.

27 "Megatest appoints two new members to its board of directors," *Business Wire*, 3 May 1995. Id.

28 Intel Facts and Figures, *Online*, 1994 and 1995.

29 Carolyn Caddes, *Portraits of Success, Impressions of Silicon Valley Pioneers*, Palo Alto, 42, 1986.

30 "Anti-immigration laws."

31 "In memory of John Heinz, Teresa Heinz bestows five $250,000 awards for bettering society," *Pittsburgh Post-Gazette*, 27 January 1995, National. The award honors those who have changed society for the good.

32 "Anti-immigration laws."

33 "LSI Logic's New Gresham Oregon Campus Underway," *PR Newswire*, 9 October 1995.

34 "New Chip on the Block, Business Dateline," *Oregonian*, 10 October 1995.

35 Caddes, *Portraits of Success*

36 "It's Asians' Turn in Silicon Valley," *New York Times*, 14 January 1992.

37 "Wang Awarded $2.2 million contract from Hewlett-Packard to provide imaging software and professional services to improve Italy's companies register program," *Business Wire*, 8 February 1995.

38 "Wang's great leap out of limbo," *Business Week*, no. 3361, (7 March 1994): 68.

39 "Microsoft makes $90 million Wang investment," United Press International, 12 April 1995, Regional News. Id.

40 "Cash is King, cash management," *Chief Executive*, no. 104, (June 1995): 40. Information provided by Corporate Communication Wang Laboratories, 13 December 1995. Id. The number of employees in the United States was not available. Microsoft makes $90 million Wang investment, United Press International, 12 April 1995, Regional News.

41 "Wang chief wins inventor award; An Wang", *MIS Week*, 9, 13, (28 March 1988): 8. Id.

42 "Corporate Profile, AST refocuses efforts, relying on Samsung relationship," *Infoworld*, Hardware, (21 August 1995): 25.

43 "Caught in the Cross-fire; Plagued by losses and a gun-shy reputation, AST's chief seeks a safe return to prosperity," *Los Angeles Times*, 17 September 1995, Business.

44 "Recognized where you want to lead," *Orange County Business Journal*, Vol. 14, pg 1, 2 December 1991.

45 "Profiles of Top Firms," *San Francisco Chronicle*, 24 April 1995, Business (F). "The Cutting Edge: Computing/Technology/Innovation; The chips are flying; Semiconductor industry is on a surprising roll," *Los Angeles Times*, 5 July 1995, Business.

46 "David Lam: Asian immigrant presses quest for leadership diversity," *Business Journal-San Jose*, 12, No. 18, Sec.1, (8 August 1994): 12.

47 "Quest for leadership diversity.' Id.

48 "David Lam: Asian immigrant presses quest for leadership diversity," *Business Journal-San Jose*, 12, No. 18, Sec.1, (8 August 1994): 12.

49 "David Lam's Career Path Winds to Presidential Commission Spot," *San Francisco Business Times*, 4, No. 42, (18 June 1990): 12.

50 Borland Company Information, 12 December 1995. This represents a drop in revenues from 1994, $394 million. The company has since reorganized and changed its product strategy. "Borland's Chairman Will Resign," *San Francisco Chronicle*, 23 November 1995, Business. Borland Company Information Online, 1 December 1995. "Chairman Will Resign." Id.

51 "Founder Quits as Chairman at Borland," *New York Times*. 23 November 1995, Business. "Newcomers Put Stamp on Silicon Valley," *San Francisco Chronicle*, 8 July 1991, Business. "Founder Quits."

52 Komag Incorporated, *Online*, 1995. "Komag announces record third quarter results," *PR Newswire*, 19 October 1995, Financial News. "Profiles of Top Firms," *San Francisco Chronicle*, 24 April 1995.

53 "Who's who in high-tech—a directory of high-ranking executives in Silicon Valley: Peripherals Manufacturers," *Business Journal-San Jose*, 12, no. 49 (27 February 1995): 18. Komag Incorporated, *Online*, 1995.

54 "Arthur Young Awards, Arthur Young and Co. and Venture announce 1988 Bay Area Entrepreneurs of the Year," *Business Wire*, 14 June 1988. "Who's who in high-tech."

55 Cadence Design Systems, *Online*, 1995.

56 "It's Asians' Turn in Silicon Valley." "Cadence Reorganizes for 1990 Debut as Full Line EDA Software Supplier," *PR Newswire*, 16 November 1989. "Cadence Reorganizes for 1990 Debut." "Asians' Turn in Silicon Valley."

57 "Asians' Turn in Silicon Valley." Kingston Technology Corporation, Press Release, *Online*, 10 October 1995. "The Changing Face of Orange County's Economy: Biggest minority companies grow revenue, jobs," *Orange County Business Journal*, 31 January 1994.

58 Kingston Technology Corporation, Company Overview, *Online*, 1995.

59 Advanced Logic Research, Inc. Press Release, *Online*, 2 November 1995. The increase has been attributed to a 61% increase in sales to domestic and OEM customers. Business Dateline, *Orange County Business Journal*, 5 December 1995. *Orange County Business Journal*, 14, no. 9 (30 May 1994): 1.

60 Two others who had capital were recruited to start the company. "VCR Literacy Dawns During Bush Administration; President applauds VCR++ and its CalTech alumni creators in commencement address," *PR Newswire*, 14 June 1991. Daniel Kwoh questionnaire completed by co-founder of Gemstar, 11 December 1995.

61 "Inventing Technology to Make Technology Simple," *Los Angeles Business Journal*, 14, no. 9, (2 March 1992): 1.

62   "Chiron and Genelabs announce worldwide diagnostics alliance," Business Wire, 10 March 1995. "Genelabs and the Taiwan, ROC Ministry of Finance announce investment plan in Genelabs Biotechnology Limited," *Business Wire*, 14 July 1995.

63   "Who's who in high tech."

64   "Profiles of Top Firms."

65   Another co-founder was Steve Winegarden of the United States. "Asians' Turn in Silicon Valley. "Sigma Designs announces third quarter results," *Business Wire*, 16 November 1995. Thinh Tran questionnaire, 11 December 1995. Revenue was unchanged from 1994. The company announced a net loss of $1.2 million, however, for the third quarter of 1995.

66   "Asians' Turn in Silicon Valley." Company information based on telephone interview, 11 December 1995.

67   "Instrumental in growth industry measures up as a boon to economy," *San Diego Union-Tribune*, 19 September 1995, Business. "Instrumental in growth industry." The company incurred losses in 1989, 1990, and 1991.

68   "Many immigrants demonstrate flair for creating jobs," *San Diego Union-Tribune*, 31 January 1995, Perspective.

Vietnamese-Owned Manicure Businesses in Los Angeles

by Craig Trinh-Phat Huynh[*]

Some 30 percent of the 22,000 nail salons in the United States are owned by Vietnamese Americans; in Los Angeles, the proportion is a staggering 80 percent. And the Vietnamese Americans involved are essentially all women. These figures are remarkable since Vietnamese Americans make up only 0.2 percent of the U.S. population and did not begin entering the country in significant numbers until 1975.[1]

Recent scholarship on small business activities in the United States suggests a significant contribution to the economy by various immigrant and ethnic groups.[2] Most of these studies have focused on immigrants who may have entered for economic reasons. Since 1975, however, about 20 percent of the documented entrants to the United States are political or religious refugees.[3] Many of these refugees came from Southeast Asia as a legacy of the U.S. involvement in the Vietnam War, and their arrival has generated a growing body of literature on socioeconomic adaptation in America.[4] Yet few studies have considered the development of refugee women's entrepreneurial activities.

While feature stories on California Vietnamese and New York Korean manicurists have appeared in newspapers and other popular periodicals, scholarly articles on the topic based on empirical research are lacking.[5] These popular accounts describe Vietnamese refugee manicurists as eagerly embracing and becoming successful in a glamorous profession, yet one cannot help but wonder whether all Vietnamese manicurists regard their profession as appealing or comfortable, and whether this niche of nail salons in mini-malls throughout California suburbs is their idea of the American dream. The women featured in the articles came to the attention of the media because they were perceived as having met all the objective criteria for success. One goal of the ongoing research that forms the basis for this paper is to define more clearly the unique issues and concerns

[*] Craig Trinh-Phat Huynh is an M.A. Candidate at the Asian American Studies Center, University of California at Los Angeles. The author gratefully acknowledges the valuable comments made on earlier drafts of this paper by Paul Ong and Bill Ong Hing.

faced by these Vietnamese women. The research may yield information to educate refugee service providers and policy makers about any special needs the women might have and to help other women learn from the experiences of these Vietnamese entrepreneurs.

Economic activity among Vietnamese American women as manicurists over the past 20 years raises a number of questions, including the following: (1) How and why do Vietnamese women enter the manicure business? (2) Since Vietnamese refugees are eligible for federally-funded social services, what types of resources and networks are available to assist them in obtaining appropriate training and licensing to work in this type of business? (3) What issues do Vietnamese manicurists face in the workplace? This research project begins to address aspects of these questions.

Background and Methodology

Ten women manicurists working in Los Angeles County nail salons were interviewed between March 1994 and September 1995. Respondents were identified and asked to participate in the study through personal contacts.[6] Most were Vietnamese, but one woman was of Chinese ethnicity born in Vietnam. Their ages ranged from 24 to 55 years of age. Eight of the women (seven married and one divorced) had children ages 3 to 27. The other two women were single and had no children. Three women owned their nail salons; the other seven were salon employees.

Length of U.S. residence varied greatly. Two women arrived in the first refugee wave immediately at the end of the Vietnam War in 1975. Three women came during the second wave (often referred to as the "boat people's wave") from the late 1970s to the 1980s. The remaining five women came to this country under the Orderly Departure Program[7] that began in the early 1980s.

Discussion

Vietnamese Manicure Business in California

Southern California, Los Angeles and Orange Counties in particular, has become a major center of the manicure industry. It is also home to most beauty schools that train nail technicians and many national and international manufacturers and distributors of nail products. At the same time, the number of professional manicurists in the area has surged, with Vietnamese refugees entering the Los Angeles industry in the late 1970s. From

1984 to 1989, licensed manicurists in Los Angeles County alone increased 50 percent from 9,755 to 15,238, of which Vietnamese Americans comprise approximately 80 percent.

The proliferation of Vietnamese nail salons can be linked to the cosmetology schools in Southern California, which reported an influx of Vietnamese students in the 1980s. At one school, Vietnamese comprised about 40 percent of all students, compared to only 2 percent only ten years before.[8]

The popularity of manicuring schools among the Vietnamese has led to the establishment of a number of cosmetology schools that are managed or directed by Vietnamese Americans. These schools have transformed their programs to meet the specific needs of Vietnamese students, especially those newcomers with very limited English proficiency. Courses are offered in Vietnamese and financial aid is available. The typical cost for training as a manicurist at a beauty school can be $1,200 to $1,500, but government-sponsored job training programs can cover tuition. Finally, while most beauty colleges usually offer a complete professional cosmetology course requiring 1,600 hours of training, these Vietnamese schools offer a more specialized manicuring course with only 350 hours of training. As a result, such schools have successfully enrolled a large number of Vietnamese students in their manicuring classes.

The 350-hour programs are linked to specific licensing requirements, which vary from state to state. California requires a manicure license for nail technicians; New York does not, and presumably, anyone who knows how to give a manicure can be in the business.[9] In California, the applicant must be at least 17 years old and have 350 hours of training in an accredited cosmetology school. The proliferation of Vietnamese manicurists in the state has prompted the California State Board of Cosmetology to offer its licensing exam in Vietnamese, as well as in English and Spanish.

An informal ethnic network has facilitated the growth in the number of Vietnamese manicurists, because prospective students often learn about the availability of financial aid or job training funds from relatives and friends. When the owners of Vietnamese nail salons need additional nail technicians, they can easily find potential employees by word of mouth and from the Vietnamese students in the local beauty schools. Employers can also recruit workers by advertising for manicurists in Vietnamese-language newspapers, radio, and television programs. Help-wanted signs in Vietnamese are commonly displayed in windows of Los Angeles nail salons.

Wages vary and manicurists usually work on 60 percent commission, plus tips. One industry expert says that the average yearly salary for a manicurist is between $20,000 to $24,000.[10] For the more ambitious Vietnamese women who can accumulate a few thousand dollars, nail salon ownership is the way to become entrepreneurs and to increase income.

Although low or no cost technical assistance is available through public and private agencies, respondents in this study did not utilize these resources in establishing their own businesses.[11] Many were not familiar with the social service agencies that could help them set up a manicure business. Instead, the Vietnamese salon owners in the study used personal savings and borrowed funds from family or friends to start their businesses. Though they were aware of bank loans, for a variety of reasons — including, limited English skills, lack of trust, and unfamiliarity with the process — they did not seek bank assistance. Twenty-four-year-old Michelle Le, arrived in the United States in 1990. When she became a professional manicurist in 1994, Le was not aware of the availability of public or private assistance, and by the time she learned about the programs, she erroneously thought that services were available only to the more recently-arrived refugees. On the other hand, 55-year-old Cam Van, who has been a professional manicurist since 1981, knew about the Small Business Administration when she set up her nail salon. She did not ask for assistance, however, because she wanted to be self-reliant. "I was going through a bitter divorce from my husband, who said to me that I could not make it on my own if I left him," she said. "He thought that I would be a welfare mother with three small children. I wanted to prove myself and to show him that I could make my own business without help from anybody."

A quick glance at the West Los Angeles telephone directory suggests that fifty nail salons in the area are owned or operated by Vietnamese Americans. The five city blocks of Westwood Boulevard between Wilshire and Santa Monica Boulevards are home to eight nail salons — six of which are owned and operated by Vietnamese. Restaurants and photocopy services are the only two types of business that outnumber nail salons on this half-mile stretch. While most of the manicure shops have two or three workers, the largest shop in this business district has 10 nail technicians working on the weekends.

Few Vietnamese or other Asian Pacific American customers frequent these Vietnamese-owned manicure businesses, which are located in a variety of ethnic neighborhoods, ranging from mostly white to mostly African American, Latino, or multiethnic. The ethnic background of clients usually reflects those who reside or work in the salon's surrounding community. Thus, depending on the location, customers for a particular salon may be predominantly African American, Latino, white, or a combination of the three. On Westwood Boulevard, clients are white or Middle-Eastern (reflecting the fact that many of the ethnic businesses in this neighborhood are owned by Middle-Easterners).

Why Vietnamese Women Enter the Manicure Business

To some observers, Vietnamese refugee women may appear to lack many of the resources needed for running a successful business. They don't have investment capital, secure credit histories, U.S. business experience, English proficiency, or knowledge of American culture. In addition, the manicure business can be difficult: it involves long hours, difficult customers, business competition, and risk of robbery and business failure. Given these many disadvantages, why, then, do Vietnamese women enter this occupation?

Shortly after Lani Nguyen, 28, arrived in Los Angeles in 1980, she enrolled in Glendale City College to study English and accounting. She started looking for a job, but nobody hired her. Nguyen attributed this to her limited English skills and her lack of work experience in the United States. Another respondent said that even with good English skills, she would still be at a disadvantage when competing with mainstream workers, because of the level of work skills or cultural experiences needed in the general labor market. She first became interested in manicure after some Vietnamese friends opened nail salons in the city. According to Nguyen, among the many appealing reasons to enter the nail salon business are the following: (1) low capital (about $6,000); (2) easy state licensing process; (3) no requirement for English proficiency; and (4) a very lucrative market. She enrolled in a manicure course at a West Los Angeles beauty school, and after 600 hours of training, she passed the exam and received her state manicurist license. Her first nail business was a rented space inside a hair salon in Glendale. After the owner retired, Nguyen bought the salon and took over the whole shop. She worked there for eight years before moving in 1990 to her current location in the San Fernando Valley.

About half of the respondents started out as seamstresses and learned of the more lucrative manicure business through fellow seamstresses. Forty-six-year-old Jasmine Trinh, a schoolteacher in Vietnam, entered the United States in 1986, and found her first job as a seamstress in a downtown Los Angeles sweatshop. While working there, she heard about Vietnamese manicure businesses from her co-workers. A year later, Trinh left her sewing job and studied manicure in a local beauty college. She decided to change jobs because she earned such little money in the sweatshop, even though she frequently brought work home so her husband and children could help her sew at night. As a manicurist, Trinh has been able to make four to five times the income of her old sewing job, and she is happy that she no longer has to bring home work to help gain extra income.

Several Vietnamese women became manicurists because they felt that they were at a disadvantage in other jobs that brought them into contact with the public. In addition to more independence, the business also allows the women to limit contact with an unfamiliar culture, and care for their families.

Limiting Contact With an Unfamiliar Culture

Vietnamese refugee women are likely to become manicurists because the salon business provides a high degree of autonomy and insulation from an alien — American — culture, language and people. Ironically, the nature of their work puts them in full contact with non-Vietnamese/non-Asian clients with whom they must communicate in English and be somewhat knowledgeable of American culture. At least, however, they are more in control of the situation.

Family Factors

Vietnamese refugee women often choose the manicure business because it allows them to provide for the needs of family members. To some, this also means making use of family-based resources in a way not possible under other conditions of employment. For many of the women, the manicure business functions as an extension of the family itself, allowing the women to spend more time with their children and saving on childcare expenses. Nguyen explained, "What I like most about my work is that I can take my daughter to the shop and look after her while I work on my customers." In one corner of her nail salon — a mini childcare center — Nguyen has placed a big doll house and lots of toys for her four-year-old.

Problems Faced by Vietnamese Manicurists

Vietnamese manicure businesses face a number of problems. The business has reached a saturation point in many parts of Los Angeles and competition has become fierce. Linda Ly has seen a proliferation of Vietnamese-owned nail salons in the area where she currently works. She is not happy about the intense competition. "[Vietnamese people open] their nail salons just a couple of doors down the street from yours. Not only that, they lowered their prices and competed for the same customers in the area."

In this competitive market, when some Vietnamese manicurists have lowered their rates to attract customers, others have had to follow suit. In the early 1980s, the price of doing a full set of nails was $60. Today, most Vietnamese nail salons charge their customers only about $18-20 for the same service. Some salons have tried another strategy to bring in new customers: free service to first-time customers. This competitiveness has resulted in some shops being only marginally profitable.

Vietnamese domination of the business and their competitive prices have created resentment among some non-Vietnamese nail salon owners who decry the lowering of prices to just one-third of what they were a decade ago. Many Vietnamese manicurists, however, counter that this trend has simply made nail services more affordable for more customers.

Manicurists also face health risks. Skin infections and danger from toxic chemicals are real threats, as well as the spread of HIV/AIDS. Because their limited English proficiency keeps them from reading and understanding warning labels on nail products, many Vietnamese manicurists encounter problems. For personal health safety reasons, most Vietnamese manicurists now take some precautions, such as wearing masks to protect themselves from dust created when filing nails. Sanitation is a concern for both the customers and the manicurists. All manicurists must meet sanitary standards established by state regulation, and most customers are interested in knowing that the Vietnamese manicurists sterilize their tools properly.

Some manicurists must also work with difficult customers, who give the impression that they look down on the workers, perhaps because of poor English-speaking skills. Sometimes disagreements arise over a customer's failure to provide a gratuity. Often, customers who are unhappy about the service will express their dissatisfaction and ask for some form of compensation from the manicurists. As a result, those Vietnamese manicurists who are limited English speakers or who are less familiar with American culture tend to feel overwhelmed by such demands, sometimes accompanied by strong feelings and language, from customers. While Vietnamese manicurists are afraid of customers who become querulous and hostile, customers can become frustrated and lose patience with the manicurists who may not be able to understand the specifics of their request. This particular perception toward the customers is less common among the Vietnamese manicurists who are more acculturated and who can also speak better English. They are more familiar with customer attitudes and can communicate more effectively to address the problem.

Conclusion

These findings indicate that Vietnamese refugee women chose the manicure business when they realized that their employment opportunities in the United States were limited by a language or education gap. In many instances, the manicure business has provided Vietnamese women with good, successful jobs. If "success" is defined, however, as making millions of dollars, or even hundreds of thousands, Vietnamese manicurists could not be deemed successful. If, on the other hand, "success" means survival and modest growth to the point where many people can earn a decent living by American standards, Vietnamese manicurists are largely successful. This does not mean that all Vietnamese women are able to do this. Certainly more needs to be learned about this phenomenon, but what we know now is that some Vietnamese women have reached a level of self-sufficiency in the United States through the manicure industry.

Footnotes

1   See Shinagawa, Larry Hajime "The Impact of Immigration on the Demography of Asian Pacific Americans," in this volume and Hing (1993).

2   According to the New York-based trade publication *American Salon*, in 1988, 139.9 million manicures, pedicures, and artificial nail services were provided in the United States generating $932 million in business. See Ong, Bonacich and Cheng (1994); Tseng (1994); and Zhou (1992).

3   Office of Refugee Resettlement, 1986. *Report to Congress: Refugee Resettlement Program* (Gold, 1988).

4   See Haines (1987); Finnan (1982); and Bach and Bach (1980).

5   Some attention has been devoted to the proliferation of Vietnamese- and Korean-owned nail salons, such as newspaper feature stories (e.g., "Vietnamese women nail down their niche as manicurists in L.A.," *Los Angeles Times*, 11 June 1989; "Waiting on women hand and foot," *The Orange County Register*, 27 November 1989; "A hand up," *Mirabella*, July 1991.

6   The data is not a random or representative sample of Vietnamese manicure businesses. The women interviewed, however, were diverse in terms of age and length of residence in the United States.

7   The Orderly Departure Program (ODP) helps Vietnamese immigrants reunite with their family members living in the United States.

8   *Los Angeles Times*, 11 June 1989; *The Orange County Register*, 27 November 1989.

9   See Park (1990).

10   Dan Hoang interview, associate publisher of *Saigon Nails* — a Vietnamese-language trade magazine.

11   For a discussion on the U.S. refugee resettlement program and its policy of economic self-sufficiency for refugees, see Bach (1988); and Law and Schneiderman (1992).

References

Hing, Bill Ong *Making and Remaking Asian America Through Immigration Policy, 1850-1990* (Stanford: Stanford University Press, 1993).

Ong, Paul, Edna Bonacich and Lucie Cheng, eds. *The New Asian Immigration in Los Angeles and Global Restructuring* (Philadelphia: Temple University Press, 1994)

Tseng Yen-Fen. "Chinese Ethnic Economy: San Gabriel Valley, Los Angeles County," *Journal of Urban Affairs*, 16(2) (1994):169-189

Zhou, Ming, *Chinatown: The Social Economic Potential Of An Urban Enclave* (Philadelphia: Temple University Press, 1992)

Office of Refugee Resettlement, 1986. *Report to Congress: Refugee Resettlement Program* (Gold, 1988).

Haines, D.W. "Patterns In Southeast Asian Refugee Employment: A Reappraisal of The Existing Research," *Ethnic Groups* 7 (1987):39-63

Finnan, C.R., "Community Influences on The Occupational Assimilation of Vietnamese Refugees," *Anthropological Quarterly* 55 (1982):161-69

Bach, R.L. and J. Bach, "Employment Patterns of Southeast Asian Refugees," *Monthly Labor Review* 103 (1980):31-38.

"Vietnamese Women Nail Down Their Niche as Manicurists in L.A.," *Los Angeles Times*, 11 June 1989

Waiting on Women Hand and Foot," *The Orange County Register*, 27 November 1989

"A Hand Up," *Mirabella*, July 1991.

Park, Kyeyoung. *The Korean American Dream: Ideology and Small Business in Queens, New York* (Ph.D. diss., City University of New York, 1990).

Dan Hoang (interview), associate publisher of <u>Saigon Nails</u> — a Vietnamese-language trade magazine.

Bach, R.L. "State Intervention in Southeast Asian Refugee Resettlement in the United States," *Journal of Refugee Studies*, 1(1) (1988):38-56

Law, C.K. and L. Schneiderman, "Policy Implications of Factors Associated with Economic Self-Sufficiency of Southeast Asian Refugees," in S.M. Furuto, et al., eds., *Social Work Practice with Asian Americans* (Sage Publications, Inc., 1992), pp.167-183.

Chinese-Cambodian Donut Makers in Orange County: Case Studies of Family Labor and Socioeconomic Adaptations

by Gen Leigh Lee[*]

Tlog! Tlog! Tlog! — sounds of batter dropping into gallons of burning-hot oil to make old-fashion and devils' food donuts.[1] The time is 1:30 a.m., and the baker's daily routine has just started. A huge mixer whips the raised flour so that by the time the buttermilk and cake donuts are finished, the dough will be ready for kneading, twisting, turning, shaping, and cutting into glazed donuts, bars, twists, cinnamon rolls, butterflies, and apple-fritters. The different patterns go onto fryer screens which are positioned in a closed heater, so the dough can rise and be readied for frying.

The baker has not finished frying the first batch of raised donuts, but between 4:00 and 4:30 a.m., a regular early bird customer knocks on the door for coffee and a donut. The donut shop is open for the day. The baker calls his wife at home, and by 5:00 a.m., she begins her routine of baking muffins and croissants, stuffing fruit fillings into donuts, and handling the counter. This is the beginning of a typical morning in a Cambodian husband-wife-owned (or -managed) donut shop.

Since 1979, a large number of refugees from Cambodia, Laos, and Vietnam have resettled throughout the United States. They risked their lives and endured much hardship to escape their ancestral homelands and reach the United States. Many still struggle to adjust to a new culture, laws, and social and economic values.

The past 20 years have witnessed an increasing amount of research on immigrants' economic and social adaptation, particularly in ethnic-based or ethnic-dominated economies, and their impact on the local economic structures. Some research has included Asian Pacific Americans, but generally absent from increasing studies is consideration of contributions made by Asian refugees (Gold, 1994).

---

[*] Gen Leigh Lee is an M.A. candidate and lecturer at the Asian American Studies Department, University of California at Los Angeles.

Even less attention has been paid to Cambodian entrepreneurship. Most literature portrays Cambodians as socially and economically immobile, yet growing numbers of Cambodians have made remarkable progress socially, economically, and academically. Nearly all Cambodians who have arrived since 1979 are survivors of war and genocide. This survival has generated research about Cambodian refugees' post-traumatic stress syndrome, mental health, and poverty issues. This paper will begin to examine one of the effective economic strategies adopted by these survivors by focusing on donut shop owners and operators in California.

Since the 1980s, donut shop operation has been a growing business enterprise among these recent arrivals, particularly among Cambodians of Chinese ancestry. *The Wall Street Journal* counted about 2,450 Cambodian-owned or -operated donut shops in California in 1995; the *Los Angeles Times* placed the figure at approximately 2,000 in 1993 (Kaufman, 1995; Akst, 1993). Most are private, family-owned shops.

These donut shops are scattered throughout California and cater to a diverse group of customers, not just members of any one specific group. Some owners live close to the business (within two miles), while others might reside as far as 30 miles away. The desire to live close to the business means many do not live in a Cambodian enclave; instead, many own homes and live in white, middle-class neighborhoods.

That Cambodian refugees have come to dominate the donut shop industry in California is a remarkable phenomenon. As refugees from an agrarian, war-torn nation, they initially arrived penniless. The donut business has opened the door for some to become economically independent, creating a path for economic and social mobility. Their accomplishments in a span of ten years or less certainly deserves attention.

Linguistic and social barriers to finding good-paying jobs caused many Cambodians to seek self-employment. For them, small business ownership is a matter of economic survival as well as a path to socioeconomic status and acceptance. Operating donut shops may be labor intensive, but the skills required can be learned easily and English fluency is not necessary. Shops create employment for many family members who are unskilled or who have no transferable skills. The income also allows most of these shop owners to become homeowners and to pay the cost of higher education for their children.

Operating shops has essentially become an entrepreneurial niche that provides a base for a significant segment of the Cambodian American community. In many ways this is reminiscent of other entrepreneurial niches established by earlier Asian Pacific immigrants. Like Chinese American laundries and Japanese American farms, Cambodian American donut businesses provide a source of support for relatives and friends.

The Cambodian community is of such recent vintage that the community itself has not been able to develop any formal social and economic organizations to assist its members. The main source of financial and social support for establishing any type of business is the strong kinship, ethnic, and regional ties shared by Cambodian refugees. Most depend on this informal, word-of-mouth network among families, relatives, and friends. Whether one wants to buy a shop, needs a baker or counter help, or requires technical or financial assistance, the informal network produces desired results. The predominantly ethnic Chinese Cambodian community in Orange County, the subject of this study, is a good example of a small, tight-knit, and supportive community. Its members value the same culture and speak the same language. They have relied on one another to develop a donut shop segment due to similar economic circumstances, educational backgrounds, and societal limitations.

Goals And Objectives

This research uses case studies to explore the history of Cambodian American families' entry into the donut shop business, the relationship of the entry to their socioeconomic adaptations, and contributions to the local economy. In analyzing this work experience, the following are important considerations: (1) the institutional structure, opportunities, and resources in the local economy; (2) past experience and cultural values; and (3) the class and ethnicity of this population.

The most frequently asked questions about these Cambodian entrepreneurs are "Why the donut business?" and "How do they capitalize their business?" This research provides some initial answers to these and other questions. First, the effective economic and social strategies adopted by some families, and the division of family labor roles according to age and gender are examined. Specific questions include the following: (1) Why and how do Cambodians enter the donut business? (2) How do family members or kin and ethnic ties contribute to their entrepreneurship decisions and acquisitions, and to the maintenance of donut shops? Second, varying expectations of work and of each other among shop owners and their children in relation to acculturation and adaptation is explored. Questions include the following: (1) How does the business affect each family's socioeconomic adaptation? (2) What is the level of acculturation, by age, into the mainstream society? (3) How do they perceive themselves in this society? (4) What kind of relationship do the parents have with their children? Third, how these experiences are impacted by their status as refugees and their contributions to the larger society is considered. Some questions include the following: (1) Do they encounter discrimination? (2) What are their contributions to the local economy and to government? (3) What are implications for policymakers?

Theoretical Framework

An overview of the pertinent scholarship on immigrant and refugee small business ownership and family labor is helpful to an understanding of the Cambodian donut shop phenomenon. Immigrant and refugee groups often turn to small businesses or ethnic-based economies to find financial independence. Extremely "severe employment problems faced by refugees" contributes to the attraction of small business opportunities (Haines, 1987). The Cambodian entrepreneurs' ability to finance, cope with, and adapt to economic needs and problems depends largely on utilization of kinship and friendship ties and networks, credit rotation, and ethnic solidarity. Much of this will be illustrated in the case studies below.

Steven Gold illustrates how ethnic Chinese Vietnamese entrepreneurs in the United States have been able to take advantage of their ethnic solidarity and connections with the Chinese from Hong Kong, Taiwan, and China. They use their ethnic linkages to secure capital from some cash-rich Chinese to establish businesses, which they themselves provide labor and which cater to other immigrants, predominantly Vietnamese, Chinese, and other Southeast Asians (Gold, 1994). In contrast, Cambodians tend to remain within their own small circle, utilizing their own savings or borrowing from friends, relatives, or credit-rotation associations. Ethnic Chinese Cambodians also take advantage of their connections with Chinese from other backgrounds.

Gold's discussion of the strong family values of the ethnic Chinese Vietnamese and contributions of family members and relatives to the successful operations of their enterprises seem quite relevant to the Cambodian situation. How does a Chinese Cambodian family or household function to operate and maintain the business? What roles do cultural values, such as kin and ethnic ties, play in establishing and maintaining the business and family? What are the parents' and children's expectations and attitudes toward their businesses? What are the social costs, sacrifices, or impact of Chinese Cambodian family, labor, employees, and employment?

Research by Usha Welaratna and Marie A. Martin includes discussion of the different work ethnics of Khmer and Chinese Cambodians. Their explanations of the cultural, religious, and socioeconomic stratification of Cambodian society provide some insights into the world-view of Cambodians (Welaratna, 1993; Martin, 1994). With regard to assimilation and the notion of "success," Welaratna argues that most Western social scientists impose American values on Cambodians. Cambodian culture, values and society define success and failure differently from the United States mainstream: money is not an important measure of personal success (Welaratna, 1993). Chinese, Sino-Khmers, and Khmers all place great emphasis on the nuclear and extended family, "bound together by a variety of emotional, economic, and legal ties" (Welaratna, 1993) Khmers consider an individual's "good conduct" and "emotional fulfillment" more important than wealth and commitment.

In pre-revolutionary Cambodia, people did not have to work hard to survive. The rice, fresh or dried fish, and vegetables that made up their simple diet were abundantly available. Homelessness was not an issue: people who did not have money to build a house or a villa could make a hut made of thatch or bamboo poles. In 1970 "everyone owned a building, a villa, an apartment, a beautiful wooden house, a straw hut, or a hovel" (Martin, 1994) This gave them plenty of leisure time.

In contrast, the majority of the Chinese in Cambodia, many of whom are entrepreneurs, strived for economic stability, social status, and prestige through wealth. Welaratna argues that the Cambodians' social and cultural aspects should be analyzed from their perspectives. Both Welaratna and Martin distinguish some of the different values held by Khmer and Chinese, enabling an interpretation of differences in their socioeconomic adaption and assimilation in the United States.

The vast majority of Cambodian refugees arriving after 1979 came from an agricultural background, a society where men and elders are believed to be supreme and right. Many who entered the U.S., however, were also of middle- and upper-class backgrounds. Further, since their arrival in this country, Cambodians have experienced changes in traditional gender roles due to harsh economic realities.

Methodology

The methodology of this research is exploratory and descriptive, using multiple research methods: primary qualitative ethnography, archival research, and participant-observation. As a member of this community, the author's presence at many social gatherings in the last ten years was useful. A decade of experience and observation working in more than ten different donut shops during summers and weekends and as a temporary fill-in was an added advantage.

Interviews provided data on personal, economic, entrepreneurial, and social experiences. Secondary sources, including published materials on history, family, labor, ethnic/small business enterprise, and gender studies, provided historical and theoretical structures.[2]

Sampling Design

Officials of B&H Distributors, a donut (and restaurant) supply and equipment warehouse, provided access to the company's 1,400 accounts, including shop names, addresses, and telephone numbers. Using the B&H account information, shops were plotted on maps of Los Angeles and Orange Counties to determine the number of shops within each zip code. More than 80 percent of B&H customers were Cambodian entrepreneurs. A brief survey was conducted at B&H's annual open-house on August 26, 1994. But most participants were unresponsive and ambivalent.

Potential interviewees, selected from diverse areas, based on zip code plotting, received letters informing them of the nature of this research and study. In follow up telephone calls, appointments were set up with those who agreed to participate.

Setting up interviews was quite difficult. Most customers contacted declined because of lack of time or scheduling conflicts. Consequently, the number of interviewees was greatly reduced and the focus became ethnic Chinese Cambodians in Orange County rather than Cambodians in both Los Angeles and Orange Counties. The semi-structured, open-ended interview questions were specific but flexible enough to raise further questions or allow any necessary probing.

Seven individuals representing four families were interviewed for this study. Three interviews were conducted at the interviewees' shops, two took place both at home and at the shop, one interview was conducted at home, and another on the phone. Khmer and English were used interchangeably in four of the interviews; two interviews were in Cantonese, Khmer, and Mandarin, and one was almost entirely in English. Two families were randomly selected from the B&H accounts while two were chosen because of their personal acquaintance. Interviews were conducted between 8 December 1994 and 23 March 1995, and lasted 45 minutes to two hours, plus time for follow-up questions to clarify questions. Some interviewees were asked different questions. Three of the families are reported on in this paper.

The Families: Ly, Chau, And Vong

Long Beach has the largest concentration of Cambodians outside of Cambodia, approximately 30,000.[3] The United States census does not distinguish Cambodians of Chinese ethnicity from the indigenous Khmer, but based on observations throughout the area, including social gatherings such as large wedding banquets, Orange County is home to several hundred Chinese Cambodians. The majority of these families own donut shops. In fact, at a typical wedding banquet, when donut shop owners from Orange, Los Angeles, San Diego, and Riverside Counties attend, a major topic of conversation is the donut business.[4]

In 1977, Ted Ngoy, who entered the United States in 1975, became the first Chinese Cambodian to buy a donut shop in La Habra, California, and eventually expanded his donut empire into a chain of 32 shops from San Diego to the San Francisco Bay Area. He trained many of his relatives and helped other Chinese Cambodians enter the trade, including Ning Yen, the owner of B&H Distributors. Ngoy is now bankrupt due to heavy debts, bad investments and other problems. Though he has returned to Cambodia, his legacy continues among those he helped, particularly those in Orange County.

The Ly Family

After surviving the brutal Khmer Rouge era, the Vietnamese invasion of Cambodia, three trips walking through the land-mined, bandit-filled border jungles of Thailand and Cambodia, and more than seven months in a refugee camp, the Ly family (all names fictitious) was sponsored by a Catholic Church in Birmingham, Michigan. They arrived in 1980 penniless, ignorant of American culture, and except for the son, unable to speak a word of English.

In pre-revolutionary Cambodia, Bing Ly, 56, was a small merchant dealing in rice and fruit, while his wife Yin Ren Ly, 53, kept house, ran a smaller business on the side, and also cared for the family's vegetable garden.[5] Both studied in private Chinese schools; she attended four years and he a total of fourteen years, including four years in Hong Kong. They did not study the Khmer language.

In Birmingham, she worked as a dishwasher in a Chinese restaurant, and he was a janitor for the primary school associated with the Catholic Church that sponsored his family. Many of their Chinese friends from Cambodia residing in Holland, Michigan, encouraged them to move there in the fall of 1981. Bing Ly was unable to find employment in Holland for more than a year, while Yin Ren Ly worked two full-time jobs, as a hotel maid and an assembler in a plastics factory. Finally her parents, brothers, sister, and friends—all in the Orange County donut business—urged them to move to Southern California in 1983. Within two years, they opened their own donut shop and bakery in Orange County.

Their son Wu Ly, 30, who graduated from California State University at Fullerton in finance and business administration, manages his parents' bakery in San Diego. Younger daughter Lynn Ly, 23, is a fourth-year student at San Diego State University, majoring in child development. She helps Wu at the bakery on weekends and whenever else she can. An older sister is a graduate student at the University of California at Los Angeles and helps the parents on weekends and at other times.

The Chau Family

Sing Chau came from a family of eleven children. His parents were well-to-do Chinese in Cambodia before the Communists took over. After two attempts to escape the war-ravaged nation, he succeeded and then spent four years in a refugee camp, where he attended English classes and taught himself Mandarin. He and his older brother were sponsored in 1988 to the United States by their older sister, who now owns two donut shops with her husband.

After working for his sister, brother-in-law, and a younger brother (who owns a donut shop in northern California) for several years, Sing Chau purchased a small, busy donut-burger establishment in Mission Viejo, California, by the age of 30. Still single, he runs the business with the help of his older brother and sister-in-law.

The Vong Family

Mao Vong's family was sponsored by a Lutheran Church in Portland, Oregon. In Cambodia, Mao Vong, a Khmer, worked as the manager of a division of the government railroad system until 1975. During that time he learned French and some English. In 1984, after four years in Portland, he left a well-paying job at a saw mill and moved to California. Vao is 49-years-old. His wife is ethnic Chinese.

The Vongs bought their first shop in 1984, in Anaheim, California, with a relative. They have since bought out their partner and have acquired two more shops in Westminster, just a few miles from their Anaheim shop. One is managed by the wife, and the other by a daughter. A son, who is a junior in a nearby college, helps out in the shops whenever possible.

Some Preliminary Findings

Capital

Of those donut shop owners who responded to a preliminary survey, a majority said that they utilized personal savings and loans from friends, relatives, and credit associations to start their business. Some began with at least one partner; others began as sole proprietors. The owners interviewed for this study followed these patterns.

The Lys purchased their first shop in 1985, with three partners—Yin's younger brother and his brother-in-law, and the brother-in-law's cousin. The Lys' savings were not enough for their share of the downpayment, so Mr. Ly borrowed from his friends and distant relatives in Michigan and other states.

The Vongs used their own savings and bought their first shop as partners with Ms. Vong's cousin and the cousin's husband.

Sing Chau first partnered with his brothers to buy a shop in Watsonville, California, with financial support from his older sister and brother-in-law. When he purchased the Mission Viejo donut and burger place for himself in 1994, again his sister and brother provided interest-free loans. He intends to repay them after the balance of his shop is paid up.

While the Lys, Vongs, and Chaus did not use credit-rotation associations for capital, many Cambodian entrepreneurs have used *huis*, as they are referred to, if personal savings and loans from friends do not provide sufficient startup capital.

Family Labor

In many small businesses owned by first-generation immigrants, particularly "mom and pop" operations, family members and other relatives are important sources of cheap labor, as well as capital, for establishment and expansion of businesses. Most donut shops are family-centered: the husband bakes most of the night and sometimes helps in the morning; the wife works all day; and any teenage children help out after school or whenever possible. The Ly children, for instance, return home from college to help on weekends, vacation breaks, or whenever needed. The Vongs' employees are also Cambodians, both ethnic Khmer and ethnic Chinese, but each one of their three shops is managed by at least one member of the family.

The reliance on family is not limited to the nuclear unit. For many, members of the extended family also play major roles in the establishment and maintenance of shops. For example, as a single man, Sing Chau depends on his older brother and sister-in-law to work equally hard running the donut and burger place. The first summer, he temporarily hired three of his cousins to help because his brother's family was behind schedule in moving from Salinas. In some families, grandparents typically care for the grandchildren while both parents are at the shop. Sing Chau's parents are taking care of his brothers' children. Since January 1995, his father has also been in charge of two grandsons in Mission Viejo, while his mother cares for his younger brother's three-year-old daughter and five-month-old son in northern California.

Because of the nature of the business, employees can easily steal from the cash register or supply room, so trust is vital. Members of the immediate extended family provide trustworthy employees. Plus, they are dependable childcare providers.

Family labor is not only cheap but also flexible. Teenage children can generally help after school and during weekends, school breaks, and summer vacations. In case of an emergency, college-age children are called upon to help out, even if they must skip classes. Education may be highly valued, but the well-being of their families and businesses are more important. For instance, when Ms. Ly was unable to work for four days in February 1995, due to a bad case of the flu, an older daughter came home to work. She missed no classes, but she had to take away time from her master's thesis work. Likewise, Zhi H. C., an ethnic Chinese Cambodian graduate student at the University of California in Los Angeles, missed the first several days of spring quarter 1995, because his father had to be out of town and his mother needed Zhi's assistance in running the family donut business.

Business Problems

Despite their dominance in the industry, not all donut shops are doing well. Some are barely breaking even. Many remain small "mom and pop" stores even after many years of operation. After its explosive expansion in the 1980s, the donut shop business is in decline today. The persistent economic depression, saturation of the market, and competition have hurt many shops. Owners feel pressured to protect any profits by maximizing family labor; some are forced to lay off a baker, a helper, or both in an effort to reduce costs.

The Ly family has been hit hard by all these forces. When they acquired one store in 1987, the surrounding area was nothing but empty fields waiting to be developed. The street in front of the shop had heavy traffic, and the closest donut shops were about five miles away. Today only two miles separate theirs from two other donut shops, a couple of coffee shops, several fast-food restaurants, and an Albertson's Supermarket that offers donuts. The development of another major street took away nearly half of their daily customers. Consequently, revenue is down, and their one employee helps only on weekends, instead of six days a week; she now works full time for another Chinese Cambodian donut shop owner in Fullerton.

Competition has prevented a price increase even though prices of most supplies and ingredients have gone up. Last year's coffee price, for example, went up at least $2.00 a pound, but the Lys felt they should not raise the prices of their coffee because costumers might switch to Carl's Jr. or MacDonald's or other nearby fast-food restaurants. The belief is that donut shops that do well with coffee will prosper.

These entrepreneurs face other business problems, including debt payments, limited capital, a lack of knowledge about American business practices, and customer service problems. Many businesses are running on very low profit margins. According to Bun Tao, a former co-owner of B&H Distributors, struggling owners owe their creditors (friends, relatives, association members) as much as $700,000 (Akst, 1993). None of the interviewees in this study would reveal the exact amount of their debts; but based on certain revelations, each family likely has at least a $200,000 debt. Limited capital and lack of knowledge have thus far prevented them from pursuing other enterprises.

Health Problems

Debts, stress, anxiety, irregular eating habits, and the grueling nature of their daily routines have led to health problems. The first three months after purchasing his shop, Sing Chau slept only three to four hours a night and spent his waking hours at the shop. He worried so much that for several weeks he would wake up frequently during the night to check the clock in the kitchen, worried that he was late for work.[6] His wife is constantly in a state of extreme stress and anxiety. She and their son Wu have developed stomach ulcers.

Many bakers and counter workers have complained of muscle aches and leg and back pain because of long hours of standing, walking, and lifting.

Resulting Attitudes

The struggle of operating a donut shop has deeply affected the attitudes of the families. Most complain about the long hours. As interviewees observed, in Cambodia, "we do not have to work this hard;" "We work like crazy here." In Cambodia, they did not have to pay mortgages and bills, but they also recognize that back then they had no luxuries, a lower living standard, and there was no peace.

Younger people lament that they have no time for social life, and that they are married to their shops. Wu Ly and Sing Chau are both unattached men, yet they cannot date or go out because they have to be at the shops 15 to 18 hours day, seven days a week. Their days start at 4:30 in the morning and end about 7:00 in the evening for Ly and 9:00 for Chau. Wu Ly at least has some time off when his sister Lynn helps out.

The interviews for this project as well as years of informal conversations and observations make clear that the prevalent view among donut shop families is that operating a donut business is a means to an end. The stores provide them a livelihood and socioeconomic mobility, but many do not regard their work as important.

Contributions to the Economy

When the United States government opened its doors to starving and traumatized refugees from Cambodia nearly 15 years ago, the American public may have had little expectation of economic contributions from these newest arrivals. The government spent money for resettlement assistance and provided employment training and other social services. Private organizations and individuals played significant roles in helping with resettlement, placement, and assimilation. Since their initial arrival, many of these refugees — in this case donut shop owners — have made tremendous progress in contributing to the local and national economies, especially in the form of personal, property, business, local, state, and federal taxes.

Donut shops not only offer steady employment for owners, but also for their adolescent children, the bakers, and one or two counter helpers. This stable employment and income reduce unemployment concerns and dependence on public assistance. In addition to their payment of personal taxes, their wages enable the workers to become consumers who support other sectors of the economy and pay sales taxes. Owners also pay monthly and quarterly sales and business taxes to both state and federal governments. The Lys, for instance, pay approximately $1,300 in monthly sales and payroll taxes.

Contributions to local economies are also apparent. In 1994, B&H Distributors reported $8 million in sales of donut and restaurant supplies (Kaufman, 1995). Its clientele is comprised mostly of Cambodian entrepreneurs in Southern California. Orange County not only has one of the largest economies in the nation but also one of the biggest concentrations of small businesses. Donut businesses significantly contribute to those statistics. Their presence has contributed to the vitality of some neighborhoods and increased property values. Certainly the county's bankruptcy in 1995 was felt throughout the area and hurt donut shop business, but the shops continue to create employment and generate incomes that result in more local consumption. Donut shops remain integral to the continued economic endurance of the area.

Cambodian donut shop families are consumers. After decades of war, communism, and poverty that deprived these refugees of the luxuries the United States has to offer, many Cambodians do not hesitate to purchase new clothing, eat well, and buy homes when they have the power to consume. The trend among Cambodian entrepreneurs during the late 1980s was to purchase new cars, houses, and jewelry. The median cost of a house in Orange County is at about $200,000. New homes generally mean new furnishings, decorations, and amenities. Most families have at least two cars, more than one television set, video cassette recorders, and other entertainment products. Children are encouraged to seek higher education, and most are striving to become professionals in fields through which they contribute to society in other ways.

During periods of economic growth in the 1980s, the donut business was good to most owners. Many continue to save and invest in more than one shop, while others invest in other businesses and products. Entrepreneurial expansion and growth means more employees and tax contributions for the economy. Because of capital constraints and lack of resources, knowledge or guidance in other enterprises, most Chinese Cambodians tend to acquire more donut shops instead of diversifying their investments. Many have at least two shops. Yen Ren Ly's nephew and his wife have more than one; the Vongs have three. Mr. Vong feels that he is in a good financial situation right now, and even if his son did not complete college, the father would purchase another shop for him to run.

The August 1994 preliminary survey revealed that a majority of respondents wish to leave the industry but lack the confidence to do so. Still, some donut shop operators have moved on to Chinese fast-food establishments, liquor stores, gas stations, frozen yogurt shops, burger places, and other small businesses. Because many feel the donut market is saturated — especially in Southern California — they are considering relocation opportunities. Some have already moved to Texas, the East, and the Midwest. The Lys are considering the Midwest, where one of Ms. Ly's sisters and brother-in-law have a thriving donut business.

Implications

This research represents a preliminary look at the phenomenon of Cambodian-owned donut shops in California. Some insights into the economic activities of this group of refugees can be gleaned that are relevant to their values and goals, families, gender roles, small-business entrepreneurship, and the historical development of this particular group within the larger Asian Pacific American community.

Certainly there is a need for more exploration of different areas: a closer look at the impact on local economies, English literacy as a factor, cultural influences, social and economic cooperation within the community, sources of capital, and the relevance of government programs in this enterprise. This is, nevertheless, at least a beginning.

Notes

1   Practically every shop spells DONUT instead of doughnut. Some of the reasons for this include cost for each letter of the sign, space, and the short, familiar name would attract more costumers than the correct spelling. Therefore, in this study "donut" is used at the expense of spelling.

2   A more quantitative survey method was initially considered but eventually rejected in favor of case studies. Through informal conversations, entrepreneurs and other workers indicated that the vast majority of subjects probably would not respond to surveys because of a language barrier or lack of time. In one study of Southeast Asian businesses conducted by Orange County officials, only 2 of 100 mailed surveys were returned.

3   This is confirmed by Professor Shinagawa's demographic analysis provided in this volume.

4   If invitations announce the banquets at 12 noon, many of these "donut people" traditionally arrive one to two hours late because they cannot leave the morning rush and must clean up for the next day. Food will not be served until 2 pm to accommodate their schedule.

5   The author has worked summers, vacations and weekends for the Lys since 1987.

6   Mr. Chau and I lived in the same household for six months. Because I sometimes stayed up late watching television during the summer, I was able to witness his nightly anxiety ritual.

References

Akst, Daniel. "Cruller Fates," *Los Angeles Times*, 9 March 1993, D: 1, 6.

Gold, Steven. "Vietnamese-Chinese Entrepreneurs in Orange County," In Ong, Paul, Edna Bonacich and Lucie Cheng (Eds.) *The New Immigrant Economy and Global Restructuring*. Philadelphia: Temple University Press, 1994.

Haines, David W. "Patterns in Southeast Asian Refugee Employment: A Reappraisal of the Existing Research." *Ethnic Groups*, Vol. 7, pp. 39-63, 1987.

Kaufman, Jonathan. "How Cambodians Came to Control California Doughnuts," *Wall Street Journal*, 22 February 1995, A: 1, 6.

Martin, Marie Alexandrine. *Cambodia: A Shattered Society*. Translated by Mark W. McLeod. Berkeley and Los Angeles: University of California Press, pp. 7-28, 1994.

Welaratna, Usha. *Beyond the Killing Fields: Voices of Nine Cambodian Survivors in America*. California: Stanford University Press, pp. 26-32, 1993.

Part III.
Education

The Social Contract to Educate All Children

by Paul Ong and Linda C. Wing*

Education has enormous transformative power. Through education children come to realize they can broaden their lives if they have equitable opportunities to develop their capacities to the fullest. Through education children first make connections with individuals outside of their families and form communities across differences and diversities of neighborhoods, ideas, language, ethnicity, race, and class. Through education human progress is made when one generation transmits knowledge, culture, and skills to the next, enabling children to add to the richness of what we collectively know, value, and are able to do.

Education shapes the future. Children educated in public schools today will one day find the cure for cancer, end hunger and homelessness, and win the Nobel Prize for Peace. Publicly-supported and accessible education is essential to the constant renewal of our sense of shared identity and destiny. This educational system works to maximize our country's productivity and standard of living. It is indispensable to the vitality of our democracy. Put another way, education makes possible the attainment of the American dream. In a nation where the common good is derived from socioeconomic mobility based upon individual merit, and from political participation based upon informed consent, public schools provide the means by which all children can achieve their maximum level of potential.

Although our schools have yet to fulfill these grand ideals, the people of the United States have placed their highest hopes for the future in the provision of a free education open to all children. Education is at the very core of the American social contract.

Some question the commitment to providing public education to every single child. This view was apparent in California when Proposition

---

* Paul Ong is Professor and Chair of the Department of Urban Planning at UCLA's School of Public Policy and Social Research. Linda Wing is lecturer at the Harvard Graduate School of Education, where she is also coordinator of the Urban Superintendents Program. We are indebted to Shu-ling Chen, Betsy Hasegawa, Ke Wen (Rose) Li, all of whom assisted in this project.

187 passed in 1994. Proposition 187 called for public schools to verify the immigration status of students and their parents, to notify state and federal governmental officials of those "reasonably suspected" to be in the country without documents, and to deny education to undocumented immigrant children. Although all provisions in Proposition 187 relating to elementary and secondary education were ruled unconstitutional by a federal district court judge in November 1995,1 the debate about whose education deserves public support has not subsided. After considering legislation that would have excluded individuals who are legal immigrants from federally subsidized loans to college students, Congress instead decided to require legal immigrants to have U.S. citizens co-sign their loans, a criterion not imposed upon students who are citizens. Meanwhile, the very youngest legal immigrants, preschool children, are barred from Head Start under another Congressional bill.2

Public sentiment toward, and public policy affecting, immigrants has historically been related to the state of the economy. Economic woes between the 1880s and 1920s were often laid on immigrants, who were blamed for taking away jobs from those born in this country. The United States is again in a period of economic unease, and public opinion polls show that the majority of Americans think that immigration is "bad" for the country. Current policy discourse about immigrants, however, has an added dimension: contemporary immigrants, especially their children, are said to be a burden on the social services system. Many residents and politicians in California and Florida contend that immigrants use social services that cost more than they contribute in tax payments.3 The largest cost is said to be associated with education. Estimates of the cost of educating undocumented immigrant children in California run as high as $3.6 billion.

These estimates fuel efforts such as Proposition 187 and Congressional proposals to limit the access of documented immigrant children and youth to federally-supported education. They suggest that the nation can "no longer afford" to be a major receiving country of even legal immigrants. Certainly, debate over immigration policy is legitimate, as is debate over any other public policy affecting the course of the country's future. The aspect of the immigration debate that targets children who are utterly vulnerable and dependent upon adults, is disturbing. The liberating mission of education appears in danger of being corrupted for another end.

This paper seeks both to inform and reframe the conversation. We do so by using three approaches to an examination of the education of children of Asian Pacific immigrants.

First, we seek to strengthen the empirical basis for discussion. Background information on our data is included in Appendix A. Current cost-oriented perspectives rest on "guesstimates" of the number of children who may be involved and expenditures on their education. We provide demographic information on Asian Pacific American children in 1970 and on their 1990 counterparts. The population has doubled every decade, a growth driven directly and indirectly by immigration. We also look closely at the available evidence on the additional cost associated with the children's education. The incremental expenditures where they exist at all, are minor.

Second, we focus on education over a span of years. Current perspectives on the schooling of children of immigrants are extremely short-term. We examine the income of parents in 1970 and 1990 as a proxy for their likely contributions to the education of their children. Their average family income compares favorably to the metropolitan average, but Asian Pacific Americans can be found throughout the income spectrum. Additionally, this study investigates how well the Asian Pacific American children of two decades ago are faring today as a way to examine the society's profit from long-term returns on their education. Their educational and economic accomplishments are considerable.

Third, we discuss the education of children of Asian Pacific immigrants as a policy issue in itself and not as a pretext for influencing immigration policy. We look at what is known about their level of learning. Students who have most recently arrived are often poor and limited English-proficient, but overall, the school performance of Asian Pacific American students is relatively high. Immigrant background may be positively associated with educational achievement.

The Population Growth of Asian Pacific American Children

The Asian Pacific American population has grown tremendously over the last quarter century. As shown in Table 1, the Asian Pacific American population has roughly doubled over the last two or three decades. Immigration has been and will continue to be a major force behind this growth. Over time, however, immigration will become a decreasing factor, as growth from births in the United States becomes more important (Ong and Hee, 1993).

The rapid population growth has also been evident among school-age children. This population increased more than six-fold from 212,900 in

1960 to almost 1.3 million by 1990. According to the Bureau of the Census, by the year 2020, the number of Asian Pacific American children will reach about 4.4 million. By the early part of the next century, Asian Pacific Americans will comprise nearly 8 percent of all children in the United States, compared to their current 3 percent proportion.

Table 1. Population Trends (in 1,000's)
Asian Americans Asian AmericansAll Children

	Total	Ages 5 to 17	Ages 5 to 17
1960	882.6	212.9	43,978
1970	1,356.6	315.9	52,489
1980	3,466.9	733.6	47,406
1990	6,908.6	1,395.4	45,249
2020	22,548.0	4,3825.0	4,915

(Based on 1960, 1970, 1980, 1990 Census and population projection)

When Asian Pacific American children are sorted by generation, their growth rates are quite different. Looking at specific generations is crucial because each group can differ in language, self-defined ethnic identity, and acculturation level. These differences, in turn, influence educational needs and concerns. For the purpose of this study, disaggregating by generations also allows us to have a more refined way of analyzing the children of Asian immigrants. The analysis uses three major classifications:

1) immigrant children of immigrant parents,4 or first generation Asian Pacific Americans;

2) U.S.-born children of immigrant parents, or second generation Asian Pacific Americans;5 and

3) U.S.-born children of U.S.-born parents, or third generation Asian Pacific Americans. (For convenience, the third generation also includes the fourth and subsequent generations of Asian Pacific Americans.)

Table 2 provides estimates of the number of Asian Pacific American school-age children by generation for 1970 and 1990.6 The changes from 1970 to 1990 capture the growth due to the renewal of large-scale immigration after the elimination of racially biased quotas in 1965. (Numbers in the table do not match those in published census reports because the table includes only those children living at home with a parent, parents or a custodial adult). Over the two decades, the population increased four-fold, with a net increase of about 1.1 million. The 1970 figure underestimates the total because it includes only those of Japanese, Chinese, Filipino and Korean descent — the only four Asian groups identified in Census data at the time. The downward bias created by the limited number of categories is small because in 1970 these four groups comprised the vast majority of Asian Pacific Americans. By 1990, the Census used 19 categories, including an "other Asian" category.

Table 2. Asian Pacific American Children (in 1,000's)

	1970	1990	% Change
Total	341.2	1,466.2	+330%
First Generation	65.2	579.8	+790%
Second Generation	85.9	651.3	+658%
Third Generation	187.6	219.6	+17%
Not Elsewhere Classified	2.6	15.5	—
% Distribution			
First Generation	19%	40%	—
Second Generation	25%	44%	—
Third Generation	55%	15%	—
Not Elsewhere Classified	1%	1%	—

(Estimates by authors from 1970 and 1990 PUMS. Includes those between ages 5 and 18, and living at home with parent, parents, or a custodial adult.)

Immigration was clearly the cause of the rapid growth in the number of Asian Pacific American children. Obviously the entry of immigrant children increased the number: between 1970 and 1990, the number of first generation children increased by over a half million, accounting for nearly half of the total net increase. The remaining increase was attributable to the dramatic increase in the number of U.S.-born children of immigrants. In 1970, second-generation children numbered 87,000; 20 years later, the total was 651,000.

Unlike the first and second generations, third generation Asian Pacific Americans increased only slightly. Their numbers in 1990 were scarcely larger than two decades earlier. Because of the vast difference in growth rates, the third generation became a proportionately smaller part of the population, declining from a majority of 55 percent to a minority of 15 percent. Two factors may account for the slow growth. The first is a decline in the fertility rate among U.S.-born Asian Pacific American women due to both acculturation and higher economic status (Ong and Hee, 1993; and

Appendix B). The second is the increase in inter-racial marriages between U.S.-born Asian Pacific Americans and non-Asian Pacific Americans (see Appendix B). In 1990, nearly a half million interracial couples, where one spouse or partner was an Asian Pacific Islander, were counted. An unknown, but perhaps sizable, number of children from these families is not classified as Asian Pacific American. As a consequence of these and other factors, the third generation declined in relative importance.

Table 3. Ethnic Composition of Asian Pacific American Children

	First Generation	Second Generation	Third Generation
1970			
Japanese	12%	8%	60%
Chinese	45%	51%	19%
Filipino	35%	38%	13%
Korean	9%	3%	8%
SE Asians	n.a.	n.a.	n.a.
Other	n.a.	n.a.	n.a.
1990			
Japanese	4%	3%	32%
Chinese	21%	22%	15%
Filipino	15%	26%	21%
Korean	12%	11%	20%
SE Asians	33%	16%	2%
Other	16%	22%	10%

(Estimates by authors from 1970 and 1990 PUMS.)

The category of Asian Pacific American children has experienced significant ethnic recomposition and diversification as well as tremendous growth. Among the third generation, the relative number of Japanese Americans declined from a large majority in 1970 to only a plurality in 1990. Chinese Americans also experienced a decline, dropping slightly from 19 percent to 15 percent of the third generation. On the other hand, Koreans, Filipinos, and other Asians increased both absolutely and relatively.

The second generation also became more diverse. Japanese Americans comprised a small and shrinking share (9 percent in 1970 and only 3 percent in 1990) due to the absence of large-scale immigration from Japan after 1965. While both second generation Chinese and Filipinos experienced an absolute growth, their proportions declined. Consider Chinese

Americans, who constituted a small majority in 1970 but less than one quarter in 1990. On the other hand, the relative number of second generation Koreans, Southeast Asians, and "other Asians" increased to the point where they collectively comprised nearly one-half of all second generation Asian Pacific American children.

The ethnic recomposition of the first generation paralleled the pattern of the second generation, with a decline for Japanese, Chinese, and Filipinos. One unique characteristic of immigrant children is the substantial increase in the number of Southeast Asians, who accounted for one-third of the first generation in 1990. Between 1975 and 1991, over one million Southeast Asian refugees came to the United States, and a significant number were children. Their increased presence was due to the influx of political refugees after the end of the Vietnam War.

The Education of Asian Pacific American Children: Needs, Policies, and Costs

Few recognize the distinct educational needs of first and second generation children. When the immigrant children and U.S.-born children of immigrants are Asian Pacific Americans, the absence of attention is especially evident. In this context, we attempt to bring light to the discussion of the education of children of Asian immigrants in three areas: (1) their needs for particular kinds of educational services; (2) federal, state, and local educational policies that might address these needs; and (3) the degree to which children of Asian immigrants benefit from these policies and the potential cost of the services provided.

Educational Needs

The absence of basic data that would permit an assessment of educational needs of first and second generation Asian Pacific American students is problematic. Until recently, school districts with substantial Asian Pacific American enrollments categorized Asian Pacific Americans as "other" when identifying students by race. Many school districts with relatively small numbers of Asian Pacific American students continue to follow this practice. School districts that count Asian Pacific American children often fail to disaggregate the students by ethnicity. For example, Japanese American students have different characteristics and educational experiences than Cambodian American students. Thus, the lack of ethnic-specific data about Asian Pacific American students prevents a careful look at the diversity of their needs, as well as the range of educational opportunities provided to them and the variability in outcomes.

National educational data sets are similarly flawed. Asian Pacific Americans are not identified as such, data on Asian Pacific Americans by ethnicity are not collected, or samplings collected are not large enough to permit more than superficial analyses. For example, 15 percent of the "Asian American" students in the National Educational Longitudinal Survey of 8th Grade Students do not fit the census definition of "Asian Pacific American." Those surveyed include Iranian, Afghani, Turkish, Iraqi, Israeli, Lebanese, and other youngsters from West Asian and Middle Eastern backgrounds.

Local school districts and state and national educational agencies make no effort to collect comprehensive data on any first and second generation students. Since California's Proposition 187 is currently blocked, no school districts anywhere in the country are required to identify students by their immigration status or by the immigration status of their parents. Public schools open their doors to all children, including undocumented immigrants, who are constitutionally entitled to a public school education under the U.S. Supreme Court's ruling in Plyer v. Doe, 457 U.S. 202 (1982).

Since appropriate data on Asian Pacific American students are scarce, their needs have been little studied. We are forced, therefore, to survey the scant literature on the educational achievement of Asian Pacific Americans to deduce the needs of those who are first and second generation. Appendix C contains the literature review in full, but key points are summarized below.

Asian Pacific American students in elementary school, middle school, high school, and college appear to earn higher grades and grade point averages than many other categories of students. In some studies, they have higher grades and grade point averages than whites and all other first and second generation students. Other studies indicate that, among Asian Pacific Americans, first and second generation students have higher grades than U.S.-born students of U.S.-born parents. Some evidence points to variations in ethnicity and subject matter. Chinese Americans, for instance, earn higher grades in mathematics compared to other subjects; while Filipino Americans may earn higher grades in English compared to other subjects.

With the exception only of the children of the most recent Asian immigrants, Asian Pacific Americans seem to score higher on mathematics achievement tests than whites and other first and second generation students. Eighth grade Asian Pacific Americans, both as a group and when disaggregated by ethnicity, perform at the same level as whites on reading tests. The average reading score of Asian Pacific American tenth graders with at least six years of residency in the country is also the same as that of their white counterparts. The limited evidence suggests, however, that other categories of Asian Pacific American students score lower than whites on measures of language, reading, and verbal ability. The level of reading achievement among Cambodian, Laotian, and Hmong children is particularly low.

Among Asian Pacific Americans, first and second generation students seem to have higher mathematics and reading test scores than U.S.-born students of U.S.-born parents. Students from low socioeconomic status do poorly on reading and mathematics tests compared to those from high socioeconomic status. Those for whom English is not their best language, or who have low English proficiency, score lower on reading tests than those for whom English is their best language or who have high English proficiency. On mathematics tests, however, students whose native language is not English do not appear to be disadvantaged.

Cambodian, Laotian, and Hmong children receive relatively high grades despite performing poorly on reading and mathematics achievement tests. Vietnamese students seem to be doing quite well in terms of grades and mathematics test scores. Nevertheless, some anecdotal evidence supports a high dropout rate among Southeast Asian students in Massachusetts and California.

Several caveats must accompany this brief description of Asian Pacific American student achievement. The description is based on relatively little research, much of which is situationally specific. For example, most of what we know about the educational achievement of Cambodian, Laotian, and Hmong students comes from only two studies of youngsters attending schools in the San Diego school district. The information about Asian Pacific American eighth graders is open to question because the National Educational Longitudinal Survey of 8th Grade Students (NELS:88) contains data on "Asian Americans" who do not fit the census definition of Asian Pacific Americans. The survey also excludes Asian Pacific American (and other) students whose educational needs may be most in need of attention, namely, those judged by teachers as lacking the English competency needed to complete the survey questionnaire. Existing literature on Asian Pacific American students, however, forms the only available basis for a thoughtful analysis of their educational needs.

As the summary of the literature indicates, many Asian Pacific American students are doing relatively well in school. Of note are recent findings that first and second generation students do better than third generation students. The evidence indicates, however, that Asian Pacific American students who are limited English proficient, living in poverty, or who most recently immigrated—in particular, Cambodian, Laotian, and Hmong children—require educational services in order to raise their achievement.

Sizable proportions of Asian Pacific American children fall into one or more categories of concern. Table 2 above gives some indication of the number of Cambodian, Laotian, and Hmong school-age children. Along with other Southeast Asians, they were 33 percent of the total number of first generation Asian Pacific American children in the 1990 census. Vietnamese began to arrive in large numbers only after 1975, while Cambodians and Laotians began to enter in large numbers only after 1980. Given the recency of their arrival, 100 percent of Southeast Asian school-age children are probably either first or second generation Americans.

In 1990, 14 percent of the total population of Asian Pacific Americans in the United States were below the poverty line (Ong and Hee 1994). The Asian Pacific American subpopulations most likely to experience poverty were Southeast Asians and immigrants who arrived in 1985, or later. Among Southeast Asian households, 46 percent were in poverty, while 26 percent of recent immigrants lived in poverty. We deduce from these figures that first and second generation Asian Pacific American students most likely to be in poverty are Southeast Asians or children whose families have resided in the country for less than five years. This is important since educational research has long established that, all else being equal, socioeconomic status of children is related to academic achievement.

Census data can be used to estimate the number of limited-English-proficient (LEP) students among Asian Pacific Americans. In the 1990 Census, respondents were asked to evaluate their ability to speak English. For this analysis, the LEP population can be defined to include those who fell into the categories "not well" or "not at all."[7] Approximately a quarter of all Asian Pacific American children, over 300,000 in absolute numbers, fell into the categories "not well" or "not at all."[8]

As with the total number of Asian Pacific American children, the number of LEP children increased dramatically between 1970 and 1990. Although the 1970 Census did not collect data on English language proficiency, one estimate can be provided by applying the generation-specific proportions found in 1990 to the 1970 counts. This method leads to an estimate of about 42,000. This would mean that the number of LEP children increased by more than seven-fold over two decades.

The relative size of the limited English-proficient population varies by generation, as evident in Table 4. Over two-thirds were first generation Asian Pacific American children. Among first generation students, four in ten were LEP. Variation by other factors is apparent. Of the Asian Pacific American eighth grade students who were language minorities in 1988, 33.5 percent said they had moderate or low English proficiency, as opposed to high English proficiency (National Center for Education Statistics 1992).9 High proficiency varied according to ethnicity, once socioeconomic status was controlled. Only 59 percent of Chinese language minority eighth graders and 56 percent of Southeast Asian language minority eighth graders rated their English proficiency as high. On the other hand, 75 percent of Korean eighth graders and 78 percent of South Asian eighth graders reported they had high English proficiency.

Table 4. English Language Ability of Asian Pacific American Children, 1990

	First Generation	Second Generation	Third Generation
Native English Speaker	10%	42%	90%
Very good	6%	38%	46%
Good	2%	13%	28%
Poor	1%	7%	14%
Non-English	0%	0%	2%

(Estimates by authors from 1990 PUMS.)

Educational Policies

What educational policies address the needs of Asian Pacific American children who are limited English proficient, poor, and/or brand-new immigrants? This section describes federal, state, and local programs that specifically or potentially address students with these characteristics.

The only current federal program specifically intended to serve immigrant students is the 1984 Emergency Immigrant Education Act (EIEA). Funds are designated for immigrant students who have lived in the United States for less than three years. School districts cannot apply for EIEA funds unless either 500 eligible students are enrolled or 3 percent of their total enrollment consist of eligible students.

Previously, Asian Pacific American immigrant students who entered the country as refugees qualified for assistance under the 1979 Indochina Refugee Children Assistance Program. Grants were made to elementary and secondary schools that enrolled eligible refugee children in school year 1979-80. The following year, Congress replaced the Indochina Refugee Children Assistance Program with the Transition Program for Refugee Children (TPRC), which operated until 1989-90. Children could receive TPRC services if they resided in the country for no more than three years.

Since 1965, the Bilingual Education Act (Title VII of the Elementary Secondary Education Act) has assisted limited-English-proficient students. In 1990, most of the Title VII appropriation of $115.8 million was awarded to school districts for 800 projects of three years duration (McDonnell and Hill 1993). A majority of these projects were designed to provide "transitional bilingual education," in which students are given subject matter instruction in their native language while they learn English. Over time, they transition to English-only instruction.

Chapter 1 is the largest, federally funded Elementary Secondary Education Act program, with an appropriation of $5.2 billion in fiscal year 1990. Its intent is to serve educationally disadvantaged students in school districts with high concentrations of children from low-income families. Both immigrant and limited-English-proficient (LEP) students in 1990 were nearly twice as likely as other students to be poor (U.S. Government Accounting Office, January 1994). Approximately 30 percent of immigrant students and 37 percent of LEP students were in poverty, compared with only 17 percent of all students. Since immigrant and LEP students are concentrated in relatively few—primarily urban—school systems, many are likely eligible for Chapter 1-funded programs and services.

In Lau v. Nichols, 414 U.S. 563 (1974), the U.S. Supreme Court mandated schools to pay attention to the educational needs of children who are limited English proficient. As a result, many states with sizable populations of LEP students gave their support to school districts operating bilingual education programs. Two such states with numerous Asian Pacific American LEP students are Illinois and New York. Another is California, whose 1976 Bilingual-Bicultural Act made funds available for a decade to school districts providing services to limited-English-proficient children. Funding for the education of such students was then included in Economic Impact Aid (EIA) block grants to school districts (McDonnell and Hill 1993). The number of LEP students in a school district triggers the award level of EIA funds.

Given the paucity of federal and state policies concerning the education of first generation children, local school districts carry primary responsibility for insuring equitable learning opportunities. They do this by focusing almost exclusively on the English language needs of the students. Few school systems attend to the children's distinctive characteristics that are rooted in their immigration experiences. Among these traits are: (1) physical and mental health conditions stemming from the trauma of war and refugee camp life; (2) lack of previous schooling if the children have come from countries without educational systems; (3) transiency if the children's families are struggling to find housing; and (4) little or no awareness or understanding by parents of how U.S. schools function and what the expectations are for both students and parents. School districts that do acknowledge special needs of immigrant students usually establish an intake center or a newcomer school.

An intake center is intended to serve as an immigrant family's first point of contact with a U.S. school system. Essential information about the system is available multilingually. An assessment of the child's English proficiency is conducted, and the child is enrolled and placed in a school. At newcomer schools, immigrant students are provided—usually for no more than one academic year—intensive instruction in academics and English as a second language, as well as extensive orientation to the local community and American culture. Health screening, mental health counseling, and social service assistance may also be provided.

School district responses to educational needs of immigrant students are best labeled idiosyncratic, not coherent and consistent. The Rand Corporation studied 55 schools in eight school districts that together enrolled the majority of immigrant students in the nation. Researchers found that programs and services provided are a function of "situational imperatives that individual principals and teachers face in trying to meet these students needs" (McDonnell and Hill 1993:11). Put differently, few school systems have designed and implemented comprehensive strategies to address the needs of immigrant students. By default, responsibility falls to principals and teachers in the specific schools where immigrant families enroll their children.

Additional Costs

The basic cost of educating the children of Asian immigrants is similar to that for all other children. Potential additional costs are related to programs that meet specialized needs of Asian children who are new immigrants, limited English proficient, or poor. As noted above, however, only one federal educational policy focuses on immigrant children; and only a few other federal and state programs encompass add-on services or programs for first or second generation children based on language or socioeconomic status. The available evidence suggests, moreover, that few Asian Pacific American children have benefited from any of these federal and state policies.

For example, less than 6 percent of Asian Pacific American language minorities in the National Educational Longitudinal Survey of 8th Graders reported receiving instruction in mathematics, science, literature, or social studies in a language other than English (National Center for Education Statistics 1992). Less than a quarter reported ever enrolling in an English language assistance program. Nearly 34 percent, however, lack high English proficiency.

The Emergency Immigrant Education Act (EIEA) probably is also underused.10 During academic year 1989-90, an estimated 700,000 immigrant students lived in the country for less than three years (U.S. Government Accounting Office 1994). About 20 percent were thought to be Asian Pacific Americans, and 90 percent were considered limited English proficient. They were enrolled in 4,500 different school districts. About 564,000 children, 85 percent of the total number of eligible, were enrolled in the 529 school districts that received EIEA funds, yet EIEA dollars did not reach all eligible students in these districts. Los Angeles public schools had 61,648 EIEA-eligible students in 1989-90, but only 12,000 were served with the funds (McDonnell and Hill 1993). Of the 9,284 EIEA-eligible students enrolled in New York City high schools, only 1,800 were served by EIEA funds.

This sporadic placement of children of Asian immigrants in programs to address their education needs is due to three main reasons.11 The first relates to deficiencies in the identification of students who are limited English proficient. The National Center for Education Statistics (1992) found that 73 percent of the nation's Asian Pacific American eighth grade students were language minorities, but only 27 percent were recognized as such by their teachers. In 1990, the Council of Chief State School Officers estimated that only 36 percent of all students in the country who were limited English proficient had been identified as such.

The second reason for underservice stems from the misperception among educators that limited-English-proficient children are not eligible for Chapter 1 services. Only 35 percent of limited-English-proficient students in 1993 received Chapter 1 services (U.S. Government Accounting Office January 1994).12

The third reason is the increasingly inadequate funding. For example, under EIEA, Congress can appropriate up to $500 per immigrant student, but actual appropriations have fallen fall short of this figure. In 1984-85, school districts that received funds were given only about $86 per student, and by 1993-94, allocations had fallen to just $27 per student (U.S. General Accounting Office April 1994). Furthermore, appropriations stayed flat while the eligible student population skyrocketed. Similarly, while the population of limited-English-proficient students grew by 25 percent over the last ten years, funding of the federal Bilingual Education Act decreased by 40 percent (U.S. Government Accounting Office 1994).

The problem is compounded by a lack of meaningful support at the state level. Illinois and New York, for example, provide less than $150 per student for bilingual education programs (McDonnell and Hill 1993). Even though the number of limited-English-proficient (LEP) students is used as one of the triggers for California's Economic Impact Aid (EIA) to school districts, EIA funds are not required to be used to serve such students. California also does not provide school systems with special funds to enable them to conform to state policies regarding the development of English competency among LEP students and insuring their access to the core curriculum.

General funding of local school districts, especially urban systems that enroll most of the nation's Asian Pacific American children and most of the nation's immigrant children, is abysmally inadequate as well. California school systems are especially hard strapped to provide high quality basic education to any student. Only eight states in 1993-94 ranked lower than California in terms of the proportion of state revenues spent on K-12 education (California Tomorrow, November 1993); only four spent fewer dollars on public schools per $1,000 of personal income. In such a fiscal climate, California school districts with large populations of immigrant students find it difficult to respond to their needs. For example, intake centers and newcomer schools are uncommon. San Francisco's four newcomer schools have the capacity to serve less than 20 percent of newly enrolled immigrants (McDonnell and Hill 1993).

If educational programs and services to children of immigrants were systematically provided, what might be the incremental cost? While potential added costs of intake centers or newcomer schools has not been studied, few estimates have been made of the incremental costs of bilingual education programs, such as programs intended to increase English proficiency and to provide content instruction in a non-English language at the same time.

Parrish (1994) compared services received by limited-English-proficient students to those received by all students in 15 elementary schools in 11 different California school districts. He found that the total supplementary cost was $361 per student, of which $60 was the supplementary cost of instruction alone. Schools in the study provided different forms of English-only instruction, as well as bilingual instruction; but the cost for each specific instructional approach was not estimated. Carpenter-Huffman and Samulon (1981) focused on the total added cost of bilingual education in 60 schools in six school districts in California, Texas, and Washington. They estimated the total added cost to be $200 to $700 per student, of which $100 to $500 was the added cost of instruction alone.

Determining the total amount of funds per student served that school districts in California and New York receive from federal and state sources is quite difficult. Some data is available from 1986 awards for EIEA, Title VII, and TPRC. California school districts won federal EIEA and Title VII grants amounting to $79 per student served, the figure for New York was $193.13 Grant awards included dollars for administration, staff salaries, teacher training, curriculum materials, and overhead. Information on the amount that went specifically to classroom instruction or about the types of programs and services provided was not available.

Federal dollars for add-on services must be viewed in the context of overall state spending on K-12 students. The average per pupil expenditure in California in 1986 was $3,728; in New York the figure was $6,497. Funding for basic education continues to be so low in California that the issue of the cost of any add-on service or program pales in comparison, yet 39 percent of the total national population of Asian Pacific Americans reside in California, as do 41 percent of the country's total number of immigrant children (Population Reference Bureau 1992).

Parental Contributions to Public Education

This section examines Asian immigrant parents' various contributions to public education in general and to the academic achievement of their children in particular. First, parents' financial contributions to school systems is analyzed by family income. Second, the question of how immigrant parents might positively influence their children's education through explicitly clear and high expectations for learning is explored.

The amount of relevant taxes paid by Asian Pacific American parents is difficult to calculate, given enormous variations in the way revenues are collected and distributed by local governments and school districts. Examining family income, however, seems a fair proxy of what is the likely contributions from Asian Pacific American parents. A reasonable correlation between family income and taxes can be drawn, although differences in consumption patterns, savings rate, and sources of income can affect the relationship. Evidence suggests that Asian Pacific Americans, including immigrants, tend to invest more in housing and home ownership than the general population. Since many school districts rely on property taxes as a major source of revenue, Asian Pacific Americans are consequently likely to contribute more of each income dollar to public education.

For this analysis, parents are classified in three categories: (1) U.S.-born parents; (2) immigrant parents with at least one U.S.-born child; and (3) immigrant parents with only immigrant children. Note that a family in the second group can also have a foreign-born child or foreign-born children. The third category by definition includes individuals who started their families prior to immigration. This third category also is not a static one; over time a parent can move into the second category if he or she has an additional child born in this country. The analysis is based on one Asian Pacific American parent, usually the head of the household, but a minority of cases is based on the Asian Pacific American spouse in an interracial family.

Table 5. Asian Pacific American Parents

	Immigrants w/Immigrant Children only	Immigrants w/U.S.-Born Children	U.S.-Born
In 1970	26.6	42.8	85.8
In 1990	269.4	418.2	94.6
Percent Increase	913%	877%	10%

(Based on head of household or Asian Pacific American parent in an inter-racial family. Estimates by authors from 1970 and 1990 PUMS.)

Table 6 provides statistics on family incomes for Asian Pacific American parents relative to a prevailing median family income figure. Data for 1970 and 1990 were used to estimate medians for all families for each of the twelve metropolitan areas with the largest number of Asian Pacific American children in 1990.14 (See Appendix D for listing and discussion of method used in this analysis.) For all other metropolitan areas and non-metropolitan areas, national medians for families in all metropolitan areas were used as the prevailing median. Overall, median family income for Asian Pacific Americans increased from $40,545 in 1969 to $43,770 in 1989. As a comparison, general population medians for the twelve metropolitan areas were $40,545 in 1969 and $38,856 in 1979. This simple comparison suggests that, on average, Asian Pacific American parents contribute at least as much taxes as other parents to the public schools.

Using the median, however, does not reveal the diversity within the Asian Pacific American population. Asian Pacific American parents can be found throughout the income spectrum. About 20 percent had an income that was less than half of the metropolitan median. At the same time, a slightly smaller proportion had an income more than twice the metropolitan median. This means that some parents contributed proportionately less, while others contributed proportionately more.

Table 6. Asian Pacific American Parents by Family Income

	Immigrants w/Immigrant Children only	Immigrants w/U.S.-Born Children	U.S.-Born
Median in 1989			
1970	$30,578	$35,815	$44,599
1990	$32,330	$49,000	$53,083
Relative to Prevailing Median			
1970			
below 50%	38%	19%	20%
50%-84%	26%	27%	17%
85%-115%	16%	20%	22%
116%-200%	17%	26%	33%
over 200%	3%	8%	8%
1990			
below 50%	30%	14%	10%
50%-84%	22%	17%	16%
85%-115%	14%	15%	16%
116%-200%	23%	32%	39%
over 200%	10%	22%	19%

(Estimates by authors from 1970 and 1990 PUMS.)

The wide variance in relative family income is not surprising. Diversity in such characteristics such as years in the United States, English language ability, and educational attainment influence an individual's earnings (Borjas, 1990). These diversity factors for Asian Pacific parents are tabulated in Table 7. The most disadvantaged group is comprised of immigrants with only immigrant children; a larger percentage of this group was also more likely to be comprised of newcomers and individuals with little education. One-third did not have an effective command of the English language, which limited employment opportunities.

Table 7. Characteristics of Asian Pacific American Parents, 1990

	Immigrants w/Immigrant Children only	Immigrants w/U.S.-Born Children	U.S.-Born
English Language			
Native English	3%	7%	75%
Very good	31%	49%	17%
Good	31%	30%	5%
Poor	28%	13%	2%
Non-English	7%	2%	0%
Years of Schooling			
Less than H.S.	28%	19%	9%
High School Degree	16%	14%	20%
Some College	18%	22%	33%
Bachelor's Degree	22%	21%	24%
Graduate Degree	14%	23%	14%
Years in the U.S.			
0-5 yrs	40%	3%	NA
6-10 yrs	35%	19%	NA
11-15 yrs	17%	28%	NA
16+ yrs	7%	49%	NA

While Asian Pacific American parents — either on average or as a group — are contributing at least the same tax revenues to public education, two additional and offsetting factors should be addressed. First, Asian immigrants tend to have larger families and, second, Asian immigrants transfer human capital, such as educational backgrounds, to the United States.

The size of the family is an important consideration. Families with more than the average number of children would receive a net gain through public education, assuming no greater tax contribution. Among all family-based households with school-age children in the twelve metropolitan areas,15 the average number of school-age children in 1990 was 1.7. For Asian Pacific American family-based households with school-age children, the average was slightly higher, 1.9. Interestingly, since the higher average number of school-age children for Asian Pacific Americans is roughly equal to those with higher income, one can infer that the proportionately greater demand placed on the school system is offset by their higher contributions to school revenues.

The average number of school-age children for the U.S.-born Asian Pacific Americans is higher (2.3) than that for immigrants (1.8). This is interesting given that fertility rates drop with acculturation into U.S. society. This apparent contradiction can be explained in part by the fact that immigrant parents tend to be older and are more likely to have adult-age children not included in the calculations.16 While Asian Pacific American parents who are U.S.-born had proportionately more school-age children, they also have considerably higher family income. The group that arguably receives a net subsidy is comprised of immigrants with only immigrant children.

On the other hand, the U.S. economy benefits from the many immigrant parents who received their schooling abroad. For non-immigrants, the cost of educating parents can be ignored because the cost and eventual returns (e.g., through taxes) are integral to, or internalized within, the educational system and economy. Over two-thirds of immigrant parents with at least one U.S.-born child, however, received their primary and secondary education abroad, and about nine-tenths of immigrant parents with only immigrant children received their primary and secondary education abroad.17. The cost of educating these immigrant parents is external to the U.S. educational system because the schooling was paid for by a foreign government. When an individual migrates, he or she essentially transfers the benefits of that education to the United States, both as gains in individual earnings and to the society as a whole.

Similarly, immigrant children who have obtained some schooling in Asia transfer the benefit of their education to this country as well. Compared to their parents, where the identifiable U.S. gains are seen in earnings, the observable gains associated with the pre-U.S. education of immigrant students may be visible through higher mathematics achievement18

Recent research on the education of first and second generation children suggests another factor that offsets the demands placed on public education by immigrants. Kao and Tienda (1995) looked at the relationship between a student's immigrant status, on the one hand, and grades, test scores, and aspirations, on the other. They determined that having an immigrant parent, specifically, an immigrant mother, significantly promoted academic achievement and high educational aspirations. Students with U.S.-born parents did less well in school and had lower aspirations than students with immigrant parents. These findings were most pronounced for Asian students, although they pertained to Latino students as well.

To explain the effect of having immigrant parents, Kao and Tienda (1995) maintain that an "immigrant optimism" is operative: Immigrant parents are confident about their children's prospects of achieving upward mobility in a country to which parents have voluntarily moved with the goal of improving their life. This optimism is somehow imbued in their children, with education being identified as the key to success.

How does immigrant optimism manifest itself? With respect to Asian Pacific American parents, especially clear and high expectations for their children's academic achievement may be communicated. These expectations are highly correlated with their children's school performance (see, e.g., Peng and Wright 1994).

- Asian Pacific American youngsters in a large-scale high school study conducted by Steinberg, Dornbusch, and Brown (1992) were more likely than all other groups of students to state that their parents had high, explicitly defined standards for academic performance. These students reported that "their parents would be angry if they came home with less than an A minus" (p. 726).
- Schneider and Lee (1990) found that 100 percent of Asian Pacific American parents, compared to 67 percent of white parents of elementary and middle school children, said that "C" or "satisfactory" grades were not acceptable. These expectations were clearly understood by Asian Pacific American children. One child reported (p. 370): "If I get a 'B,' my parents say it isn't that good. They get mad. They want all As."
- In the same study, one parent observed: "I think there will be discrimination against my children because they are minorities.... Therefore I tell my children to study for two hours when white children study for one hour. If they ask me the reason, I tell them I will let them know later" (Schneider and Lee 1990:370).19

- Vietnamese immigrant parents interviewed in New Orleans said they believed that education was their children's chief way out of "the poorest part of a poor area in a poor city in a poor State [sic]" (Zhou and Bankston 1994: 828). Researchers observed that parents had "adjusted their cultural patterns to orient the younger generation toward educational and occupational attainment." If they did not, their children might become permanent members of the underclass.20

Immigrants add value to their children's education and U.S. society through their parenting. Certainly financial contributions to school systems are important in an analysis of the financial demands placed on public education by immigrants. The parents' social contributions to the high level of their children's learning somehow seems relevant as well.

Economic Returns to Educating Children of Immigrants

The short-run costs of education generate long-term benefits because of the role schools play in preparing children to be productive adult workers. Despite severe constraints on the availability of relevant data, this section represents a preliminary attempt to calculate types of returns for Asian Pacific Americans.

Longitudinal data following children of immigrants as they mature and enter the labor market would be helpful. Unfortunately, census data only refer to the characteristics of a sample at one point in time. Asian Pacific American adults, however, who received at least a part of their primary and secondary education in the United States can be examined. This inquiry can be initiated by taking those between the ages of 25 and 38 in 1990, who had resided in the United States in 1970, the year when these individuals would have been between ages 5 and 18. This sample includes all U.S.-born Asian Pacific Americans and Asian immigrants who entered the country in 1970 or earlier.

Because of data limitations, certain generational categories cannot be determined. For U.S.-born Asian Pacific Americans not living at home, the second and subsequent generation cannot be distinguished. The best that can be done is to examine whether an individual spoke a language other than English at home. A person who did is likely to be second generation, and this group is used to represent the achievements of the second generation. This group is labeled as U.S.-born and bilingual.

This approach is far from being ideal. A large number of second generation persons may no longer use their parents' native language, but a good guess is that only half of the second generation Asian Pacific Americans in the sample used a language other than English. The analysis uses two other categories: monolingual, or those who were U.S.-born but spoke only English at home; and all Asian immigrants.

The Census data show that children of Asian immigrants do become highly educated adults, thus adding to the skill base of our labor force. Table 8 compares the educational attainment of U.S.-born non-Hispanic whites with Asian Pacific Americans who were children in 1970. As the figures show, Asian Pacific Americans in all three categories were more likely to be better educated than non-Hispanic whites. While two in five non-Hispanic whites had no more than a high school education, only one in five Asian Pacific Americans did. At the other end of the spectrum, Asian Pacific Americans were twice as likely to have a graduate or professional degree. While some differences among the three Asian Pacific American categories listed in Table 8 are apparent, distributions by educational attainment are remarkably similar.

Table 8. Educational Attainment, 1990
Selected Persons Ages 25-38

| | Non-Hispanic Whites | Asian Pacific Americans | | |
		Monolingual U.S. born	Bilingual U.S. born	Pre-1971 Immigrants
Years of Schooling				
Less than H.S.	10%	5%	7%	6%
High School	31%	16%	12%	14%
Some College	32%	34%	30%	36%
B.S. Degree	19%	33%	36%	30%
Grad. Degree	7%	13%	15%	14%

(Estimates by author from 1990 PUMS.)

Annual earnings are used as a measure of an individual's contribution to the economy. Table 9 shows that Asian Pacific Americans fared better than non-Hispanic whites. Distributions by income category in the top panel include those with zero and negative earnings. While a majority of non-Hispanic whites had earnings below $20,000 per year, only a minority of Asian Pacific Americans did (a difference of about 10 percentage points).

Although only a minority of Asian Pacific Americans had earnings that placed them in the top income category (16 percent in the $40,000 or more per year category), they were roughly one-and-a-half times more likely than non-Hispanic whites to be in that category.

A higher level of labor force participation by Asian Pacific American women contributed to the higher earnings reported in Table 9. Annual earnings of $1,000 is placed at zero or trivial level of paid work. While 24 percent of non-Hispanic white women fell into this category, only 11 percent of Asian Pacific American women did. Not only did proportionately more Asian Pacific American women work, but they had higher earnings. This can be seen in the bottom panel in Table 9, which reports the median for those with at least $1,000 in earnings. While Asian Pacific American males fared moderately better than non-Hispanic white males, Asian Pacific American females fared considerably better than non-Hispanic white females.

Table 9. Annual Earnings, 1989
Selected Persons Ages 25-38

	Non-Hispanic Whites	Asian Pacific Americans		
		Monolingual U.S. born	Bilingual U.S. born	Pre-1971 Immigrants
Less than $10k	30%	20%	27%	24%
$10k-$19,999	25%	22%	20%	20%
$20k-$39,999	34%	42%	39%	38%
$40k or more	11%	16%	13%	18%
% with at least $1k				
Males & Females	86%	91%	86%	88%
Males	94%	94%	90%	93%
Females	77%	87%	81%	83%
Median Earnings*				
Males & Females	$20,000	$24,300	$24,300	$25,000
Males	$25,000	$28,000	$26,000	$29,000
Females	$15,000	$21,000	$21,700	$21,000

(Median earnings is calculated for those with at least $1,000 in income. Estimates by authors from 1990 PUMS.)

Higher earnings of Asian Pacific Americans are tied to educational attainment. Table 10 summarizes results from a statistical analysis. The analysis uses the same sample of 25-to-28-year-old Asian Pacific Americans and non-Hispanic whites, with the additional restriction of including only those with at least $1,000 in income. While findings are not directly comparable to earnings data in Table 9, patterns are consistent: figures show that Asian Pacific Americans on the average earned more than non-Hispanic whites, although variations by gender and the listed Asian Pacific American subgroups are evident.

Monolingual U.S.-born and pre-1971 immigrant Asian Pacific American males earned at least a 10 percent more than non-Hispanic males. Nearly all of that difference is due to higher levels of education. After adjusting for education, no statistical difference in the earnings of these Asian Pacific Americans and non-Hispanic whites appears. Bilingual U.S.-born Asian Pacific American males, on the other hand, did not have higher incomes than non-Hispanic white males. In fact, after adjusting for educational attainment, this group of Asian Pacific Americans earned less, and this remains true regardless of age. This indicates that education is relied upon to compensate for whatever disadvantage is associated with being bilingual. A weaker command of the English language is likely translated into poorer employment opportunities and lower salaries. Whether this applies to all second generation Asian Pacific Americans is unclear.

Estimates in Table 10 show that Asian Pacific American women earned about a third more than non-Hispanic white females. Only a third of those higher earnings is explained by higher educational attainment. Regardless of schooling, Asian Pacific American women still earned 20 percent to 25 percent more. Unlike their male counterparts, differences among the subgroups of Asian Pacific American women (monolingual U.S. born, bilingual U.S. born, and immigrants) are small.

Table 10. Earnings Relative to Non-Hispanic Whites
Selected Persons Ages 25-38

| | Asian Pacific Americans | | |
	Monolingual U.S. born	Bilingual U.S. born	Pre-1971 Immigrants
Males			
Unadjusted Difference	+14%*	-2%	+11%*
Adjusted for Education	+2%	-14%*	+1%
Adjusted Ed. and Age	+3%	-8%*	+3%
Females			
Unadjusted Difference	+36%*	+36%*	+34%*
Adjusted for Education	+25%*	+22%*	+22%*
Adjusted Ed. and Age	+25%*	+22%*	+22%*

(Based on the log of 1989 annual earnings. Statistically significant differences are marked by an asterick*. Estimates from regressions by authors from 1990 PUMS.)

As noted, the three categories used in Tables 8, 9, and 10 are not substitutes for generational categories. Viewing the bilingual U.S.-born as a proxy for the second generation and viewing the monolingual U.S.-born as a proxy for the third plus generation is problematic. A large number of second generation persons may no longer use their parents' native language. This problem can create a bias in interpreting the above analysis if the findings are attributed to generational differences. The issue comes down to whether the bilingual U.S.-born group is representative of all second generation Asian Pacific Americans, ages 25 to 38.

An analysis of the 1994 Current Population Survey indicates that the answer is no. This data set contains information on the respondent's nativity and parents' place of birth. The number of Asian Pacific Americans in the survey is too small for reasonable estimates similar to statistics in Tables 9 and 10; but the survey sample is sufficient to test for any statistical difference in earnings between the third and second generation. The analysis shows that the second generation earned on the average about 13 percent more than the third generation, with most of the difference due to higher educational attainment. In other words, the U.S.-born children of Asian immigrants, along with other Asian Pacific American children, grew up to be well-educated and highly productive.

Conclusion

The American social contract is predicated upon an intergenerational commitment to providing public education to each and every child. Through education, the United States endeavors to enable all children to develop their intellect, spirit, and capacity for action, both for their individual interests and for the interests of the common good. To consider excluding the children of immigrants from the social contract based upon a transitory economic problem or a perceived marginal cost is to begin the unraveling of the social fabric. If we deny one child an education, then we put all children, and our collective future, at risk. This is not to say that economic exigencies do not matter with respect to the public good. Rather, this is an argument that the obligation to make responsible, well-considered, comprehensive analyses and decisions where children are concerned is a sacred one.

The analysis in this paper does not reveal any fiscal or educational crisis that would even remotely suggest that this nation should limit its promise to educating the next generation. Although relevant short-term or long-term costs and benefits have not been quantified, the evidence supports the argument that providing public education for the children of Asian immigrants makes good sense. The additional costs are minimal; the contributions of Asian Pacific American parents are at least equal to that of other parents; and Asian Pacific American children mature to become highly educated and productive. The children of Asian immigrants and their parents enhance, rather than diminish, the vitality of our nation.

Appendix A: Data

The main source of information for this chapter comes from the decennial Census. While we use published information when appropriate, published reports seldom provide statistics in a form that directly addresses the issues in this chapter. We overcome this problem by using the public use microdata samples (PUMS) from the 1970 and 1990 census. These are large data sets containing individual records that can be tabulated and analyzed according to the needs of the researcher. When possible, the two 1 percent samples from 1970 are combined. In that census, two long forms were used. Although the two forms shared many questions in common, each also asked a different set of questions. For example, one form asked immigrants when they entered the United States, but the other did not. For 1990, the 5 percent sample was used for Asian Pacific Americans, and the 1 percent sample is used for non-Hispanic whites.

Before any analysis can be done, the PUMS data have to be rearranged. The hierarchical structure required the creation of working data set in two steps: one for all Asian Pacific American children and one for all Asian Pacific American parents. The children and parents in the same household were then merged together for the analysis. For the majority of the Asian Pacific American children in the samples, this approach yields appropriate matches. This approach presents a problem, however, for Asian Pacific American children in a household with a single parent who is not Asian Pacific American, and for Asian Pacific American children with adopted parents who are not Asian Pacific American.

For both censuses, individuals who were U.S. citizens at birth were classified as U.S.-native. This includes those born in the United States or U.S. territory and those born abroad to U.S. citizens. This approach is consistent with the categories and definitions in governmental publications for the 1990 Census. The characteristic of the heads of the household is used to determine if the parent is U.S.-born or foreign-born. In cases where the head of the household is not Asian, the spouse is used to determine the nativity of the parent. (Also language ability is used when there is no match.) The term foreign-born and immigrants are used interchangeably.

This study used the Current Population Survey for March 1994. This is a monthly survey whose main purpose is to track the economy, particularly employment and unemployment. The data set for the March survey is known as the "Annual Demographic File," which contains detailed demographic information and income data for the previous year. The survey includes responses from approximately 57,000 households. Because this is a national survey, the sample size for Asian Pacific Americans is small. For the earnings analysis of Asian Pacific American adults by generation, the sample size was between only 400 and 500.

Appendix B: Additional Tables

Fertility Rates: The effects of acculturation can be seen in Table A2, which reports average fertility rates based on 1990 data. For every age category, the fertility rate for U.S.-natives is lower than those for immigrants. The difference is particularly noticeable for those over the age of 55.

Table B1. Fertility Rates of Asian American Women

	US-natives	Pre-1980 Immigrants	1980-90 Immigrants
Age			
25-34 years	1.18	1.07	0.74
35-44	1.98	1.97	1.51
45-54	2.30	3.05	2.17
55+	3.32	4.65	2.63

(Estimates by authors from 1990 PUMS.)

Interracial Marriage Rates

The effects of acculturation on interracial marriages can be seen in Table A2. The figures are based on Asian Pacific Americans who were married with the spouse being present. Because our sample includes all Asian Pacific Americans from the 5 percent PUMS for 1990, we were able to match married couples with both spouses being Asian Pacific American. Those without a match were consider to be married to a non-Asian Pacific American. The summary statistics show that for every age group, the interracial marriage rate is higher for U.S.-born natives than for immigrants; and among immigrants, the rate is higher for those in the country longer than for newcomers.

Table B2. Asian Americans Married to Non-Asian-Americans

	Pre-1980	1980-90	US-natives
By Age Groups			
15 & over	20%	12%	33%
25-34	24%	14%	52%
35-44	20%	9%	44%
45-54	17%	7%	28%
55+	19%	11%	12%

(Estimates by authors from 1990 PUMS)

Appendix C: Review Of Literature on Asian Pacific American Student Achievement

This review contains two major sections. The first focuses on small-scale, local studies of Asian Pacific American students. The second focuses on large-scale, national studies. In the main, the studies did not identify whether the youngsters were first or second generation, and slightly different definitions of the research subjects were used. Based on the time frame when most of the studies were conducted, and based on our analyses of census data discussed in the first section of this paper, we believe that the majority of Asian Pacific American children included in the studies surveyed were either immigrants or children of immigrants.

The Achievement of Students in Specific Localities

During school year 1982-83, Korean, Chinese, and Japanese American youngsters in a Chicago K-8 school and a suburban middle school for grades six through eight earned higher grades than Anglo students (Schneider and Lee 1990). Students in the middle school had achievement test scores higher than those of their Anglo classmates during 1981-82 and 1982-83. Children who had immigrated to the United States after 1978 were excluded from the study.

Lao, Hmong, and Cambodian students scored the lowest on a reading achievement test among 5,000 foreign-born children and children of foreign-born parents attending schools in San Diego, and Dade and Broward Counties, Florida (Rumbaut 1994). The sample consisted of Asian, Latin American, and Caribbean youngsters enrolled in the eighth and ninth grades in the spring 1992. Specifically, Cambodian students scored at the 14.0 percentile, Hmong at the 15.2 percentile, and Lao at the 22.3 percentile. Other Asians, primarily Chinese, Japanese, Korean, and East Indian, had the highest reading achievement test scores, followed by Filipino students. They scored at the 62 percentile and at the 51.1 percentile respectively.

The Hmong students scored at the 29.7 percentile on a mathematics achievement test, the lowest among all students in the study. Both Laotians and Cambodians scored below the national norm, at the 42.1 percentile and 35.7 percentile, respectively. Other Asians did the best on the mathematics test, scoring at the 74.3 percentile. The second highest scoring students were Vietnamese youngsters, who scored at the 60.4 percentile. Filipino students followed, scoring at the 59.1 percentile.

Although Hmong students scored well below national norms in reading and mathematics, they earned an average grade point average of 2.95. Their grade point average was exceeded only by those of their Vietnamese classmates, who had a grade point average of 3.04, and their Other Asian classmates, who had a grade point average of 3.24.

Put another way, Asian students in the study, nearly all of them San Diego students, did both the best and the worst in terms of reading and mathematics achievement test scores. Youngsters from Mexico, Cuba, Nicaragua, Colombia, Haiti, Jamaica, and the West Indies scored in between. All Asian students, however, earned higher grade point averages than all the Latin American and Caribbean students. The lowest grade point average earned by a group of Asian students was 2.93 among Filipinos. Jamaican students earned the highest grade point, 2.58, average among Latin American and Caribbean students.

In academic year 1987-88, East Asian 11th and 12th graders had the highest grade point average of all groups of language minority students in San Diego high schools (Ima and Rumbaut 1989). East Asians included as Chinese, Japanese, and Korean American students. Students with the second highest grade point average were Southeast Asians. Southeast Asians were defined as Khmer, Lao, Hmong, and ethnic Chinese and Vietnamese from Vietnam. Other language minority students in the 11th and 12th grades were Hispanics and other immigrants. "Other immigrants" included those who came from Iran and India, as well as Arab and European nations.

An analysis of spring 1985 data on California schools with the highest concentrations of limited-English-proficient students revealed that the "highest average attrition rate was for the schools with large concentrations of Southeast Asians" (Olsen 1988:88). An astounding 48 percent of Southeast Asians in such schools dropped out. Unfortunately, "Southeast Asians" were not precisely defined.

In 1986, every 12th grade California student was tested as part of a statewide assessment program. Among language minority students who were categorized as fluent English proficient, Southeast Asian students had the lowest reading scores of any group of students (Olsen 1988), with a score of 28.5 percentile. The second lowest scoring group of fluent-English-proficient language minority students were Spanish-speaking students, who scored at the 30.9 percentile. Once again, the term "Southeast Asian" was not delineated.

For all Asian language minority groups categorized as fluent English proficient, reading and writing test scores were lower than their mathematics test scores. For example, fluent-English-proficient Chinese language minority group students scored at the 71.2 percentile in mathematics, but only at the 50.0 percentile in writing and the 38.3 percentile in reading.

A large survey of 6,750 Southeast Asian refugees living in Seattle, Houston, Chicago, Boston, and Orange County, California was conducted in the early 1980s by Caplan, Choy, and Whitmore (1992). They looked at the academic performance of 536 school age youngsters who, on average, had been in the U.S. for three and one-half years. The children were evenly spread across all the grade levels. The researchers did not exactly describe their population of "Southeast Asians." Given the time frame when the study was conducted and the average amount of time the subjects had lived in the U.S., we guess that the children were predominantly, if not exclusively, Vietnamese.

The average grade point was 3.05. Only one-fifth earned grade point averages of C or lower. Almost 50 percent earned A's in math; another one-third earned B's. The youngsters did less well in English, history, and social studies. In those subject areas, the average combined grade point was 2.64. One-half of the children scored in the top quartile on a mathematics achievement test, with 27 percent scoring in the highest decile. The mean score on the language and reading achievement test, however, was a little below the national average.

The Achievement of Students in the Nation

Eighth Grade Student Achievement. In 1988, the federal government launched the National Educational Longitudinal Survey of 8th Grade Students, called NELS:88. This survey oversampled Asian Pacific American students and is considered by some to be the first and only national education survey that includes an adequate sample of Asian Pacific Americans. There were 1,505 Asian Pacific American eighth graders in a total sample of 25,000 eight graders enrolled in 1,000 public and private schools. Seventeen percent were Chinese Americans, 20 percent Filipino, 13 percent Southeast Asian, and 11 percent Korean. Pacific Islanders and South Asians were 9 percent each, and 6 percent were Japanese. The remaining 15 percent encompassed students not usually categorized as Asian Pacific American, namely, Iranian, Afghani, Turkish, Iraqi, Israeli, Lebanese, and other West Asian and Middle Eastern youngsters. It is unclear if or how the inclusion of West Asian and Middle Eastern students skewed the data about the more generally accepted categories of Asian Pacific Americans. Nearly 80 percent of the Asian Pacific Americans in NELS:88, including West Asian and Middle Eastern youngsters, were first or second generation students. Children with extremely limited English proficiency were *excluded* from the study. Peng and Wright (1994), Kao and Tienda (1995) and Kao (1995) and the National Center for Education Statistics (1992) have all done analyses of the educational achievement of Asian Pacific American students in this dataset.

Peng and Wright (1994) did not distinguish among Asian Pacific American eighth graders by generation, ethnicity, or language proficiency. They found that Asian Pacific Americans had higher combined reading and mathematics achievement test scores than all other minority students. There was no significant difference between Asian Pacific American and white achievement test scores.

The mathematics achievement test scores, reading achievement test scores, and grades of Asian Pacific American eighth graders as a group and by ethnicity were examined by Kao (1995). As a group, Asian Pacific Americans earned higher mathematics scores but had comparable reading scores relative to whites, when gender and parental socioeconomic status were controlled. By ethnicity, Chinese, Koreans, and Southeast Asian eighth graders earned higher mathematics scores than white eighth graders from comparable family backgrounds. Students from Filipino, Japanese, South Asian, and West Asian backgrounds had mathematics scores that were the same as white students. All Asian Pacific American ethnic groups earned reading scores equivalent to whites. Additionally, Asian Pacific American eighth graders, as a group, had higher grades than whites at each level of educational aspiration, with aspirations divided into four categories: high school graduation or less, some college, college graduation, and college graduation.

Kao and Tienda (1995) compared eighth grade achievement levels and educational aspirations of U.S.-born children of U.S.-born mothers, on the one hand, with the eighth grade achievement levels and educational aspirations of immigrant children of immigrant mothers and U.S.-born children of immigrant mothers on the other hand. They included black, Hispanic, and Asian youth in their study. With respect to Asian Pacific Americans, first and second generation eighth graders had higher grades, mathematics test scores, reading test scores, and educational aspirations than U.S.-born eighth graders with U.S.-born mothers. First generation students earned the same mathematics test scores as second generation students, but second generation students scored higher on the reading test than first generation students. U.S.-born students with U.S.-born mothers had the worst reading test scores of the three groups of students.

In the analyses of Asian Pacific American eighth graders done by the National Center for Education Statistics (1992), the main finding was that socioeconomic status correlated with students' English proficiency and scores on reading and mathematics tests. For example, those from low socioeconomic backgrounds were more likely than those from high socioeconomic backgrounds to fail to score at the basic level on the reading achievement test (38 percent versus 12 percent, respectively). On the mathematics achievement test, 39 percent of low socioeconomic status students failed to score at the basic level, in contrast to 14 percent of high socioeconomic status students. Even after English proficiency was controlled, socioeconomic status adversely affected both reading and mathematics performance levels.

Among Asian Pacific American language minority students, after socioeconomic status was adjusted, level of English proficiency correlated with reading achievement levels. Sixty-three percent of eighth graders with the least English proficiency did not perform at the basic level on the reading test, compared to 19 percent of those with highest English proficiency. Mathematics performance appeared not to be affected by English proficiency among language minority eighth graders, after socioeconomic status was controlled.

High School Student Achievement. Another national longitudinal survey of students conducted by the federal government is called High School & Beyond (HS&B). Data collection began in 1980 with respect to 10th and 12th grade students and did not oversample Asian Pacific Americans. Peng, Owings, and Fetters (1984) and Wong (1990) have examined this data set.

Peng et al. (1984) found that both 10th and 12th grade Asian Pacific American students had lower verbal but higher mathematics scores than their white classmates. Verbal skills were even lower among Asian Pacific American 10th and 12th graders who had lived in this country from one to five years. Asian Pacific American 10th graders with six years to less than lifetime U.S. residency, however, had higher verbal scores than both U.S.-born Asian Pacific American and white 10th grade students. The highest average mathematics score among 12th graders was achieved by Asian Pacific Americans with six to 10 years of residence in the United States.

Peng et al. also compared percentages of correct answers and nonresponses of sophomores on the achievement tests administered in 1980 to the percentages of correct answers and nonresponses on achievement tests administered to the same students two years later when they were seniors. Researchers determined that the verbal skill growth rate of Asian

Pacific Americans with only one to five years of U.S. residency was slow compared to those with six or more years of residency. Both groups of students, however, demonstrated the same rate of growth in mathematics.

HS&B seniors who were Chinese, Filipino, and Japanese Americans were studied by Wong (1990). More than 58 percent of Chinese American seniors and about 52 percent of the Filipino American seniors were foreign born. A greater proportion of Chinese American 12th graders received As and Bs in mathematics than whites, and greater proportions of Japanese and Filipino American students received As and Bs in English compared to whites.

The federal National Assessment of Educational Progress (NAEP), in 1983-84, conducted a special project on the achievement of language minority youngsters. Asian Pacific American language minority students in the 11th grade read significantly less well than their Asian Pacific American non-language-minority counterparts (Baratz-Snowden and Duran 1987). While approximately 50 percent of Asian Pacific American non-language minorities and whites scored at the advanced reading level, only 20 percent of Asian Pacific American language minorities did so. Since the assessment did not include students considered by their school systems to be too limited English proficient to take the reading test, it is likely that the performance of Asian Pacific American language minority students was gauged higher than in reality.

In 1983, 46 percent of Asian Pacific American freshmen enrolled as first-time, full-time students in four-year colleges and universities had earned an A average in high school (Hsia 1988). Only 29.4 percent of their white counterparts and only 27.6 percent of all their classmates earned the same average in high school.

SAT Scores of College-Bound High School Students. Since 1981, the College Board has published SAT profiles by race and ethnicity, as well as family income. Hsia looked closely at these profiles. In 1985, 42,000 Asian Pacific Americans took the SAT, representing 4.2 percent of all SAT takers and more than 50 percent of all Asian Pacific American 18-year-olds. Asian Pacific American performance on the test's verbal portion was related to whether English was the test taker's best language. Approximately 27 percent reported that English was not their best language.

In particular, there was a difference of 162 points in the verbal portion—more than one standard deviation—between median scores of Asian Pacific Americans with English as their best language and those for whom English is not their best language. When English was not their best language, 90 percent of Asian Pacific Americans scored in the two lowest score intervals, between 200 and 400, on the verbal part of the test. The verbal scores of both groups of Asian Pacific Americans were lower than their white counterparts.

The same pattern was not discernible on the test's mathematics portion. The median score of Asian Pacific Americans for whom English was their best language was only one point higher than that of Asian Pacific American for whom this was not the case. Hsia observed that, subsequent to 1985, median math scores of Asian Pacific Americans for whom English was not their best language rose above those of their counterparts for whom English was their best language. Math scores for both Asian Pacific American groups continued to be higher than those of white SAT takers and all SAT test takers.

A spot check of performance on the test since Hsia's 1988 analysis shows that Asian Pacific Americans as a group continued to score lower on the verbal than on the math portion and to underperform whites on the former and outperform them on the latter. For example, the average Asian Pacific American 1992 verbal score was 413, while the average math score was 532 (*The Chronicle of Higher Education* 1992). The average white verbal score was 442, and the average white math score was 491.

Appendix D: Earnings Regressions

Definitions: (1) Monolingual U.S. Asian Pacific American, Bilingual U.S. Asian Pacific American, and Asian Immigrants are dummy variables taking on the value of one if the respondent falls into the category, otherwise zero. The excluded category is non-Hispanic white; (2) Years of Schooling is based on the categories reported in the 1990 PUMS, with the mid-point used when there is more than one year of schooling is used in a category; (3) Professional Degree is a dummy variable for those with a post-bachelor's professional degree; (4) Years of Experience is calculated as age minus the years of schooling and minus five years, and this value denotes the potential years of experience; (5) Experience Squared is the years of experience squared, and then divided by 100.

Table D1. Annual Earnings of Selected Asian Pacific Americans and Non-Hispanic Whites, 1989

Dependent Variable: Log of Annual Earnings

Independent Variables	(1)	(2)	(3)
Male			
Constant	10.017	8.757	7.608
Monolingual U.S. Asian American	0.140	0.020	0.032
Bilingual U.S. Asian American	-0.023	0.141	-0.086
Asian Immigrants	0.106	0.005	0.030
Years of Schooling	—	0.091	0.119
Professional Degree	—	0.229	0.258
Years of Experience	—	—	0.104
Experience Squared	—	—	0.290
Adjusted R-squared	.0002	.1025	.1472
Female			
Constant	9.478	7.776	7.659
Monolingual U.S. Asian American	0.356	0.250	0.250
Bilingual U.S. Asian American	0.364	0.217	0.220
Asian Immigrants	0.342	0.215	0.218
Years of Schooling	—	0.122	0.127
Professional Degree	—	0.062	0.059
Years of Experience	—	—	0.001
Experience Squared	—	—	0.020
Adjusted R-squared	.0017	.1044	.1052

Notes

1   The judge invoked the U.S. Supreme Court's decision in Plyer v. Doe, 457 U.S. 202 (1982), when ruling against Proposition 187's denial of public education to undocumented immigrant children. Also cited was the federal, not state, responsibility to establish immigration policy under the U.S. Constitution. No ruling was made on Proposition 187 provisions having to do with the access of undocumented immigrants to public colleges and universities or public social and health services. Lawsuits challenging these aspects of the proposition are pending. It is also likely that the federal court ruling on elementary and secondary school education will be appealed. Meanwhile, due to court injunctions, no aspect of Proposition 187 has yet been implemented.

2   As of December 1995, the bill pertaining to student loans may be vetoed by the president. Proposals to lower the ceiling on, and alter the priorities for, future legal immigration have been introduced in the House by Lamar Smith (R-Texas) and in the Senate Alan Simpson (R-Wyoming).

3   Huddle (1994), Fix and Passel (1994), and, most recently, Simon (1995) are among those who have weighed in on the issue of cost.

4   In a few households, the head of the household is not a parent but some other relative, such as a grandparent. The three classifications capture the situation of the vast majority of Asian American children. The "Not Elsewhere Classified" category, below, includes, for example, Asian children adopted by non-Asian parents.

5   The term "U.S.-born" encompasses individuals born in the United States, in a U.S. territory, or abroad to U.S. citizens.

6   The number of school-age children is not identical to the number of children attending school because a few are too young to attend and some older teenagers are no longer in school. For example, among Asian Americans in 1990, approximately 30 percent of the five-year-olds and 10 percent of the 18 year-olds were not enrolled in school. Among those between 6 and 17, only 4 percent were not enrolled.

7   Responses to census questions can provide only rough estimates of the population of LEP students. Limited English proficiency is a function of several dynamic factors, among them are educational opportunities for limited-English-proficient students to acquire English, the rate of English proficiency attainment among students enrolled in school, the social context within which the standard for full English proficiency is determined, the quality of instruments used to assess proficiency, the inflow of new immigrant students from non-English-speaking countries, and the birthrate among immigrant parents and the degree to which they speak English at home. Research has shown that it takes a limited-English-proficient child three to seven years to attain the level of English proficiency needed to succeed in an all-English class.

8   The National Center for Education Statistics (NCES, 1992) estimated there were 429,000 children between the ages of 8 and 15 in 1989 who spoke an Asian language at home. Of this number, 118,000 were thought to be limited English proficient. The fact that our figure differs from that of NCES is indicative of the lack of a common definition of limited English proficiency. For example, estimates of the total population of LEP students in the nation range from 2.3 million to 3.5 million. In calculating the lower figure, the U.S. Government Accounting Office (1994) defined LEP students as children between the ages of 5 and 17 who lived in families in the 1990 census, who did not speak English only, and who spoke English well, not well, or not at all. In contrast, our working definition of limited English proficiency among Asian children between the ages of 5 and 17 is more narrow.

9   In educational parlance, a child from a home where a non-English language is spoken is called a "language minority." Language minority students who are also lacking in English competency are considered LEP. In the national survey of eighth grade students done by the National Center for Educational Statistics (1992), 73 percent of Asian American eighth graders reported they were language minorities.

10 It is likely that first generation Asian American children were the primary beneficiaries of the federal Transitional Program for Refugee Children (TPRC), which expired in 1990. Southeast Asians were the dominant refugee population during the program's lifetime.

11 A fourth major factor has to do with the perception that Asian American children are "model minority" students. We will not discuss this factor here except to note that the portrayal of Asian Americans as the "model minority" is used to stigmatize other students of color. The assertion that the relatively high educational achievement of Asian Americans is endemic to their culture is meant to suggest that the relatively low educational achievement of other children of color is similarly endemic to their cultures. In other words, from the model minority perspective, children are held responsible for their own successes and failures as students. Responsibility is deflected from school systems to provide educational excellence to all children regardless of their backgrounds.

12 Some school districts automatically exclude children with low English proficiency (LEP) from Chapter 1 based on the perception that Chapter 1 bars them from providing remedial instruction in the student's native language (Urban Institute 1993). It is also the case that inclusion in Chapter 1 has generally been dependent upon a student's score on a standardized achievement test. Nearly all such tests are written in English. Many school districts do not administer them to LEP students, who consequently have not been placed in Chapter 1 programs. Recent changes in federal Chapter 1 policy may result in greater inclusion of LEP students. Chapter 1 funds are now to be used for school-wide efforts. All children in a school eligible to receive Chapter 1 funds are to receive Chapter 1 services even if some of the children do not meet Chapter 1 eligibility criteria.

13 If California districts had instead combined Title VII monies with TPRC monies, the amount per student served would total $206. The New York figure would be $232. TPRC provided around $650 per student during the early 1980s (McDonnell and Hill 1993). By 1989-90, funding had decreased to $200 per student.

14 Although it is possible to calculate the distribution of Asian Pacific American family incomes relative to the national median, this distribution would be misleading and upwardly biased due to considerable variation in the median family income across metropolitan areas and because Asian Pacific Americans are heavily concentrated in the larger and higher income metropolitan areas. To minimize this problem, the relative distribution is first determined within the 12 metropolitan areas with the largest numbers of Asian Pacific American children: Los Angeles-Long Beach; New York; Honolulu; San Francisco-Oakland; Anaheim-Santa Ana; San Jose; Chicago; Washington, D.C.; San Diego; Seattle; Houston; and Sacramento. Collectively, these metropolitan areas contained over two-thirds of the Asian Pacific population in 1970 and a large majority of the populatin in 1990. For each metropolitan area, the following steps are done:

a) The prevailing median family income for all families with school age children is estimated from the Public Use Microdata Samples (PUMS) for both 1970 and 1990.

b) The estimated metropolitan-specific prevailing median is then used to determine the relative ranking of Asian Pacific American families with school-age children. The rankings are below 50 percent of prevailing median, 50 percent to 84 percent of the prevailing median, etc.

Because the definitions of some metropolitan areas changed between 1970 and 1990, the actual number of metropolitan areas used is greater than 12. For example, the analysis is done separately for Oakland and San Francisco in 1990. For Asian Pacific American families in areas not listed in the table, the national median family income for urbanized areas is used as the prevailing median in determining relative ranking. The rankings of all Asian Pacific American families (relative to either the metropolitan-specific or national median) are then aggregated and normalized to produce Table 6 in the text.

15   The term "family-based" household is used because the mean average is calculated using all school-age children who are related to the head of the household rather than just sons and daughters.

16   There are other factors that contribute to the apparent discrepancy between fertility rate and observed number of school-age children: (1) a higher infant and child mortality rate in Asia;, and (2) children remaining in the sending country.

17   These are rough but conservative approximations based on 1990 Census data. Unfortunately, the data do not indicate the precise age at which an immigrant entered the country, because the year-of-entry data are reported in two- to five-year categories. We use the mid-point to estimate the number of years in the United States, which is then subtracted from the reported chronological age to derive an estimated age at time of entry. We assume that an immigrant had received his or her primary and secondary education if that person was 19 or older at the time of entry. Immigrants also transfer an enormous amount of human capital in the form of post-secondary education received abroad (Ong and Blumenberg, 1994).

18   Immigrant students of all ages come to the United States. We speculate that those who received at least part of their K-12 education in Asian countries may be relatively advantaged in mathematics compared to their U.S. counterparts. International assessments of mathematics performance among students in different countries regularly indicate that Asian youngsters achieve at higher levels than American youngsters (e.g., American School Board Journal and the Executive Educator 1989). Until recently, the pedagogy provided by teachers in Asia is designed to meet higher standards than those in place in this country, and Asian teachers throughout their careers appear to have more opportunities than their American counterparts to continue refining their skills (e.g., Stevenson and Stigler 1992). Mathematics is international in its conceptual content and emphasis on problem-solving skills. Immigrant students may thus experience a relatively seamless transition from learning mathematics in an Asian country to learning it here, and, although new to U.S. schools, they may tend to have a superior mathematics foundation upon which to draw. This foundation may pay off not only in terms of their mathematics achievement but also in other areas. Sue and Abe (1988) found that, among Asian Americans whose best language is not English, performance on the mathematics portion of the SAT is a better predictor of college freshman grade point average than their performance on the verbal portion of the SAT, regardless of college major.

19   We believe it is indeed through hours spent studying that Asian American children respond to their parents' expectations. Several studies indicate that Asian American children spend more time doing homework than other students (see, e.g., Olsen 1988, Caplan, Choy, and Whitemore 1992, Steinberg, Dornbusch, and Brown 1992, Rumbaut 1994). Time spent on homework is correlated with academic achievement (see, e.g., Peng and Wright 1994, Hsia 1988).

20   We are not unmindful of the possible negative effects of high parental expectations. Lee (1994) found that Korean and other Asian high school students suffered anxiety in trying to live up to parental expectations for academic achievement. They felt embarrassed and depressed if they could not meet expectations.

References

American School Board Journal and The Executive Educator. (1989/1990). "Innumeracy." *Education Vital Signs*, V, A9-All.

Baratz-Snowden, Joan C. and Duran, Richard. (1987, January). The *Educational Progress of Language Minority Students: Findings from the 1983-84 NAEP Reading* Survey. Princeton, NJ: Educational Testing Service. Cited in U.S. Commission on Civil Rights (1992, February), *Civil Rights Issues Facing Asian Americans in the 1990s*. Washington, D.C.: Author.

Borjas, George. (1990). *Friends or Strangers: The Impact of Immigrants on the U.S.* Economy. New York: Basic Books, Inc.

Caplan, Nathan., Choy, Marcella H., and Whitmore, John K. (1992, February). "Indochinese Refugee Families and Academic Achievement." *Scientific* American, 266, 36-42.

Council of Chief State School Officers/Resource Center on Educational Equity. (1990, February). *School Success for Limited-English-Proficient Students: The Challenge and State* Response. Washington, D.C.: Author.

Fix, Michael and Passell, Jeffrey S. (1994). *Immigration and Immigrants, Setting the Record* Straight. Washington D.C.: The Urban Institute.

Hsia, Jayjia. (1988). *Asian Americans in Higher Education and at* Work. Hillsdale, NJ: Lawrence Erlbaum Associates, Publishers.

Huddle, Donald (1994). *The Net National Costs of Immigration in 1993*. Houston: Rice University.

Ima, Kenji and Rumbaut, Ruben (1995). "Southeast Asian Refugees in American Schools: A Comparison of Fluent-English-Proficient and Limited-English-Proficient Students." In Nakanishi, Don T. and Nishida, Tina Yamano (eds.), *The Asian American Educational Experience, a Source Book for Teachers and* Students. New York: Routledge.

Internal Services Division (ISD), Los Angeles County (1992, November). *Impact of Undocumented Persons and Other Immigrants on Costs, Revenues and Services in Los Angeles County: A Report Prepared for Los Angeles County Board of Supervisors*.

Kao, Grace. (1995, February). "Asian Americans as Model Minorities? A Look at Their Academic Performance." *American Journal of Education* 103, 121-159.

Kao, Grace and Tienda, Marta. (1995, March). "Optimism and Achievement: The Educational Performance of Immigrant Youth." *Social Science Quarterly*, 76 (1), 1-19.

Lee, Stacey J. (1994). "Behind the Model-Minority Stereotype: Voices of High- and Low-Achieving Asian American Students." *Anthropology & Education Quarterly* 25 (4), 413-429.

McDonnell, Lorraine M., and Hill, Paul T. (1993). Newcomers *in American Schools: Meeting the Educational Needs of Immigrant* Youth. Santa Monica, CA: RAND.

National Center for Education Statistics. (1992, February). Statistical Analysis Report, *Language Characteristics and Academic Achievement: A Look at Asian and Hispanic Eighth Graders in NELS:88*, US Department of Education, Office of Educational Research and Improvement, NCES 92-479. Washington, D.C.: U.S. Government Printing Office, Superintendent of Documents.

Olsen, Laurie. (1988). *Crossing the Schoolhouse Border: Immigrant Students and the California Public* Schools. San Francisco: California Tomorrow.

Ong, P. and Blumenberg, Evelyn. (1994). "Scientist and Engineers." In Ong, P. (ed.), *The State of Asian Pacific America: Economic Diversity, Issues & Policies* (pp. 165-189). Los Angeles: LEAP Asian American Public Policy Institute and UCLA Asian American Studies Center.

Ong, P. and Hee S. (1993). "The Growth of the Asian Pacific American Population: Twenty Million in 2020." In Ong, P. (ed.), *The State of Asian Pacific America: Policy Issues to the Year 2020* (pp. 11-23). Los Angeles: LEAP Asian American Public Policy Institute and UCLA Asian American Studies Center.

Ong, P. and Hee, S. (1994). "Economic Diversity." In Ong, P. (ed.),*The State of Asian Pacific America: Economic Diversity, Issues & Policies* (pp. 31-56). Los Angeles: LEAP Asian American Public Policy Institute and UCLA Asian American Studies Center.

Peng, Samuel S., Owings, J.A., and Fetters, W.B. (1994, April). "School experiences and performance of Asian American high school students," paper presented at the Annual Meeting of the American Educational Research Association. Cited in Hsia, Jayjia (1988), *Asian Americans in Higher Education and at Work.* Hillsdale, NJ: Lawrence Erlbaum Associates, Publishers.

Peng, Samuel S. and Wright, DeeAnn. (1994, July-August). "Explanation of Academic Achievement of Asian American Students." *Journal of Educational* Research, 87(6), 346-352.

Population Reference Bureau. (1992, September). *The Challenge of Change: What the 1990 Census Tells Us About Children,* a report prepared for the Center for the Study of Social Policy (CSSP). Washington, D.C.: CSSP.

Rumbaut, Ruben G. (1994, Winter). "The Crucible Within: Ethnic Identity, Self-Esteem, and Segmented Assimilation Among Children of Immigrants." International *Migration* Review, XXVIII(4), 748-794.

Schneider, Barbara and Lee, Yongsook. (1990, December). "A Model for Academic Success: The School and Home Environment of East Asian Students." Anthropology & *Education Quarterly*, 21(4), 358-377.

Shea, Christopher. (1992, September 2). "SAT Scores Rise 1 Point on Verbal Section, Ending Steady Drop; 2-Point Gain in Math." *The Chronicle of Higher* Education, A41-A43.

Simon, Julian. (1995). Immigration: *The Demographic and Economic Facts,* Washington, D.C.: The Cato Institute and the National Immigration Forum.

Steinberg, Laurence, Dornbusch, Sanford, and Brown, B. Bradford. (1992, June). "Ethnic Differences in Adolescent Achievement: An Ecological Perspective." American Psychologist, 47(6), 723-729.

Stevenson, Harold W. and Stigler, James W. (1992). *The Learning* Gap. New York: Summit Books.

Sue, Stanley and Jennifer Abe. (1988). Predictors *of Academic Achievement Among Asian American and White Students*, College Board Report No. 88-11. NY: College Entrance Examination Board.

The Urban Institute. (1993, Summer). "Educating Immigrant Children," *Policy and Research* Report. Washington, D.C.: Author.

U.S. Bureau of the Census (1973). 1970 *Census of Population: Subject Reports: Japanese, Chinese, and Filipinos in the United States* PC(2)-1G. Washington, D.C.: U.S. Government Printing Office.

U.S. Bureau of the Census, (1984). *U.S. Census of the Population: 1980 Subject Reports-Asian and Pacific Islander Population in the United States PC(802)-1E*. Washington, D.C.: U.S. Government Printing Office.

U.S. Bureau of the Census, (1992). *Current Population Reports, P25-1092, Population Projection of the U.S., by Age, Sex, Race, and Hispanic Origin: 1992-2050*. Washington, D.C.: U.S. Government Printing Office.

U.S. Bureau of the Census, (1993). *1990 U.S. Census of the Population: Subject Reports-Asian and Pacific Islander in the United States 1990 CP-3-5*. Washington, D.C.: U.S. Government Printing Office.

U.S. General Accounting Office. (1994, January). *Limited English Proficiency: A Growing and Costly Educational Challenge Facing Many School* Districts. Washington, D.C.: Author.

U.S. General Accounting Office. (1994, April). *Immigrant Education: Federal Funding Has Not Kept Pace With Student Increases, Testimony Before the Subcommittee on Education, Arts and the Humanities, Committee on Labor and Human Resources, U.S.* Senate. Washington, D.C.: Author.

Wong, Morrison G. (1990). "The Education of White, Chinese, Filipino, and Japanese Students: A Look at 'High School and Beyond.'" Socio *logical* Perspectives, 33, 355-374.

Zhou, Min and Bankston III, Carl L. (1994, Winter). "Social Capital and the Adaptation of the Second Generation: The Case of Vietnamese Youth in New Orleans." *International Migration* Review, XXVIII(4), 821-845.

Interviews of Three
Asian Pacific Immigrants

by Irene Chang[*]

In the preceding article, Paul Ong and Linda Wing have set forth empirical support for the view that providing public education for immigrant children makes sense. The children mature and become productive members of society. In short, the fair way of assessing costs and benefits of educational expense is over the life time of the individual. In economic terms, public education is an investment in human capital. Furthermore, when the children of immigrants mature, their reliance on welfare is highly unlikely compared to the general population. This is further evidence of the dividends the nation receives from its educational investments in immigrant children. For many, the productivity is also a dividend from the public assistance that some immigrant families need.

Presented here are three real examples of Asian Pacific immigrants and refugees who entered as children and relied upon public school education. They were interviewed in the spring of 1995.

Khanh Phan

When Khanh Phan was eight, he and his two younger siblings came to the United States from Vietnam in 1975. Though it was not an easy transition for Phan to go from a developing country to modern America, he received a lot of encouragement from his parents, especially when it came to attending school and learning English. "At first, coming here was a scary experience because you feel alienated," he said. "One problem was the language barrier. It was intimidating just going to the store to buy things... I remember my parents stressing how it's important to try to learn English as soon as possible to do better in school and to communicate in public. I don't recall how I learned English. It came naturally. I guess I picked it up fairly easily and also retained my Vietnamese."

As the children went to school, Phan's parents went to work. His mother — a housewife in Vietnam — became a hairstylist and eventually set up

---

[*]   Irene Chang has a J.D. from Stanford University Law School.

her own shop in Gardena, just south of Los Angeles. His dad — a civil engineer back in Vietnam — used the little money they had brought over with them to buy some rental property and went into property management. They received neither government assistance nor community support; instead, they "started everything on their own."

Phan paid his own college tuition by doing part-time general office work for $8 an hour at the Nissan Motor Corporation; his parents helped him by buying some of his books. He graduated in 1991 from California State University, Long Beach, with a Bachelor degree in sociology. Now 27, Phan earns over $3,000 a month as a social worker in Los Angeles. He assists mentally disabled clients with their SSI applications. "We act as their voice." Through his work in the county, he also joined in the occasional activities of the Vietnamese Employees Association which tries to educate people about community issues.

"I've grown up the majority of my lifetime as an American and affiliate myself more with the American side of it. I have mixed friends; most are Asian or Vietnamese. . . .If you're going to adapt and survive in a new environment, you need to learn the language and custom of that environment. For someone coming here, you need to learn English to get a job and for basic activities." After more than two decades in this country, Phan has adapted and is thriving in his adopted home.

David Mao

Born in Taiwan, 11 year old David Mao and his mother came to the United States in 1956 to join his father, who was on the military staff committee of the United Nations. David began his American education in Washington, DC, public schools, which were still racially segregated at the time, and eventually finished up his secondary school experience in San Francisco.

"I didn't speak English when we came," said Mao, 48, of his DC years. "I was thrown into the fifth grade. The teacher would take time out with one Yugoslavian child, me and another Chinese. She gave us special lessons — Dick and Jane, etc. They give you tests for tracking. Just coming from China, not knowing the language, I didn't do very well on the tracking tests for junior high school and ended up in the lowest remedial class in seventh grade. I was almost learning disabled, and that was a great handicap."

Fortunately, however, Mao earned good grades and every year was able to "climb one level higher" and eventually even managed to take college prep courses. Taiwan schools begin teaching algebra in elementary school, so Mao found American math classes to be much easier. Because education is so highly valued, it was not surprising that his father also tutored him at home, or that the family jointly decided that Mao should take physics, trigonometry and calculus to help him get into college. "People in school and people in church told me this is what I had to do. In Chinese families, they expect you to go to college and complete a bachelor's degree."

Mao attended American University, University of Maryland and San Francisco State University, with a detour into the U.S. Army and a tour in Vietnam. With most of his assistance coming from the G.I. bill, plus earnings from his part-time work, Mao finally graduated in 1974 in international business from San Francisco State University. Active with R.O.T.C. while in school, Mao is still a Major in the army reserves and serves one weekend a month. "This is the best country in the world, and I should put something back into it."

In 1975, shortly after graduating, the federally-funded Comprehensive Employment Training Act enabled Mao to find a job as a placement counselor for the California Employment Development Department. About five years later, he switched to law enforcement. Now a supervising criminal investigator for the department, he looks into and prosecutes medical, tax and unemployment fraud cases. In 1995, he paid about $4,800 in federal taxes, $1,800 in state taxes, and almost $28.000 in mortgage payments and property taxes.

Katherine Chan

When the Saigon government fell in 1975, Katherine Chan, then just a young teenager, found her family separated by thousands of miles: some members relocated to New Jersey; others, including two siblings and her father remained in Vietnam and were unable to come to the United States until many years later. Uprooted from all that was familiar — including what Chan described as a "wealthy" lifestyle — introduction to American life was difficult. The first year, the family lived on welfare, including food stamps and Medicaid; their clothing came from the Red Cross. "No one in my family liked being on welfare." The family got off welfare after that one year.

Through her mother's business acumen and perseverance, and through long hours of hard work, from 7 am to 11 pm, the family's small candy store in New York's Chinatown eventually expanded into a grocery store. Earnings grew from $100 a day to $1,000 a day.

Chan remembered that life was "miserable." "I attended public schools in New Jersey until the 11th grade. I didn't do well. I hated public school The students teased us, and we couldn't answer back. I had no friends. I was the only immigrant or refugee in school. That school was not prepared for me at all, because I was in that first wave of refugees." For her senior year, she received a scholarship to attend a private school across the river in New York. There in the smaller school of 120 students, she blossomed and was even was elected student body vice president.

A creative combination of grants, national student loans, and work study — which involved spending 40 hours a week working in a biology lab — enabled Chan to attend a private university in Texas. After college, she went to the Philippines, first as a Peace Corps worker and then as a staff member in the United Nations refugee camp. In the Peace Corps, she organized a clinic for eye and harelip operations and worked as a midwife; in the camp, she provided mental health counseling to refugees. "Some of these were boat people; others were sponsored by United States residents. In the camp, for six months, they had to learn about U.S. culture, etc., before coming here."

When she finally returned to the United States, Chan went on to graduate school and earned a master's in social work in 1992 from the University of California at Berkeley. Chan, 33, is a psychiatric social worker for an Alameda County outpatient mental health clinic and provides therapy and case management for severely mentally ill people, most of whom are indigent Medi-Cal patients. She earns over $40,000 a year.

Though she has voted in every major election, Chan admitted that in 1982 when she became a citizen, she was motivated out of fear: she hoped that her U.S. status would protect her from any harm during her visit to China. It was not until she went to the Philippines, where "we were doing good for people," that she developed "patriotic feelings." There, she became proud to proclaim she was from the United States.

Part IV.
Citizenship and
Civic Participation

Becoming Citizens, Becoming Voters: The Naturalization and Political Participation Of Asian Pacific Immigrants

by Paul Ong and Don Nakanishi[*]
University of California, Los Angeles

In his address to the national conference of the Southwest Voter Registration Project in 1995, Vice President Albert Gore heralded naturalization as the final stage of incorporating an immigrant into American society.[1] Naturalization is not merely a technical change in immigration status. The passage to citizenship also is more than the required level of acculturation defined by a basic command of the English language and knowledge of U.S. history and its political institutions. With this act, immigrants abandon allegiance to their country of origin and pledge loyalty to the United States.

The acquisition of citizenship marks the beginning of full political and social membership in this country. The individual acquires new civil and legal rights, with the opportunity to vote and to participate in the electoral process perhaps the most important. The stakes are also economic. In today's growing anti-immigrant climate, citizenship has become a litmus test for inclusion in America's social contract. Consider, for instance, current proposals to require citizenship for programs such as SSI (Supplementary Security Income) for the elderly and AFDC (Aid to Families with Dependent Children) for families with children.[2]

Naturalization and political participation have profound implications for groups, as well as individuals. The political strength of an immigrant-dominated population within our electoral system hinges on two interrelated but distinct processes: (1) the group's naturalization rate, that is, the relative proportion of immigrants with citizenship; and (2) the rates by

---

[*]   Paul Ong is professor and chair of the Department of Urban Planning at UCLA's School of Public Policy and Social Research. Don Nakanishi is director of the UCLA Asian American Studies Center and associate professor at the UCLA Graduate School of Education.

which naturalized and native-born citizens both register to vote and actually vote during elections. Low rates in either situation dilute an immigrant-dominated group's potential electoral power, and thus diminishes its influence on legislation and public policy. Citizenship and civic participation also are regarded by the general public as indicators of the ability and willingness of a group to assimilate and become "Americanized" rather than to separate from the mainstream. While high rates of naturalization and civic participation do not guarantee that members of a group will be accepted as equals, low rates foster a sense of political isolation and provide fodder for nativist movements.

Although becoming a citizen and a voter are often viewed as simultaneous processes, they are distinct and temporally distant forms of membership and participation. Most adult immigrants and refugees acquired their fundamental political values, attitudes, and behavioral orientations in countries that have sociopolitical systems, traditions, and expectations that are different from those in the United States. Indeed, many came from countries where voting was not permitted, limited to a privileged few, or was widely viewed as being inconsequential because of the dominance of a single political party. As a result, these immigrants must undergo a process of political acculturation beyond the rudimentary exposure to the basic structure of the U.S. government presented in adult citizenship classes. The general notion of participating in electoral politics is a prolonged and complicated process of social learning for immigrants—as it may be for many native-born citizens as well.

Using an empirical approach, this essay examines rates of naturalization, voter registration, and voting behavior for Asian Pacific immigrants and refugees. The first section explores the overall trends in naturalization between Asian and other groups of immigrants during the past three decades. Factors that have the greatest influence on whether Asian immigrants become naturalized are also measured. The second section analyzes the political participation of immigrant and native-born Asian Pacific Americans, with special attention to voter registration and electoral involvement. Comparisons are made between Asian Pacific Americans and other groups in American society, and the analysis explores factors that account for differences in participation rates. A concluding section summarizes major findings and offers several policy recommendations.

Becoming Citizens:
Naturalization and Asian Immigrants

The status of Asian Pacific Americans, as an immigrant-dominated population, is greatly affected by the rate of naturalization. While the number of U.S.-born citizens doubled between 1970 and 1990, the foreign-born population grew over eight-fold because of the Immigration Act of 1965. As a consequence, the proportion of U.S.-born citizens in Asian Pacific America declined from 52 percent to 21 percent. Although U.S.-born citizens continued to comprise a large majority of the Japanese American community from 1970 to 1990, newer and rapidly growing groups such as Southeast Asians, Koreans, and Asian Indians were predominantly foreign-born. Since the early 1970s, immigrants have constituted a growing majority of the Asian Pacific American adult population; each decade the number of foreign-born adults has more than doubled (See Table 1. All tables located at the end of this essay.). Given these demographic trends, naturalization rates very directly determine the size of the Asian Pacific American population eligible to vote and also its political future.

This section of the report examines naturalization rates and influences for Asian Pacific immigrants over the minimum eligibility age of 18.[3] The analysis is based on samples from the three census periods that looked at individuals. The advantage of this data source is the large sampling which allows for detailed tabulations and reasonable estimates of the characteristics of the entire population.[4] While the 1970 sample includes only 1 percent of the total U.S. population, the 1980 and 1990 samples include 5 percent of the population. The samples also contain information on nativity, racial and ethnic identity, demographic characteristics, educational attainment, and a host of other variables.

There are limitations, however. The census does not distinguish between legal immigrants, undocumented aliens, and some foreign visitors. Foreign tourists (without an established residence) are excluded, but those on employment or student visas are included. Thus the immigrant population in the census can be best described as the foreign-born population with an established U.S. residence. The census data also do not follow individuals over a period of time; the data refer to the characteristics of the sample at one point in time. But profiles, rates, and other demographic features of the 1970, 1980 and 1990 populations can be compared.

The census uses five categories to define U.S. citizenship: (1) those born in the United States (citizens by *jus solis*), (2) those who are citizens through birth in a U.S. territory, (3) those born abroad to U.S. citizens (citizens by *jus sanguini*), (4) alien immigrants, and (5) naturalized immigrants.[5] For the purpose of this report, the foreign-born population is comprised of those in the last two categories, and the naturalized population is comprised of those in the last category. The terms "foreign-born" and "immigrant" are used interchangeably.

The data reveal the following: (1) Asian Pacific immigrants are naturalizing at a rate comparable to that of non-Hispanic white immigrants. (2) Length of residence in the United States is the single most important factor in determining naturalization rates. (3) This time-dependent process, along with the underlying acculturation process, appears remarkably stable over the decades. (4) While time is the most important factor, ethnicity, age, and level of education are among other influential factors.

Overall Pattern of Naturalization

Between 1970 and 1990, the naturalization rate for all immigrants fell 24 percentage points from 67 percent to 43 percent (See Table 2). Two factors are behind this decline. The first relates to a resumption of large-scale immigration in 1960s, and the second simply reflects actual changes in naturalization rates within certain groups.

After the 1965 immigration changes, the adult immigrant population more than doubled from less than 8.5 million in 1970 to over 17.5 million in 1990. Renewed large-scale immigration altered the proportion of immigrants who resided in the United States for a lengthy period of time.[6] A majority (55 percent) of the 1970 adult immigrants had lived in the United States for 21 or more years, but two decades later only about a third (35 percent) had lived in the United States for that length of time. This decline in the number of long-term immigrants occurred despite an increase in the absolute number of long-term residents from 4.9 million to 6.2 million. On the other hand, newer immigrants (those in the country for no more than 10 years) increased from 25 percent to 39 percent of all adult immigrants. In absolute numbers, their ranks grew from 2.2 million to 6.9 million.

Given the large number of recent immigrants, the decline in the relative number of citizens among adult immigrants from 1970 to 1990 is no surprise. In fact, this recomposition accounts for nearly half of the overall decline.[7]

The rest of the decline is attributable to the second factor, changes in the naturalization rate. Comparing groups who have resided in the United

States for different periods of time presents a clear picture. In 1970, 20 percent of those who had been in the country for ten years or less were naturalized. In 1990, only 15 percent of that group was naturalized. For those who had resided in the country for more than two decades, the naturalization figure dropped from 90 percent in 1970 to 74 percent in 1990.[8] Some social, cultural, and economic explanations for this decline are considered below.

Racial Variations

A racial recomposition of the foreign-born population has accompanied the renewal of large-scale immigration.[9] Sources of modern immigration differ dramatically from that of earlier immigration. For the first two-thirds of the century, Europeans dominated immigration flows into the United States. After the elimination of racially biased quotas in 1965, people from the Asia Pacific and Latin America have dominated. Non-Hispanic whites comprised 75 percent of all adult immigrants in 1970 but less than 20 percent in 1990. Latinos and Asian Pacific Islanders were less than a quarter of all immigrants in 1970, but today they constitute the vast majority.[10]

The racial recomposition has favored some populations that have low naturalization rates. Mexicans, for example, are not only the single largest group of recent immigrants but also a group with a substantially lower than average rate of naturalization (Skerry, 1993; Tomas Rivera Center, 1994). They generally are not proficient in English; they maintain ties to Mexico through occasional visits; and, relative to other immigrants, they are less educated. These factors may contribute to their low naturalization rate. The shift to non-European immigrants, however, cannot solely explain the drop in naturalization rates, because recent non-Hispanic white immigrants *also* maintain a lower than average naturalization rate.

Naturalization rates for Asian immigrants over three decennial censuses did not decrease. Overall rates have fluctuated around 40 percent (See Table 2). Although all non-Hispanic white immigrants exhibited higher overall rates, rates are directly related to the fact that most long-term residents for the three census years were non-Hispanic whites (See Table 3). On the other hand, newer immigrants were predominantly Asian and Pacific Islanders.

Over time, naturalization rates for Asian Pacifics have changed for both new and long-term residents. In 1970, Asian rates were consistently low for all cohorts, especially for long-term residents. The substantially lower rate for long-term Asian residents versus non-Hispanic whites (68 percent versus 92 percent, Table 3) is a historical legacy. Prior to 1952, most Asian immigrants were ineligible for citizenship (Hing, 1993). Historical restrictions not only delayed naturalization for those who wanted to become citizens, but years of discrimination alienated many other Asian immigrants and dampened their desire to naturalize. By 1980, however, the naturalization rates for non-Hispanic whites declined while those for Asians improved. Asians had a higher rate among those in the country for ten years or less. By 1990, all Asian rates were at least equal to, or considerably higher than, those of non-Hispanic whites.

The fact that many immigrants return to their native lands permanently should be taken into account for a more accurate naturalization rate calculation. Return migration is more extensive for non-Hispanic whites than for Asians (Liang, 1994; Jasso and Rosenzweig, 1990). Calculations by the Immigration and Naturalization Service that include return-migrants show that immigrants from Asian Pacific countries have the highest naturalization rates (INS, 1990). The top three Asian Pacific communities are Vietnamese (78 percent), Chinese (63 percent), and Filipino Americans (63 percent).[11] Among the bottom five nationality groups are Canadians (12 percent), the British (20 percent), and Italians (23 percent).[12]

Time-Dependent Acculturation

As noted, length of residence in the United States is the most powerful determinant of whether a person will naturalize. This is partly a product of the residency requirement for naturalization, which is usually five years, although the period for spouses of citizens is reduced to three. Other constraints on naturalization may be more important. Acculturation, the broad process of learning and adopting the language, values, and norms of the host society, is a central factor.

A strong correlation between time in the United States and the level of assimilation has been demonstrated. The level of economic assimilation, as measured by immigrant earnings compared to that of U.S.-born ethnic counterparts with similar education and years of work experience, starts from a low point at the time of entry and gradually improves over a fifteen-year period; at that point, immigrants reach parity (See Borjas, 1990). Understanding English and societal institutions also improve over time.

Naturalization rates of Asian immigrants show a remarkably similar pattern for all three censuses. Graph 1 compares the rates in five-year increments.[13] Prior to five years, few naturalizations occur, due largely to the five-year residency requirement for most immigrants.[14] The greatest increase occurs among those in the country between 5 and 15 years. The data suggest that two-thirds of all naturalizations take place within this range.[15] The naturalization rate continues to increase after residency of more than 15 years, but in smaller increments. The one exception to the overall pattern is for those who have been in the country for over a quarter century. In 1970, only a third of this cohort were citizens, due to the legacy of discrimination encountered by earlier immigrants. Over time, this effect faded as the number of pre-World War II immigrants declined. By 1990, 84 percent of the Asian Pacific immigrants in the country for more than 25 years were citizens.

The influence of length of residence on the naturalization rate can also be seen in data for comparable groups in different census years. Although the census does not identify and follow the same groups each census, a dynamic process can be inferred from observed differences among groups at the same point in time. For example, because the naturalization rate in 1990 for those in the country for 11 to 15 years was higher than the rate for those in the country for 6 to 10 years, the inference is that the increase was due to being in the country an additional five years.[16] This is a reasonable assumption given the relative stability of the pattern of naturalization rates observed in Graph 1.

This type of analysis allows a further step in determining how naturalization rates change with time. While the census data are not longitudinal, samples can be used to estimate changes for a given cohort over time. For example, the group whose members were from 18 and 40 years old in 1970 would be roughly the same group with members from 28 and 50 in 1980, and 38 and 60 in 1990.[17] While the census sample does not include the same individuals in all three decades, statistical principles permit the use of the data to develop representative profiles as this cohort aged over time. This method can be further refined by dividing the cohort by period of entry into the United States and tracking each group over time. Using this approach, longitudinal changes in naturalization for each cohort can be estimated. Table 4 compares the results of this exercise with the rates observed in cross-sectional analysis. In spite of minor differences, patterns are remarkably similar.

While time in the United States is perhaps the single most important factor in determining the naturalization rate, the entire process is not simple. Changes in the rate are based on a more fundamental phenomenon: acculturation that unfolds over time, such as learning English language, acquiring a knowledge of U.S. institutions, and strengthening one's sense of identity as an American. These changes are no doubt influenced by demands of everyday life. Like most residents, immigrants work to earn a living, while coping with family responsibilities.

Larger societal forces also influence the process. Historically, the dampening effect of discrimination was clear. More recently, the growth of anti-immigrant sentiments, particularly in California, has also affected the behavior of immigrants. The fear created by efforts such as Proposition 187 has led to a noticeable increase in naturalization applicants.

Intra-Cohort Variations

In addition to length of residence and the acculturation process, naturalization rates are also affected by ethnicity, age, English language ability, and education. Table 5 presents an analysis on those falling between the ages of 6 and 20, the range when changes in rates are most dramatic.

Among major ethnic groups, the difference between the highest and lowest naturalization rates is about 50 percentage points. Japanese immigrants exhibited the lowest rates: for those in the country from 6 to 10 years, only 1 in 14 was a citizen. Although the rate increased as residency increased, only 1 in 3 Japanese immigrants in the country 16 to 20 years was a citizen. This strikingly low level of naturalization may be tied to Japanese transnational corporations. With increased trade with the United States, many of these companies establish operations in the country and bring a significant number of nationals to work. Sizable and visible communities of these employees and their families have been established in places like New York City and parts of Southern California. This transpacific movement in turn fostered the migration of other Japanese who work in restaurants, clubs, and other businesses serving corporate-based Japanese communities. Many of these Japanese do not regard themselves as immigrants, even after residing in the country for a number of years.

Filipinos represent the other end of the spectrum with the highest naturalization rates. In many respects, they are the most "Americanized" of Asian Pacific immigrants. The history of U.S. colonization from 1898 to 1946 has left a legacy in the Philippines where English, once the official language, remains the language of choice for many Filipinos. Many aspects of U.S. culture also have become deeply embedded in Filipino society and identity. This pre-migration acculturation has facilitated the naturalization process for Filipino immigrants in the United States. This "headstart" is reflected in the 1990 census, in which nearly half of those who had been here for 6 to 10 years were citizens.

Naturalization rates of other Asian Pacific immigrant groups fall between those of the Japanese and Filipinos (See Table 5). As length of residence increased, however, the naturalization level for the other groups approached that for Filipinos. In other words, the early advantage enjoyed by Filipinos in terms of "Americanization" disappeared as the other groups acculturated. The rate for Southeast Asians was similar to that of Chinese and Koreans. This may be surprising because Southeast Asians are less likely to have formed a pre-migration sense of attachment to the United States because they are predominantly refugees. On the other hand, refugees may be more likely to sever ties with the home country because of a revolutionary change in government, thus prompting the formation of allegiance to the United States.

Younger immigrants are also more likely to be citizens (See Table 5). Having spent most of their lives in another society and culture, older immigrants may find that breaking their attachment is not easy. Middle-age immigrants are also burdened by the daily demands of working and raising a family. Younger immigrants, on the other hand, are being raised and educated in the United States, so *American* behaviors and values become *their* behaviors and values.

Differences in English-language ability also generate variations in the naturalization rates (See Table 5). Among those who do not speak English, only 1 in 10 was a citizen in 1990. Even among those who had lived in the country for 16 to 20 years, only 1 in 4 was naturalized. Rates generally increased with improved English language ability. Those whose English proficiency was "very good," for example, were 3 to 6 times more likely to be naturalized than those who did not speak English.

Educational attainment also influences the likelihood of being a citizen but not in a linear fashion. The naturalization rate increased with years of schooling up to an undergraduate education. For example, among immigrants in the country for 6 to 10 years, those with some college education were more than twice as likely to be naturalized than those with no more than an elementary school education. This pattern suggests that more formal education enabled an immigrant to acquire more quickly the knowledge required to pass the naturalization exam. This educational effect, however, was smaller among those in the country for 16 to 20 years.

Graduate school experience played a different role. Those with a doctorate degree had lower naturalization rates than those with a master's degree,[18] who in turn had lower rates than those with a bachelor's degree. This outcome was particularly noticeable among those in the country for 6 to 10 years. Although this pattern may be puzzling at first glance, the result in fact is not surprising since many of those with more than an undergraduate education are in the country on temporary visas to pursue additional graduate and post-doctorate training, and thus are not eligible for citizenship (Ong, et al., 1992). Naturalization rates of doctorate degree holders—even those with over 11 years U.S. residency—were lower than those with bachelor's degrees.

The data support the thesis that age, English language ability, and education influence the naturalization rate in an interrelated way. Elderly immigrants, for example, may be more likely to have a poor command of English or to have less education. Those with advanced degrees may be more likely to have a better command of English. An analysis to determine if these factors have an independent effect on odds of an immigrant becoming a citizen sheds some light.[19] Results are consistent with patterns discussed above: (1) the likelihood of naturalization decreases with age but increases with English language ability, and (2) the effect of education is nonlinear, with the odds increasing up to an undergraduate education and then decreasing with additional graduate training. Moreover, ethnic variations discussed earlier also hold, with Filipinos having the highest probability of being citizens and the Japanese the lowest.

Becoming Voters:
The Electoral Participation
of Asian Immigrants

In recent years, a number of political commentators and scholars have speculated about whether Asian Pacific Americans will become a major new force in American electoral politics, because of their dramatic demographic growth and concentration in certain key electoral states like California, New York, and Texas (Tachibana, 1986; Cain, 1988; Stokes, 1988; Nakanishi, 1991; Karnow, 1992; Miller, 1995). Many believe that if Asian Pacific American — like American Jewish — voters come to represent a proportion of the electorate that is comparable to, if not greater than, their share of the total population, then they could become a highly influential "swing vote" in critical local, state, and presidential elections. In California, for example, the state with the most congressional seats and electoral college votes, if Asian Pacific Americans, who are 1-in-10 residents of the state also became 1-in-10 voters, then they could play a strategically important role in national and local elections. Indeed, their voting potential coupled with their proven record of campaign funding could elevate Asian Pacific Americans to the status of leading players in the grand theater of American politics (*Asianweek*, 1984).

During the past decade, the increase in the political participation and presence of Asian Pacific Americans in electoral politics is unmistakable. The 1995 edition of the "Asian Pacific American Political Roster and Resource Guide" (Nakanishi and Lai, 1995) listed over 1,200 Asian Pacific American elected and major appointed officials for the federal government and 31 different states. In contrast, the first edition of this directory, published in 1978, listed several hundred politicians, primarily holding offices in Hawaii and California (Nakanishi, 1978). The vast majority of 1978 officials were second and third generation Asian Pacific Americans, primarily Japanese Americans. Today, a growing number of recently elected officeholders are immigrants, such as Jay Kim of Walnut, California, the first Korean American elected to Congress; David Valderrama, the first Filipino American elected as a delegate to the Maryland Assembly; and City Councilmember Tony Lam of Westminster, California, the first Vietnamese American elected to public office. In the past few years, Asian Pacific American candidates also have run well-financed, professional — though ultimately unsuccessful — mayoral campaigns for some of the nation's largest cities, including Los Angeles, San Francisco, and Oakland.

There is more, however, to this seemingly optimistic and glowing assessment of Asian Pacific American electoral achievements. In reality, this immigrant-dominant population has yet to reach its full political potential, especially in transforming its extraordinary population growth into comparable proportions of registered voters who actually vote. In California, for example, Asian Pacific Americans may represent 1-in-10 residents but are no more than 1-in-20 of the state's registered voters and only 3 out of 100 of those who actually vote (The Field Institute, 1992).

The size, characteristics, and impact of the Asian Pacific American electorate are constantly evolving in relation to historical and contemporary conditions. Institutional structures as well as individual personalities are relevant at both the grassroots and leadership levels. Early Chinese and Japanese immigrants were disenfranchised and excluded from fully participating in American life because of discriminatory laws and policies, such as the 1870 naturalization law, *Ozawa v. United States* (1922), and *Thind v. United States* (1923), which forbade Asian immigrants from becoming naturalized citizens. These legal barriers prevented early Asian Pacific immigrants from being involved in electoral politics of any form—be it the type of ward politics practiced by European immigrants in East Coast and Midwest cities or simply to vote for their candidate in a presidential election. Barriers significantly delayed the development of electoral participation and representation by Asian Pacific Americans until the second and subsequent generations, decades after their initial period of immigration. Early Asian immigrants and their descendants were scapegoated for political gain by opportunistic politicians and anti-Asian social movements and political parties. The most disastrous example was the wholesale incarceration of 120,000 Japanese Americans during World War II.

This legacy of political exclusion and isolation has many contemporary manifestations. Asian Pacific American civil rights groups remain vigilant in seeking the elimination of a number of "political structural barriers" (Kwoh and Hui, 1993), such as the unfair redistricting of Asian Pacific American communities and the lack of bilingual ballots and voting materials, which prevents less English-proficient Asian Pacific Americans from exercising their full voting rights (Bai, 1991). Likewise, grassroots voter registration campaigns in Asian Pacific American communities have had to confront and overcome deep-seated views of political inefficacy, political alienation, and mistrust of government held by large segments of the immigrant Asian Pacific American population. And elected officials and major political parties pay little attention to the unique public policy and quality-of-life needs and issues of Asian Pacific Americans (Nakanishi, 1992).

This section of the report analyzes levels and determinants of voter registration and voting by naturalized Asian Pacific immigrants over the age of 18, compared to native-born Asian Pacific Americans and other racial and ethnic populations. The analysis is based on the Census Bureau's 1990, 1992, and 1994 Current Population Surveys (CPS). The 1994 CPS data, which will be the primary focus of analysis, was particularly useful because it provided detailed information on the citizenship status of individuals similar to the decennial census, as mentioned in the previous section on naturalization. This made it possible to differentiate between Asian Pacific Americans who were foreign-born and native-born, as well as immigrants and refugees who were naturalized and those who were not.

Unfortunately, this data source does not enable an analysis of differences in electoral participation among the array of Asian Pacific ethnic communities. Previous studies have found that rates of voter registration vary markedly, with Japanese Americans having the highest proportion of registered voters and Southeast Asians having the lowest percentage (Nakanishi, 1991). Despite their limitations, advantages of the CPS data are that they allow an examination of both national and regional trends with a sufficiently large sample of Asian Pacific Americans,[20] and an analysis of potential differences in registration and voting rates in relation to native-born and naturalized citizens, which has rarely been examined rigorously (Din, 1984; Nakanishi, 1991; Horton, 1995; Shinagawa, 1995; Tam, 1995).

Major findings are that naturalized Asian Pacific immigrants and refugees have lower rates of voter registration than native-born citizens. Asian Pacific naturalized citizens who have been in the country for over 20 years, however, have registration rates that are comparable to, or exceed those of, the native-born, while those who arrived over 30 years ago have higher rates for both registration and voting. As in the case of naturalization rates, statistical analysis revealed that year of entry was the single most important factor in determining voter registration rates. In terms of actual voting, best predicators included not only year of entry but also educational attainment and age. And finally, characteristics of Asian Pacific American voters as a whole, as well as between native-born and foreign-born, reflect an ethnic electorate that is far from being monolithic with respect to political party affiliations, ideological preferences, and voting preferences. Rather, these groups have many dimensions of diversity, which are influencing their continued development.

Rates of Voter Registration

The Asian Pacific population in the United States is characterized by the largest proportion of individuals over the age of 18 who cannot take the first step towards participating in American electoral politics, that is, registering to vote, because they are not citizens. In 1994, 55 percent of adult Asians were not citizens in contrast to 44 percent of the Latinos, 5 percent African Americans, and 2 percent Non-Hispanic whites. The proportion of non-citizens varied by geographic region, with Honolulu having the lowest percentage of non-citizens among its adult Asian population (21 percent), and New York (73 percent) having the highest. Sixty-three percent of adult Asians in Los Angeles County and 52 percent in the Oakland-San Francisco region also were not citizens.

Nationwide, in 1994, approximately 1,166,450 Asian Pacific American were registered to vote, of whom 58 percent (680,750) were U.S.-born and 42 percent (485,700) were foreign-born (Table 6). California's Asian Pacific American electorate, which accounted for 40 percent of the country's

Asian Pacific American registered voters, mirrored the nation's composition of U.S.-born (58 percent) to foreign-born (42 percent) voters. Hawaii, on the other hand, which has witnessed far less recent immigration than many mainland states, had an overwhelmingly U.S.-born Asian Pacific American electorate (88 percent).

Native and naturalized Asian Pacific American citizens exhibited very low overall rates of voter registration. Nationally, 1994 CPS census data estimated that only 53 percent of all Asian Pacific American citizens — as well as 53 percent of Latino citizens — were registered in contrast to 61 percent of African Americans and 69 percent of Non-Hispanic whites. Similar patterns were observed in 1992 for these population groups in Los Angeles, Oakland-San Francisco, New York, and Honolulu. Indeed, in some regions, differences in voter registration rates between Asian Pacific Americans and Non-Hispanic whites, who usually have the highest rates of registration, were quite substantial. In 1992, for example, in the Oakland-San Francisco region, 56 percent of all adult Asian Pacific American citizens were registered to vote compared to 86 percent of Non-Hispanic whites, 73 percent African Americans, and 63 percent Latino American citizens. At the same time, regional differences in voter registration rates for Asian Pacific American communities were apparent, with Los Angeles having the highest (64 percent) and New York having the lowest (54 percent).

Many previous studies have found that Asian Pacific Americans have lower rates of voter registration than African Americans and non-Hispanic whites, and usually the same or somewhat lower rates than that of Latinos. The findings here are consistent, and remain extremely puzzling, because of the relatively high, group-level attainment levels of Asian Pacific Americans in education and other socioeconomic variables. These factors have been long associated with active electoral participation in political science research (Nakanishi, 1986a, 1991; Cain, 1988; Field Institute, 1992; Erie and Brackman, 1993; Lien, 1994).

Among Asian Pacific American citizens, those who were born in the United States have a higher *overall* rate of voter registration than those who were born abroad and have become naturalized. In 1994, as Table 7 illustrates, 56 percent of all U.S.-born Asian Americans were registered compared to 49 percent of those who were naturalized. Indeed, foreign-born Asian Pacific American citizens had among the lowest rates of any group, including Latino naturalized citizens (53 percent). In terms of electoral participation beyond registration, however, both Asian Pacific American naturalized and native-born voters had among the highest rates of voting during the 1994 elections. Therefore, Asian Pacific immigrants appear to reflect a provocative series of discrete, non-linear trends from becoming citizens to becoming registered voters and then to becoming actual voters: they have one of the highest rates of naturalization after immigrating, but one of the lowest rates of voter registration after becoming citizens. Once registered, however, Asian Pacific American naturalized citizens have among the highest rates of voting of any group.

A closer and more detailed examination of Asian naturalized citizens indicates that those who immigrated over 20 years ago, prior to 1975, have rates of voter registration comparable to, if not greater than, those who were born in the United States (See Tables 8 and 9). Indeed, this was the case for practically all age groups, educational attainment levels, and for women. On the other hand, Asian Pacific naturalized citizens who immigrated within the past twenty years have rates of registration that are substantially lower than native-born citizens and naturalized citizens who arrived before 1975. This was consistent for practically all age and educational attainment levels, as well as for men and women. Like naturalization, statistical analysis revealed that year of entry was the best predictor of voter registration for Asian naturalized citizens. For voting, year of entry, educational attainment, and age were the strongest explanatory variables for Asian naturalized registered voters.

Like the process of naturalization, the importance of time-dependent variables for electoral participation is consistent with the view that immigrants and refugees must often undergo a prolonged and multifaceted process of social adaptation and learning before fully participating in their newly-adopted country. Becoming actively involved in American electoral politics and politically acculturated may be one of the most complex, lengthy, and least understood learning experiences. Adult Asian Pacific immigrants and refugees, like other groups of migrants (Gittleman, 1982), largely acquired their core political values, attitudes, and behavioral orientations in sociopolitical systems that differed from that of the United States. Some of their countries of origin did not have universal suffrage, others were dominated by a single political party (which made voting nearly inconsequential), and still others were in extreme political upheaval as a result of civil war or international conflict. Indeed, one of the major reasons why many Asian refugees left their homelands was to escape some of the most horrendous political situations like the killing fields in Cambodia.

As a result, previously learned lessons and orientations toward government and political activities may not be easily supplanted nor supplemented.

For example, adult education classes in American civics and government which immigrants usually take to prepare for naturalization examinations expose them to the most rudimentary facts about American government. At the same time, though, they probably have little or no impact on preexisting political belief systems, the general sense of political efficacy and distrust toward government, or knowledge of American political traditions, current policy debates, and political party agendas. Learning about and becoming actively involved in politics "American style" through registering to vote and voting in elections take place through a range of personal and group experiences that go beyond citizenship classes. Over time, this evolution occurs in conjunction with other aspects of acculturating to American life and society.

The Asian Pacific American electorate is clearly in the process of transformation and change. Its future characteristics and impact will be largely determined by the extent to which newly naturalized Asian immigrants and refugees are incorporated into the political system and encouraged to register to vote and to cast their ballots. An electorate that "looks like Asian Pacific America," in all of its dimensions of diversity, especially in becoming predominantly foreign-born rather than reflecting its current native-born majority profile, may have far different partisan preferences and public policy priorities.

The Asian Pacific American voters in the city of Monterey Park in Los Angeles County may be illustrative (See Table 10). In 1984, the city had a plurality of Democrats (43 percent) over Republicans (31 percent) among Chinese American voters, and also a high proportion of individuals (25 percent) who specified no party affiliations and considered themselves to be independents.[21] By 1989, Chinese American voters, who accounted for the vast majority of new registered voters in Monterey Park since 1984, were nearly evenly divided among Democrats (35 percent), Republicans (37 percent), and independents (26 percent) (Nakanishi, 1986a, 1991). The Asian Pacific American electorate in the city changed its overall partisan orientation through the addition of these new, largely Chinese American registered voters. In 1984, the city's Asian Pacific American voters as a whole showed a slight majority for the Democrats. By 1989, with an increase of over 2,500 new registered voters, the Asian Pacific American electorate in the city could no longer be characterized in this manner. In an analogous fashion, the Asian Pacific American electorate at both the grassroots and leadership levels nationally have undergone, and will continue to undergo, significant changes with the increased future political participation of Asian Pacific immigrants and refugees.

Conclusion and Recommendations

Large-scale immigration from Asia since the enactment of the Immigration Act of 1965 has had a dramatic impact on many states and regions across the nation, as well as on the Asian Pacific American population.[22] From a largely native-born group of 1.5 million in 1970, Asian Pacific Americans became a predominantly immigrant population of 3.5 million in 1980. By 1990, the population had doubled again to 7.2 million nationwide, of which 66 percent were foreign-born. Recent projections estimate that Asian Pacific Americans will continue to increase to nearly 12 million by 2000, and nearly 20 million by 2020. The foreign-born sector is expected to remain the majority beyond 2020 (Ong and Hee, 1993).

The issues of naturalization and electoral participation will remain compelling and critical for both the Asian Pacific American population and for American society generally for many years to come. Asian immigrants have the highest rates of naturalization of any group, including those who came from Europe, and do not remain permanent aliens in this country. They "Americanize," become full citizens, participate actively in all sectors of American life, and should be entitled to all their citizenship rights and privileges. At the same time, Asian Pacific immigrants like their native-born counterparts have extremely low overall rates of voter registration when compared with other groups. Asian Pacific immigrants appear, however, to attain levels of political involvement that are the same, if not better, than those of native-born Asian citizens with the passage of a substantial period of time—over two decades—and with increased acculturation.

The political incorporation of naturalized (*and* native-born) Asian Pacific Americans into the American electoral system needs to be accelerated. Challenging contemporary remnants of the political exclusion and isolation that Asian Pacific Americans experienced in the past is a responsibility to be shared with the two major political parties and others who believe that citizens should be able to exercise fully their right to vote. Unfair redistricting of Asian Pacific American communities, lack of bilingual voter registration application forms and ballots, and opposition to the implementation of legislation like the National Voter Registration Act of 1993 (a.k.a. the Motor Voter Act) perpetuate "political structural barriers," which must be challenged and replaced by fair and inclusive political practices and policies. Asian immigrants have much to contribute to all aspects of American political life—as voters, campaign workers, financial donors, policy experts, and elected officials—and must be allowed and encouraged to participate fully. To do so is to continue a political tradition as old as the nation itself of benefiting from the special leadership talents and contributions of individuals who came to the United States from all corners of the world and shaped its domestic and international programs and policies.

In recent years, the incentive and necessity for Asian Pacific immigrants and their native-born counterparts to naturalize and become more involved in electoral politics have been greatly enhanced in both obvious and unexpected ways. Politicians and the major political parties, who had long neglected to address the unique interests and concerns of Asian Pacific Americans, have become increasingly responsive and attentive, especially to the growing sector of the Asian Pacific American population that contributes sizable donations to campaign coffers. Less interest, however, has been shown toward augmenting the long-term voting potential of Asian Pacific Americans, and few attempts have been made by either the Democratic or Republican party to finance voter registration and education campaigns in Asian Pacific American communities.

The increasing number of Asian Pacific Americans, especially those of immigrant background, who are seeking public office appears, however, to be stimulating greater electoral participation among Asian Pacific Americans at the grassroots level. For example, Asian Pacific American candidates are now regularly making special efforts to seek monetary donations and register new voters among Asian Pacific Americans in jurisdictions in which they are running for office. These activities provide Asian immigrants with important and direct vantage points from which to understand the workings of the American political system, thereby facilitating their political acculturation. At the same time, a wide array of advocacy and social services groups have formed in Asian Pacific American communities across the nation, and a number of different community-based outreach campaigns have been launched to promote citizenship and to register individuals, particularly those who have just been naturalized. Finally, disastrous events like the 1992 civil unrest in Los Angeles, in which over 2,000 Korean American and Asian-owned businesses were destroyed, have underscored the need for immigrant-dominant communities to place greater organizational and leadership activities toward augmenting their access to, and influence in, local government and other policy arenas, as well as to increasing their representation in voter registration rolls.

The decade of the 1990s and the start of the new century are often viewed in glowing and optimistic terms because of seemingly positive demographic trends. The period will be important to witness and analyze because of the extraordinary challenges and opportunities that it will undoubtedly present for Asian Pacific Americans in seeking realization of their full potential as citizens and electoral participants. The level of success that they will achieve in the future, however, will not be solely determined by the Asian Pacific American population, or its leaders and organizations. Success will require the partnership, assistance, and intervention of a wide array of groups and leaders in both private and public sectors. Whether Asian Pacific Americans become a major new political force in the American electoral system is nearly impossible to predict with any precision. Our ability to raise and seriously entertain such a question in the context of the disenfranchisement and exclusion that Asian Pacific Americans faced in the past is quite revealing in itself.

Notes

1   Albert Gore, "Keynote Address." (Pasadena, Calif., 14 July 1995).

2   The 1995 Personal Responsibility Act.

3   To become citizens, immigrants: (1) must be at least 18 years of age; (2) have been lawfully admitted to the United States for permanent residence; (3) have lived in the United States continuously for five consecutive years; (4) are able to speak, read and write English; (5) pass an exam on U.S. government and history; (6) be of good moral character; and (7) are able to show loyalty to the United States by taking an oath of allegiance. There are exceptions to these rules: (1) the spouse or child of a United States citizen becomes eligible in three years; (2) a child who immigrates with his or her parent may become a citizen when the parent naturalizes; (3) an adopted children is eligible for administrative naturalization; (4) an alien who served in World War I, World War II, Korean War, Vietnam, or Grenada may naturalize without permanent residence requirements in some situations; (5) an alien who has served in the Armed Forces for three years may be able to naturalize without meeting certain requirements; (6) former U.S. citizens may waive some requirements; and (7) employees of organizations that promote the U.S. interests in foreign countries may naturalize without meeting these requirements.

4   The number of adult Asian immigrants in the samples are over 10,000 for 1970, 87,000 for 1980, and 182,000 for 1990.

5   The 1970 Census used only four categories: naturalized U.S. citizen, alien, born abroad of American parents, and native-born.

6   The number of years in this country is estimated based on time of entry into the United States. The census does not report whether a respondent has been in the country continuously.

7   The observed change can be decomposed into three components: (1) the difference due to a change in the composition of the population holding naturalization rates for each subgroup constant, (2) the difference due to a change in naturalization rates holding the composition constant, and (3) the difference due to the interaction of the changes in rates and composition. Calculations indicate the compositional shift accounts for just slightly less than half of the decline—that is, 11.2 of the 23.5 percentage points difference in the 1970 and 1990 naturalization rates.

8   The contribution of lower rates with each cohort can be estimated through decomposition with one component being the change in within-group rates between 1970 and 1990, holding the composition by years in the United States to that observed for 1970. Calculations indicate that the within-group drop in naturalization rates accounts for 53 percent of the overall decline for all immigrants—that is, 12.5 of the 23.5 percentage points difference in the naturalization rates for 1970 and 1990.

9   For the purpose of this paper, the four major racial groups are defined as Asians, African Americans, non-Hispanic whites, and Hispanics. The Hispanic classification is nominally an ethnic classification, but being Hispanic in U.S. society is often ascriptive in a manner similar to membership in a racial group.

10   Editor's note: see the articles by Larry Shinagawa and Robert Jiobu in the demographic section of this volume.

11   Rates are based on administrative records on the total number of legal immigrants admitted and the total number of persons who naturalized. Rates reported in the text are for the cohort of immigrants who entered between 1970 and 1979. The number of persons from this cohort who naturalized is based on INS records from 1970 to 1990.

12   The two other nations are Mexico (14 percent) and the Dominican Republic (22 percent).

13   Categories beyond 20 years for the 1980 Census differ from those for the other two censuses. For the 1980 Census, the categories are 21-29 and 30-plus years.

14   The low rate is also due to the inclusion of foreign-born persons on temporary visas in the United States. As stated earlier, the census does not differentiate between permanent immigrants and those on temporary visas. The latter are likely to be here for a short time and thus are concentrated among newly-arrived aliens.

15   The estimate depends on assumptions regarding the naturalization rate in the fifth year and the fifteenth year and the relative number who would never naturalize. One difficulty making an estimate is the nonlinear nature of the naturalization rates, with a noticeable decrease in the change with more years in the United States. If we assume that the rates are 10 percent in the fifth year and 70 percent in the fifteenth year, and that 10 percent would never naturalize, then two-thirds of all naturalization would have occurred in the 5-15 year range.

16   Repeated for the 6-to-10 year group over the next five years; consequently, the difference in the naturalization rates between the two groups observed in the cross-sectional data would not be an accurate predictor of the increase in rate experienced by the 6-to-10 year group over the subsequent five years.

17   There are changes in the cohort from one census to another due to death, emigration and changes in how respondents report their time of entry into the United States. It is, however, beyond the scope of this study to examine how these factors may affect our estimates.

18   This includes those with a non-doctorate professional degree.

19   The results of this multivariate analysis based on logit regressions are available from the authors.

20   The 1994 CPS included 3,317 Asians out of a total sample of 102,197. The 1990 survey included 2,914 Asians among 105,875; and the 1992 had 3,443 Asians among 102,901. Both weighted and unweighted data were analyzed for this report.

21   Other studies have also found that some groups of Asian American voters register in higher than expected proportions as "no party" or independents. See Din, 1984, and Chen, *et al.*, 1989.

22   These population figures include both Asian Americans and Pacific Islanders (*e.g.*, Hawaiians, Samoans, Guamanians, Tongans, Fijians, Palauans, Northern Mariana Islands, and Tahitians). From 1980 to 1990, Pacific Islanders increased by 41 percent from 259,566 to 365,024.

Table 1 Nativity of Asian Pacific Americans
18 years and older

	1970	1980	1990
Population (in thousands)			
Total Asian Pacific Americans	969	2,498	4,938
U.S.-born Citizens	502	741	1,022
Immigrants	468	1,758	3,916
Percent U.S.-Born Citizens	52%	30%	21%
Distribution by Ethnicity			
Japanese	411	567	706
Chinese	288	598	1,261
Filipino	214	538	1,033
Koreans	57	227	548
SE Asians	—	143	592
Asian Indians	—	274	555
Percent U.S.-born Citizens			
Japanese	73%	68%	65%
Chinese	39%	26%	19%
Filipino	30%	19%	20%
Koreans	43%	7%	8%
SE Asians	—	2%	2%
Asian Indians	—	17%	6%

Estimates from Public Use Micro Samples
U.S.-born category includes those born to U.S. citizens

Table 2
Naturalization Rates by Years in U.S. and by Race
All Immigrants 18 years and older

	1970	1980	1990
All Immigrants (in thousands)	8,468	12,423	17,612
Distribution by Years in U.S.			
0 to 10 years	25%	34%	39%
11 to 20 years	19%	23%	26%
21 or more years	55%	43%	35%
Distribution by Race			
Non-Hispanic Whites	76%	53%	37%
Blacks	2%	5%	7%
Latinos	16%	27%	37%
Asians	6%	14%	22%
Overall Naturalization Rates	67%	54%	43%
Naturalization Rates by Years in U.S.			
0 to 10 years	20%	20%	15%
11 to 20 years	64%	49%	45%
21 or more years	90%	85%	74%
Naturalization Rates by Race			
Non-Hispanic Whites	77%	71%	63%
Blacks	45%	43%	36%
Latinos	35%	31%	28%
Asians	41%	36%	43%

Estimates from Public Use Micro Samples
Excluding those born abroad to U.S. Citizens

Table 3
Naturalization Rates
Asian and Non-Hispanic White Immigrants 18 years and older

	1970	1980	1990
Years in U.S.			
Non-Hispanic Whites			
0-10 years	17%	16%	20%
11-20 years	19%	18%	16%
over 20 years	64%	66%	64%
Asians			
0-10 years	56%	66%	54%
11-20 years	19%	20%	32%
over 20 years	25%	13%	14%
Naturalization Rate By Years in U.S.			
Non-Hispanic Whites			
0-10 years	20%	16%	15%
11-20 years	69%	53%	48%
over 20 years	92%	89%	81%
Asians			
0-10 years	17%	19%	19%
11-20 years	67%	67%	66%
over 20 years	68%	79%	81%

Estimates from Public Use Micro Samples

Table 4
Estimated Naturalization Rates of Asian Immigrants

	Cross-section Average (70-90)	Pseudo Panel Estimates
Years in U.S.		
0-5	7%	8%
6-10	36%	33%
11-15	63%	64%
16-20	74%	77%
21-25	81%	81%

Estimates from Public Use Micro Samples

Table 5
Detailed Naturalization Rates of Asian Immigrants

	Years in the United States		
	6-10	11-15	16-20
By Ethnicity			
Japanese	7%	18%	35%
Chinese	34%	67%	80%
Filipinos	45%	73%	83%
Koreans	27%	62%	82%
SE Asians	32%	62%	N.A.
Asian Indians	26%	53%	68%
By Age			
18-29	34%	67%	80%
30-39	35%	65%	76%
40-49	33%	64%	77%
50-59	29%	59%	75%
60 plus	23%	44%	60%
By Education Level			
0-8 years	17%	36%	56%
9-11 years	29%	54%	69%
High School	34%	61%	71%
Some College	43%	70%	77%
Bachelor's	39%	73%	83%
Master's	25%	67%	79%
Doctorate	15%	49%	75%
By English Language Ability			
None	6%	12%	26%
Poor	22%	47%	66%
Good	39%	69%	76%
Very Good	38%	68%	79%
Only English	33%	62%	77%

Estimates from Public Use Micro Samples

Table 6 Distribution of Naturalized and U.S. Born Asian Pacific American Registered Voters, 1994

	California	Hawaii	Rest of Nation	National Total
U.S.-Born	271, 820 (58%)	218,580 (88%)	189,790 (42%)	680,190 (58%)
Naturalized	194,840 (42%)	29,170 (12%)	261,680 (58%)	485,710 (42%)
Total	466,660	247,770	451,470	1,165,990
% of national Total	40%	21%	39%	100%

Current Population Survey, 1994

Table 7 Voter Registration and Turnout Rates, 1994

	% Registered to Vote	% Voted in 1994 Elections
Asian Pacific Americans		
U.S.-Born	56%	78%
Foreign Born	49%	74%
Overall	53%	76%
Latinos		
U.S.-Born	53%	62%
Foreign Born	53%	74%
Overall	53%	64%
African Americans		
U.S.-Born	61%	63%
Foreign Born	58%	78%
Overall	61%	63%
Non-Hispanic Whites		
U.S.-Born	69%	73%
Foreign Born	68%	78%
Overall	69%	73%

Current Population Survey, 1994

Table 8 Registration and Voting by Year of Immigration for Naturalized and U.S. born Citizens, 1994

	% Registered to Vote Year of Immigration for Naturalized Citizens	% Actually Voted
Pre-1965	77%	92%
1965-1974	57%	66%
1975-1985	43%	71%
1986-1994	26%	81%
Overall	49%	74%
U.S.-Born	56%	78%

Current Population Survey, 1994

Table 9 Detailed Rates of Voter Registration of Asian Pacific American Naturalized and Native-Born Citizens, 18 years and older

	Number of Years in the U.S. (Naturalized Citizens)				
	6-10	11-14	15-19	20+	U.S.-Born
By Age					
18-24	0%	20%	15%	10%	26%
25-29	13%	16%	0%	31%	25%
30-39	3%	15%	4%	40%	31%
40-49	8%	37%	42%	20%	24%
50-59	0%	19%	20%	51%	22%
60 plus	0%	0%	12%	41%	40%
By Education Level					
0-8 years	0%	11%	26%	33%	24%
9-12 years	0%	0%	13%	45%	16%
High School	16%	20%	33%	28%	16%
Some college	1%	18%	23%	28%	32%
BA	5%	12%	27%	45%	43%
Graduate					
Degree	0%	66%	18%	41%	35%
By Gender					
Males	6%	20%	23%	29%	32%
Females	6%	21%	27%	39%	29%

Current Population Survey, 1994

**Table 10: Asian Pacific American Registered Voters,
Monterey Park, California, 1984 and 1989**

	# Registered	Democrats	Republicans	Other No.	Parties
'84 Citywide	22,021	13,657	5,564	368	2,290
	(100%)	(62%)	(25%)	(2%)	(10%)
'89 Citywide	23,184	13,243	6,684	369	2,888
	(100%)	(57%)	(29 %)	ˋ (2 %)	(13%)
'84-'89 Net Gain/Loss	+1,163	-414	+1,120	+1	+598
'84 Asian Pacific Total	6,441	3,265	1,944	54	1,178
	(100%)	(51%)	(30%)	(1%)	(18%)
'89 Asian Pacific Total	8,988	3,754	3,198	168	1,868
	(100%)	(42%)	(36%)	(2%)	(21%)
'84-'89 Net Loss/Gain	+2547	+489	+1254	+114	+690
'84 Non-Asian Pacific Total	15,438	10,392	3,620	314	1,112
	(100%)	(67%)	(23%)	(2%)	(7%)
'89 Non-Asian Pacific Total	14,196	9,489	3,486	201	1,020
	(100%)	(67%)	(25%)	(1%)	(7%)
'84-'89 Net Loss/Gain	-1,242	-903	-134	-113	-92
'84 Chinese Americans	3,152	1,360	972	23	797
	(100%)	(43%)	(31%)	(1%)	(25%)
'89 Chinese Americans	5,356	1,868	1,989	100	1,399
	(100%)	(35%)	(37%)	(2%)	(26%)
'84-'89 Net Gain/Loss	+2,204	+508	+1,017	+77	+602
'84 Japanese Americans	2,586	1,429	838	21	298
	(100%)	(55%)	(32%)	(1%)	(12%)
'89 Japanese Americans	2,919	1,516	991	42	370
	(100%)	(52%)	(34%)	(1%)	(13%)
'84-'89 Net Gain/Loss	+343	+87	+153	+21	+72

Source: UCLA Asian Pacific American Voter Registration Project, 1995

Graph 1

Naturalization Rates Among Asian Pacific Immigrants by Years in the United States

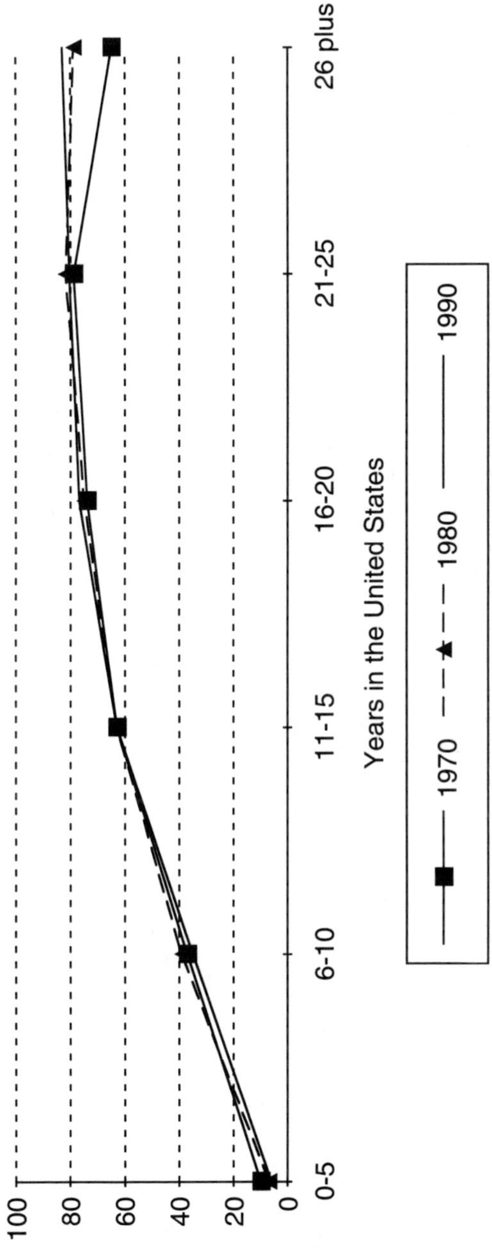

References

Asianweek, "Asians Called a 'Major National Force' in Political Fund-raising," 1 June 1994.

Bai, Su Sun. "Affirmative Pursuit of Political Equality for Asian Pacific Americans: Reclaiming the Voting Rights Act." *University of Pennsylvania Law Review* 139, no. 3 (1991): 731-767.

Borjas, G. *Friends or Strangers: The Impact of Immigrants on the U.S. Economy*. New York: Basic Books, Inc. (1990)

Cain, Bruce E. "Asian-American electoral power: imminent or illusory?" *Election Politics* 5 (1988): 27-30.

Chen, Marion, Woei-Ming New, and John Tsutakawa. "Empowerment in New York Chinatown: Our Work as Student Interns." *Amerasia Journal* 15 (1989): 299-306.

Din, Grant. "An Analysis of Asian/Pacific American Registration and Voting Patterns in San Francisco." Master's Thesis, Claremont Graduate School, 1984.

Erie, Steven P. and Harold Brackman. *Paths to Political Incorporation For Latinos and Asian Pacifics in California*. Berkeley: The California Policy Seminar, 1993.

The Field Institute. "A Digest on California's Political Demography," 1992.

Gittleman, Zvi. *Becoming Israelis: Political Resocialization of Soviet and American Immigrants*, New York: Praeger, 1982.

Gurwitt, Rob. "Have Asian Pacific Americans Arrived Politically? Not Quite." *Governing*, November (1990): 32-38.

Hammer, Tomas. "Migration and Politics: Delimitation and Organization of a Research Field." Paper presented to the Workshop on International Migration and Politics, European Consortium on Political Research, Grenoble, France, 1978.

Hing, Bill Ong. *Making and Remaking Asian Pacific America Through Immigration Policy 1850-1990*, Stanford: Stanford University Press, 1993.

Isaacs, Stephen D. *Jews and American Politics* (Garden City: Doubleday and Company), 1974.

Jasso, Guillermina and Mark R. Rosenzweig. *The New Chosen People: Immigrants in the United States* (The Population of the U.S. in the 1980's Census Monograph Series). For the National Committee for Research on the 1980 Census. New York: Russel Sage Foundation, 1990.

Karnow, Stanley. "Apathetic Asian Pacific Americans? Why Their Success Hasn't Spilled Over into Politics," *Washington Post*, 29 November 1992, sec. C.

Kwoh, Stewart and Mindy Hui. "Empowering Our Communities: Political Policy." *The State of Asian Pacific America: Policy Issues to the Year 2020*. Los Angeles: LEAP Asian Pacific American Public Policy Institute and the UCLA Asian Pacific American Studies Center, (1993): 189-197.

Liang, Zai. "On the Measurement of Naturalization." *Demography*, 32, no. 3 (1994): 525-548.

Lien, Pei-te. "Ethnicity and Political Participation: A Comparison Between Asian and Mexican Americans." *Political Behavior* 16, no. 2 (1994): 237-264.

Miller, John. "Asian Pacific Americans Head For Politics," *The American Enterprise*, 6 (1995): 56-58.

Nakanishi, Don T. "Asian Pacific American Politics: An Agenda for Research." *Amerasia Journal* 12 (1986a): 1-27.

_____. *The UCLA Asian Pacific American Voter Registration Study*. Los Angeles: Asian Pacific American Legal Center, 1986b.

_____. "A Quota on Excellence? The Debate on Asian American Admissions." *Change,* November/December (1989): 38-47.

_____. "The Next Swing Vote? Asian Pacific Americans and California Politics." In *Racial and Ethnic Politics in California,* edited by Byran Jackson and Michael Preston. Berkeley: Institute for Governmental Studies, 1991, 25-54.

_____. "Surviving Democracy's 'Mistake': Japanese Americans and Executive Order 9066." *Amerasia Journal* 19 (1993): 7-35.

Ong, Paul, Lucie Cheng, and Leslie Evans. "Migration of Highly-Educated Asians and Global Dynamics." *Asian and Pacific Migration Journal* 1, nos. 3-4 (19__): 543-584.

Ong, Paul and Suzanne Hee. "The Growth of the Asian Pacific American Population: 20 million in 2020." In *The State of Asian Pacific America: Policy Issues to the Year 2020*. Los Angeles: LEAP Asian Pacific American Public Policy Institute and the UCLA Asian Pacific American Studies Center, 1993, 11-24.

Skerry, Peter. *Mexican Americans: The Ambivalent Minority*. New York: The Free Press, 1993.

Stokes, Bruce. "Learning the Game." *National Journal,* no. 43 (22 October 1988): 2649-2654.

Tachibana, Judy. "California's Asians: Power from a Growing Population." *California Journal* 17 (1986): 534-543.

Tam, Wendy. "Asians—A Monolithic Voting Bloc?" *Political Behavior* 17, no. 2 (1995): 223-249.

Tomas Rivera Center. *Mexican Americans: Are They an Ambivalent Minority*. Claremont, CA: The Tomas Rivera Center, 1994.

U.S. Immigration & Naturalization Service. *Statistical Yearbook of the Immigration and Naturalization Service, 1990*. Washington D.C.: U.S. Government Printing Office, 1991.

Yang, Philip Q. "Explaining Immigrant Naturalization." *International Migration Review* 28, no. 3 (1994a): 449-477.

—. "Ethnicity and Naturalization." *Ethnic & Racial Studies* 17, no. 4 (1994b): 593-618.

The Editors

Bill Ong Hing is an Associate Professor at Stanford Law School and volunteers as the Executive Director of the Immigrant Legal Resource Center. He is the author of three books: Making and Remaking Asian America Through Immigration Policy 1850-1990 (Stanford University Press 1993), Handling Immigration Cases, 2nd ed. (Wiley 1995), and To Be An American: Cultural Pluralism and the Rhetoric of Assimilation (NYU Press forthcoming). He is currently serving on the Citizens' Advisory Panel of the Department of Justice which scrutinizes the Immigration and Naturalization Service and Border Patrol training and misconduct.

Ronald Lee is a Professor of Demography and Economics at the University of California at Berkeley, where he is the Chair of the Demography Department. He is a member of the National Academy of Sciences, and chairs the Academy's Committee on Population. Lee is an editor of the Journal of Population Economies as well as Mathematical Population Studies. He is also a member of the American Economic Association, Population Association of America, International Union for the Scientific Study of the Population, and European Society for Population Economies. He has written extensively on issues related to demography, population, economic development, and fertility.

Leadership Education for Asian Pacifics (LEAP)

Leadership Education for Asian Pacifics (LEAP) is a nonprofit, non-partisan, educational, community based organization founded in 1982 to develop, strengthen, and expand the leadership roles played by Asian Pacific Americans within their own communities as well as in the mainstream institutions.

LEAP's mission to achieve full participation and equality for Asian Pacific Americans through leadership, empowerment, and policy is being realized through the creation of the nationally recognized Asian Pacific American Policy Institute (APA•PPI), the innovative Leadership Management Institute (LMI), and the newly created Community Development Institute (CDI).

Board of Directors

William H. "Mo" Marumoto, *Chair*
Peter Wiersma, *Vice Chair*
Gay Yuen Wong, *Vice Chair*
Yoon Hee Kim, *Secretary*
Janice T. Koyama, *Treasurer*
John T. Nagai, *Legal Counsel* (non-voting)

David R. Barclay
Rockwell "Rocky" Chin
June Choi
Enrique B. de la Cruz
Kenneth S. Kasamatsu
Glenn M. Kawafuchi
Stewart Kwoh
Shirley Komoto Maimoni
Ngoan Thi Le
Robert Lee
Juanita Tamayo Lott
Peggy A. Nagae
Cao K. O
Nampet Panichpant-M
Frank J. Quevedo
Prany Sananikone
Tritia Toyota
Nghia Trung Tran
Leland Wong
Audrey Yamagata-Noji

J.D. Hokoyama
President and Executive Director

Staff

Linda Akutagawa, *Executive Assistant*
Suzanne J. Hee, *Program Associate*
Gena A. Lew, *Program Associate*

Consultants

Graham S. Finney
John Y. Tateishi

Leadership Education
for Asian Pacifics (LEAP), Inc.
327 East Second Street, Suite 226
Los Angeles, CA 90012-4210
Tel: (213) 485-1422
Fax: (213) 485-0050
E-mail: leap90012@aol.com
World Wide Web:
http://www.leap.org

UCLA Asian American Studies Center

Don T. Nakanishi, *Director*

The UCLA Asian American Studies Center, founded in 1969, is one of the oldest Asian American Studies programs in the nation. It has the largest, mulltidisciplinary faculty in the field, with specialists in areas ranging from history to public health, who pursue basic, applied, and policy-oriented research on the Asian American experience. The Center also offers over sixty classes annually in its undergraduate BA and graduate MA programs; maintains active relationships with student and community organizations; publishes Amerasia Journal and other publications; and maintains one of the world's largest research archives and libraries in Asian American Studies.

Center Staff

Cathy Castor, *Administrative Assistant of Center Management*

Enrique de la Cruz, *Assistant Director*

Yuji Ichioka, *Research & Adjunct Professor in History*

Mary Kao, *Graphics and Production Assistant*

Marjorie Lee, *Librarian & Library Coordinator*

Russell C. Leong, *Editor, Amerasia Journal*

Darryl Mar, *Publications Business Manager*

Glenn Omatsu, *Associate Editor, Amerasia Journal*

Steve Ropp, *Associate Librarian*

Meg Thornton, *Coordinator, Student/Community Projects*

Maria Ventura, *Administrative Assistant, Center Management*

Christine Wang, *Coordinator, Center Management*

Eric Wat, *Assistant Coordinator, Student/Community Projects*

UCLA Asian American Studies Center
3230 Campbell Hall, 405 Hilgard Avenue
Los Angeles, CA 90095-1546
Tel.: (310) 825-2974
Fax: (310) 206-9844
e-mail: dtn@ucla.edu
World Wide Web:
http://www.sscnet.ucla.edu/aasc

Faculty Advisory Committee

James Lubben, *Social Welfare*
Pauline Agbayani-Siewert, *Social Welfare*
Emil Berkanovic, *Public Health*
Lucie Cheng, *Sociology*
King-Kok Cheung, *English*
Clara Chu, *Library & Information Science*
Cindy Fan, *Geography*
Wei-Yin Hu, *Economics*
Yuji Ichioka, *Asian American Studies Center/History*
Marjorie Kagawa-Singer, *Public Health*
Jerry Kang, *Law*
Snehendu Kat, *Public Health*
Harry Kitano, *Emeritus, Social Welfare*
Jinqi Ling, *English*
David Wong Louie, *English*
Mitchell Maki, *Social Welfare*
Takashi Makinodan, *Medicine*
Valerie Matsumoto, *History*
Ailee Moon, *Social Welfare*
Robert Nakamura, *Film & Television*
Kazuo Nihira, *Psychiatry & Biobehavorial Sciences*
William Ouchi, *Management*
Paul Ong, *Urban Planning*
Geraldine Padilla, *Nursing*
Kyeyoung Park, *Anthropology*
Julie Roque, *Urban Planning*
Michael Salman, *History*
Shu-mei Shih, *East Asian Languages & Cultures*
Zhixin (Justine) Su, *Education*
Stanley Sue, *Psychology*
David Takeuchi, *Psychiatry*
James Tong, *Political Science*
Cindy Yee-Bradbury, *Psychology*
Henry Yu, *History*
Min Zhou, *Sociology*
Don T. Nakanishi, *Education & Center Director, ex-officio*
Shirley Hune, *Urban Planning & Associate Dean, Graduate Programs*